Eastern Philosophy/Religion

USA $24.95
CAN $35.50

Worldwide Acclaim for This Rendition

".... every sincere translator of the Universal Gita should have Dr. Ramananda Prasad's translation for constant reference. **This rendition of Gita is original and authoritative.** It is a concise reference tool for every seeker, and every translator. The Eternal Truth is plainly brought forward, and, at the same time the best and most easily read translation in English ...."

— Dr. Philippe De Coster, D.D, Belgium

" .... **A wonderful translation**. It's about time that we get a new translation of the Bhagavad-Gita. Dr. Prasad takes a much more low-key approach, simply translating the Gita to the best of his ability and allowing the reader to make sense of it rather than forcing his own opinions on others. Any time there is the possibility of confusion, Prasad defines his terms and goes to the extra effort to make sure that what Vyasa was trying to describe is clear to even ones not familiar with Indian/Eastern philosophy. **More accurate than most other translations and rendered into modern prose,** this makes an excellent place to start with if you're new to Eastern thought."

— Gsibbery, Baton Rouge, LA.

" .... American Gita Society now offers a translation, rendering thought provoking delicacy for the scholar, and at the same time provides unbiased commentaries that can be easily understood by the layperson. This rendition does not endorse, propagate, or oppose any causes, and **delivers a translation that is devoid of all personal motivation and speculation ....** "

— Douglas Remington, Los Angeles, 1997

" .... this translation has an excellent format. **It is very simple, compact, nice, and comfortable to read**. Your book is Maha Prasada. I like it very much ...."

— Ojasvi Dasa, Divine Life Society of Brazil

"…. I want to implore your organization to continue spreading the truth found in the Gita to those who seek **spiritual transcendence from the fetters of commercialism….**"

— Steven Blackwell, New York

" … **this rendition is a product of a meditative brooding to convey the spirit of the original.** As a result, clarity and simplicity characterize the translation. The author's explanation of the verses does not suffer from any distortion of meaning or interpretation. Judicious use of Sanskrit in the translation conveys its majestic beauty to the reader. His lucid English prose style makes a pleasant reading. **It is marked by terseness and clarity and is devoid of superfluity.** This book is refreshingly free from any sectarian slant ."

— Vedanta Kesari, Calcutta, May 1997

" .... I am currently creating a textbook on ancient world cultures on the World-Wide Web. I would like to include the translation of the Gita by Dr. Ramananda Prasad in my site. I am interested in representing India fairly, and I fear that the translation of the Gita by Sir Edwin Arnold that is distributed all over the net will do more to **turn students away rather than introduce them fairly to the text....**"

— Prof. Anthony Beavers, University of Evansville, Indiana, USA

"..... Dr. Prasad brings the ancient wisdom and insights of divine message into modern applicability. **A beautiful blend of melodic and compelling commentary......"**

— H. H. Swami Chidanand Sarasawati (Muniji)
Rishikesh, India

"......I have read several editions of the Gita, and never have I sprung upon such **a simple and lucid description of the essence of the Gita** and its background......"

— R. Puran, Williamsville, Trinidad

Henry David Thoreau said:

"In the morning I bathe my intellect in the stupendous and cosmogonal philosophy of the Bhagavad-Gita, in comparison with which our modern world and its literature seem puny and trivial"

Mahatma Gandhi said:

"When disappoint stares me in the face and all alone I see not one ray of light, I go back to the Bhagavad-Gita. I find a verse here and a verse there, and I immediately begin to smile in the midst of overwhelming tragedies."

ABOUT THIS RENDITION

This lucid rendition allows the average person and the scholar an easy entry into a vast ocean of transcendental knowledge. The important verses are printed in red for the convenience of the first time readers and concise commentaries are made only on key verses that enables a reader to get directly to the point. Simultaneously, this work is intended for advanced readers, presenting the original Sanskrit text in an easy to read format along with the Roman transliteration. The sayings of saints and sages of major religious denominations as well as world leaders and scholars are included.

Quotations from the Vedas, Upanishads, BrahmaSutra, YogaSutra, BhaktiSutras, Puranas, ManuSmriti, Ramayanas, Mahabharata, as well as other major scriptures of the world such as the Bible, Dhammapada, and Koran have been incorporated to highlight the basic unity of all religious views and help propagate the Universal Fellowship of humankind. Several mantras, a guide to meditation, and forty verses of the Holy Gita (Gita Chalisa) are included for daily reading and contemplation.

AIMS AND OBJECTIVES

of

International Gita Society

(Formerly: American Gita Society)

Founded in 1984, the International Gita Society (IGS) is a registered, non-profit, tax-exempt, spiritual institution in the United States of America under Section 501(c) (3) of the IRS Code. Membership is free of charge and open to all. The Aims and Objectives of IGS include:

1. Publish and distribute, free if possible, The Bhagavad-Gita in simple and easy to understand languages, to any one interested in the Gita.

2. Spread the basic Non-sectarian Universal teachings of Shrimad Bhagavad-Gita and other Vedic scriptures in easy to understand languages by establishing branches of the Society in other countries.

3. Provide support and guidance in establishing Gita Study and Discussion (Satsang) Groups, including a free Gita correspondence course.

4. To provide inspiration, cooperation, and support to persons and non-profit organizations engaged in the study and propagation of Vedic knowledge.

5. To break the barriers between faiths, and establish unity of races, religions, castes, and creeds through the immortal non-sectarian teachings of the Vedas, Upanishads, Gita, Ramayana, as well as other major world scriptures such as the Dhammapada, the Bible, the Koran, etc.; and to promote the Universal Brotherhood.

Readers interested in promoting the ideals of the society are invited to correspond with the secretary: **gita@gita-society.com**

The International Gita Society
511 Lowell Place
Fremont, California 94536-1805 117, USA
Visit us: www.gita-society.com, www.gita4free.com

THE BHAGAVAD-GITA

(The Sacred Song)

The Fourth Edition

With Introduction, Original Sanskrit Text and Roman Transliteration, A Lucid English Rendition in two colors, Paragraph Headings, Guide for the Beginners and Daily Reading, Explanation with Verses from Other Religious Scriptures, and Index.

by
Ramananda Prasad, Ph.D.

INTERNATIONAL GITA SOCIETY

First Edition, 1988
Second Revised and Enlarged Edition, 1996
(Published by Motilal Banarsidass in India)
Second Printing, 1997
Third Printing, 1998
Third Revised Edition, 1999
Free Pocket size editions, 2000, 2001,2003,2004
Hindi Translation, 2004 (In Print)
Fourth Revised and Enlarged Edition, 2004

International Gita Society
511 Lowell Place, Fremont, Ca 94536
Phone (510) 791 6953, 6993
Mail2@gita-society.com
Visit: www.gita-society.com
www.GitaInternational.com
www.gita4free.com

ISBN 0-9621099-5-9 (Paperback)
ISBN 0-9621099-2-4 (Hardcover)

INTERNATIONAL GITA SOCIETY

PREFACE

The **First Edition** of our work was published in 1988. The **Second** revised and enlarged edition, with Sanskrit verses, was published in 1996 by Motilal Banarsidass in India with a view to underline the harmony and unity between major teachings of the great religions of the world. All scriptures draw the water of truth from the same ocean. The teachings of Gita are non-sectarian and do not belong to any particular creed, cult, or country. They are meant for the people of the whole world. In this edition similar verses and teachings of major Hindu as well as non-Hindu scriptures of the world such as the Vedas, the Upanishads, the Puranas, the Mahabharata, the Bhakti Sutras, Yoga Sutra, Brahma Sutra, Manu Smriti, and Ramayanas, as well as the Dhammapada, the Bible, and the Koran, were added. A short commentary of selected verses, as well as the teachings of saints and sages, was included to aid the understanding of difficult verses. The **Third Edition** was substantially revised and improved. In this edition both Sanskrit and English words were used, within parentheses, for the clarity and convenience of our readers. In the **Fourth Edition** additional material and paragraph headings have been added, and the use of Sanskrit words is kept to a minimum. The Fourth edition is suitable also for those who are not familiar with Indian Philosophy.

The writer wishes to offer adoration to saints and sages of all religions, and to the commentators on the Gita, through whose grace and blessings alone I was able to write this commentary. I also wish to acknowledge the immeasurable contributions made to my spiritual life by my gurus, under whose guidance I had an opportunity and privilege to start the study of the Gita and Kriya-yoga. They are: Swami Prabhupada, Swami Chinmayananda, Swami Dayananda, Swami Arjun Puri, Paramahamsa Hariharanandaji, and Swami Chidanand Sarasawati (Muniji). I wish to express my heart-felt appreciation and acknowledgment to Sayeed Chaudhury, Dr. Ved Prakash Vatuk, my wife Sadhana, daughter Reeta, and sons Abhinav and Sanjay, for providing valuable suggestions, moral support, help, and encouragement during the development and preparation of this manuscript. Brother BrahmaSwarup Varma provided valuable guidance whenever it was needed. I would like to give special thanks to Avkash Chauhan and Shyamala Raveendran for their support and timely help in cover design, to Doret Kollerer for her editorial help and to Denise Notley for her promotional efforts. The writer wishes to express his gratefulness to Chimanbhai Patel who reviewed the manuscript and made valuable suggestions. The last, but not the least, the writer expresses his gratitude to a great soul, late Shri Mulkraj Dhamija, who inspired this publication by his immortal words:

"The best translation of Gita is your own translation."

Ramananda Prasad
Fremont, California
Gita Jayanti, Dec 25, 2003

CONTENTS

Contents

The Message of Peace, Solace, and Guidance for the:

(See index for more details)

LIST OF ABBREVIATIONS

AiU	Aitareya Upanishad
AV	Atharvaveda
BP	Bhagavata Maha Purana
BrU	Brihadaranyaka Upanishad
BS	BrahmaSutra
ChU	Chaandogya Upanishad
DB	Devi Bhagavatam
IsU	Ishavasya Upanishad
KaU	Katha Upanishad
KeU	Kena Upanishad
MaU	Mandukya Upanishad
MB	Mahabharata
MS	Manu Smriti
MuU	Mundaka Upanishad
NBS	Narada BhaktiSutra
PrU	Prashna Upanishad
PYS	Patanjali YogaSutra
RV	Rigveda
SBS	Shandilya BhaktiSutra
ShU	Shvetashvatara Upanishad
SV	Samaveda
TaU	Taittiriya Upanishad
TR	Tulasi Ramayana
VP	Vishnu Purana
VR	Valmiki Ramayanam
YV	Yajurveda, Vajasaneyi Samhita

INTRODUCTION

The Gita is a doctrine of universal truth. Its message is universal, sublime, and non-sectarian although it is a part of the scriptural trinity of Sanaatana Dharma, commonly known as Hinduism. The Gita is very easy to understand in any language for a mature mind. A repeated reading with faith will reveal all the sublime ideas contained in it. A few abstruse statements are interspersed here and there, but they have no direct bearing on practical issues or the central theme of Gita. The Gita deals with the most sacred metaphysical science. It imparts the knowledge of the Self and answers two universal questions: Who am I, and how can I lead a happy and peaceful life in this world of dualities? It is a book of yoga, the moral and spiritual growth for mankind, based on the cardinal principles of the Hindu religion.

The message of the Gita came to humanity because of Arjuna's unwillingness to do his duty as a warrior because fighting involved destruction and killing. Nonviolence or Ahimsa is one of the most fundamental tenets of Hinduism. All lives, human or non-human, are sacred. This immortal discourse between the Supreme Lord, Krishna, and His devotee-friend, Arjuna, occurs not in a temple, a secluded forest, or on a mountain top but on a battlefield on the eve of a war and is recorded in the great epic, Mahaabhaarata. In the Gita Lord Krishna advises Arjuna to get up and fight. This may create a misunderstanding of the principles of Ahimsa if the background of the war of Mahaabhaarata is not kept in mind. Therefore, a brief historical description is in order.

In ancient times there was a king who had two sons, Dhritaraashtra and Paandu. The former was born blind; therefore, Paandu inherited the kingdom. Paandu had five sons. They were called the Paandavs. Dhritaraashtra had one hundred sons. They were called the Kauravs. Duryodhana was the eldest of the Kauravs.

After the death of king Paandu, the eldest son of Paandu became the lawful King. Duryodhana was a very jealous person. He also wanted the kingdom. The kingdom was divided into two halves between the Paandavs and the Kauravs. Duryodhana was not satisfied with his share of the kingdom. He wanted the entire kingdom for himself. He unsuccessfully planned several foul plots to kill the Paandavs and take away their kingdom. He unlawfully took possession of the entire kingdom of the Paandavs and refused to give back even an acre of land without a war. All mediation by Lord Krishna and others failed. The big war of Mahaabhaarata was thus inevitable. The Paandavs were unwilling participants. They had only two choices: Fight for their right as a matter of duty or run away from war and accept defeat in the name of peace and nonviolence. Arjuna, one of the five Paandava brothers, faced the dilemma in the battlefield whether to fight or run away from war for the sake of peace.

Arjuna's dilemma is, in reality, the universal dilemma. All human beings face dilemmas, big and small, in their everyday life when performing their duties. Arjuna's dilemma was a big one. He had to make a choice between fighting the war and killing his most revered guru who was on the other side, very dear friends, close relatives, and many innocent warriors; or running away from the battlefield for the sake of preserving the peace and nonviolence. The entire seven hundred verses of the Gita are a discourse between Lord Krishna and the confused Arjuna on the battlefield of Kurukshetra near New Delhi, India, about 3,100 years BCE. This discourse was narrated to the blind king, Dhritaraashtr, by his charioteer, Sanjaya, as an eyewitness war report.

The main objective of the Gita is to help people — struggling in the darkness of ignorance — cross the ocean of transmigration and reach the spiritual shore of liberation while living and working in society. The central teaching of the Gita is the attainment of freedom or happiness from the bondage of life by doing one's duty. Always remember the glory and greatness of the Creator and do your duty efficiently without being attached to or affected by the results, even if that duty may at times demand unavoidable violence. Some people neglect or give up their duty in life for the sake of a spiritual life while others excuse themselves from spiritual practices because they believe that they have no time. The Lord's message is to sanctify the entire living process itself. Whatever a person does or thinks, ought to be done for the glory and satisfaction of the Maker. No effort or cost is necessary for this process. Do your duty as a service to the Lord and humanity, and see God alone in everything in a spiritual frame of mind. In order to gain such a spiritual frame of mind, personal discipline, austerity, penance, good conduct, selfless service, yogic practices, meditation, worship, prayer, rituals, and study of scriptures, as well as the company of holy persons, pilgrimage, chanting of the holy names of God, and Self-inquiry are needed to purify the body, mind, and intellect. One must learn to give up lust, anger, greed, and establish mastery over the mind and five senses (hearing, touch, sight, taste, smell) by the purified intellect. One should always remember that all works are done by the energy of nature and that one is not the doer but only an instrument. One must strive for excellence in all undertakings but maintain equanimity in success and failure, gain and loss, and pain and pleasure.

The ignorance of metaphysical knowledge is humanity's greatest predicament. A scripture, being the voice of transcendence, cannot be translated. Language is incapable and translations are defective to clearly impart the knowledge of the Absolute. In this rendering, an attempt has been made to keep the style as close as possible to the original Sanskrit poetry and yet make it easy to read and understand. An attempt has been made to improve the clarity by adding words or phrases, within parentheses, in the English translation of the verses. One hundred and thirty-three (133) key verses are printed in **red** for the convenience of beginners. We suggest all our readers to ponder, contemplate, and act upon these verses. The beginners and the busy executives should first read and understand the meaning of these key verses before delving deep into the bottomless ocean of transcendental knowledge of the Gita.

According to the scriptures, no sin, however heinous, can affect one who reads, ponders, and practices the teachings of Gita any more than water affects the lotus leaf. The Lord Himself resides where Gita is kept, read, chanted, or taught. One who reads, ponders, and practices the teachings of Gita with faith and devotion will attain Moksha (or Nirvana) by the grace of God.

This book is dedicated to all the gurus whose blessings, grace, and teachings have been invaluable. It is offered to the greatest Guru, Lord Krishna, with love and devotion. May the Lord accept it, and bless those who repeatedly read this with peace, happiness, and the true knowledge of the Self.

OM TAT SAT

श्री हनुमते नमः

अथ श्रीमद् भगवद्गीता

अथ प्रथमोऽध्यायः

CHAPTER 1

अर्जुनविषादयोगः

ARJUNA'S DILEMMA

The war of Mahaabhaarata had begun after all negotiations by Lord Krishna and others to avoid it failed. Sage Vyasa, the author of Mahaabhaarata, wanted to give the blind King (Dhritaraashtra) the boon of eyesight so that the King could see the horrors of the war for which he was responsible. But the King refused the offer. He did not want to see the horrors of the war; but preferred to get the war report through his charioteer, Sanjaya. Sage Vyasa granted the power of clairvoyance and clairvision to Sanjaya. With this power Sanjaya could see, hear, and recall the events of the past, present, and future. He was able to give an instant replay of the eye-witness war report to the blind King sitting in the palace.

Bhishma, the mightiest man and the commander-in-chief of the Kaurava's army, is disabled by Arjuna and dying on the battleground on the tenth day of the eighteen-day war. Upon hearing this bad news from Sanjaya, the blind King loses all hope for victory by his sons. Now the King wants to know the details of the war from the beginning, including how the mightiest man, the commander-in-chief of his superior army — who had a boon of dying at his own will — was defeated in the battlefield. The teaching of the Gita begins with the inquiry of the blind King, after Sanjaya described how Bhishma was defeated, as follows:

धृतराष्ट्र उवाच
धर्मक्षेत्रे कुरुक्षेत्रे समवेता युयुत्सवः ।
मामकाः पाण्डवाश्चैव किम् अकुर्वत संजय ।।१।।

dhṛtarāṣṭra uvāca
dharmakṣetre kurukṣetre samavetā yuyutsavaḥ
māmakāḥ pāṇḍavāś cai'va kim akurvata Saṁjaya

The King inquired: Sanjaya, please, now tell me in detail, what did my people (the Kauravas) and the Pandavas do in the battlefield before the war started? (1.01)

संजय उवाच
दृष्ट्वा तु पाण्डवानीकं व्यूढं दुर्योधनस् तदा ।
आचार्यम् उपसंगम्य राजा वचनम् अब्रवीत् ॥२॥

saṁjaya uvāca
dṛṣṭvā tu pāṇḍavānīkaṁ vyūḍhaṁ duryodhanas tadā
ācāryam upasaṁgamya rājā vacanam abravīt

Sanjaya said: O King, After seeing the battle formation of the Pandava's army, your son approached his guru and spoke these words: (1.02)

NOTE: Beginners should not become lost in the jungle of historic proper nouns, or the names of the characters of Mahābhārata in this chapter and the Sanskrit names of various celestial controlling forces (Devas) in Chapter 10 of the Bhagavad-Gita. These names have no bearing on the main theme of the Gita; therefore, these names are either omitted or substituted by generic names in this rendition.

पश्यैतां पाण्डुपुत्राणाम् आचार्य महतीं चमूम् ।
व्यूढां द्रुपदपुत्रेण तव शिष्येण धीमता ॥३॥

paśyaitāṁ pāṇḍuputrāṇām ācārya mahatīṁ camūm
vyūḍhāṁ drupada putreṇa tava śiṣyeṇa dhīmatā

अत्र शूरा महेष्वासा भीमार्जुनसमा युधि ।
युयुधानो विराटश्च द्रुपदश्च महारथः ॥४॥

atra śūrā maheṣvāsā bhīmārjunasamā yudhi
yuyudhāno virāṭaśca drupadaśca mahārathaḥ

धृष्टकेतुश् चेकितानः काशिराजश्च वीर्यवान् ।
पुरुजित् कुन्तिभोजश्च शैब्यश्च नरपुङ्गवः ॥५॥

dhṛṣṭaketuś cekitānaḥ kāśirājaśca vīryavān
purujit kuntibhojaśca śaibyaśca narapuṅgavaḥ

युधामन्युश्च विक्रान्त उत्तमौजाश्च वीर्यवान् ।
सौभद्रो द्रौपदेयाश्च सर्व एव महारथाः ।।६।।

yudhāmanyuśca vikrānta uttamaujāśca vīryavān
saubhadro draupadeyāśca sarva eva mahārathāḥ

O Master, behold this mighty army of the Pandavas, arranged in battle formation by your other talented disciple! There are many great warriors, valiant men, heroes, and mighty archers. (1.03-06)

INTRODUCTION OF THE ARMY COMMANDERS

अस्माकं तु विशिष्टा ये तान् निबोध द्विजोत्तम ।
नायका मम सैन्यस्य संज्ञार्थं तान् ब्रवीमि ते ।।७।।

asmākaṁ tu viśiṣṭā ye tān nibodha dvijottama
nāyakā mama sainyasya saṁjñārthaṁ tān bravīmi te

भवान् भीष्मश्च कर्णश्च कृपश्च समितिंजयः ।
अश्वत्थामा विकर्णश्च सौमदत्तिस् तथैव च ।।८।।

bhavān bhīṣmaśca karṇaśca kṛpaśca samitiṁjayaḥ
aśvatthāmā vikarṇaśca saumadattis tathaiva ca

अन्ये च बहवः शूरा मदर्थे त्यक्तजीविताः ।
नानाशस्त्रप्रहरणाः सर्वे युद्धविशारदाः ।।९।।

anye ca bahavaḥ śūrā madarthe tyakta jīvitāḥ
nānā śastra praharaṇāḥ sarve yuddha viśāradāḥ

Also there are many heroes on my side who have risked their lives for me. I shall name a few distinguished commanders of my army for your information. He named all the officers of his army and said: They are armed with various weapons and are skilled in warfare. (1.07-09)

अपर्याप्तं तद् अस्माकं बलं भीष्माभिरक्षितम् ।
पर्याप्तं त्विदम् एतेषां बलं भीमाभिरक्षितम् ॥१०॥

aparyāptaṁ tad asmākaṁ balaṁ bhīṣmābhi rakṣitam
paryāptaṁ tvidam eteṣāṁ balaṁ bhīmābhi rakṣitam

अयनेषु च सर्वेषु यथाभागम् अवस्थिताः ।
भीष्मम् एवाभिरक्षन्तु भवन्तः सर्व एव हि ॥११॥

ayaneṣu ca sarveṣu yathā bhāgam avasthitāḥ
bhīṣmam evā'bhirakṣantu bhavantaḥ sarva eva hi

The army protecting our commander-in-chief is insufficient, whereas my archrival on the other side is well protected. Therefore all of you, occupying your respective positions, protect our commander-in-chief. (1.10-11)

WAR STARTS WITH THE BLOWING OF CONCH SHELLS

तस्य संजनयन् हर्षं कुरुवृद्धः पितामहः ।
सिंहनादं विनद्योच्चैः शङ्खं दध्मौ प्रतापवान् ॥१२॥

tasya saṁjanayan harṣaṁ kuruvṛddhaḥ pitāmahaḥ
siṁha nādaṁ vinadyo ccaiḥ śaṅkhaṁ dadhmau pratāpavān

The mighty commander-in-chief and the eldest man of the dynasty, roared as a lion and blew his conch loudly, bringing joy to your son. (1.12)

ततः शङ्खाश्च भेर्यश्च पणवानकगोमुखाः ।
सहसैवाभ्यहन्यन्त स शब्दस् तुमुलोऽभवत् ॥१३॥

tataḥ śaṅkhāś ca bheryaś ca paṇavānaka gomukhāḥ
sahasai'vā'bhyahanyanta sa śabdas tumulo'bhavat

Soon after that, conches, kettledrums, cymbals, drums, and trumpets were sounded together. The commotion was tremendous. (1.13)

ततः श्वेतैर् हयैर् युक्ते महति स्यन्दने स्थितौ ।
माधवः पाण्डवश्चैव दिव्यौ शङ्खौ प्रदध्मतुः ॥१४॥

tataḥ śvetair hayair yukte mahati syandane sthitau
mādhavaḥ pāṇḍvaś cai'va divyau śaṅkhau pradadhmatuḥ

After that, Lord Krishna and Arjuna, seated in a grand chariot yoked with white horses, blew their celestial conches. (1.14)

पाञ्चजन्यं हृषीकेशो देवदत्तं धनंजयः ।
पौण्ड्रं दध्मौ महाशङ्खं भीमकर्मा वृकोदरः ॥१५॥

pāñcajanyaṁ hṛṣīkeśo devadattaṁ dhanaṁjayaḥ
pauṇḍraṁ dadhmau mahā śaṅkhaṁ bhīma karmā vṛkodaraḥ

अनन्तविजयं राजा कुन्तीपुत्रो युधिष्ठिरः ।
नकुलः सहदेवश्च सुघोषमणिपुष्पकौ ॥१६॥

anantavijayaṁ rājā kuntī putro yudhiṣṭhiraḥ
nakulaḥ sahadevaś ca sughoṣa maṇipuṣpakau

काश्यश्च परमेष्वासः शिखण्डी च महारथः ।
धृष्टद्युम्नो विराटश्च सात्यकिश्चापराजितः ॥१७॥

kāśyaś ca parameṣvāsaḥ śikhaṇḍī ca mahā rathaḥ
dhṛṣṭadyumno virāṭaś ca sātyakiś cā'parājitaḥ

द्रुपदो द्रौपदेयाश्च सर्वशः पृथिवीपते ।
सौभद्रश्च महाबाहुः शङ्खान् दध्मुः पृथक् पृथक् ॥१८॥

drupado draupadeyāś ca sarvaśaḥ pṛthivī pate
saubhadraś ca mahābāhuḥ śaṅkhān dadhmuḥ pṛthak pṛthak

स घोषो धार्तराष्ट्राणां हृदयानि व्यदारयत् ।
नभश्च पृथिवीं चैव तुमुलो व्यनुनादयन् ॥१९॥

sa ghoṣo dhārtarāṣṭrāṇāṁ hṛdayāni vyadārayat
nabhaś ca pṛthivīṁ caiva tumulo vyanunādayan

Krishna blew His conch; then Arjuna and all other commanders of various divisions of the army of Pandavas

blew their respective conches. The tumultuous uproar, resounding through the earth and sky, tore the hearts of your sons. (1.15-19)

ARJUNA WANTS TO INSPECT THE ARMY AGAINST WHOM HE IS ABOUT TO FIGHT

अथ व्यवस्थितान् दृष्ट्वा धार्तराष्ट्रान् कपिध्वजः ।
प्रवृत्ते शस्त्रसंपाते धनुर् उद्यम्य पाण्डवः ॥२०॥

atha vyavasthitān dṛṣṭvā dhārtarāṣṭrān kapidhvajaḥ
pravṛtte śastrasaṁpāte dhanur udyamya pāṇḍavaḥ

हृषीकेशं तदा वाक्यम् इदम् आह महीपते ।
सेनयोर् उभयोर् मध्ये रथं स्थापय मेऽच्युत ॥२१॥

hṛṣīkeśaṁ tadā vākyam idam āha mahīpate
senayor ubhayor madhye rathaṁ sthāpaya me'cyuta

यावद् एतान् निरीक्षेऽहं योद्धुकामान् अवस्थितान् ।
कैर् मया सह योद्धव्यम् अस्मिन् रणसमुद्यमे ॥२२॥

yāvad etān nirīkṣe'haṁ yoddhu kāmān avasthitān
kair mayā saha yoddhavyam asmin raṇasamudyame

Seeing your sons standing and the war about to begin with the hurling of weapons, Arjuna took up his bow and spoke these words to Lord Krishna: O Lord, please stop my chariot between the two armies until I behold those who stand here eager for the battle and with whom I must engage in this act of war. (1.20-22)

योत्स्यमानान् अवेक्षेऽहं य एतेऽत्र समागताः ।
धार्तराष्ट्रस्य दुर्बुद्धेर् युद्धे प्रियचिकीर्षवः ॥२३॥

yotsyamānān avekṣe'haṁ ya ete'tra samāgatāḥ
dhārtarāṣṭrasya durbuddher yuddhe priyacikīrṣavaḥ

I wish to see those who are willing to serve and appease the evil-minded Kauravas by assembling here to fight the battle. (1.23)

संजय उवाच
एवम् उक्तो हृषीकेशो गुडाकेशेन भारत ।
सेनयोर् उभयोर् मध्ये स्थापयित्वा रथोत्तमम् ॥२४॥

saṁjaya uvāca
evam ukto hṛṣīkeśo guḍākeśena bhārata
senayor ubhayor madhye sthāpayitvā rathottamam

भीष्मद्रोणप्रमुखतः सर्वेषां च महीक्षिताम् ।
उवाच पार्थ पश्यैतान् समवेतान् कुरून् इति ॥२५॥

bhīṣma droṇa pramukhataḥ sarveṣāṁ ca mahīkṣitām
uvāca pārtha paśyai'etān samavetān kurūn iti

Sanjaya said: O King, Lord Krishna, as requested by Arjuna, placed the best of all the chariots in the midst of the two armies facing Arjuna's grandfather, his guru and all other Kings, and said to Arjuna: Behold these assembled soldiers! (1.24-25)

तत्रापश्यत् स्थितान् पार्थः पितन् अथ पितामहान्
आचार्यान् मातुलान् भ्रातन् पुत्रान् पौत्रान् सखींस् तथा ॥२६॥

tatrā'paśyat sthitān pārthaḥ pitṝn atha pitāmahān
ācāryān mātulān bhrātṝn putrān pautrān sakhīṁs tathā

Arjuna saw his uncles, grandfathers, teachers, maternal uncles, brothers, sons, grandsons, and other comrades in the army. (1.26)

ARJUNA'S DILEMMA

श्वशुरान् सुहृदश्चैव सेनयोर् उभयोर् अपि ।
तान् समीक्ष्य स कौन्तेयः सर्वान् बन्धून् अवस्थितान् ॥२७॥

śvaśurān suhṛdaś cai'va senayor ubhayor api
tān samīkṣya sa kaunteyaḥ sarvān bandhūn avasthitān

कृपया परयाविष्टो विषीदन्न् इदम् अब्रवीत् ।
दृष्ट्वेमं स्वजनं कृष्ण युयुत्सुं समुपस्थितम् ।।२८।।

kṛpayā parayāviṣṭo viṣīdann idam abravīt
dṛṣṭvemaṁ svajanaṁ kṛṣṇa yuyutsuṁ samupasthitam

सीदन्ति मम गात्राणि मुखं च परिशुष्यति ।
वेपथुश्च शरीरे मे रोमहर्षश्च जायते ।।२९।।

sīdanti mama gātrāṇi mukhaṁ ca pariśuṣyati
vepathuś ca śarīre me romaharṣaś ca jāyate

After seeing fathers-in-law, companions, and all his kinsmen standing in the ranks of the two armies, Arjuna was overcome with great compassion and sorrowfully spoke these words: O Krishna, seeing my kinsmen standing with a desire to fight, my limbs fail and my mouth becomes dry. My body quivers and my hairs stand on end. (1.27-29)

गाण्डीवं स्रंसते हस्तात् त्वक् चैव परिदह्यते ।
न च शक्नोम्य् अवस्थातुं भ्रमतीव च मे मनः ।।३०।।

gāṇḍīvaṁ sraṁsate hastāt tvak caiva paridahyate
na ca śaknomy avasthātuṁ bhramatīva ca me manaḥ

निमित्तानि च पश्यामि विपरीतानि केशव ।
न च श्रेयोऽनुपश्यामि हत्वा स्वजनम् आहवे ।।३१।।

nimittāni ca paśyāmi viparītāni keśava
na ca śreyo'nupaśyāmi hatvā svajanam āhave

The bow slips from my hand and my skin intensely burns. My head turns, I am unable to stand steady, and O Krishna, I see bad omens. I see no use of killing my kinsmen in battle. (1.30-31)

न काङ्क्षे विजयं कृष्ण न च राज्यं सुखानि च ।
किं नो राज्येन गोविन्द किं भोगैर् जीवितेन वा ।।३२।।

na kāṅkṣe vijayaṁ kṛṣṇa na ca rājyaṁ sukhāni ca
kiṁ no rājyena govinda kiṁ bhogair jīvitena vā

येषाम् अर्थे काङ्क्षितं नो राज्यं भोगाः सुखानि च ।
त इमेऽवस्थिता युद्धे प्राणांस् त्यक्त्वा धनानि च ।।३३।।

yeṣām arthe kāṅkṣitaṁ no rājyaṁ bhogāḥ sukhāni ca
ta ime'vasthitā yuddhe prāṇāṁs tyaktvā dhanāni ca

I desire neither victory nor pleasure nor kingdom, O Krishna. What is the use of the kingdom or enjoyment or even life, O Krishna; because all those — for whom we desire kingdom, enjoyments, and pleasures — are standing here for the battle, giving up their lives? (1.32-33)

आचार्याः पितरः पुत्रास् तथैव च पितामहाः ।
मातुलाः श्वशुराः पौत्राः श्यालाः संबन्धिनस् तथा ।।३४।।

ācāryāḥ pitaraḥ putrās tathaiva ca pitāmahāḥ
mātulāḥ śvaśurāḥ pautrāḥ śyālāḥ saṁbandhinas tathā

एतान् न हन्तुम् इच्छामि घ्नतोऽपि मधुसूदन ।
अपि त्रैलोक्यराज्यस्य हेतोः किं नु महीकृते ।।३५।।

etān na hantum icchāmi ghnato'pi madhusūdana
api trailokya rājyasya hetoḥ kiṁ nu mahīkṛte

I do not wish to kill my teachers, uncles, sons, grandfathers, maternal uncles, fathers-in-law, grandsons, brothers-in-law, and other relatives who are about to kill us, even for the sovereignty of the three worlds, let alone for this earthly kingdom, O Krishna. (1.34-35)

निहत्य धार्तराष्ट्रान् नः का प्रीतिः स्याज् जनार्दन ।
पापम् एवाश्रयेद् अस्मान् हत्वैतान् आततायिनः ।।३६।।

nihatya dhārtarāṣṭrān naḥ   kā prītiḥ syāj janārdana
pāpam evāśrayed asmān   hatvaitān ātatāyinaḥ

O Lord Krishna, what pleasure shall we find in killing our cousin brothers? Upon killing these felons, we shall incur only sin. (1.36)

तस्मान् नार्हा वयं हन्तुं धार्तराष्ट्रान् स्वबान्धवान् ।
स्वजनं हि कथं हत्वा सुखिनः स्याम माधव ॥३७॥

tasmān nārhā vayaṁ hantuṁ   dhārtarāṣṭrān svabāndhavān
svajanaṁ hi kathaṁ hatvā   sukhinaḥ syāma mādhava

Therefore, we should not kill our cousin brothers. How can we be happy after killing our relatives, O Krishna? (1.37)

यद्यप्येते न पश्यन्ति लोभोपहतचेतसः ।
कुलक्षयकृतं दोषं मित्रद्रोहे च पातकम् ॥३८॥

yady apy ete na paśyanti   lobhopahata cetasaḥ
kulakṣayakṛtaṁ doṣaṁ   mitradrohe ca pātakam

कथं न ज्ञेयम् अस्माभिः पापाद् अस्मान् निवर्तितुम् ।
कुलक्षयकृतं दोषं प्रपश्यद्भिर् जनार्दन ॥३९॥

kathaṁ na jñeyam asmābhiḥ   pāpād asmān nivartitum
kulakṣaya kṛtaṁ doṣaṁ   prapaśyadbhir janārdana

Though they are blinded by greed and do not see evil in the destruction of the family or sin in being treacherous to friends, why should not we, who clearly see evil in the destruction of the family, think about turning away from this sin, O Krishna? (1.38-39)

ARJUNA DESCRIBES THE EVILS OF WAR

कुलक्षये प्रणश्यन्ति कुलधर्माः सनातनाः ।
धर्मे नष्टे कुलं कृत्स्नम् अधर्मोऽभिभवत्युत ॥४०॥

kulakṣaye praṇaśyanti kuladharmāḥ sanātanāḥ
dharme naṣṭe kulaṁ kṛtsnam adharmo'bhibhavatyuta

Eternal family traditions and codes of moral conduct are destroyed with the destruction of (the head of the) family in a war. And immorality prevails in the family due to the destruction of family traditions. (1.40)

अधर्माभिभवात् कृष्ण प्रदुष्यन्ति कुलस्त्रियः ।
स्त्रीषु दुष्टासु वार्ष्णेय जायते वर्णसंकरः ।।४१।।

adharmābhibhavāt kṛṣṇa praduṣyanti kula striyaḥ
strīṣu duṣṭāsu vārṣṇeya jāyate varṇasaṁkaraḥ

And when immorality prevails, O Krishna, people become corrupted. And when people are corrupted, unwanted progeny are born. (1.41)

संकरो नरकायैव कुलघ्नानां कुलस्य च ।
पतन्ति पितरो ह्येषां लुप्तपिण्डोदकक्रियाः ।।४२।।

saṁkaro narakāyaiva kulaghnānāṁ kulasya ca
patanti pitaro hyeṣāṁ lupta piṇḍodaka kriyāḥ

This brings the family and the slayers of the family to hell because the spirits of their ancestors are degraded when deprived of ceremonial offerings of love and respect by the unwanted progeny. (1.42)

दोषैर् एतैः कुलघ्नानां वर्णसंकरकारकैः ।
उत्साद्यन्ते जातिधर्माः कुलधर्माश्च शाश्वताः ।।४३।।

doṣair etaiḥ kulaghnānāṁ varṇa saṁkara kārakaiḥ
utsādyante jātidharmāḥ kula dharmāśca śāśvatāḥ

The everlasting qualities of social order and family traditions of those who destroy their family are ruined by the sinful act of illegitimacy. (1.43)

उत्सन्नकुलधर्माणां मनुष्याणां जनार्दन ।
नरकेऽनियतं वासो भवतीत्यनुशुश्रुम ।।४४।।
utsanna kula dharmāṇāṁ manuṣyāṇāṁ janārdana
narake'niyataṁ vāso bhavatī'ty anuśuśruma

We have been told, O Krishna, that people whose family traditions are destroyed necessarily dwell in hell for a long time. (1.44)

अहो बत महत् पापं कर्तुं व्यवसिता वयम् ।
यद् राज्यसुखलोभेन हन्तुं स्वजनम् उद्यताः ।।४५।।
aho bata mahat pāpaṁ kartuṁ vyavasitā vayam
yad rājya sukha lobhena hantuṁ svajanam udyatāḥ

Alas! We are ready to commit a great sin by striving to slay our relatives because of greed for the pleasures of the kingdom. (1.45)

यदि माम् अप्रतीकारम् अशस्त्रं शस्त्रपाणयः ।
धार्तराष्ट्रा रणे हन्युस् तन् मे क्षेमतरं भवेत् ।।४६।।
yadi mām apratīkāram aśastraṁ śastrapāṇayaḥ
dhārtarāṣṭrā raṇe hanyus tan me kṣemataraṁ bhavet

It would be far better for me if my cousin brothers kill me with their weapons in battle while I am unarmed and unresisting. (1.46)

WHEN THE GOING GETS TOUGH, EVEN TOUGH ONES CAN GET DELUDED

संजय उवाच
एवम् उक्त्वाऽर्जुनः संख्ये रथोपस्थ उपाविशत् ।
विसृज्य सशरं चापं शोकसंविग्नमानसः ।।४७।।

saṁjaya uvāca
evam uktvā'rjunaḥ saṁkhye rathopastha upāviśat
visṛjya saśaraṁ cāpaṁ śokasaṁvignamānasaḥ

Sanjaya said: Having said this in the battlefield and casting aside his bow and arrow, Arjuna sat down on the seat of the chariot with his mind overwhelmed with sorrow. (1.47)

ॐ तत्सदिति श्रीमद्भगवद्गीतासूपनिषत्सु ब्रह्मविद्यायां योगशास्त्रे
श्रीकृष्णार्जुनसंवादे अर्जुनविषादयोगो नाम प्रथमोऽध्यायः ॥
OM tatsaditi śrīmadbhagavadgītāsūpaniṣatsu brahmavidyāyāṁ
yogaśāstre śrīkṛṣṇārjuna saṁvāde arjunaviṣādayogo
nāma prathamo'dhyāyaḥ

Thus ends the first chapter named "Arjuna's Dilemma" of the Upaniṣad of the Bhagavadgītā, the scripture of yoga, dealing with the science of the Absolute in the form of the dialogue between Śrīkṛṣṇa and Arjuna.

अथ द्वितीयोऽध्यायः
CHAPTER 2
सांख्ययोगः
TRANSCENDENTAL KNOWLEDGE

संजय उवाच
तं तथा कृपयाविष्टम् अश्रुपूर्णाकुलेक्षणम् ।
विषीदन्तम् इदं वाक्यम् उवाच मधुसूदनः ॥१॥
saṁjaya uvāca
taṁ tathā kṛpayāviṣṭam aśrupūrṇākulekṣaṇam
viṣīdantam idaṁ vākyam uvāca madhusūdanaḥ

Sanjaya said: Lord Krishna spoke these words to Arjuna whose eyes were tearful and downcast and who was overwhelmed with compassion and despair. (2.01)

श्रीभगवानुवाच
कुतस्त्वा कश्मलम् इदं विषमे समुपस्थितम् ।
अनार्यजुष्टम् अस्वर्ग्यम् अकीर्तिकरम् अर्जुन ॥२॥
śrī bhagavān uvāca
kutas tvā kaśmalam idaṁ viṣame samupasthitam
anāryajuṣṭam asvargyam akīrtikaram arjuna

Lord Krishna said: How has the dejection come to you at this juncture? This is not fit for a person of noble mind and deeds. It is disgraceful, and it does not lead one to heaven, O Arjuna. (2.02)

क्लैब्यं मा स्म गमः पार्थ नैतत् त्वय्य् उपपद्यते ।
क्षुद्रं हृदयदौर्बल्यं त्यक्त्वोत्तिष्ठ परंतप ॥३॥
klaibyaṁ mā sma gamaḥ pārtha naitat tvayy upapadyate
kṣudraṁ hṛdaya daurbalyaṁ tyaktvottiṣṭha paraṁtapa

Do not become a coward, O Arjuna, because it does not befit you. Shake off this trivial weakness of your heart and get up for the battle, O Arjuna. (2.03)

ARJUNA CONTINUES HIS REASONING AGAINST THE WAR

अर्जुन उवाच
कथं भीष्मम् अहं संख्ये द्रोणं च मधुसूदन ।
इषुभिः प्रतियोत्स्यामि पूजार्हाव् अरिसूदन ॥४॥
arjuna uvāca
kathaṁ bhīṣmam ahaṁ saṁkhye droṇaṁ ca madhusūdana
iṣubhiḥ prati yotsyāmi pūjārhāv arisūdana

Arjuna said: How shall I strike my grandfather, my guru, and all other relatives — who are worthy of my respect — with arrows in battle, O Krishna? (2.04)

Arjuna had a valid point. In Vedic culture, gurus, the elderly, honorable personalities, and all other superiors are to be respected. One should not fight or even joke or speak sarcastically with superiors, even if they hurt you. But the scriptures also say that anyone who is engaged in abominable activities or supports misdeeds against you or others, is no longer to be respected, but punished.

गुरून् अहत्वा हि महानुभावान्
श्रेयो भोक्तुं भैक्ष्यम् अपीह लोके ।
हत्वार्थकामांस् तु गुरून् इहैव
भुञ्जीय भोगान् रुधिरप्रदिग्धान् ॥५॥
gurūn ahatvā hi mahānubhāvān
śreyo bhoktuṁ bhaikṣyam apī'ha loke
hatvā'rthakāmāṁs tu gurūn ihai'va
bhuñjīya bhogān rudhirapradigdhān

It would be better, indeed, to live on alms in this world than to slay these noble personalities because by killing them I would enjoy wealth and pleasures stained with their blood. (2.05)

न चैतद् विद्मः कतरन् नो गरीयो
यद् वा जयेम यदि वा नो जयेयुः ।
यान् एव हत्वा न जिजीविषामस्
तेऽवस्थिताः प्रमुखे धार्तराष्ट्राः ॥६॥
na caitad vidmaḥ kataran no garīyo
yad vā jayema yadi vā no jayeyuḥ
yān eva hatvā na jijīviṣāmas
te'vasthitāḥ pramukhe dhārtarāṣṭrāḥ

We do not know which alternative— to fight or to quit— is better for us. Further, we do not know whether we will conquer them or they will conquer us. We should not even wish to live after killing our cousin brothers who are standing in front of us. (2.06)

Arjuna was unable to decide what to do. It is said that expert guidance of a guru, the spiritual counselor, should be sought during a moment of crisis or to overcome the perplexities of life. Arjuna now requests Krishna for guidance.

कार्पण्यदोषोपहतस्वभावः
पृच्छामि त्वां धर्मसंमूढचेताः ।
यच्छ्रेयः स्यान् निश्चितं ब्रूहि तन् मे
शिष्यस् तेऽहं शाधि मां त्वां प्रपन्नम् ॥७॥
kārpaṇyadoṣopahatasvabhāvaḥ
pṛcchāmi tvāṁ dharmasaṁmūḍhacetāḥ
yacchreyaḥ syān niścitaṁ brūhi tan me
śiṣyas te'haṁ śādhi māṁ tvāṁ prapannam

My senses are overcome by the weakness of pity, and my mind is confused about duty (Dharma). Please tell me what is better for me. I am Your disciple, and I take refuge in You. (2.07)

NOTE: 'Dharma' may be defined as the eternal law governing, upholding, and supporting creation and the world order. It is the eternal relationship between the creator and His creatures. It also means way of life, doctrine, principle, prescribed duty, righteousness, right action, integrity, ideal conduct, custom, virtue, nature, essential quality, commandments, moral principles, spiritual truth, spirituality, spiritual values, and a function within the scriptural injunction or religion.

न हि प्रपश्यामि ममापनुद्याद्
यच्छोकम् उच्छोषणम् इन्द्रियाणाम् ।
अवाप्य भूमाव् असपत्नम् ऋद्धं
राज्यं सुराणाम् अपि चाधिपत्यम् ॥८॥

na hi prapaśyāmi mamāpanudyād
yacchokam ucchoṣaṇam indriyāṇām
avāpya bhūmāv asapatnam ṛddhaṁ
rājyaṁ surāṇām api cādhipatyam

I do not perceive that gaining an unrivaled and prosperous kingdom on this earth, or even lordship over all the celestial controllers, will remove the sorrow that is drying up my senses. (2.08)

संजय उवाच
एवम् उक्त्वा हृषीकेशं गुडाकेशः परंतप ।
न योत्स्य इति गोविन्दम् उक्त्वा तूष्णीं बभूव ह ॥९॥

saṁjaya uvāca
evam uktvā hṛṣīkeśaṁ guḍākeśaḥ paraṁtapa
na yotsya iti govindam uktvā tūṣṇīṁ babhūva ha

Sanjaya said: O King, after speaking like this to Lord Krishna, the mighty Arjuna said to Krishna: I shall not fight, and became silent. (2.09)

तम् उवाच हृषीकेशः प्रहसन्न् इव भारत ।
सेनयोर् उभयोर् मध्ये विषीदन्तम् इदं वचः ॥१०॥
tam uvāca hṛṣīkeśaḥ prahasann iva bhārata
senayor ubhayor madhye viṣīdantam idaṁ vacaḥ

O King, Lord Krishna, as if smiling, spoke these words to the distressed Arjuna in the midst of the two armies. (2.10)

THE TEACHINGS OF THE GITA BEGIN WITH THE TRUE KNOWLEDGE OF THE SELF AND THE PHYSICAL BODY

श्रीभगवानुवाच
अशोच्यान् अन्वशोचस् त्वं प्रज्ञावादांश्च भाषसे ।
गतासून् अगतासूंश्च नानुशोचन्ति पण्डिताः ॥११॥
śrī bhagavān uvāca
aśocyān anvaśocas tvaṁ prajñāvādāṁśca bhāṣase
gatāsūn agatāsūṁśca nānuśocanti paṇḍitāḥ

Lord Krishna said: You grieve for those who are not worthy of grief and yet speak words of wisdom. The wise grieve neither for the living nor for the dead. (2.11)

People meet and depart in this world as two pieces of wood flowing down the river come together and then separate from each other (MB 12.174.15). The wise, who know that the body is mortal and the Spirit is immortal, have nothing to moan about (KaU 2.22).

NOTE: The Self (or Atma) is also called soul or consciousness and is the source of life and the cosmic power behind the body-mind complex. Just as our body exists in space, similarly, our thoughts, intellect, emotions, and psyche exist in the Self, the space of consciousness. Self cannot be perceived by our physical senses because Self is beyond the domain of the senses. The senses were designed only to comprehend physical objects.

The word 'Atma' has been also used in the 'Gita' for the lower self (body, mind, and senses), psyche, intellect, soul, spirit, subtle senses, oneself, ego, heart, human beings, Eternal Being (Brahma), Absolute Truth, individual soul, and the supersoul or the supreme Self, depending on the context.

न त्वेवाहं जातु नासं न त्वं नेमे जनाधिपाः ।
न चैव न भविष्यामः सर्वे वयम् अतः परम् ॥१२॥

na tvevāhaṁ jātu nāsaṁ na tvaṁ neme janādhipāḥ
na caiva na bhaviṣyāmaḥ sarve vayam ataḥ param

There was never a time when these monarchs, you, or I did not exist, nor shall we ever cease to exist in the future. (2.12)

देहिनोऽस्मिन् यथा देहे कौमारं यौवनं जरा ।
तथा देहान्तरप्राप्तिर् धीरस् तत्र न मुह्यति ॥१३॥

dehino'smin yathā dehe kaumāraṁ yauvanaṁ jarā
tathā dehāntaraprāptir dhīras tatra na muhyati

Just as the soul acquires a childhood body, a youth body, and an old-age body during this life, similarly, the soul acquires another body after death. This should not delude the wise. (See also 15.08) (2.13)

मात्रास्पर्शास् तु कौन्तेय शीतोष्णसुखदुःखदाः ।
आगमापायिनोऽनित्यास् तांस् तितिक्षस्व भारत ॥१४॥

mātrāsparśās tu kaunteya śītoṣṇa sukha duḥkhadāḥ
āgamāpāyino'nityās tāṁs titikṣasva bhārata

The contacts of the senses with sense objects give rise to the feelings of heat and cold, and pain and pleasure. They are transitory and impermanent. Therefore, one should learn to endure them bravely. (2.14)

यं हि न व्यथयन्त्येते पुरुषं पुरुषर्षभ ।
समदुःखसुखं धीरं सोऽमृतत्वाय कल्पते ॥१५॥

yaṁ hi na vyathayantyete puruṣaṁ puruṣarṣabha
sama duḥkha sukhaṁ dhīraṁ so'mṛta tvāya kalpate

Because a calm person — who is not afflicted by these sense objects and is steady in pain and pleasure — becomes fit for salvation. (2.15)

Nothing can hurt one if the mind can be trained to withstand the impulse of the pairs of opposites — joys and sorrows, pains and pleasures, loss and gain. The phenomenal world cannot exist without the pairs of opposites. Good and evil, pain and pleasure will always exist. The universe is a playground designed by God for the living entities. It takes two to play a game. The game cannot continue if the pairs of opposites are altogether eliminated. Before one can feel joy, one must know sorrow. Both negative and positive experiences are needed for our growth and spiritual development. Cessation of pain brings pleasure, and cessation of pleasure results in pain. Thus, pain is born in the womb of pleasure. Peace is born in the womb of war. Sorrow exists because the desire for happiness exists. When the desire for happiness disappears, so does the sorrow. Sorrow is only a prelude to happiness and vice versa. Even the joy of going to heaven is followed by the sorrow of coming back to the earth; therefore, worldly objects should not be the main goal of human life. If one chooses material pleasures, it is like giving up nectar and choosing poison instead.

Change is the law of nature— change from summer to winter, from spring to fall, from the light of the full moon to the darkness of the new moon. Neither pain nor pleasure last forever.

Pleasure comes after pain, and pain is followed again by pleasure. Reflecting like this, one must learn to tolerate the blows of time with patience and learn not only to endure, but also to expect, welcome, and enjoy both the joys as well as the sorrows of life. Sow the seed of hope in the soil of sorrow. Find your way in the darkness of the night of adversity with the torch of the scriptures and faith in God. There would be no opportunities if there were no problems. Destiny is born out of crisis. Einstein said: Opportunity lies in the middle of difficulties.

THE SELF IS ETERNAL, BODY IS TRANSITORY

नासतो विद्यते भावो नाभावो विद्यते सतः ।
उभयोर् अपि दृष्टोऽन्तस् त्व् अनयोस् तत्त्वदर्शिभिः ॥१६॥

nāsato vidyate bhāvo nābhāvo vidyate sataḥ
ubhayor api dṛṣṭo'ntas tv anayos tattvadarśibhiḥ

The invisible Self (Atma, Atman, the soul, spirit, the life-force) is eternal. The visible physical body is transitory, and it undergoes changes. The reality of these two is indeed certainly seen by the seer of the truth (who knows that we are not this body, but the Atma). (2.16)

The Self exists everywhere and at all times — past, present, and future. The human body and the universe both have a temporary existence, but appear permanent at first sight. Webster defines Atman or Atma as the 'World Soul', from which all souls derive and the Supreme Abode to which they return. Atma is also called 'Jivatma' or 'Jiva', which is the ultimate source of all individual selves. We have used the English words: Self, Spirit, spirit, soul, or individual soul interchangeably for different aspects of Atma.

Our physical body is subject to birth, growth, maturity, reproduction, decay, and death; whereas the Self is eternal, indestructible, pure, unique, all knower, substratum, unchangeable, self-luminous, the cause of all causes, all pervading, unaffectable, immutable, and inexplicable.

अविनाशि तु तद् विद्धि येन सर्वम् इदं ततम् ।
विनाशम् अव्ययस्यास्य न कश्चित् कर्तुम् अर्हति ॥१७॥
avināśi tu tad viddhi yena sarvam idaṁ tatam
vināśam avyayasyāsya na kaścit kartum arhati

The Spirit, by whom this entire universe is pervaded, is indestructible. No one can destroy the imperishable Spirit. (2.17)

अन्तवन्त इमे देहा नित्यस्योक्ताः शरीरिणः ।
अनाशिनोऽप्रमेयस्य तस्माद् युध्यस्व भारत ॥१८॥
antavanta ime dehā nityasyoktāḥ śarīriṇaḥ
anāśino'prameyasya tasmād yudhyasva bhātata

The physical bodies of the eternal, immutable, and incomprehensible Spirit are mortal. Spirit (Atma) is immortal. Therefore, as a warrior, you must fight, O Arjuna. (2.18)

य एनं वेत्ति हन्तारं यश्चैनं मन्यते हतम् ।
उभौ तौ न विजानीतो नायं हन्ति न हन्यते ॥१९॥
ya enaṁ vetti hantāraṁ yaścainaṁ manyate hatam
ubhau tau na vijānīto nāyaṁ hanti na hanyate

One who thinks that the Spirit is a slayer, and one who thinks the Spirit is slain are both ignorant because the Spirit neither slays nor is slain. (2.19)

न जायते म्रियते वा कदाचिन्
नायं भूत्वा भविता वा न भूयः ।
अजो नित्यः शाश्वतोऽयं पुराणो
न हन्यते हन्यमाने शरीरे ॥२०॥
na jāyate mriyate vā kadācin
nāyaṁ bhūtvā bhavitā vā na bhūyaḥ
ajo nityaḥ śāśvato'yaṁ purāṇo
na hanyate hanyamāne śarīre

The Spirit is neither born, nor does it die at any time. It does not come into being nor cease to exist. It is unborn, eternal, permanent, and primeval. The Spirit is not destroyed when the body is destroyed. (2.20)

वेदाविनाशिनं नित्यं य एनम् अजम् अव्ययम् ।
कथं स पुरुषः पार्थ कं घातयति हन्ति कम् ॥२१॥

vedāvināśinaṁ nityaṁ ya enam ajam avyayam
kathaṁ sa puruṣaḥ pārtha kaṁ ghātayati hanti kam

O Arjuna, how can a person who knows that the Spirit is indestructible, eternal, unborn, and immutable, kill anyone or causes anyone to be killed? (2.21)

DEATH AND TRANSMIGRATION OF THE SOUL

वासांसि जीर्णानि यथा विहाय
नवानि गृह्णाति नरोऽपराणि ।
तथा शरीराणि विहाय जीर्णान्य्
अन्यानि संयाति नवानि देही ॥२२॥

vāsāṁsi jīrṇāni yathā vihāya
navāni gṛhṇāti naro'parāṇi
tathā śarīrāṇi vihāya jīrṇāny
anyāni saṁyāti navāni dehī

Just as a person puts on new garments after discarding the old ones, similarly, the living entity or the individual soul acquires new bodies after casting away the old bodies. (2.22)

Just as a caterpillar takes hold of another object before leaving an object, similarly, the living entity (or soul) obtains a new body before or after leaving the old one (BrU 4.4.03). The physical body has also been compared to a cage, a vehicle, an abode, as well as a garment of the subtle body that needs to be changed frequently. Death is the separation of the subtle body from the physical body. The living entity is a traveler. Death is not the end of the journey of the living entity. Death is like a rest area where the individual soul changes vehicles and the journey continues. Life is continuous and endless. Inevitable death is not the end of life; it is only an end of a perishable, physical body.

नैनं छिन्दन्ति शस्त्राणि नैनं दहति पावकः ।
न चैनं क्लेदयन्त्यापो न शोषयति मारुतः ॥२३॥

nai'naṁ chindanti śastrāṇi nai'naṁ dahati pāvakaḥ
na cai'naṁ kledayanty āpo na śoṣayati mārutaḥ

अच्छेद्योऽयम् अदाह्योऽयम् अक्लेद्योऽशोष्य एव च ।
नित्यः सर्वगतः स्थाणुर् अचलोऽयं सनातनः ॥२४॥

acchedyo'yam adāhyo'yam akledyo'śoṣya eva ca
nityaḥ sarvagataḥ sthāṇur acalo'yaṁ sanātanaḥ

Weapons do not cut this Spirit, fire does not burn it, water does not make it wet, and the wind does not make it dry. The Spirit cannot be cut, burned, wet, or dried. It is eternal, all-pervading, changeless, immovable, and primeval. Atma is beyond space and time. (2.23-24)

अव्यक्तोऽयम् अचिन्त्योऽयम् अविकार्योऽयम् उच्यते ।
तस्माद् एवं विदित्वैनं नानुशोचितुम् अर्हसि ॥२५॥

avyakto'yam acintyo'yam avikāryo'yam ucyate
tasmād evaṁ viditvainaṁ nā'nuśocitum arhasi

The Spirit is said to be unexplainable, incomprehensible, and immutable. Knowing the Spirit as such, you should not grieve for the physical body. (2.25)

In the previous verses Krishna asked us not to worry about the indestructible spirit. A question may arise: Should one lament the death of (the destructible body of) our near and dear ones at all? The answer comes:

अथ चैनं नित्यजातं नित्यं वा मन्यसे मृतम् ।
तथापि त्वं महाबाहो नैवं शोचितुम् अर्हसि ।।२६।।

atha cainaṁ nityajātaṁ nityaṁ vā manyase mṛtam
tathā'pi tvaṁ mahābāho naivaṁ śocitum arhasi

जातस्य हि ध्रुवो मृत्युर् ध्रुवं जन्म मृतस्य च ।
तस्माद् अपरिहार्येऽर्थे न त्वं शोचितुम् अर्हसि ।।२७।।

jātasya hi dhruvo mṛtyur dhruvaṁ janma mṛtasya ca
tasmād aparihārye'rthe na tvaṁ śocitum arhasi

Even if you think that the physical body takes birth and dies perpetually, even then, O Arjuna, you should not grieve like this because death is certain for one who is born, and birth is certain for one who dies. Therefore, you should not lament over the inevitable death. (2.26-27)

One should not lament the death of anybody at all. Lamentation is due to attachment, and attachment binds the individual soul to the wheel of transmigration. Therefore, the scriptures suggest one should not mourn, but pray for several days after the person's death for salvation of the departed soul.

The inevitability of death and indestructibility of the soul, however, does not and cannot justify lawful but unnecessary killing of any creature, unjust war, or even suicide. The Vedic scriptures are very clear on this point in regard to killing human beings or any other living entity. The scripture says: One should not commit violence towards anyone. Unauthorized killing is punishable in all circumstances: A life for life. Lord Krishna is urging Arjuna to fight — but not to kill wantonly — in order to establish peace and law and order on earth as a matter of a warrior's duty.

अव्यक्तादीनि भूतानि व्यक्तमध्यानि भारत ।
अव्यक्तनिधनान्येव तत्र का परिदेवना ।।२८।।

avyaktādīni bhūtāni vyakta madhyāni bhārata
avyakta nidhanāny eva tatra kā paridevanā

All beings are unmanifest (or invisible) to our physical eyes before birth and after death. They manifest between birth and death only. What is there to grieve about? (2.28)

THE INDESTRUCTIBLE SPIRIT TRANSCENDS MIND AND SPEECH

आश्चर्यवत् पश्यति कश्चिद् एनम्
आश्चर्यवद् वदति तथैव चान्यः ।
आश्चर्यवच्चैनम् अन्यः शृणोति
श्रुत्वाप्येनं वेद न चैव कश्चित् ॥२९॥
āścaryavat paśyati kaścid enam
āścaryavad vadati tathai 'va cānyaḥ
āścaryavac cainam anyaḥ śṛṇoti
śrutvāpyenaṁ veda na caiva kaścit

Some look upon this Spirit as a wonder, another describes it as wonderful, and others hear of it as a wonder. Even after hearing about it, very few people know what the Spirit is. (See also KaU 2.07) (2.29)

देही नित्यम् अवध्योऽयं देहे सर्वस्य भारत ।
तस्मात् सर्वाणि भूतानि न त्वं शोचितुम् अर्हसि ॥३०॥
dehī nityam avadhyo'yaṁ dehe sarvasya bhārata
tasmāt sarvāṇi bhūtāni na tvaṁ śocitum arhasi

O Arjuna, the Spirit that dwells in the body of all beings is eternally indestructible. Therefore, you should not mourn for anybody. (2.30)

LORD KRISHNA REMINDS ARJUNA OF THE DUTY OF A WARRIOR

स्वधर्मम् अपि चावेक्ष्य न विकम्पितुम् अर्हसि ।
धर्म्याद्धि युद्धाच्छ्रेयोऽन्यत् क्षत्रियस्य न विद्यते ॥३१॥

svadharmam api cāvekṣya na vikampitum arhasi
dharmyāddhi yuddhāc chreyo'nyat kṣatriyasya na vidyate

Considering also your duty as a warrior, you should not waver because there is nothing more auspicious than one's personal duty in life. (2.31)

यदृच्छया चोपपन्नं स्वर्गद्वारम् अपावृतम् ।
सुखिनः क्षत्रियाः पार्थ लभन्ते युद्धम् ईदृशम् ॥३२॥

yadṛcchayā copapannaṁ svargadvāram apāvṛtam
sukhinaḥ kṣatriyāḥ pārtha labhante yuddham īdṛśam

Only the fortunate warriors, O Arjuna, get such an opportunity for a righteous war against evil that is like an open door to heaven. (2.32)

The righteous war is not a religious war against the followers of other religions. The righteous war may be waged even against our own evil-doer kith and kin (RV 6.75.19). Life is a continuous battle between the forces of evil and goodness. A valiant person must fight with the spirit of a warrior — with a will and determination for victory — and without any compromise with the forces of evil and difficulties. God helps the valiant who adhere to morality. Dharma (righteousness) protects those who protect Dharma (morality, justice, and righteousness).

It is better to die for a right cause and acquire the grace of sacrifice than to die an ordinary but compulsory death. The gates of heaven open wide for those who stand up to vindicate justice and righteousness (Dharma). Not to oppose an evil is to indirectly support it. Very similar ideas are expressed in other scriptures of the world. The Koran says: Allah loves those who battle for His cause in ranks (Surah 61.04). The Bible says: Happy are those who suffer persecution because they do what God requires. The kingdom of heaven belongs to them (Matthew 5.10). There is no sin in killing an aggressor. Whosoever helps and supports an aggressor is also an aggressor. Thus, all those who supported Kauravas were basically aggressors and deserved to be eliminated.

अथ चेत् त्वम् इमं धर्म्यं संग्रामं न करिष्यसि ।
ततः स्वधर्मं कीर्तिं च हित्वा पापम् अवाप्स्यसि ।।३३।।

atha cet tvam imaṁ dharmyaṁ saṁgrāmaṁ na kariṣyasi
tataḥ svadharmaṁ kīrtiṁ ca hitvā pāpam avāpsyasi

If you will not fight this battle of good over evil, you will fail in your duty, lose your reputation as a warrior, and incur sin by not doing the right action. (2.33)

अकीर्तिं चापि भूतानि कथयिष्यन्ति तेऽव्ययाम् ।
संभावितस्य चाकीर्तिर् मरणाद् अतिरिच्यते ।।३४।।

akīrtiṁ cāpi bhūtāni kathayiṣyanti te'vyayām
saṁbhāvitasya cākīrtir maraṇād atiricyate

People will talk about your disgrace for a long time. To the honorable, dishonor is worse than death. (2.34)

भयाद् रणाद् उपरतं मंस्यन्ते त्वां महारथाः ।
येषां च त्वं बहुमतो भूत्वा यास्यसि लाघवम् ।।३५।।

bhayād raṇād uparataṁ maṁsyante tvāṁ mahārathāḥ
yeṣāṁ ca tvaṁ bahumato bhūtvā yāsyasi lāghavam

The great warriors will think that you have retreated from the battle out of fear. Those who have greatly esteemed you will lose respect for you. (2.35)

अवाच्यवादांश्च बहून् वदिष्यन्ति तवाहिताः ।
निन्दन्तस् तव सामर्थ्यं ततो दुःखतरं नु किम् ।।३६।।

avācyavādāṁśca bahūn vadiṣyanti tavāhitāḥ
nindantas tava sāmarthyaṁ tato duḥkhataraṁ nu kim

Your enemies will speak many unmentionable words and scorn your ability. What could be more painful to you than this? (2.36)

हतो वा प्राप्स्यसि स्वर्गं जित्वा वा भोक्ष्यसे महीम् ।
तस्माद् उत्तिष्ठ कौन्तेय युद्धाय कृतनिश्चयः ॥३७॥

hato vā prāpsyasi svargaṁ jitvā vā bhokṣyase mahīm
tasmād uttiṣṭha kaunteya yuddhāya kṛta niścayaḥ

You will go to heaven if killed in the line of duty, or you will enjoy the kingdom on the earth if victorious. No matter what happens, you win. Therefore, get up with a determination to fight, O Arjuna. (2.37)

सुखदुःखे समे कृत्वा लाभालाभौ जयाजयौ ।
ततो युद्धाय युज्यस्व नैवं पापम् अवाप्स्यसि ॥३८॥

sukha duḥkhe same kṛtvā lābhālābhau jayājayau
tato yuddhāya yujyasva naivaṁ pāpam avāpsyasi

Treating pleasure and pain, gain and loss, and victory and defeat alike, engage yourself in your duty. By doing your duty this way, you will not incur any sin. (2.38)

Lord Krishna says here that even the violence done in the line of duty with a proper frame of mind, as discussed in the above verse, is sinless. This is the starting verse of the theory of KarmaYoga, the main theme of the Gita.

The wise should wholeheartedly welcome pleasure and pain, joy and sorrow, without becoming discouraged (MB 12.174.39). Two types of people are happy in this world: those who are completely ignorant and those who are truly wise. All others are unhappy (MB 12.174.33).

THE SCIENCE OF KARMA-YOGA, THE SELFLESS ACTION

एषा तेऽभिहिता सांख्ये बुद्धिर् योगे त्व् इमां शृणु ।
बुद्ध्या युक्तो यया पार्थ कर्मबन्धं प्रहास्यसि ॥३९॥

eṣā te'bhihitā sāṁkhye buddhir yoge tv imāṁ śṛṇu
buddhyā yukto yayā pārtha karma bandhaṁ prahāsyasi

The science of transcendental knowledge has been imparted to you, O Arjuna. Now listen to the science of God-dedicated, selfless action (Seva), endowed with which you will free yourself from all Karmic bondage, or sin. (2.39)

नेहाभिक्रमनाशोऽस्ति प्रत्यवायो न विद्यते ।
स्वल्पम् अप्य् अस्य धर्मस्य त्रायते महतो भयात् ॥४०॥
nehābhikramanāśo'sti pratyavāyo na vidyate
svalpam apy asya dharmasya trāyate mahato bhayāt

No effort ever goes to waste in selfless service, and there is no adverse effect. Even a little practice of this discipline protects one from the cycle of repeated birth and death. (2.40)

The selfless action is also called Seva, KarmaYoga, sacrifice, yoga of work, science of proper action, and yoga of equanimity. A KarmaYogi works with love for the Lord as a matter of duty without a selfish desire for the fruits of work or selfish attachment to the results, and becomes free from all fear. The word Karma also means duty, action, deeds, work, endeavor, or the results of past deeds.

व्यवसायात्मिका बुद्धिर् एकेह कुरुनन्दन ।
बहुशाखा ह्य् अनन्ताश्च बुद्धयोऽव्यवसायिनाम् ॥४१॥
vyavasāyātmikā buddhir ekeha kurunandana
bahuśākhā hy anantāśca buddhayo'vyavasāyinām

A selfless worker has resolute determination only for God-realization, but the desires of one who works to enjoy the fruits of work are endless, which makes the mind unsteady. (2.41)

THE VEDAS DEAL WITH BOTH MATERIAL AND SPIRITUAL ASPECTS OF LIFE

याम् इमां पुष्पितां वाचं प्रवदन्त्य् अविपश्चितः ।
वेदवादरताः पार्थ नान्यद् अस्तीति वादिनः ॥४२॥

yām imāṁ puṣpitāṁ vācaṁ pravadanty avipaścitaḥ
vedavādaratāḥ pārtha nānyad astīti vādinaḥ

The misguided ones who delight in the melodious chanting of the Vedas — without understanding the real purpose of the Vedas — think, O Arjuna, there is nothing else in the Vedas except the rituals for the sole purpose of obtaining heavenly enjoyment. (2.42)

कामात्मानः स्वर्गपरा जन्मकर्मफलप्रदाम् ।
क्रियाविशेषबहुलां भोगैश्वर्यगतिं प्रति ॥४३॥

kāmātmānaḥ svargaparā janma karma phala pradām
kriyā viśeṣa bahulāṁ bhogaiśvarya gatiṁ prati

They are dominated by material desires and consider the attainment of heaven as the highest goal of life. They engage in specific rites for the sake of material prosperity and enjoyment. Rebirth is the result of their action. (2.43)

भोगैश्वर्यप्रसक्तानां तयापहृतचेतसाम् ।
व्यवसायात्मिका बुद्धिः समाधौ न विधीयते ॥४४॥

bhogaiśvarya prasaktānāṁ tayā'pahṛtacetasām
vyavasāyātmikā buddhiḥ samādhau na vidhīyate

Self-realization, the real goal of life, is not possible for those who are attached to pleasure and power and whose judgment is obscured by ritualistic activities for fulfillment of selfish desires. (2.44)

Self-realization is to know one's relationship with the Supreme Lord and His true transcendental nature. The promise of material benefits of Vedic rituals is like the promise of candy to a child by the mother to induce him or her to take the medicine of detachment from the material life; it is necessary in most instances. Rituals must be changed with time and backed up by devotion and good deeds. People may pray and meditate anytime, anywhere, without any ritual. Rituals have played a great role in spiritual life, but they have been greatly abused. Lord Krishna and Lord Buddha both disapproved the misuse of Vedic rituals, not the rituals as such. Rituals create a holy and blissful atmosphere. They are regarded as a heavenly ship (RV 10.63.10) and criticized as a frail raft (MuU 1.2.07).

त्रैगुण्यविषया वेदा निस्त्रैगुण्यो भवार्जुन ।
निर्द्वन्द्वो नित्यसत्त्वस्थो निर्योगक्षेम आत्मवान् ॥४५॥

traiguṇya viṣayā vedā nistraiguṇyo bhavārjuna
nirdvandvo nitya sattvastho niryogakṣema ātmavān

A portion of the Vedas deals with three modes — goodness, passion, and ignorance — of material Nature. Rise above these three modes, and be Self-conscious. Become free from the tyranny of pairs of opposites. Remain tranquil and unconcerned with the thoughts of acquisition and preservation of material objects. (2.45)

यावानर्थ उदपाने सर्वतः संप्लुतोदके ।
तावान् सर्वेषु वेदेषु ब्राह्मणस्य विजानतः ॥४६॥

yāvān artha udapāne sarvataḥ saṁplutodake
tāvān sarveṣu vedeṣu brāhmaṇasya vijānataḥ

To the enlightened person, who has realized the true nature of the Self within, the Vedas become as useful as a small reservoir of water when the water of a huge lake becomes available. (2.46)

A scripture is like a finite pond that derives its water from the infinite ocean of Truth. Therefore, scriptures become unnecessary only after enlightenment in much the same way that a reservoir of water has no use when one is surrounded by floodwater. One who has realized the Supreme Being will not desire the attainment of heaven mentioned as the fruits of performing Vedic rituals. Scriptures, such as the Vedas, are necessary means, but not the end. Scriptures are meant to lead and guide us on the spiritual path. Once the goal is reached, they have served their purpose.

THEORY AND PRACTICE OF KARMAYOGA

कर्मण्येवाधिकारस्ते मा फलेषु कदाचन ।
मा कर्मफलहेतुर् भूर् मा ते सङ्गोऽस्त्व् अकर्मणि ॥४७॥

karmaṇy evādhikāraste mā phaleṣu kadācana
mā karma phala hetur bhūr mā te saṅgo'stv akarmaṇi

You have control over doing your respective duty only, but no control or claim over the results. The fruits of work should not be your only motive, and you should never be inactive. (2.47)

This key verse of the Gita has confused some commentators and common people who interpret it to mean that one should work without expecting a fruit. This would mean that Lord Krishna should not expect Arjuna to understand and follow His teachings! No one can perform action without expecting some result. This verse means that one should not expect only favorable results of your choice and should accept all results as Prasada (Grace) from God. This is called Prasada Buddhi, BuddhiYog or KarmaYog.

The right outlook on life develops when we fully understand that we have the ability to put our best effort into all endeavors, but we cannot pick the results of our work. We have absolutely no control over all the factors that determine the results. The affairs of the world would not run if all were given the power to choose the results of their actions or to satisfy all their desires.

One is given the power and the ability to do one's respective duty in life, but one is not free to choose the desired results. To work without expecting success or good results would be meaningless, but to be fully prepared for the unexpected should be an important part of any planning. Swami Karmananda says: The essence of KarmaYoga is to go to work just to please the creator; mentally renounce the fruits of all action; and let God take care of the results. Do your duty in life — to the best of your ability — as God's personal servant without any regard for the personal enjoyment of the fruits of your work.

Fear of failure, caused by being emotionally attached to the fruits of work, is the greatest impediment to success because it robs efficiency by constantly disturbing equanimity of mind. Therefore, duty should be performed with detached attachment. Success in any undertaking becomes easier if one works hard without being bothered by the outcome. Work is done more efficiently when the mind is not bothered continuously — consciously or subconsciously — with the outcome, good or bad, of an action.

One has to discover this fact personally in life. A person should work without selfish motives as a matter of duty for a greater cause of helping humanity rather than just helping oneself, one's children, or a few individuals. Equanimity and spiritual progress result from selfless service, whereas work with selfish motives create the bonds of Karma as well as great disappointments. Dedicated selfless service for a greater cause leads to everlasting peace and happiness here and hereafter.

The boundary of one's jurisdiction ends with the completion of duty; it never crosses the garden of fruit. A hunter has control over the arrow only, never over the deer. Harry Bhalla says: A farmer has control over how he works his land, yet no control over the harvest. But he cannot expect a harvest if he does not work his land.

When one has no desire for the pleasure of victory, one is not affected by the pain of defeat. Questions of the pleasure of success or the pain of failure do not arise because a KarmaYogi is always on the path of service without waiting to enjoy the fruit or even the flower of work. He or she has learned to enjoy the joy of service. The myopia of short-term, personal gain, caused by ignorance of metaphysics, is the root of all evils in society and the world. The bird of righteousness cannot be confined in the cage of personal gain. Dharma and selfishness cannot stay together.

The desire for fruit takes one to the dark alley of sin and prevents one's real growth. Acting only in one's own self-interest is sinful. The welfare of the individual lies in the welfare of society. The wise work for all of society, whereas the ignorant work only for themselves or their children and grandchildren. One who knows the Truth does not let the shadow of personal gain fall on the path of duty. The secret art of living a meaningful life is to be intensely active without any selfish motive, as stated below:

योगस्थः कुरु कर्माणि सङ्गं त्यक्त्वा धनंजय ।
सिद्ध्यसिद्ध्योः समो भूत्वा समत्वं योग उच्यते ।।४८।।

yogasthaḥ kuru karmāṇi saṅgaṁ tyaktvā dhanaṁjaya
siddhy asiddhyoḥ samo bhūtvā samatvaṁ yoga ucyate

Do your duty to the best of your ability, O Arjuna, with your mind attached to the Lord, abandoning worry and selfish attachment to the results, and remaining calm in both success and failure. Selfless service brings peace and equanimity of mind that lead to the union with God. (2.48)

KarmaYoga is defined as doing one's duty while maintaining equanimity under all circumstances. Pain and pleasure, birth and death, loss and gain, union and separation are inevitable, being under the control of one's past deeds or Karma, like the coming of day and night. Fools rejoice in prosperity and mourn in adversity, but a KarmaYogi remains tranquil under all circumstances (TR 2.149.03-04). The word 'yoga' has also been defined in the following verses of the Gita: 2.50, 2.53, 6.04, 6.08, 6.19, 6.23, 6.29, 6.31, 6.32, and 6.47. Any practical technique of understanding the Supreme Reality and uniting with Him is called spiritual practice, or yoga.

दूरेण ह्यवरं कर्म बुद्धियोगाद् धनंजय ।
बुद्धौ शरणम् अन्विच्छ कृपणाः फलहेतवः ॥४९॥

dūreṇa hyavaraṁ karma buddhiyogād dhanaṁjaya
buddhau śaraṇam anviccha kṛpaṇāḥ phalahetavaḥ

Work done with selfish motives is inferior by far to selfless service. Therefore, be a selfless worker, O Arjuna. Those who work only to enjoy the fruits of their labor are unhappy (because one has no control over the results). (See also 2.48, 6.03, 10.10, and 18.57) (2.49)

बुद्धियुक्तो जहातीह उभे सुकृतदुष्कृते ।
तस्माद् योगाय युज्यस्व योगः कर्मसु कौशलम् ॥५०॥

buddhiyukto jahātīha ubhe sukṛta duṣkṛte
tasmād yogāya yujyasva yogaḥ karmasu kauśalam

A KarmaYogi or the selfless person becomes free from both vice and virtue in this life itself. Therefore, strive for selfless service. Working to the best of one's abilities without becoming selfishly attached to the fruits of work is called KarmaYoga or Seva. (2.50)

Peace, composure, and freedom from Karmic bondage await those who work for a noble cause with a spirit of detachment and do not seek any personal reward or recognition. Such persons enjoy the joy of selfless service that ultimately leads them to the bliss of salvation. KarmaYoga purifies the mind and is a very powerful and easy spiritual discipline that one can practice while living and working in society. There is no religion better than selfless service. The fruits of vice and virtue grow only on the tree of selfishness, not on the tree of selfless service.

Generally, it is thought that one works harder when one is deeply interested in, or attached to, the fruits of work. Therefore,

KarmaYoga or selfless service may not be very conducive to the material progress of the individual or society. This dilemma can be solved by developing a hobby of selfless service to a noble cause of one's choice, never letting greed for the fruits dilute the purity of action. Dexterity or skillfulness in work lies in not getting bound by the bonds of one's Karma or worldly duty.

कर्मजं बुद्धियुक्ता हि फलं त्यक्त्वा मनीषिणः ।
जन्मबन्धविनिर्मुक्ताः पदं गच्छन्त्य् अनामयम् ॥५१॥
karmajaṁ buddhiyuktā hi phalaṁ tyaktvā manīṣiṇaḥ
janma bandha vinirmuktāḥ padaṁ gacchanty anāmayam

KarmaYogis are freed from the bondage of rebirth due to renouncing the selfish attachment to the fruits of all work and they attain a blissful divine state of salvation or Nirvana. (2.51)

यदा ते मोहकलिलं बुद्धिर् व्यतितरिष्यति ।
तदा गन्तासि निर्वेदं श्रोतव्यस्य श्रुतस्य च ॥५२॥
yadā te moha kalilaṁ buddhir vyatitariṣyati
tadā gantāsi nirvedaṁ śrotavyasya śrutasya ca

When your intellect completely pierces the veil of confusion regarding Self and non-Self, then you will become indifferent to what has been heard and what is to be heard from the scriptures. (2.52)

Scriptures become dispensable after enlightenment. According to Shankara, this verse means one who has rent asunder the veil of ignorance and realized the Truth, becomes indifferent to the Vedic texts that prescribe details of performing rituals for the attainment of desired fruits.

श्रुतिविप्रतिपन्ना ते यदा स्थास्यति निश्चला ।
समाधावचला बुद्धिस् तदा योगम् अवाप्स्यसि ॥५३॥
śruti vipratipannā te yadā sthāsyati niścalā
samādhāvacalā buddhis tadā yogam avāpsyasi

When your intellect that is confused by the conflicting opinions and the ritualistic doctrine of the Vedas shall stay steady and firm, concentrating on the Supreme Being, then you will be enlightened and completely united with God in trance. (2.53)

Non-scriptural reading or reading of different philosophical writings is bound to create confusion. Ramakrishna said: "One should learn from the scriptures that God alone is real and the world is illusory." A beginner should know that only God is eternal and everything else is temporal. After Self-awareness, one finds God alone has become everything. Everything is His manifestation. He is sporting in various forms. In trance, or the superconscious state of mind, the confusion arising from conflicting views ceases, and mental equipoise is attained.

Different schools of thought, cults, systems of philosophy, ways of worship, and spiritual practices found in the Vedic culture are different rungs in the ladder of yoga. Such a wide choice of methods does not exist in any other system, religion, or way or life. People's temperaments are different due to differences in their stages of spiritual development and understanding. Therefore, different schools of thought are necessary to suit different individuals, as well as the same individual as he or she grows and develops. The highest philosophy of pure monism is the topmost rung of the ladder. The vast majority cannot comprehend it. All schools and cults are necessary. One should not be confused because different methods are not meant to confuse, but one should choose wisely.

अर्जुन उवाच
स्थितप्रज्ञस्य का भाषा समाधिस्थस्य केशव ।
स्थितधीः किं प्रभाषेत किम् आसीत व्रजेत किम् ।।५४।।

arjuna uvāca
sthita prajñasya kā bhāṣā samādhisthasya keśava
sthitadhīḥ kiṁ prabhāṣeta kim āsīta vrajeta kim

Arjuna said: O Krishna, what are the marks of an enlightened person whose intellect is steady? What does a person of steady intellect think and talk about? How does such a person behave with others, and live in this world? (2.54)

The answers to all of the above questions are given by Lord Krishna in the remaining verses of this chapter.

MARKS OF A SELF-REALIZED PERSON

श्रीभगवानुवाच
प्रजहाति यदा कामान् सर्वान् पार्थ मनोगतान् ।
आत्मन्येव् आत्मना तुष्टः स्थितप्रज्ञस् तदोच्यते ॥५५॥

śrī bhagavān uvāca
prajahāti yadā kāmān sarvān pārtha manogatān
ātmanyev ātmanā tuṣṭaḥ sthita prajñas tadocyate

Lord Krishna said: When one is completely free from all desires of the mind and is satisfied with the bliss of knowing the Supreme Being, then one is called an enlightened person, O Arjuna. (2.55)

According to mother Sarda, desires for knowledge, devotion, and salvation cannot be classed as desires because they are higher desires. One should first replace the lower desires with higher desires and then renounce the highest desires also and become absolutely free. It is said that the highest freedom is the freedom from becoming free.

दुःखेष्व् अनुद्विग्नमनाः सुखेषु विगतस्पृहः ।
वीतरागभयक्रोधः स्थितधीर् मुनिर् उच्यते ॥५६॥

duḥkheṣv anudvignamanāḥ sukheṣu vigataspṛhaḥ
vīta rāga bhaya krodhaḥ sthitadhīr munir ucyate

A person is called an enlightened sage of steady intellect whose mind is unperturbed by adversity, who does not crave pleasures, and who is completely free from attachment, fear, and anger. (2.56)

Attachment to people, places, and objects takes away the intellect, and one becomes myopic. People are helplessly tied with the rope of attachment. One has to learn to cut this rope with the sword of knowledge of the Absolute and become detached and free.

यः सर्वत्रानभिस्नेहस् तत् तत् प्राप्य शुभाशुभम् ।
नाभिनन्दति न द्वेष्टि तस्य प्रज्ञा प्रतिष्ठिता ।।५७।।

yaḥ sarvatrā'nabhisnehas tat tat prāpya śubhāśubham
nābhinandati na dveṣṭi tasya prajñā pratiṣṭhitā

The mind and intellect become steady in a person who is not attached to anything, who is neither elated by getting desired results nor perturbed by undesired results. (2.57)

True spiritualists have a peaceful and happy look on their faces under all circumstances.

यदा संहरते चायं कूर्मोऽङ्गानीव सर्वशः ।
इन्द्रियाणीन्द्रियार्थेभ्यस् तस्य प्रज्ञा प्रतिष्ठिता ।।५८।।

yadā saṁharate cāyaṁ kūrmo'ṅgānīva sarvaśaḥ
indriyāṇī'ndriyārthebhyas tasya prajñā pratiṣṭhitā

When one can completely withdraw the senses from sense objects, as a tortoise withdraws its limbs into the shell for protection from calamity, then the intellect of such a person is considered steady. (2.58)

When a person learns to control or withdraw the senses from sense objects, as a tortoise retracts its limbs inside its shell in time of danger and cannot be forced to extend its limbs again until the trouble is over, the lamp of Self-knowledge becomes lighted, and one perceives the self-effulgent Supreme Being within (MB 12.174.51). A Self-realized person enjoys the beauty of the world, keeping the senses under complete control like a tortoise. The best way to purify the senses and control them perfectly like a tortoise, is to engage them in the service of God at all times.

विषया विनिवर्तन्ते निराहारस्य देहिनः ।
रसवर्जं रसोऽप्यस्य परं दृष्ट्वा निवर्तते ॥५९॥

viṣayā vinivartante nirāhārasya dehinaḥ
rasavarjaṁ raso'pyasya paraṁ dṛṣṭvā nivartate

The desire for sensual pleasures fades away if one abstains from sense enjoyment, but the craving for sense enjoyment remains in a very subtle form. This subtle craving also completely disappears from one who knows the Supreme Being. (2.59)

The desire for sensual pleasure becomes dormant when one abstains from sense enjoyment, or incurs physical limitations imposed by disease or old age. But the craving remains as a subtle mental impression. Those who have tasted the nectar of unity with the Supreme Being no longer find enjoyment in the lower-level sensual pleasures. The subtle craving lurks like a robber ready to rob the striver at the appropriate opportunity, as explained below:

DANGERS OF UNRESTRAINED SENSES

यततो ह्यपि कौन्तेय पुरुषस्य विपश्चितः ।
इन्द्रियाणि प्रमाथीनि हरन्ति प्रसभं मनः ॥६०॥

yatato hyapi kaunteya puruṣasya vipaścitaḥ
indriyāṇi pramāthīni haranti prasabhaṁ manaḥ

Restless senses, O Arjuna, forcibly carry away the mind of even a wise person striving for perfection. (2.60)

The wise always keep vigilance over the mind. The mind can never be fully trusted. It can mislead even a Self-realized person (BP 5.06.02-05). One has to be very alert and closely witness the wanderings of the mind. Never relax your vigilance until the final goal of God-realization is reached. Mother Sarda said: It is the very nature of the mind to go to lower objects of enjoyment, just as it is the nature of water to flow downwards. The grace of God can make the mind go towards higher objects, just as the sun's rays lift the water to the sky.

The human mind is ever ready to deceive and play tricks. Therefore, discipline, constant vigilance, and sincere spiritual practice are needed. The mind is like an unruly horse that needs to be broken in. Never let the mind roam unwatched into the realm of sensuality. The path of spiritual life is very slippery and has to be trodden very carefully to avoid falls. It is not a joyous ferryboat ride, but a very difficult path to tread like the sharp edge of a sword. Many obstacles, distractions, and failures come on the path to help the devotee become stronger and more advanced on the path, just like iron is turned into steel by alternate heating, cooling, and hammering. One should not get discouraged by failures, but carry on with determination.

तानि सर्वाणि संयम्य युक्त आसीत मत्परः ।
वशे हि यस्येन्द्रियाणि तस्य प्रज्ञा प्रतिष्ठिता ।।६१।।

tāni sarvāṇi saṁyamya yukta āsīta matparaḥ
vaśe hi yasye'ndriyāṇi tasya prajñā pratiṣṭhitā

One should fix one's mind on Me with loving contemplation after bringing the senses under control. One's intellect becomes steady when one's senses are under complete control. (2.61)

ध्यायतो विषयान् पुंसः सङ्गस् तेषूपजायते ।
सङ्गात् संजायते कामः कामात् क्रोधोऽभिजायते ।।६२।।

dhyāyato viṣayān puṁsaḥ saṅgas teṣū'pajāyate
saṅgāt saṁjāyate kāmaḥ kāmāt krodho'bhijāyate

One develops attachment to sense objects by thinking about sense objects. Desire for sense objects comes from attachment to sense objects, and anger comes from unfulfilled desires. (2.62)

क्रोधाद् भवति संमोहः संमोहात् स्मृतिविभ्रमः ।
स्मृतिभ्रंशाद् बुद्धिनाशो बुद्धिनाशात् प्रणश्यति ॥६३॥
krodhād bhavati saṁmohaḥ saṁmohāt smṛti vibhramaḥ
smṛti bhraṁśād buddhināśo buddhināśāt praṇaśyati

Delusion or wild ideas arise from anger. The mind is bewildered by delusion. Reasoning is destroyed when the mind is bewildered. One falls from the right path when reasoning is destroyed. (2.63)

ATTAINMENT OF PEACE AND HAPPINESS THROUGH SENSE CONTROL AND KNOWLEDGE

रागद्वेषवियुक्तैस्तु विषयान् इन्द्रियैश्चरन् ।
आत्मवश्यैर् विधेयात्मा प्रसादम् अधिगच्छति ॥६४॥
rāga dveṣa viyuktais tu viṣayān indriyaiś caran
ātmavaśyair vidheyātmā prasādam adhigacchati

A disciplined person, enjoying sense objects with senses that are under control and free from attachments and aversions, attains tranquility. (2.64)

Real peace and happiness are achieved, not by sense gratification, but by sense control.

प्रसादे सर्वदुःखानां हानिर् अस्योपजायते ।
प्रसन्नचेतसो ह्याशु बुद्धिः पर्यवतिष्ठते ॥६५॥
prasāde sarva duḥkhānāṁ hānir asyo'pajāyate
prasannacetaso hyāśu buddhiḥ paryavatiṣṭhate

All sorrows are destroyed upon attainment of tranquility. The intellect of such a tranquil person soon becomes completely steady and united with the Supreme. (2.65)

नास्ति बुद्धिर् अयुक्तस्य न चायुक्तस्य भावना ।
न चाभावयतः शान्तिर् अशान्तस्य कुतः सुखम् ॥६६॥
nāsti buddhir ayuktasya na cāyuktasya bhāvanā
na cābhāvayataḥ śāntir aśāntasya kutaḥ sukham

There is neither Self-knowledge nor Self-perception for those who are not united with the Supreme. Without Self-perception there is no peace, and without peace there can be no happiness. (2.66)

इन्द्रियाणां हि चरतां यन् मनोऽनुविधीयते ।
तदस्य हरति प्रज्ञां वायुर् नावम् इवाम्भसि ॥६७॥
indriyāṇāṁ hi caratāṁ yan mano'nuvidhīyate
tad asya harati prajñāṁ vāyur nāvam ivāmbhasi

The mind, when controlled by the roving senses, steals away the intellect as a storm takes away a boat on the sea from its destination — the spiritual shore of peace and happiness. (2.67)

A person without control over the mind and senses drifts like a ship without its rudder, becomes a reactor instead of an actor, and develops negative Karma.

Greed for the pleasure of enjoying the light leads bugs to destruction; similarly, desire for the enjoyment of sensual pleasures keeps one away from Self-knowledge and leads into the net of transmigration (MB 3.02.69).

तस्माद् यस्य महाबाहो निगृहीतानि सर्वशः ।
इन्द्रियाणीन्द्रियार्थेभ्यस् तस्य प्रज्ञा प्रतिष्ठिता ॥६८॥

tasmād yasya mahābāho nigṛhītāni sarvaśaḥ
indriyāṇī'ndriyārthebhyas tasya prajñā pratiṣṭhitā

Therefore, O Arjuna, one's intellect becomes steady when the senses are completely withdrawn from sense objects. (2.68)

या निशा सर्वभूतानां तस्यां जागर्ति संयमी ।
यस्यां जाग्रति भूतानि सा निशा पश्यतो मुनेः ॥६९॥
yā niśā sarvabhūtānāṁ tasyāṁ jāgarti saṁyamī
yasyāṁ jāgrati bhūtāni sā niśā paśyato muneḥ

A yogi, the person of self-restraint, remains wakeful when it is night for all others. It is night for the yogi who sees when all others are wakeful. (2.69)

Ascetics keep awake or detached in the night of mundane existence of life because they are in quest of the highest truth. One is considered awake when one is free from worldly desires (TR 2.92.02). A yogi is always aware of the Spirit about which others are unaware. A sage who sees is unaware of the experience of sense objects about which others are aware. The life of an ascetic is entirely different from the life of a materialistic person. What is considered real by a yogi is of no value for a worldly person. While most people sleep and make dream plans in the night of the illusory world, a yogi keeps awake because he or she is detached from the world while living in it.

आपूर्यमाणम् अचलप्रतिष्ठं
समुद्रम् आपः प्रविशन्ति यद्वत् ।
तद्वत् कामा यं प्रविशन्ति सर्वे
स शान्तिम् आप्नोति न कामकामी ॥७०॥

āpūryamāṇam acalapratiṣṭhaṁ
samudram āpaḥ praviśanti yadvat
tadvat kāmā yaṁ praviśanti sarve
sa śāntim āpnoti na kāmakāmī

One attains peace when all desires dissipate within the mind without creating any mental disturbance, just as river waters enter the full ocean without creating any disturbance. One who desires material objects is never peaceful. (2.70)

Torrents of the river of desire can carry away the mind of a materialistic person as a river carries away wood and other objects in its path. The tranquil mind of a yogi is like an ocean that takes in the rivers of desire without being disturbed by them because a yogi does not think about personal gain or loss. Human desires are endless. To satisfy a desire is like drinking salt water that will never quench thirst, but will increase it. It is like trying to extinguish a fire with gasoline.

Trying to fulfill material desires is like adding more wood to the fire. The fire will go out if no more wood is added to it (MB 12.17.05). If one dies without conquering the great enemy — desires — one has to reincarnate to fight this enemy again and again till victory (MB 12.16.24). One cannot see one's face in a pot of water that is disturbed by the wind, similarly, one is unable to realize one's true Self when the mind and senses remain perturbed by the winds of material desires (MB 12.204.03).

विहाय कामान् यः सर्वान् पुमांश्चरति निःस्पृहः ।
निर्ममो निरहंकारः स शान्तिम् अधिगच्छति ॥७१॥
vihāya kāmān yaḥ sarvān pumāṁś carati niḥspṛhaḥ
nirmamo nirahaṁkāraḥ sa śāntim adhigacchati

One who abandons all desires and becomes free from longing and the feeling of 'I' and 'my', attains peace. (2.71)

एषा ब्राह्मी स्थितिः पार्थ नैनां प्राप्य विमुह्यति ।
स्थित्वाऽस्याम् अन्तकालेऽपि ब्रह्मनिर्वाणम् ऋच्छति ॥७२॥
eṣā brāhmī sthitiḥ pārtha nai'nāṁ prāpya vimuhyati
sthitvā'syām antakāle'pi brahma nirvāṇam ṛcchati

O Arjuna, this is the superconscious state of mind. Attaining this state, one is no longer deluded. Gaining this state, even at the end of one's life, a person attains the very goal of human life by becoming one with God. (2.72).

The Supreme Being is the ultimate Reality and truth, knowledge and consciousness, and is limitless and blissful (TaU 2.01.01). The individual soul becomes blissful and filled with joy after knowing God. The giver of bliss is nothing but the bliss itself like the giver of wealth must have wealth. That from which the origin, sustenance, and dissolution of this universe are derived is called the Absolute (BS 1.01.02, TaU 3.01.01). Knowledge is not a natural quality (Dharma) of the Absolute; it is the intrinsic nature of the Absolute (DB 7.32.19). The Absolute is the substratum, or material as well as efficient cause of the universe. It is both the source and the sink of energy in one. It is also called the Unified Field, Supreme Spirit, Divine Person, and Total Consciousness that is responsible for the sense perceptions in all living beings by functioning through mind and intellect.

The word 'Salvation' in Christianity means deliverance from the power and penalty of sin. Sin in Hinduism is nothing but the Karmic bondage responsible for transmigration. Thus, salvation is equivalent to the Sanskrit word 'Mukti' in Hinduism — the final emancipation of the living entity from transmigration. Mukti means the complete destruction of all impressions of desires from the causal body. It is the uniting of the individual soul with the Supersoul. Some say that the all-pervading Supersoul is the causal body who is conducting everything and remains compassionately detached. The Sanskrit word 'Nirvana' in Buddhism is thought to be the cessation of worldly desires and ego. It is a state of being in which worldly desires and personal likes and dislikes have been absolutely extinguished. It is getting out of body-consciousness and attaining a state of Self-consciousness. It is liberation from attachment to the material body and achieving a state of bliss with God.

ॐ तत्सदिति श्रीमद्भगवद्गीतासूपनिषत्सु ब्रह्मविद्यायां योगशास्त्रे
श्रीकृष्णार्जुनसंवादे सांख्ययोगो नाम द्वितीयोऽध्यायः ॥
OM tatsaditi śrīmadbhagavadgītāsūpaniṣatsu brahmavidyāyāṁ
yogaśāstre śrīkṛṣṇārjuna saṁvāde sāṁkhyayogo
nāma dvitīyo'dhyāyaḥ

Thus ends the second chapter named "Transcendental Knowledge"
of the Upaniṣad of the Bhagavadgītā, the scripture
of yoga, dealing with the science of the
Absolute in the form of the dialogue
between Śrīkṛṣṇa and Arjuna.

अथ तृतीयोऽध्यायः
CHAPTER 3
कर्मयोगः
PATH OF SELFLESS SERVICE

अर्जुन उवाच
ज्यायसी चेत् कर्मणस् ते मता बुद्धिर् जनार्दन ।
तत् किं कर्मणि घोरे मां नियोजयसि केशव ।।१।।

arjuna uvāca
jyāyasī cet karmaṇas te matā buddhir janārdana
tat kiṁ karmaṇi ghore māṁ niyojayasi keśava

व्यामिश्रेणेव वाक्येन बुद्धिं मोहयसीव मे ।
तद् एकं वद निश्चित्य येन श्रेयोऽहम् आप्नुयाम् ।।२।।

vyāmiśreṇeva vākyena buddhiṁ mohayasīva me
tad ekaṁ vada niścitya yena śreyo'ham āpnuyām

Arjuna asked: If You consider that acquiring transcendental knowledge is better than working, then why do You want me to engage in this horrible war, O Krishna? You seem to confuse my mind by apparently conflicting words. Tell me, decisively, one thing by which I may attain the Supreme. (3.01-02)

Arjuna was in the mode of delusion; he thought that Lord Krishna meant a contemplative life was better than doing one's normal duty in life. Some people are often confused and think that salvation is possible only by leading a life devoted to scriptural study, contemplation, and acquiring Self-knowledge. Lord Krishna clarifies this by mentioning two major paths of spiritual practice — depending on the nature of the individual — in the following verse:

श्रीभगवानुवाच
लोकेऽस्मिन् द्विविधा निष्ठा पुरा प्रोक्ता मयाऽनघ ।
ज्ञानयोगेन सांख्यानां कर्मयोगेन योगिनाम् ।।३।।

śrī bhagavān uvāca
loke'smin dvividhā niṣṭhā purā proktā mayā'nagha
jñānayogena sāṁkhyānāṁ karmayogena yogināṃ

Lord Krishna said: In this world I have stated a twofold path of spiritual discipline in past — the path of Self-knowledge for the contemplative ones and the path of unselfish work (Seva, KarmaYoga) for all others. (3.03)

'Seva' or 'KarmaYoga' means sacrifice, selfless service, unselfish work, meritorious deeds, giving away something to others. Some people often get confused like Arjuna and think that leading a life devoted to scriptural study, contemplation, and acquiring transcendental knowledge may be better for spiritual progress than doing one's worldly duty.

A God-realized person does not consider oneself the doer of any action, but only an instrument in the hands of the divine for His use. It should be further pointed out that both metaphysical knowledge and selfless service are means to attain the Supreme Being. These two paths are not separate, but complementary. In life a combination of these two modes is considered the best. Carry both selfless service and a spiritual discipline of acquir ing Self-knowledge with you as stated in the following verses:

न कर्मणाम् अनारम्भान् नैष्कर्म्यं पुरुषोऽश्नुते ।
न च संन्यसनाद् एव सिद्धिं समधिगच्छति ।।४।।

na karmaṇām anārambhān naiṣkarmyaṁ puruṣo'śnute
na ca saṁnyasanād eva siddhiṁ samadhigacchati

न हि कश्चित् क्षणमपि जातु तिष्ठत्य् अकर्मकृत् ।
कार्यते ह्य् अवशः कर्म सर्वः प्रकृतिजैर् गुणैः ।।५।।

na hi kaścit kṣaṇam api jātu tiṣṭhaty akarmakṛt
kāryate hy avaśaḥ karma sarvaḥ prakṛtijair guṇaiḥ

One does not attain freedom from the bondage of Karma by merely abstaining from work. No one attains perfection by merely giving up work because no one can remain actionless even for a moment. Everything in the universe is driven to action — helplessly indeed — by the forces of Nature. (3.04-05)

It is not possible for anybody to completely abandon action by thought, word, and deed. Therefore, one should always be active in serving the Lord by various means of one's choosing, and never be without work because an idle mind is the devil's workshop. Performing action till death with a desireless frame of mind is better than abandoning work and leading the life of an ascetic, even after God-realization because even an ascetic cannot escape the impulse of action.

कर्मेन्द्रियाणि संयम्य य आस्ते मनसा स्मरन् ।
इन्द्रियार्थान् विमूढात्मा मिथ्याचारः स उच्यते ।।६।।
karmendriyāṇi saṁyamya ya āste manasā smaran
indriyārthān vimūḍhātmā mithyācāraḥ sa ucyate

Anyone who restrains the senses but mentally thinks of sense pleasures, is called a pretender. (3.06)

One's growth comes from working selflessly rather than giving up work and practicing sense-control before one is naturally ready for it. Bringing the mind under control is difficult, and spiritual life becomes a mockery without mastery over the senses. Desires may become dormant and rise again to give trouble, just as a sleeping person wakes up in due course of time.

The four goals of human life — doing one's duty, earning wealth, material and sensual enjoyment, and attaining salvation — were designed in the Vedic tradition for gradual and systematic growth of the individual and the progress of society. Success in spiritual life does not come from prematurely wearing saffron clothes just to maintain an Ashram or livelihood without first conquering the six enemies — lust, anger, greed, pride, attachment, and envy. It is said that such pretenders do a great disservice to God, society, and themselves and become bereft of happiness in this world and the next (BP 11.18.40-41) A pretending monk is considered sinful and a destroyer of the ascetic order of life.

WHY ONE SHOULD SERVE OTHERS

यस् त्व् इन्द्रियाणि मनसा नियम्यारभतेऽर्जुन ।
कर्मेन्द्रियैः कर्मयोगम् असक्तः स विशिष्यते ।।७।।

yas tv indriyāṇi manasā niyamyā'rabhate'rjuna
karmendriyaiḥ karmayogam asaktaḥ sa viśiṣyate

One who restrains the senses — by a trained and purified mind and intellect — and engages the organs of action to selfless service, is considered superior. (3.07)

नियतं कुरु कर्म त्वं कर्म ज्यायो ह्य् अकर्मणः ।
शरीरयात्रापि च ते न प्रसिद्ध्येद् अकर्मणः ।।८।।

niyataṁ kuru karma tvaṁ karma jyāyo hy akarmaṇaḥ
śarīrayātrāpi ca te na prasiddhyed akarmaṇaḥ

Perform your obligatory duty because working is indeed better than sitting idle. Even the maintenance of your body would be impossible without work. (3.08)

यज्ञार्थात् कर्मणोऽन्यत्र लोकोऽयं कर्मबन्धनः ।
तदर्थं कर्म कौन्तेय मुक्तसङ्गः समाचर ।।९।।

yajñārthāt karmaṇo'nyatra loko'yaṁ karma bandhanaḥ
tad arthaṁ karma kaunteya mukta saṅgaḥ samācara

Human beings are bound by work (Karma) that is not performed as a selfless service (Seva, Yajna). Therefore, becoming free from selfish attachment to the fruits of

work, do your duty efficiently as a service to Me for the good of humanity. (3.09)

TO HELP EACH OTHER IS THE FIRST COMMANDMENT OF THE CREATOR

सहयज्ञाः प्रजाः सृष्ट्वा पुरोवाच प्रजापतिः ।
अनेन प्रसविष्यध्वम् एष वोऽस्त्व् इष्टकामधुक् ॥१०॥
sahayajñāḥ prajāḥ sṛṣṭvā purovāca prajāpatiḥ
anena prasaviṣyadhvam eṣa vo'stv iṣṭa kāmadhuk

In the beginning the Creator created human beings together with selfless service (Seva, Yajna, sacrifice) and said: By serving each other you shall prosper, and the sacrificial service shall fulfill all your desires. (3.10)

देवान् भावयतानेन ते देवा भावयन्तु वः ।
परस्परं भावयन्तः श्रेयः परम् अवाप्स्यथ ॥११॥
devān bhāvayatānena te devā bhāvayantu vaḥ
parasparaṁ bhāvayantaḥ śreyaḥ param avāpsyatha

Nourish the celestial controllers with selfless service, and they will nourish you. Thus nourishing one another, you shall attain the Supreme goal. (3.11)

इष्टान् भोगान् हि वो देवा दास्यन्ते यज्ञभाविताः ।
तैर् दत्तान् अप्रदायैभ्यो यो भुङ्क्ते स्तेन एव सः ॥१२॥
iṣṭān bhogān hi vo devā dāsyante yajñabhāvitāḥ
tair dattān apradāyaibhyo yo bhuṅkte stena eva saḥ

The celestial controllers, being nourished and pleased by selfless service, will give you all desired objects. One who enjoys the gift of celestial controllers without sharing with others is, indeed, a thief. (3.12)

lestial controller or guardian angel means a ıler, a celestial person, an angel, an agent of God, the cosmic forces that control, protect, and fulfill desires. Even the gates of heaven shall be closed to those who try to enter alone. According to the ancient scriptures, helping others is the best meritorious deed one can do. The wise seek to serve themselves in the service of others while the ignorant serve themselves at the cost of others. To serve each other is the original or first commandment of the creator that has been restated by Lord Krishna in the Gita. God has given us talents to help us serve, and in serving others we grow spiritually. We take birth to help each other, to understand, care, love, give, and forgive each other. According to Muniji "Giving is Living". Giving makes the world a better place for all humanity.

It is believed that selfishness saps our natural health and immune system also. When we take steps to move ourselves away from self and think about the needs of others and how to serve them, a physical healing process seems to set in motion. This is especially true if we personally help a person we may never meet again in life.

One who makes no sacrifice, but grabs everything without helping others, is like a thief. It is said that celestials are pleased when people help each other. The capacity of the giver increases by the grace of God, fulfilling all desires to give. The spirit of cooperation — not competition or confrontation — between human beings, between nations, and between organizations seems to be hinted here by the Lord. All the necessities of life are produced by dedicated sacrificial services of other people. We are created to depend on each other. The world has been called a cosmic wheel of cooperative action by Swami Chinmayananda. Cooperation, not competition, is more conducive to overall progress of the individual, as well as society. Nothing worthwhile can be achieved without cooperation and help from others. The world would be a much better place if all inhabitants cooperated and helped each other, rather than fight or compete with each other. It is the selfish motive that prevents cooperation even between spiritual organizations. One who can truly say all organizations, temples, mosques, and churches are our own, is a true leader and a real saint.

यज्ञशिष्टाशिनः सन्तो मुच्यन्ते सर्वकिल्बिषैः ।
भुञ्जते ते त्व् अघं पापा ये पचन्त्यात्मकारणात् ॥१३॥
yajñaśiṣṭāśinaḥ santo mucyante sarva kilbiṣaiḥ
bhuñjate te tv aghaṁ pāpā ye pacanty ātmakāraṇāt

The righteous who eat after sharing with others are freed from all sins, but the impious who cook food only for themselves (without first offering to God or sharing with others), in truth, eat sin. (3.13)

Food should be cooked for the Lord and offered first to Him with love before consuming. Children should be taught to pray before taking food. The house rule should be: No food before prayer and thanking the Lord. Lord further states that helping others is divine:

अन्नाद् भवन्ति भूतानि पर्जन्याद् अन्नसंभवः ।
यज्ञाद् भवति पर्जन्यो यज्ञः कर्मसमुद्भवः ॥१४॥
annād bhavanti bhūtāni parjanyād annasaṁbhavaḥ
yajñād bhavati parjanyo yajñaḥ karma samudbhavaḥ

कर्म ब्रह्मोद्भवं विद्धि ब्रह्माक्षरसमुद्भवम् ।
तस्मात् सर्वगतं ब्रह्म नित्यं यज्ञे प्रतिष्ठितम् ॥१५॥
karma brahmodbhavaṁ viddhi brahmā'kṣara samudbhavam
tasmāt sarvagataṁ brahma nityaṁ yajñe pratiṣṭhitam

Living beings are sustained from food grains; grains are produced by sacrificial work (or duty performed by farmers and other field workers). Duty is prescribed in the scriptures. Scriptures come from the Supreme Being. Thus the all-pervading Supreme Being or God is ever present in selfless service. (3.14-15)

एवं प्रवर्तितं चक्रं नानुवर्तयतीह यः ।
अघायुर् इन्द्रियारामो मोघं पार्थ स जीवति ॥१६॥

evaṁ pravartitaṁ cakraṁ nānuvartayatīha yaḥ
aghāyur indriyārāmo moghaṁ pārtha sa jīvati

One who does not help to keep the wheel of creation in motion by sacrificial duty (Seva) and rejoices in sense pleasures, that sinful person lives in vain. (3.16)

A grain of wheat is a single grain unless it is dropped into the ground and dies. If it does die, then it produces many grains (John 12.24). Saints, trees, rivers, and earth are for the use of others. However, there is no prescribed duty for the enlightened ones as explained below:

यस् त्वात्मरतिर् एव स्याद् आत्मतृप्तश्च मानवः ।
आत्मन्येव च संतुष्टस् तस्य कार्यं न विद्यते ॥१७॥

yas tv ātmaratir eva syād ātmatṛptaśca mānavaḥ
ātmanyeva ca saṁtuṣṭas tasya kāryaṁ na vidyate

नैव तस्य कृतेनार्थो नाकृतेनेह कश्चन ।
न चास्य सर्वभूतेषु कश्चिद् अर्थव्यपाश्रयः ॥१८॥

naiva tasya kṛtenārtho nākṛteneha kaścana
na cāsya sarvabhūteṣu kaścid arthavyapāśrayaḥ

For one who rejoices only with the Supreme Being, who is delighted with the Supreme Being, and who is content with the Supreme Being alone, for such a Self-realized person there is no duty. Such a person has no interest, whatsoever, in what is done or what is not done. A Self-realized person does not depend on anybody, except God, for anything. (3.17-18)

All duties, obligations, prohibitions, regulations, and injunctions are meant to lead one to perfection. Therefore, a perfect yogi who has Self-knowledge, detachment, and devotion has nothing more to gain in this world by doing worldly duty.

LEADERS SHOULD SET AN EXAMPLE

तस्माद् असक्तः सततं कार्यं कर्म समाचर ।
असक्तो ह्याचरन् कर्म परम् आप्नोति पूरुषः ॥१९॥

tasmād asaktaḥ satataṁ kāryaṁ karma samācara
asakto hyācaran karma param āpnoti pūruṣaḥ

Always perform your duty efficiently and without any selfish attachment to the results because by doing work without attachment, one reaches the supreme goal of life. (3.19)

In no other scripture, written before the Bhagavad-Gita, has the philosophy of KarmaYoga — unselfish devotion for the welfare of humanity — been so beautifully expounded. Lord Krishna has elevated the idea of altruism to the highest form of worship and spiritual practice. By altruism, one obtains grace, by grace one gets faith, and by faith the ultimate Truth is revealed. One immediately feels better by helping others and comes one step closer to perfection. Swami Vivekananda said: Work done for others awakens the subtle and dormant divine power, Kundalini, within our body. An example of attaining Self-realization by persons while doing their worldly duties is given below:

कर्मणैव हि संसिद्धिम् आस्थिता जनकादयः ।
लोकसंग्रहमेवापि संपश्यन् कर्तुम् अर्हसि ॥२०॥

karmaṇaiva hi saṁsiddhim āsthitā janakādayaḥ
lokasaṁgraham evāpi saṁpaśyan kartum arhasi

King Janaka and many others attained perfection of Self-realization by selfless service (KarmaYoga) alone. You

also should perform your duty with a view to guide people and for the welfare of society. (3.20)

Those who do selfless service are not bound by Karma and attain salvation (VP 1.22.52). Nothing is beyond the reach of those who have others' interest in mind. Swami Harihar says: Selfless service to humanity is the true service to God and the highest form of worship.

यद् यद् आचरति श्रेष्ठस् तत् तद् एवेतरो जनः ।
स यत् प्रमाणं कुरुते लोकस् तद् अनुवर्तते ॥२१॥
yad yad ācarati śreṣṭhas tat tad evetaro janaḥ
sa yat pramāṇaṁ kurute lokas tad anuvartate

Because whatever noble persons do, others follow. Whatever standard they set up, the world follows. (3.21)

People follow whatever great persons do (BP 5.04.15). Jesus said: I have set an example for you, so that you will do just what I have done for you (John 13.15). A leader is obliged to set higher ethical, moral, and spiritual standards for the general population to follow. If the leader fails in this regard, the quality of the nation's life declines, and the progress of society is greatly hampered. Therefore, leaders have a great burden on their shoulders. The life of a true leader is the life of service and sacrifice. Leadership should not be an enterprise for becoming rich or famous.

न मे पार्थास्ति कर्तव्यं त्रिषु लोकेषु किंचन ।
नानवाप्तमवाप्तव्यं वर्त एव च कर्मणि ॥२२॥
na me pārthāsti kartavyaṁ triṣu lokeṣu kiṁcana
nānavāptam avāptavyaṁ varta eva ca karmaṇi

O Arjuna, there is nothing in the three worlds — heaven, earth, and the lower regions — that should be done by Me,

nor there is anything unobtained that I should obtain, yet I engage in action. (3.22)

यदि ह्यहं न वर्तेयं जातु कर्मण्यतन्द्रितः ।
मम वर्त्मानुवर्तन्ते मनुष्याः पार्थ सर्वशः ।।२३।।

yadi hy ahaṁ na varteyaṁ jātu karmaṇy atandritaḥ
mama vartmā'nuvartante manuṣyāḥ pārtha sarvaśaḥ

उत्सीदेयुर् इमे लोका न कुर्यां कर्म चेद् अहम् ।
संकरस्य च कर्ता स्याम् उपहन्याम् इमाः प्रजाः ।।२४।।

utsīdeyur ime lokā na kuryāṁ karma ced aham
saṁkarasya ca kartā syām upahanyām imāḥ prajāḥ

If I do not engage in action relentlessly, O Arjuna, people would follow the same path in every way. These worlds would perish if I did not work, and I would be the cause of confusion and destruction. (3.23-24)

WHAT SHOULD THE WISE DO TO THE IGNORANT?

सक्ताः कर्मण्य् अविद्वांसो यथा कुर्वन्ति भारत ।
कुर्याद् विद्वांस् तथासक्तश् चिकीर्षुर् लोकसंग्रहम् ।।२५।।

saktāḥ karmaṇy avidvāṁso yathā kurvanti bhārata
kuryād vidvāṁs tathāsaktaś cikīrṣur lokasaṁgraham

The ignorant work with attachment to the fruits of work for themselves, and the wise should work without attachment for the welfare of the society. (3.25)

न बुद्धिभेदं जनयेद् अज्ञानां कर्मसङ्गिनाम् ।
जोषयेत् सर्वकर्माणि विद्वान् युक्तः समाचरन् ।।२६।।

na buddhibhedaṁ janayed ajñānāṁ karma saṅginām
joṣayet sarva karmāṇi vidvān yuktaḥ samācaran

The wise should not unsettle the minds of the ignorant who are attached to the fruits of work, but should inspire others by performing all works efficiently without selfish attachment. (See also 3.29) (3.26)

Doing one's duty without a personal, selfish motive is an exalted state given only to the enlightened ones. This may be beyond comprehension of ordinary people. The mark of genius lies in the ability to handle two opposed ideas and paradoxes, such as living in the world with detached attachment. Most people work hard only when they have some motivating force, such as enjoyment of the fruits of work. Such persons should not be discouraged or condemned. They should be introduced slowly to the beginning stages of selfless service. The excessive attachment to possessions, not the possessions themselves, becomes the source of misery.

Just as one has to pray and worship with single-minded attention, similarly, one should perform worldly duties with full attention, even while knowing full well that the world and its affairs are transitory. One should not live thinking only of God and neglecting one's duty in the world. Yogananda said: Be as earnest about meditation as about earning money. One should not live a one-sided life. The importance of controlling the senses and ways to combat ego are given below:

ALL WORKS ARE THE WORKS OF NATURE

प्रकृतेः क्रियमाणानि गुणैः कर्माणि सर्वशः ।
अहंकारविमूढात्मा कर्ताहम् इति मन्यते ।।२७।।

prakṛteḥ kriyamāṇāni guṇaiḥ karmāṇi sarvaśaḥ
ahaṁkāra vimūḍhātmā kartāham iti manyate

The forces (Gunas) of Nature do all work, but due to delusion of ignorance people assume themselves to be the doer. (See also 5.09, 13.29, and 14.19) (3.27)

Indirectly, God is the doer of everything. The power and the will of God do everything. One is not free even to kill oneself. One cannot feel the presence of the omnipresent God as long as one feels: "I am the doer". If one realizes — by the grace of God — that one is not the doer, but just an instrument, one at once becomes free. A Karmic bondage is created if we consider ourselves the doer and enjoyer. The same work done by a Self-realized master and an ordinary person produces different results. The work done by a Self-realized master becomes spiritualized and produces no Karmic bondage because a Self-realized person does not consider oneself the doer or the enjoyer. The work done by an ordinary person produces Karmic bondage.

तत्त्ववित् तु महाबाहो गुणकर्मविभागयोः ।
गुणा गुणेषु वर्तन्त इति मत्वा न सज्जते ॥२८॥

tattvavit tu mahābāho guṇa karma vibhāgayoḥ
guṇā guṇeṣu vartanta iti matvā na sajjate

One who knows the truth about the role of the forces of Nature in getting work done, does not become attached to work. Such a person knows that it is the forces of Nature that get their work done by using our organs as instruments. (3.28)

प्रकृतेर् गुणसंमूढाः सज्जन्ते गुणकर्मसु ।
तान् अकृत्स्नविदो मन्दान् कृत्स्नविन् न विचालयेत् ॥२९॥

prakṛter guṇa saṁmūḍhāḥ sajjante guṇa karmasu
tān akṛtsnavido mandān kṛtsnavin na vicālayet

Those who are deluded by the illusive power (Maya) of Nature become attached to the work done by the forces of Nature. The wise should not disturb the mind of the ignorant whose knowledge is imperfect. (See also 3.26) (3.29)

The enlightened one should not try to dissuade or detract ignorant ones from performing selfish actions that they do, deluded by the forces of Nature, because doing work — and not the renunciation of work in the initial stages — will ultimately lead them to realize the truth that we are not the doers, but divine instruments only. Working with attachment also has a place in the development of society and in the life of common people. People can easily transcend selfish desires by working for a noble goal of their choice.

मयि सर्वाणि कर्माणि संन्यस्याध्यात्मचेतसा ।
निराशीर् निर्ममो भूत्वा युध्यस्व विगतज्वरः ।।३०।।

mayi sarvāṇi karmāṇi saṁnyasyā'dhyātma cetasā
nirāśīr nirmamo bhūtvā yudhyasva vigatajvaraḥ

Do your prescribed duty, dedicating all work to Me in a spiritual frame of mind, free from desire, attachment, and mental grief. (3.30)

ये मे मतम् इदं नित्यम् अनुतिष्ठन्ति मानवाः ।
श्रद्धावन्तोऽनसूयन्तो मुच्यन्ते तेऽपि कर्मभिः ।।३१।।

ye me matam idaṁ nityam anutiṣṭhanti mānavāḥ
śraddhāvanto'nasūyanto mucyante te'pi karmabhiḥ

ये त्वेतद् अभ्यसूयन्तो नानुतिष्ठन्ति मे मतम् ।
सर्वज्ञानविमूढांस् तान् विद्धि नष्टान् अचेतसः ।।३२।।

ye tv etad abhyasūyanto nā'nutiṣṭhanti me matam
sarvajñāna vimūḍhāṁs tān viddhi naṣṭān aceta saḥ

Those who always practice this teaching of Mine — with faith and free from cavil — become free from the bondage of Karma. But those who carp at this teaching and do not practice it, should be considered ignorant, senseless, and confused. (3.31-32)

सदृशं चेष्टते स्वस्याः प्रकृतेर् ज्ञानवान् अपि ।
प्रकृतिं यान्ति भूतानि निग्रहः किं करिष्यति ॥३३॥

sadṛśaṁ ceṣṭate svasyāḥ prakṛter jñānavān api
prakṛtiṁ yānti bhūtāni nigrahaḥ kiṁ kariṣyati

All beings follow their nature. Even the wise act according to their own nature. If we are but pawns of our nature, what, then, is the value of sense restraint? (3.33)

While we cannot and should not suppress our nature, we must not become victims but rather controllers and masters of the senses by using the discriminative faculties of human life for gradual improvement. The best way to control the senses is to engage all our senses in the service of God.

TWO MAJOR STUMBLING BLOCKS ON THE PATH OF PERFECTION

इन्द्रियस्येन्द्रियस्यार्थे रागद्वेषौ व्यवस्थितौ ।
तयोर् न वशम् आगच्छेत् तौ ह्यस्य परिपन्थिनौ ॥३४॥

indriyasye'ndriyasyā 'rthe rāgadveṣau vyavasthitau
tayor na vaśam āgacchet tau hy asya paripanthinau

Attachments and aversions for sense objects remain in the senses. One should not come under the control of these two because they are two major stumbling blocks, indeed, on one's path of Self-realization. (3.34)

'Attachment' may be defined as a very strong desire to experience sensual pleasures again and again. 'Aversion' is the strong dislike for the unpleasant. The search for peace of mind, comfort, and happiness is the basis of all human endeavors, including the acquisition and propagation of knowledge. Desire — like any other power given by the Lord — is not the problem. We can have desires with a proper frame of mind that gives us control over attachments and aversions. If we can manage our wants, most of the things we possess become dispensable rather than essential. With a right attitude, we can get mastery over all our attachments and aversions. The only necessity is to have a frame of mind that makes most items unnecessary. Those who have knowledge, detachment, and devotion have neither likes nor dislikes for any worldly object, person, place, or work. Personal likes and dislikes disturb the equanimity of mind and become a hindrance on the path of spiritual progress.

One should act with a sense of duty without being governed by personal likes and dislikes. Selfless service is the only austerity and penance in this age by which anyone can reach God while living and working in modern society without going to the mountains and jungles.

Everybody benefits if work is done for the Lord, just as every part of the tree gets water when water is put at the root of the tree rather than on individual leaves. Attachments and aversions are destroyed in a noble person at the onset of Self-knowledge and detachment. Personal likes and dislikes are two major obstacles on the path of perfection. One who has conquered attachments and aversions becomes a free person and attains salvation by doing one's natural duty as stated below:

श्रेयान् स्वधर्मो विगुणः परधर्मात् स्वनुष्ठितात् ।
स्वधर्मे निधनं श्रेयः परधर्मो भयावहः ॥३५॥

śreyān svadharmo viguṇaḥ paradharmāt svanuṣṭhitāt
svadharme nidhanaṁ śreyaḥ paradharmo bhayāvahaḥ

One's inferior natural work is better than superior unnatural work. Even death in carrying out one's (natural) duty is useful. Unnatural work produces too much stress. (See also 18.47) (3.35)

One who does the duty ordained by nature is freed from the bonds of Karma and slowly rises above the worldly plane (BP 7.11.32). One who takes on work that was not meant for him or her certainly courts failure. One evolves by the work best suited to one's own nature or inborn tendencies. There is no perfect occupation. Every occupation in this world has some faults. One should keep oneself free from concern over the faults of one's duty in life. One should carefully study one's nature to determine an appropriate occupation. Natural work does not produce stress and is conducive to creativity. Walking uphill, vocationally, against one's natural tendencies is not only more stressful but also less productive, and it does not provide opportunity and leisure time for spiritual growth and development. On the other hand, if one follows a very easy or artistic path, one may not be able to earn enough to satisfy the basic necessities of (family) life. Therefore, lead a simple life by limiting unnecessary luxuries, and develop a hobby of selfless service to balance the material and spiritual needs of life. The balanced life is a happy life.

LUST IS THE ORIGIN OF SIN

अर्जुन उवाच
अथ केन प्रयुक्तोऽयं पापं चरति पूरुषः ।
अनिच्छन् अपि वार्ष्णेय बलाद् इव नियोजितः ।।३६।।

arjuna uvāca
atha kena prayukto'yaṁ pāpaṁ carati pūruṣaḥ
anicchann api vārṣṇeya balād iva niyojitaḥ

Arjuna said: O Krishna, what impels one to commit sin or selfish deeds as if unwillingly and forced against one's will? (3.36)

श्रीभगवानुवाच
काम एष क्रोध एष रजोगुणसमुद्भवः ।
महाशनो महापाप्मा विद्ध्येनम् इह वैरिणम् ।।३७।।

śrī bhagavān uvāca
kāma eṣa krodha eṣa rajoguṇa samudbhavaḥ
mahāśano mahāpāpmā viddhy enam iha vairiṇam

Lord Krishna said: It is the lust, born out of passion, that becomes anger when unfulfilled. Lust is insatiable and is a great devil. Know this as the enemy. (3.37)

The mode of passion is the absence of mental equilibrium leading to vigorous activity to achieve desired fruits. Lust, the passionate selfish desire for all sensual and material pleasures, is the product of the mode of passion. Lust becomes anger if it is unfulfilled. When the attainment of fruits is hindered or interrupted, the intense desire for their achievement turns into fierce rage. Hence, the Lord says that lust and anger are two mighty enemies that can lead one to commit sin and turn one astray from the path of Self-realization, the supreme goal of human life. Actually, mundane desire compels a person to engage in sinful activities in spite of his or her will. Control your wants because whatever you want wants you. Lord Buddha said: Selfish desire is the root of all evils and misery.

धूमेनाव्रियते वह्निर् यथादर्शो मलेन च ।
यथोल्बेनावृतो गर्भस् तथा तेनेदम् आवृतम् ।।३८।।
dhūmenā'vriyate vahnir yathā'darśo malena ca
yatho'lbenā'vṛto garbhas tathā tenedam āvṛtam

आवृतं ज्ञानम् एतेन ज्ञानिनो नित्यवैरिणा ।
कामरूपेण कौन्तेय दुष्पूरेणानलेन च ।।३९।।
āvṛtaṁ jñānam etena jñānino nitya vairiṇā
kāmarūpeṇa kaunteya duṣpūreṇā'nalena ca

As a fire is covered by smoke, as a mirror by dust, and as an embryo by the amnion, similarly, Self-knowledge gets covered by different degrees of this insatiable lust, the eternal enemy of the wise. (3.38-39)

Lust and Self-knowledge are eternal enemies. Lust can be destroyed only by Self-knowledge. Where lust resides and how one should control the senses to subjugate lust, are given below:

इन्द्रियाणि मनो बुद्धिर् अस्याधिष्ठानम् उच्यते ।
एतैर् विमोहयत्य् एष ज्ञानम् आवृत्य देहिनम् ।।४०।।
indriyāṇi mano buddhir asyā'dhiṣṭhānam ucyate
etair vimohayaty eṣa jñānam āvṛtya dehinam

The senses, the mind, and the intellect are said to be the seat of lust. Lust deludes a person by controlling the senses, the mind, and the intellect and veils Self-knowledge. (3.40)

तस्मात् त्वम् इन्द्रियाण्यादौ नियम्य भरतर्षभ ।
पाप्मानं प्रजहि ह्येनं ज्ञानविज्ञाननाशनम् ।।४१।।
tasmāt tvam indriyāṇyādau niyamya bharata rṣabha
pāpmānaṁ prajahi hy enaṁ jñānavijñāna nāśanam

Therefore, by controlling the senses, first kill this devil of material desires (or lust) that destroys Self-knowledge and Self-realization. (3.41)

The mighty enemy, lust, enslaves the intellect by using the mind as its friend and senses and sense objects as its soldiers. These soldiers keep the individual soul deluded and obscure Absolute Truth as a part of the drama of life. The success or failure of our role in action depends on how we handle our individual role and reach our destiny.

All desires cannot — and need not — be eliminated, but selfish desires and motives must be eliminated for spiritual progress. All our actions by thought, word and deed, including desires, should be directed to glorify God and for the good of humanity. The scriptures say: The mortal, when freed from the captivity of selfish desires, becomes immortal and attains liberation even in this very life (KaU 6.14, BrU 4.04.07).

HOW TO CONTROL LUST

इन्द्रियाणि पराण्याहुर् इन्द्रियेभ्यः परं मनः ।
मनसस् तु परा बुद्धिर् यो बुद्धेः परतस् तु सः ॥४२॥
indriyāṇi parāṇy āhur indriyebhyaḥ paraṁ manaḥ
manasas tu parā buddhir yo buddheḥ paratas tu saḥ

The senses are said to be superior to the body; the mind is superior to the senses; the intellect is superior to the mind; and the Self is superior to the intellect. (3.42)

एवं बुद्धेः परं बुद्ध्वा संस्तभ्यात्मानम् आत्मना ।
जहि शत्रुं महाबाहो कामरूपं दुरासदम् ॥४३॥
evaṁ buddheḥ paraṁ buddhvā saṁstabhyā'tmānam ātmanā
jahi śatruṁ mahābāho kāmarupaṁ durāsadam

Thus, knowing the Self to be the highest, and controlling the mind by the intellect that is purified by spiritual practices, one must kill this mighty enemy, lust, O Arjuna, with the sword of true knowledge of the Self. (3.43)

Uncontrolled worldly desires will ruin the beautiful spiritual journey of life. The scriptures provide ways and means of keeping the desires born in the mind under proper control. The body may be compared to a chariot upon which the individual soul — as passenger, owner, and enjoyer — is riding on a spiritual journey towards the Supreme Abode of the Lord. Duty and Self-knowledge are the two wheels of the chariot, and devotion is its axle. Selfless service is the road, and the divine qualities are the milestones. The scriptures are the guiding lights to dispel the darkness of ignorance. The five senses are the horses of this chariot. Sense objects are the roadside green grasses; attachments and aversions are the stumbling blocks; and lust, anger, and greed are the plunderers. Friends and relatives are fellow travelers whom we temporarily meet during the journey. Intellect is the driver of this chariot. If intellect, the charioteer, is not made pure and strong by Self-knowledge and will power, then strong desires for sensual and material pleasures — or the senses — will control the mind (See 2.67) instead of the intellect controlling the mind. The mind and senses will attack and take control of intellect, the weak charioteer, and lead the passenger away from the goal of salvation into the ditch of transmigration.

If the intellect is well trained and purified by the fire of Self-knowledge and discrimination, the intellect will be able to control the sense-horses with the help of spiritual practice and detachment, the two reins of mind, and the whip of moral conduct and spiritual practices. The charioteer should hold the reins under control at all times; otherwise, the sense-horses will lead one into the ditch of transmigration. A single moment of carelessness leads to the downfall of the seeker. Finally, one must cross the river of illusion (Maya) and, by using the bridge of meditation and the silent repetitive chanting of Lord's name or a mantra to still the ripples of mind waves, reach the spiritual shore of trance. Those who cannot control the senses will not be able to attain Self-realization, the goal of human birth.

One must not spoil oneself by wrongful temporary pleasures of the senses. One who can control the senses can control the whole world and achieve success in all endeavors. Passion cannot be completely eliminated, but is subdued by Self-knowledge. The intellect becomes polluted during the youthful years, just as the clear water of a river becomes muddy during the rainy season. Keeping good company and setting a higher goal of life prevent the mind and intellect from becoming tainted by the distractions of sensual pleasures.

ॐ तत्सदिति श्रीमद्भगवद्गीतासूपनिषत्सु ब्रह्मविद्यायां योगशास्त्रे
श्रीकृष्णार्जुनसंवादे कर्मयोगो नाम तृतीयोऽध्यायः ॥

OM tatsaditi śrīmadbhagavadgītāsūpaniṣatsu brahmavidyāyāṁ
yogaśāstre śrīkṛṣṇārjuna saṁvāde karmayogo
nāma tṛtīyo'dhyāyaḥ

Thus ends the third chapter named "Path of Selfless Service" of
the Upaniṣad of the Bhagavadgītā, the scripture of yoga,
dealing with the science of the Absolute in the
form of the dialogue between
Śrīkṛṣṇa and Arjuna.

अथ चतुर्थोऽध्यायः
CHAPTER 4
ज्ञानकर्मसंन्यासयोगः
PATH OF RENUNCIATION WITH KNOWLEDGE

श्रीभगवानुवाच

इमं विवस्वते योगं प्रोक्तवान् अहम् अव्ययम् ।
विवस्वान् मनवे प्राह मनुर् इक्ष्वाकवेऽब्रवीत् ।।१।।

śrī bhagavān uvāca
imaṁ vivasvate yogaṁ proktavān aham avyayam
vivasvān manave prāha manur ikṣvākave'bravīt

एवं परम्पराप्राप्तम् इमं राजर्षयो विदुः ।
स कालेनेह महता योगो नष्टः परंतप ।।२।।

evaṁ paramparā prāptam imaṁ rājarṣayo viduḥ
sa kāleneha mahatā yogo naṣṭaḥ paraṁtapa

स एवायं मया तेऽद्य योगः प्रोक्तः पुरातनः ।
भक्तोऽसि मे सखा चेति रहस्यं ह्येतद् उत्तमम् ।।३।।

sa evāyaṁ mayā te'dya yogaḥ proktaḥ purātanaḥ
bhakto'si me sakhā ceti rahasyaṁ hyetad uttamam

KARMA-YOGA IS AN ANCIENT FORGOTTEN COMMANDMENT

Lord Krishna said: I taught this KarmaYoga, the eternal science of right action, to King Vivasvan. Vivasvan taught it to Manu; Manu taught it to Ikshvaku. Thus, the saintly Kings knew this science of proper action (KarmaYoga), handed down in succession. After a long time, this science was lost from this earth. Today, I have described the same ancient science to you because you are my sincere devotee and friend. This science is a supreme secret indeed. (4.01-03)

KarmaYoga, discussed in the previous chapter, is declared by the Lord as the supreme secret science of right action. According to Swami Karmananda, a practitioner of KarmaYoga, unless Lord Himself reveals this secret science, no one can practice or even understand it.

अर्जुन उवाच
अपरं भवतो जन्म परं जन्म विवस्वतः ।
कथम् एतद् विजानीयां त्वम् आदौ प्रोक्तवान् इति ।।४।।
arjuna uvāca
aparaṁ bhavato janma paraṁ janma vivasvataḥ
katham etad vijānīyāṁ tvam ādau proktavān iti

Arjuna said: You were born later, but Vivasvan was born in ancient time. How am I to understand that You taught this science in the beginning of the creation? (4.04)

Arjuna questions how Krishna, a contemporary of Arjuna, could have taught this science of KarmaYoga to King Vivasvan, who was born earlier in ancient times, long before Lord Krishna. The doctrine of Bhagavad-Gita is not just five thousand years old; it is primeval. Lord Krishna restated it in the Gita for the benefit of humanity. All great masters come to rekindle the fire of forgotten Truth. Different people have said everything we hear or read at different times.

THE PURPOSE OF INCARNATION OF GOD

श्रीभगवानुवाच
बहूनि मे व्यतीतानि जन्मानि तव चार्जुन ।
तान्यहं वेद सर्वाणि न त्वं वेत्थ परंतप ।।५।।
śrī bhagavān uvāca
bahūni me vyatītāni janmāni tava cā'rjuna
tānyahaṁ veda sarvāṇi na tvaṁ vettha paraṁtapa

Lord Krishna said: Both you and I have taken many births. I remember them all, O Arjuna, but you do not remember. (4.05)

अजोऽपि सन्न् अव्ययात्मा भूतानाम् ईश्वरोऽपि सन् ।
प्रकृतिं स्वाम् अधिष्ठाय संभवाम्यात्ममायया ।।६।।
ajo'pi sann avyayātmā bhūtānām īśvaro'pi san
prakṛtiṁ svām adhiṣṭhāya saṁbhavāmy ātma māyayā

Though I am eternal, immutable, and the Lord (Ishvara, controller) of all beings, yet I manifest Myself by controlling material Nature, using My own divine potential energy, Yoga-Maya. (See also 10.14) (4.06)

Yoga-māyā (Divine Light, Brahma-jyoti, Noor) is the creative power (Ānanda-śakti) of Lord Kṛṣṇa. Mahā-māyā is the fractional reflection of Yoga-māyā. Kāla-māyā is the reflection of Mahā-māyā. And the illusory energy (Māyā) is the supernatural, extraordinary, and mystic power of Eternal Being (Brahma). Mahā-māyā, Kāla-māyā, and Māyā are also called Ādi Prakṛti; and Prakṛti, the material Nature, is considered the reflection of Māyā. Thus Yoga-māyā is the origin of both Māyā and Prakṛti. Guru Nanak said: "He has created Māyā that deceives and controls us." The word 'Māyā' also means unreal, illusory, or deceptive image of Reality. Due to the power of Māyā, one considers the universe existent and distinct from Eternal Being (Brahma). The Eternal Light (Brahma-jyoti, Noor, Yoga-māyā) is the invisible potential energy; Māyā is kinetic energy, the force of action of Brahma. They are inseparable like fire and heat. Māyā is also used as a metaphor to explain the visible world (Jagat) to common people.

यदा यदा हि धर्मस्य ग्लानिर् भवति भारत ।
अभ्युत्थानम् अधर्मस्य तदात्मानं सृजाम्यहम् ।।७।।
yadā yadā hi dharmasya glānir bhavati bhārata
abhyutthānam adharmasya tadā'tmānaṁ sṛjāmy aham

परित्राणाय साधूनां विनाशाय च दुष्कृताम् ।
धर्मसंस्थापनार्थाय संभवामि युगे युगे ॥८॥

paritrāṇāya sādhūnāṁ vināśāya ca duṣkṛtām
dharma saṁsthāpanārthāya saṁbhavāmi yuge yuge

Whenever there is a decline of Dharma (Righteousness) and a predominance of Adharma (Unrighteousness), O Arjuna, I manifest Myself. I appear from time to time for protecting the good, for transforming the wicked, and for establishing world order (Dharma). (4.07-08)

The Supreme Being is both divine and human (AV 4.16.08). Prophets appear from time to time as divine dispensation sees the need for the welfare of society. Whenever miscreants are born to destroy world order (Dharma), the good Lord, Vishnu, incarnates to put everything in proper balance (VR 7.08.27). His compassion is the main reason for Lord's incarnation (SBS 49). There are other reasons besides the protection of righteousness (Dharma), for the Lord's incarnation. The Supreme Being, which is beyond birth and death, incarnates in human form through a great soul on earth to satisfy the longings of devotees who want to see Him and be in His personal presence. Saint Tulasidasa said: Though devoid of material attributes, unattached, and immutable, yet for the love of His votaries, the Lord assumes a form with attributes (TR 2.218.03).

Lord performs many ordinary, human, and also uncommon or controversial pastimes just to please His devotees or to set things right. Ordinary human beings cannot understand the reasons behind these pastimes and, therefore, should not pass judgment on Lord's activities when He incarnates. Great personalities and incarnations are sometimes known to be acting contrary to the scriptural rules, just as a King has the freedom to break certain rules. These acts are done for a very good purpose and with a reason beyond human comprehension. One should neither criticize nor follow such acts.

Saints and sages also reincarnate by the will of Krishna. Ramakrishna said that he would live in a subtle body for three hundred years in the hearts and minds of his devotees. Yogananda said: So long as people in this world are crying for help, I shall return to ply my boat and offer to take them to heavenly shores.

जन्म कर्म च मे दिव्यम् एवं यो वेत्ति तत्त्वतः ।
त्यक्त्वा देहं पुनर्जन्म नैति माम् एति सोऽर्जुन ।।९।।

janma karma ca me divyam evaṁ yo vetti tattvataḥ
tyaktvā dehaṁ punarjanma naiti mām eti so'rjuna

One who truly understands My transcendental appearance, and activities of creation, maintenance, and dissolution, attains My Supreme Abode and is not born again after leaving this body, O Arjuna. (4.09)

One develops love for Krishna by studying and listening to the transcendental birth and sportive acts of the Lord as narrated by the saints and sages in the scriptures. True understanding of the transcendental nature of Lord's form, His incarnation, and His activities, is the Self-knowledge that leads to salvation.

वीतरागभयक्रोधा मन्मया माम् उपाश्रिताः ।
बहवो ज्ञानतपसा पूता मद्भावम् आगताः ।।१०।।

vīta rāga bhaya krodhā manmayā mām upāśritāḥ
bahavo jñāna tapasā pūtā mad bhāvam āgatāḥ

Many have become free from attachment, fear, anger, and attained salvation by taking refuge in Me, by becoming fully absorbed in My thoughts and by getting purified by the fire of Self-knowledge. (4.10)

PATH OF WORSHIP AND PRAYER

ये यथा मां प्रपद्यन्ते तांस् तथैव भजाम्यहम् ।
मम वर्त्मानुवर्तन्ते मनुष्याः पार्थ सर्वशः ।।११।।

ye yathā māṁ prapadyante tāṁs tathaiva bhajāmy aham
mama vartmā'nuvartante manuṣyāḥ pārtha sarvaśaḥ

With whatever motive people worship Me, I fulfill their desires accordingly. People worship Me with different motives, O Arjuna. (4.11)

Ask, and you will receive; seek, and you will find; knock, and the door will be opened to you (Luke 11.09). It is due to divine illusion (Maya) that most people seek temporary material gains, such as health, wealth, and success, and not Self-knowledge and devotion to His lotus feet.

काङ्क्षन्तः कर्मणां सिद्धिं यजन्त इह देवताः ।
क्षिप्रं हि मानुषे लोके सिद्धिर् भवति कर्मजा ॥१२॥
kāṅkṣantaḥ karmaṇāṁ siddhiṁ yajanta iha devatāḥ
kṣipraṁ hi mānuṣe loke siddhir bhavati karmajā

Those who long for success in their work here on earth worship the celestial controllers, Devas. Success in work comes quickly in this human world. (4.12)

No one, including all Devas, and Brahm, has his or her own power. They all derive their powers from the Supreme Being, ParaBrahm.

Would you give to your son a stone when he asks you for bread? Your Father in heaven will give good things to those who ask Him (Matthew 7.09-11). When you ask for something in prayer, have faith and believe that you have received it, and it will be given to you (Mark 11.24). In prayer one asks the Lord's help in getting what one needs; in worship one adores, glorifies, and thanks Him for what one has. One should first be aware of and contemplate one's plight, feel helpless in getting out of the difficulty, then seek divine help — through prayer — in a state of helplessness with intense faith. Lord will take the first step if you know your plight and seek His help for transformation. Show yourself — open up, confess — to the Lord as you are in prayer; be specific in what you ask; and cry for His help.

All prayers are answered, but prayers for the benefit of others are given first priority. Lord actually knows our needs at all times and is simply waiting to be asked for help due to our free will. Meditation is listening to God by stilling the mind and assuming a receptive posture in order to hear Lord's instructions, insights, and revelations. For example, embrace the attitude: Thank You for answering my prayers and for all You have given me, but now what do You want me to do with what You have given? Then, having said that, be still and alert, and just try to listen. Pray so that you can talk to God and tell Him how you are and what you have been doing. Meditate so that God can effectively tell you what you are supposed to do.

DIVISION OF LABOR IS BASED ON THE APTITUDE OF PEOPLE

चातुर्वर्ण्यं मया सृष्टं गुणकर्मविभागशः ।
तस्य कर्तारम् अपि मां विद्ध्य् अकर्तारम् अव्ययम् ॥१३॥

cāturvarṇyaṁ mayā sṛṣṭaṁ guṇakarma vibhāgaśaḥ
tasya kartāram api māṁ viddhy akartāram avyayam

I created the four divisions of human society based on aptitude and vocation. Though I am the author of this system of division of labor, one should know that I do nothing directly, and I am eternal. (See also 18.41) (4.13)

न मां कर्माणि लिम्पन्ति न मे कर्मफले स्पृहा ।
इति मां योऽभिजानाति कर्मभिर् न स बध्यते ॥१४॥

na māṁ karmāṇi limpanti na me karmaphale spṛhā
iti māṁ yo'bhijānāti karmabhir na sa badhyate

Work or Karma does not bind Me because I have no desire for the fruits of work. One who fully understands and practices this truth is also not bound by Karma. (4.14)

Those who want to be first must place themselves last and be the servant of all (Mark 10.44). All works, including prayers, should be undertaken for a just cause, rather than just for personal gain.

एवं ज्ञात्वा कृतं कर्म पूर्वैर् अपि मुमुक्षुभिः ।
कुरु कर्मैव तस्मात् त्वं पूर्वैः पूर्वतरं कृतम् ॥१५॥
evaṁ jñātvā kṛtaṁ karma pūrvair api mumukṣubhiḥ
kuru karmai'va tasmāt tvaṁ pūrvaiḥ pūrvataraṁ kṛtam

The ancient seekers of salvation also performed their duties without concern for the fruits. Therefore, you should do your duty as the ancients did. (4.15)

ATTACHED, DETACHED, AND FORBIDDEN ACTION

किं कर्म किम् अकर्मेति कवयोऽप्य् अत्र मोहिताः ।
तत् ते कर्म प्रवक्ष्यामि यज् ज्ञात्वा मोक्ष्यसेऽशुभात् ॥१६॥
kiṁ karma kiṁ akarmeti kavayo'pya atra mohitāḥ
tat te karma pravakṣyāmi yaj jñātvā mokṣyase'śubhāt

Even the wise are confused about what is action and what is inaction. Therefore, I shall clearly explain what is action, knowing that one shall be liberated from the evil of birth and death. (4.16)

कर्मणो ह्यपि बोद्धव्यं बोद्धव्यं च विकर्मणः ।
अकर्मणश्च बोद्धव्यं गहना कर्मणो गतिः ॥१७॥
karmaṇo hyapi boddhavyaṁ boddhavyaṁ ca vikarmaṇaḥ
akarmaṇaś ca boddhavyaṁ gahanā karmaṇo gatiḥ

The true nature of action is very difficult to understand. Therefore, one should know the nature of attached action, the nature of detached action, and also the nature of forbidden action. (4.17)

Attached action is selfish work, done in the mode of passion that produces Karmic bondage and leads to transmigration. Detached action is unselfish work, done in the mode of goodness that leads to salvation. Detached action is considered to be inaction because from the Karmic viewpoint, it is as if no action was performed. Action forbidden by the scriptures, done in the mode of ignorance, is harmful to both the doer and society. It creates misfortunes here and hereafter.

A KARMA-YOGI IS NOT SUBJECT TO THE KARMIC LAWS

कर्मण्य् अकर्म यः पश्येद् अकर्मणि च कर्म यः ।
स बुद्धिमान् मनुष्येषु स युक्तः कृत्स्नकर्मकृत् ॥१८॥

karmaṇy akarma yaḥ paśyed akarmaṇi ca karma yaḥ
sa buddhimān manuṣyeṣu sa yuktaḥ kṛtsnakarmakṛt

One who sees inaction in action and action in inaction, is a wise person. Such a person is a yogi and has accomplished everything. (See also 3.05, 3.27, 5.08 and 13.29) (4.18)

All acts are the acts of Eternal Being's (Brahma's) Divine Light (BrahmaJyoti, Noor), the inactively active actor. The Bible says: The words you speak are not yours; they come from the Spirit of your Father (Matthew 10.20). The wise perceive the inactive, infinite, and invisible reservoir of potential energy of the Supreme as the ultimate source of all visible kinetic energy in the cosmos, just as invisible electricity runs a fan. The urge and power to do action come from the Supreme Being. Therefore, one should spiritualize all work by perceiving that one does nothing at all and everything is done by the energy of the Supreme Being, using us only as an instrument.

यस्य सर्वे समारम्भाः कामसंकल्पवर्जिताः ।
ज्ञानाग्निदग्धकर्माणं तम् आहुः पण्डितं बुधाः ।।१९।।
yasya sarve samārambhāḥ kāmasaṁkalpa varjitāḥ
jñānāgni dagdha karmāṇaṁ tam āhuḥ paṇḍitaṁ budhāḥ

One whose desires have become selfless by being roasted in the fire of Self-realization, is called a sage by the wise. (4.19)

त्यक्त्वा कर्मफलासङ्गं नित्यतृप्तो निराश्रयः ।
कर्मण्य् अभिप्रवृत्तोऽपि नैव किंचित् करोति सः ।।२०।।
tyaktvā karmaphalāsaṅgaṁ nityatṛpto nirāśrayaḥ
karmaṇy abhipravṛtto'pi naiva kiṁcita karoti saḥ

One who has abandoned selfish attachment to the fruits of work and remains ever content and dependent on no one but God, such a person — though engaged in activity — does nothing at all and incurs no Karmic reaction. (4.20)

निराशीर् यतचित्तात्मा त्यक्तसर्वपरिग्रहः ।
शारीरं केवलं कर्म कुर्वन् नाप्नोति किल्बिषम् ।।२१।।
nirāśīr yatacittātmā tyakta sarva parigrahaḥ
śārīraṁ kevalaṁ karma kurvan nāpnoti kilbiṣam

One who is free from desires, whose mind and senses are under control, and who has renounced all proprietorship, does not incur sin — the Karmic reaction — by doing bodily action. (4.21)

यदृच्छालाभसंतुष्टो द्वन्द्वातीतो विमत्सरः ।
समः सिद्धाव् असिद्धौ च कृत्वापि न निबध्यते ।।२२।।

yadṛcchā lābha saṁtuṣṭo dvandvātīto vimatsaraḥ
samaḥ siddhāv asiddhau ca kṛtvāpi na nibadhyate

A KarmaYogi — who is content with whatever gain comes naturally by His will, who is unaffected by pairs of opposites, and free from envy, tranquil in success and failure — is not bound by Karma. (4.22)

गतसङ्गस्य मुक्तस्य ज्ञानावस्थितचेतसः ।
यज्ञायाचरतः कर्म समग्रं प्रविलीयते ॥२३॥

gatasaṅgasya muktasya jñānāvasthita cetasaḥ
yajñāyā'carataḥ karma samagraṁ pravilīyate

All Karmic bonds of a KarmaYogi — who is free from attachment, whose mind is fixed in Self-knowledge, and who does work as a service to the Lord — dissolve away. (4.23)

ब्रह्मार्पणं ब्रह्म हविर् ब्रह्माग्नौ ब्रह्मणा हुतम् ।
ब्रह्मैव तेन गन्तव्यं ब्रह्मकर्मसमाधिना ॥२४॥

brahmā'rpaṇaṁ brahma havir brahmāgnau brahmaṇā hutam
brahmaiva tena gantavyaṁ brahmakarma samādhinā

The divine Spirit (Brahma, Eternal Being) has become everything. The Divinity (Brahma, Self, Spirit) shall be realized by one who considers everything as a manifestation (or an act) of Brahma. (Also see 9.16) (4.24)

Life itself is an ever-burning fire where sacrificial ceremony is going on constantly. Every action must be thought of as a holy sacrifice, a holy act. Everything is not the Eternal Being (Brahma), but Brahma is the root or basis of everything. One attains salvation and becomes one with Brahma, without losing one's identity, when one perceives Brahma in every action, perceives the things one uses as a transformation of Brahma, and realizes that the very process of all action is also Brahma. Thus salvation or Mukti is not the destruction of individual soul (Jeeva), but the realization of one's true nature that Jeeva is like Brahma.

DIFFERENT TYPES OF SPIRITUAL PRACTICES OR SACRIFICES

दैवम् एवापरे यज्ञं योगिनः पर्युपासते ।
ब्रह्माग्नाव् अपरे यज्ञं यज्ञेनैवोपजुह्वति ।।२५।।

daivam evā 'pare yajñaṁ yoginaḥ paryupāsate
brahmāgnāv apare yajñaṁ yajñenai'vo'pajuhvati

श्रोत्रादीनीन्द्रियाण्य् अन्ये संयमाग्निषु जुह्वति ।
शब्दादीन् विषयान् अन्ये इन्द्रियाग्निषु जुह्वति ।।२६।।

śrotrādīnī'ndriyāṇy anye saṁyamāgniṣu juhvati
śabdādīn viṣayān anye indriyāgniṣu juhvati

सर्वाणीन्द्रियकर्माणि प्राणकर्माणि चापरे ।
आत्मसंयमयोगाग्नौ जुह्वति ज्ञानदीपिते ।।२७।।

sarvāṇī'ndriya karmāṇi prāṇakarmāṇi cāpare
ātmasaṁyama yogāgnau juhvati jñānadīpite

द्रव्ययज्ञास् तपोयज्ञा योगयज्ञास् तथापरे ।
स्वाध्यायज्ञानयज्ञाश्च यतयः संशितव्रताः ।।२८।।

dravyayajñās tapoyajñā yogayajñās tathāpare
svādhyāya jñānayajñāśca yatayaḥ saṁśita vratāḥ

Some yogis perform the service of worship to celestial controllers (Devas), while others offer sacrifice (of reasoning, Viveka) to the fire of the Eternal Being (Brahma) by performing the sacrifice of Self-knowledge. (4.25)

Some offer their hearing and other senses as sacrifice in the fires of restraint; others offer sound and other objects of the senses (as sacrifice) in the fires of the senses. (4.26)

Others offer all the functions of the senses and the functions of the five bioimpulses (life forces) as sacrifice

in the fire of self-restraint that is kindled by Self-knowledge. (4.27)

Others offer their wealth, their austerity, and their practice of yoga as sacrifice, while the ascetics with strict vows offer their study of scriptures and knowledge as sacrifice. (4.28)

अपाने जुह्वति प्राणं प्राणेऽपानं तथापरे ।
प्राणापानगती रुद्ध्वा प्राणायामपरायणाः ।।२९।।

apāne juhvati prāṇaṁ prāṇe'pānaṁ tathāpare
prāṇāpāna gati ruddhvā prāṇāyāma parāyaṇāḥ

Those who engage in yogic practices reach the breathless state of trance by offering inhalation into exhalation and exhalation into inhalation as a sacrifice (by using short breathing Kriya techniques). (4.29)

Deep spiritual meaning and interpretation of the practical yogic verses (4.29, 4.30, 5.27, 6.13, 8.10, 8.12, 8.13, 8.24, and 8.25) cannot be explained here. They should be acquired from a Self-realized master of KriyaYoga.

The breathing process can be slowed down by: (1) watching the breath going in and coming out as one watches the ocean waves going up and down, (2) practicing of diaphragmatic (or deep yogic) breathing, and (3) using yogic techniques and KriyaYoga. The aim of yogic practice is to achieve the superconscious or breathless state of trance by gradually mastering the breathing process.

अपरे नियताहाराः प्राणान् प्राणेषु जुह्वति ।
सर्वेऽप्येते यज्ञविदो यज्ञक्षपितकल्मषाः ।।३०।।

apare niyatāhārāḥ prāṇān prāṇeṣu juhvati
sarve'pyete yajñavido yajñakṣapita kalmaṣāḥ

Others restrict their diet and offer their inhalations as sacrifice into their inhalations. All these people are the

knowers of sacrifice and their minds become purified by their sacrifice. (4.30)

यज्ञशिष्टामृतभुजो यान्ति ब्रह्म सनातनम् ।
नायं लोकोऽस्त्य् अयज्ञस्य कुतोऽन्यः कुरुसत्तम ॥३१॥

yajñaśiṣṭāmṛta bhujo yānti brahma sanātanam
nāyaṁ loko'sty ayajñasya kuto'nyaḥ kurusattama

Those who perform selfless service obtain the nectar of Self-knowledge as a result of their sacrifice and attain the Supreme Being. O Arjuna, if even this world is not a happy place for the non-sacrificer, how can the other world be? (See also 4.38, and 5.06). (4.31)

एवं बहुविधा यज्ञा वितता ब्रह्मणो मुखे ।
कर्मजान् विद्धि तान् सर्वान् एवं ज्ञात्वा विमोक्ष्यसे ॥३२॥

evaṁ bahuvidhā yajñā vitatā brahmaṇo mukhe
karmajān viddhi tān sarvān evaṁ jñātvā vimokṣyase

Many types of spiritual disciplines are described in the Vedas. Know that all of them are the action of body, mind, and senses prompted by the forces of Nature. Understanding this, one shall attain Nirvana or salvation. (See also 3.14) (4.32)

In order to attain salvation, spiritual discipline or sacrifice should be performed as a duty without attachment and with full understanding that oneself is not the doer.

A SUPERIOR SPIRITUAL PRACTICE

श्रेयान् द्रव्यमयाद् यज्ञाज् ज्ञानयज्ञः परंतप ।
सर्वं कर्माखिलं पार्थ ज्ञाने परिसमाप्यते ॥३३॥

śreyān dravyamayād yajñāj jñānayajñaḥ paraṁtapa
sarvaṁ karmā'khilaṁ pārtha jñāne parisamāpyate

The acquisition and propagation of Self-knowledge are superior to any material gain or gift because purification of mind and intellect eventually leads to the dawn of transcendental knowledge and Self-realization — the sole purpose of any spiritual practice. (4.33)

तद् विद्धि प्रणिपातेन परिप्रश्नेन सेवया ।
उपदेक्ष्यन्ति ते ज्ञानं ज्ञानिनस् तत्त्वदर्शिनः ॥३४॥

tad viddhi praṇipātena paripraśnena sevayā
upadekṣyanti te jñānaṁ jñāninas tattva darśinaḥ

Acquire this transcendental knowledge from a Self-realized master by humble reverence, by sincere inquiry, and by service. The empowered ones, who have realized the Truth, will teach you. (4.34)

Contact with great souls who have realized the truth is helpful. Reading scriptures, giving charity, and doing spiritual practices alone may not give God-realization. Only a God-realized soul can awaken and kindle another soul. But no guru can give a secret formula for Self-realization without His grace. The Vedas say: One who knows the land gives direction to the one who does not know and asks (RV 9.70.09). It is also said that the precepts of Truth are essentially an individual process. People discover the truth by their own efforts. One has to row his or her boat through the turbulent waters of this material world.

The Vedas prohibit the sale of God in any form. They say: O mighty Lord of countless wealth, I will not sell thee for any price (RV 8.01.05). The role of a guru is that of a guide and a giver, not of a taker. Before accepting a human guru, one must first have — or develop — full faith in the guru and leave the guru's human frailties out of consideration, take the pearls of wisdom and throw away the oyster shells. If this is not possible, it should be remembered that the word 'guru' also means the light of Self-knowledge that dispels ignorance and delusion; and the light comes — automatically — from the Supreme Being, the internal guru, when one's mind is purified by selfless service, spiritual practice, and surrender.

There are four categories of gurus: A false guru, guru, realized guru, and the divine guru. In this age too many false gurus are coming to teach or just give a mantra for a price. These false gurus are the merchants of mantra. They take money from disciples to fulfill their personal material needs without giving the true knowledge of the Supreme Being. Jesus also said: Watch out for false prophets; they come to you looking like sheep on the outside, but they are really like wild wolves on the inside (Matthew 7.15). Saint Tulasidasa said that a guru who takes money from disciples and does not remove their ignorance, goes to hell (TR 7.98.04). A guru is one who imparts true knowledge and complete understanding of the Absolute and the temporal. A realized guru is a Self-realized master mentioned in this verse here. A realized guru helps the devotee maintain God-consciousness all the time by his or her own vested spiritual power.

When the mind and intellect are purified, Supreme Lord, the divine guru, reflects Himself in the inner psyche of a devotee and sends a guru or a realized guru to him or her. A real guru is a giver. He never asks any money or a fee from a disciple because he depends on God only. A real guru would not ask anything from a disciple for personal or even for organizational gain. However, a disciple is obliged to do the best he or she can to help the cause of the guru. It is said that one should not accept any fee from a pupil without giving full instruction and understanding of the Absolute, divine kinetic energy (Maya), temporal material Nature, and the living entity (BrU 4.01.02).

The Spirit within us is the divine guru. Outside teachers only help us in the beginning of the spiritual journey. Our own intellect — when purified by selfless service, prayer, meditation, worship, silent chanting of Lord's name, congregational chanting of holy names, and scriptural study — becomes the best channel and guide for the flow of divine knowledge (See also Gita 4.38, and 13.22). The Divine Being within all of us is the real guru, and one must learn how to tune in with Him. It is said that there is no greater guru than one's own pure mind. A pure mind becomes a spiritual guide and the inner divine guru leading to a real guru and Self-realization. This is expressed by the common saying that the guru comes to a person when he or she is ready. The word 'guru' also means vast and is used to describe the Supreme Being — the divine guru and internal guide.

The wise spiritual master disapproves the idea of blind personal service, or the guru cult, which is so common in India. A Self-realized (SR) master says that God only is the guru, and all are His disciples. A disciple should be like a bee seeking honey from flowers. If the bee does not get honey from one flower, it immediately goes to another flower and stays at that flower as long as it gets the nectar. Idolization and blind worship of a human guru may become a stumbling block in spiritual progress and is harmful to both the disciple and the guru.

यज् ज्ञात्वा न पुनर् मोहम् एवं यास्यसि पाण्डव ।
येन भूतान्य् अशेषेण द्रक्ष्यस्य् आत्मन्य् अथो मयि ।।३५।।

yaj jñātvā na punar moham evaṁ yāsyasi pāṇḍava
yena bhūtāny aśeṣeṇa drakṣyasy ātmany atho mayi

After knowing the transcendental science, O Arjuna, you shall not again become deluded like this. With this knowledge you shall see the entire creation within your own higher Self and thus within Me. (See also 6.29, 6.30, 11.07, 11.13) (4.35)

The same life-force of the Supreme Being reflects in all living beings to support and activate them. Therefore, we are all part and parcel of the cosmic energy of Brahma, the Self, and connected with each other. At the dawn of enlightenment, one merges within the Absolute (Gita 18.55), and all diversities appear as nothing but the expansion of one's own higher Self.

अपि चेद् असि पापेभ्यः सर्वेभ्यः पापकृत्तमः ।
सर्वं ज्ञानप्लवेनैव वृजिनं संतरिष्यसि ।।३६।।
api ced asi pāpebhyaḥ sarvebhyaḥ pāpakṛttamaḥ
sarvaṁ jñāna plavenai'va vṛjinaṁ saṁtariṣyasi

Even if one is the most sinful of all sinners, one shall cross over the river of sin by the raft of Self-knowledge. (4.36)

यथैधांसि समिद्धोऽग्निर् भस्मसात् कुरुतेऽर्जुन ।
ज्ञानाग्निः सर्वकर्माणि भस्मसात् कुरुते तथा ।।३७।।
yathai'dhāṁsi samiddho'gnir bhasmasāt kurute'rjuna
jñānāgniḥ sarva karmāṇi bhasmasāt kurute tathā

The fire of Self-knowledge reduces all bonds of Karma to ashes, O Arjuna, like the blazing fire reduces wood to ashes. (4.37)

The Bible also says: You shall know the truth, and the truth shall make you free (John 8.32). The fire of Self-knowledge burns all past Karma — the root cause of the soul's transmigration — just as fire instantly burns a mountain of cotton. The present action does not produce any new Karma because the wise know that all work is done by the forces of nature; therefore, people are not the doer. Thus, when Self-knowledge dawns, only a part of the past Karma, known as fate that is responsible for the present birth, has to be exhausted before freedom from transmigration is attained by the enlightened person.

The physical body and mind generate new Karma; the subtle body carries the fate; and the causal body is the repository of past Karma. Karma produces body, and body generates Karma. Thus, the cycle of birth and death continues indefinitely. Only selfless service can break this cycle, and selfless service is not possible without Self-knowledge. Thus, transcendental knowledge breaks the bonds of Karma and leads to salvation. This knowledge does not manifest to a sinful person — or to any person whose time to receive the spiritual knowledge has not come.

Loss and gain, life and death, fame and infamy lie in the hands of one's Karma. Fate is all-powerful. This being so, one should neither be angry nor blame anybody (TR 2.171.01). People know virtue and vice, but one's choice is ordained by fate or Karmic footprints because the mind and intellect are controlled by fate. When success does not come in spite of best efforts, it may be concluded that fate precedes endeavor.

TRANSCENDENTAL KNOWLEDGE IS AUTOMATICALLY REVEALED TO A KARMA-YOGI

न हि ज्ञानेन सदृशं पवित्रम् इह विद्यते ।
तत् स्वयं योगसंसिद्धः कालेनात्मनि विन्दति ॥३८॥

na hi jñānena sadṛśaṁ pavitram iha vidyate
tat svayaṁ yogasaṁsiddhaḥ kālenā'tmani vindati

Truly, there is no purifier in this world like the true knowledge of the Supreme Being. One discovers this knowledge within, naturally, in course of time when one's mind is cleansed of selfishness by KarmaYoga. (See also 4.31, 5.06, and 18.78). (4.38)

The intense fire of devotion to God burns all Karma and purifies and illuminates the mind and intellect just as sunlight illumines the earth (BP 11.03.40). Selfless service should be performed to the best of one's ability until purity of mind is attained (DB 7.34.15). True knowledge of the Self is automatically reflected in a pure consciousness (Chitta). KarmaYoga cleanses the dirt of selfishness from the mind and prepares it to receive

Self-knowledge. Selfless service (KarmaYoga) and Self-knowledge are thus the two wings to take one to salvation.

श्रद्धावाँल् लभते ज्ञानं तत्परः संयतेन्द्रियः ।
ज्ञानं लब्ध्वा परां शान्तिम् अचिरेणाधिगच्छति ।।३९।।
śraddhāvāṁl labhate jñānaṁ tatparaḥ saṁyatendriyaḥ
jñānaṁ labdhvā parāṁ śāntim acireṇā'dhigacchati

One who has faith in God, is sincere in yogic practice, and has control over the mind and senses, gains this transcendental knowledge. Having gained this knowledge, one quickly attains supreme peace or liberation. (4.39)

The fires of mental grief and sorrows, born of attachment, can be completely extinguished by the water of Self-knowledge (MB 3.02.26). There is no basis for right thought and action without Self-knowledge.

अज्ञश्चाश्रद्दधानश्च संशयात्मा विनश्यति ।
नायं लोकोऽस्ति न परो न सुखं संशयात्मनः ।।४०।।
ajñaścā'śraddadhānaś ca saṁśayātmā vinaśyati
nāyaṁ loko'sti na paro na sukhaṁ saṁśayātmanaḥ

The irrational, the faithless, and the disbeliever (atheist) perish. There is neither this world nor the world beyond nor happiness for a disbeliever. (4.40)

BOTH TRANSCENDENTAL KNOWLEDGE AND KARMA-YOGA ARE NEEDED FOR NIRVANA

योगसंन्यस्तकर्माणं ज्ञानसंछिन्नसंशयम् ।
आत्मवन्तं न कर्माणि निबध्नन्ति धनंजय ।।४१।।
yogasaṁnyastakarmāṇaṁ jñānasaṁchinnasaṁśayam
ātmavantaṁ na karmāṇi nibadhnanti dhanaṁjaya

Work does not bind a person who has renounced work — by renouncing the fruits of work — through KarmaYoga and whose confusion with regard to body and Spirit is completely destroyed by Self-knowledge, O Arjuna. (4.41)

तस्माद् अज्ञानसंभूतं हृत्स्थं ज्ञानासिनात्मनः ।
छित्त्वैनं संशयं योगम् आतिष्ठोत्तिष्ठ भारत ।।४२।।
tasmād ajñānasaṁbhūtaṁ hṛtsthaṁ jñānāsinā'tmanaḥ
chittvainaṁ saṁśayam yogaṁ ātiṣṭho'ttiṣṭha bhārata

Therefore, cut the ignorance-born confusion with regard to body and Spirit by the sword of Self-knowledge, resort to KarmaYoga, and get up for the war, O Arjuna. (4.42)

ॐ तत्सदिति श्रीमद्भगवद्गीतासूपनिषत्सु ब्रह्मविद्यायां योगशास्त्रे
श्रीकृष्णार्जुनसंवादे ज्ञानकर्मसंन्यासयोगो नाम चतुर्थोऽध्यायः ।।
OM tatsaditi śrīmadbhagavadgītāsūpaniṣatsu brahmavidyāyāṁ yogaśāstre śrīkṛṣṇārjuna saṁvāde Jñānakarmasaṁnyāsayogo nāma caturtho'dhyāyaḥ

Thus ends the fourth chapter named "Path of Renunciation with Knowledge" of the Upaniṣad of the Bhagavadgītā, the scripture of yoga, dealing with the science of the Absolute in the form of the dialogue between Śrīkṛṣṇa and Arjuna.

अथ पञ्चमोऽध्यायः

CHAPTER 5

कर्मसंन्यासयोगः

PATH OF RENUNCIATION

अर्जुन उवाच
संन्यासं कर्मणां कृष्ण पुनर् योगं च शंससि ।
यच्छ्रेय एतयोर् एकं तन् मे ब्रूहि सुनिश्चितम् ॥१॥

arjuna uvāca
saṁnyāsaṁ karmaṇāṁ kṛṣṇa punar yogaṁ ca śaṁsasi
yac chreya etayor ekaṁ tan me brūhi suniścitam

Arjuna asked: O Krishna, You praise the path of transcendental knowledge, and also the path of selfless service (KarmaYoga). Tell me, definitely, which one is the better of the two paths? (See also 5.05) (5.01)

Renunciation means complete renouncement of doership, ownership, and selfish motive behind an action, not the renunciation of work or worldly objects. Renunciation comes only after the dawn of Self-knowledge. Therefore, the words 'renunciation' and 'Self-knowledge' are used interchangeably in the Gita. Renunciation is considered the goal of life. Selfless service (Seva, KarmaYoga) and Self-knowledge are the necessary means to achieve the goal. True renunciation is attaching all action and possession — including body, mind, and thought — to the service of the Supreme.

श्रीभगवानुवाच
संन्यासः कर्मयोगश्च निःश्रेयसकराव् उभौ ।
तयोस् तु कर्मसंन्यासात् कर्मयोगो विशिष्यते ॥२॥

śrī bhagavān uvāca
saṁnyāsaḥ karmayogaś ca niḥśreyasakarāv ubhau
tayos tu karmasaṁnyāsāt karmayogo viśiṣyate

Lord Krishna said: The path of Self-knowledge and the path of selfless service both lead to the supreme goal. But of the two, the path of selfless service is superior to path of Self-knowledge (because it is easier to practice for most people). (5.02)

ज्ञेयः स नित्यसंन्यासी यो न द्वेष्टि न काङ्क्षति ।
निर्द्वन्द्वो हि महाबाहो सुखं बन्धात् प्रमुच्यते ॥३॥

jñeyaḥ sa nitya saṁnyāsī yo na dveṣṭi na kāṅkṣati
nirdvandvo hi mahābāho sukhaṁ bandhāt pramucyate

A person should be considered a true renunciant who has neither attachment nor aversion for anything. One is easily liberated from Karmic bondage by becoming free from attachment and aversion. (5.03)

BOTH PATHS LEAD TO THE SUPREME

सांख्ययोगौ पृथग्बालाः प्रवदन्ति न पण्डिताः ।
एकम् अप्य् आस्थितः सम्यग् उभयोर् विन्दते फलम् ॥४॥

sāṁkhyayogau pṛthag bālāḥ pravadanti na paṇḍitāḥ
ekam apy āsthitaḥ samyag ubhayor vindate phalam

The ignorant — not the wise — consider the path of Self-knowledge and the path of selfless service (KarmaYoga) as different from each other. The person who has truly mastered one, gets the benefits of both. (5.04)

यत् सांख्यैः प्राप्यते स्थानं तद् योगैर् अपि गम्यते ।
एकं सांख्यं च योगं च यः पश्यति स पश्यति ॥५॥

yat sāṁkhyaiḥ prāpyate sthānaṁ tad yogair api gamyate
ekaṁ sāṁkhyaṁ ca yogaṁ ca yaḥ paśyati sa paśyati

Whatever goal a renunciant reaches, a KarmaYogi also reaches the same goal. Therefore, one who sees the path

of renunciation and the path of unselfish work as the same, really sees. (See also 6.01 and 6.02) (5.05)

संन्यासस् तु महाबाहो दुःखम् आप्तुम् अयोगतः ।
योगयुक्तो मुनिर् ब्रह्म नचिरेणाधिगच्छति ॥६॥
saṁnyāsas tu mahābāho duḥkham āptum ayogataḥ
yogayukto munir brahma nacireṇā'dhigacchati

But true renunciation (the renunciation of doership and ownership), O Arjuna, is difficult to attain without KarmaYoga. A sage equipped with KarmaYoga quickly attains Nirvana. (See also 4.31, 4.38, 5.08) (5.06)

Selfless service (KarmaYoga) provides the preparation, discipline, and purification necessary for renunciation. Self-knowledge is the upper limit of KarmaYoga, and renunciation of doership and ownership is the upper limit of Self-knowledge.

योगयुक्तो विशुद्धात्मा विजितात्मा जितेन्द्रियः ।
सर्वभूतात्मभूतात्मा कुर्वन्न् अपि न लिप्यते ॥७॥
yogayukto viśuddhātmā vijitātmā jitendriyaḥ
sarvabhūtātma bhūtātmā kurvann api na lipyate

A KarmaYogi, whose mind is pure, whose mind and senses are under control, and who sees one and the same Spirit in all beings, is not bound by Karma, though engaged in work. (5.07)

A TRANSCENDENTALIST DOES NOT CONSIDER ONESELF AS THE DOER

नैव किंचित् करोमीति युक्तो मन्येत तत्त्ववित् ।
पश्यञ् शृण्वन् स्पृशञ् जिघ्रन्न् अश्नन् गच्छन् स्वपञ् श्वसन् ॥८॥
naiva kiṁcit karomīti yukto manyeta tattvavit
paśyañ śṛṇvan spṛśañ jighrann aśnan gacchan svapañ śvasan

प्रलपन् विसृजन् गृह्णन्न् उन्मिषन् निमिषन्न् अपि ।
इन्द्रियाणीन्द्रियार्थेषु वर्तन्त इति धारयन् ।।९।।

pralapan visṛjan gṛhṇann unmiṣan nimiṣann api
indriyāṇī'ndriyārtheṣu vartanta iti dhārayan

The wise who know the truth think: "I do nothing at all." In seeing, hearing, touching, smelling, eating, walking, sleeping, breathing, speaking, giving, taking, as well as opening and closing the eyes; the wise believe that only the senses are operating upon their objects. (See also 3.27, 13.29, and 14.19) (5.08-09)

Senses need not be subdued if the activities of the senses are spiritualized by perceiving that all work, good or bad, is done by the powers of God.

A KARMA-YOGI WORKS FOR GOD

ब्रह्मण्य् आधाय कर्माणि सङ्गं त्यक्त्वा करोति यः ।
लिप्यते न स पापेन पद्मपत्रम् इवाम्भसा ।।१०।।

brahmaṇy ādhāya karmāṇi saṅgaṁ tyaktvā karoti yaḥ
lipyate na sa pāpena padma patram ivāmbhasā

One who does all work as an offering to God — abandoning selfish attachment to results — remains untouched by Karmic reaction or sin, just as a lotus leaf never gets wet by water. (5.10)

A KarmaYogi does not work with selfish motives and therefore does not incur any sin. Selfless service is always sinless. Selfishness is the mother of sin. One becomes happy, peaceful, purified, and enlightened by performing one's prescribed duties as an offering to God while remaining detached inwardly.

कायेन मनसा बुद्ध्या केवलैर् इन्द्रियैर् अपि ।
योगिनः कर्म कुर्वन्ति सङ्गं त्यक्त्वात्मशुद्धये ।।११।।

kāyena manasā buddhyā kevalair indriyair api
yoginaḥ karma kurvanti saṅgaṁ tyaktvā'tmaśuddhaye

The KarmaYogis perform action — without selfish attachment — with their body, mind, intellect, and senses only for the purification of their mind and intellect. (5.11)

युक्तः कर्मफलं त्यक्त्वा शान्तिम् आप्नोति नैष्ठिकीम् ।
अयुक्तः कामकारेण फले सक्तो निबध्यते ॥१२॥

yuktaḥ karmaphalaṁ tyaktvā śāntim āpnoti naiṣṭhikīm
ayuktaḥ kāmakāreṇa phale sakto nibadhyate

A KarmaYogi attains Supreme peace by abandoning attachment to the fruits of work, while others who are attached to the fruits of work become bound by selfish work. (5.12)

THE PATH OF KNOWLEDGE

सर्वकर्माणि मनसा संन्यस्यास्ते सुखं वशी ।
नवद्वारे पुरे देही नैव कुर्वन् न कारयन् ॥१३॥

sarvakarmāṇi manasā saṁnyasyā'ste sukhaṁ vaśī
navadvāre pure dehī naiva kurvan na kārayan

A person, who has completely renounced the attachment to the fruits of all work from his or her mind, dwells happily in the City of Nine Gates, neither performing nor directing action. (5.13)

The human body has been called the City of Nine Gates (or openings) in the scriptures. The nine openings are: Two openings each for the eyes, ears, and nose; and one each for the mouth, anus, and urethra. The Lord of all beings and the universe who resides in this city as an individual soul or the living entity (Jiva) is called the Spiritual Being (Purush) performing and directing all action.

न कर्तृत्वं न कर्माणि लोकस्य सृजति प्रभुः ।
न कर्मफलसंयोगं स्वभावस् तु प्रवर्तते ॥१४॥

na kartṛtvaṁ na karmāṇi lokasya sṛjati prabhuḥ
na karmaphala saṁyogaṁ svabhāvas tu pravartate

The Lord neither creates the urge for action nor the feeling of doership nor the attachment to the results of action in people. The powers of material Nature do all these. (5.14)

नादत्ते कस्यचित् पापं न चैव सुकृतं विभुः ।
अज्ञानेनावृतं ज्ञानं तेन मुह्यन्ति जन्तवः ॥१५॥

nādatte kasyacit pāpaṁ na caiva sukṛtaṁ vibhuḥ
ajñānenā'vṛtaṁ jñānaṁ tena muhyanti janta vaḥ

The Lord does not take responsibility for the good or evil deeds of anybody. The veil of ignorance covers Self-knowledge; thereby people become deluded and do evil deeds. (5.15)

God does not punish or reward anybody. We our selves do this by the misuse or the right use of our own power of reasoning and free will. Bad things happen to good people to make them better.

ज्ञानेन तु तद् अज्ञानं येषां नाशितम् आत्मनः ।
तेषाम् आदित्यवज् ज्ञानं प्रकाशयति तत् परम् ॥१६॥

jñānena tu tad ajñānaṁ yeṣāṁ nāśitam ātmanaḥ
teṣām ādityavaj jñānaṁ prakāśayati tat param

Transcendental knowledge destroys the ignorance of the Self and reveals the Supreme Being, just as the sun reveals the beauty of objects of the world. (5.16)

तद्बुद्धयस् तदात्मानस् तन्निष्ठास् तत्परायणाः ।
गच्छन्त्य् अपुनरावृत्तिं ज्ञाननिर्धूतकल्मषाः ॥१७॥

tadbuddhayas tadātmānas tanniṣṭhās tatparāyaṇāḥ
gacchanty apunarāvṛttiṁ jñānanirdhūtakalmaṣāḥ

Persons whose mind and intellect are totally merged in the Eternal Being, who are firmly devoted to the Supreme, who have God as their supreme goal and sole refuge, and whose impurities are destroyed by the knowledge of the Self, do not take birth again. (5.17)

ADDITIONAL MARKS OF AN ENLIGHTENED PERSON

विद्याविनयसंपन्ने ब्राह्मणे गवि हस्तिनि ।
शुनि चैव श्वपाके च पण्डिताः समदर्शिनः ।।१८।।
vidyāvinayasaṁpanne brāhmaṇe gavi hastini
śuni caiva śvapāke ca paṇḍitāḥ samadarśinaḥ

An enlightened person — by perceiving God in all — looks at a learned person, an outcast, even a cow, an elephant, or a dog with an equal eye. (See also 6.29) (5.18)

Just as a person does not consider parts of the body, such as arms and legs, different from the body itself, similarly a Self-realized person does not consider any living entity different from all pervading Eternal Being (BP 4.07.53). Such a person sees God everywhere, in everything, and in every being. After discovering the metaphysical truth, one looks at everything with reverence, compassion, and kindness because everything in the material world is part and parcel of the cosmic body of Lord Vishnu.

इहैव तैर् जितः सर्गो येषां साम्ये स्थितं मनः ।
निर्दोषं हि समं ब्रह्म तस्माद् ब्रह्मणि ते स्थिताः ।।१९।।
ihaiva tair jitaḥ sargo yeṣāṁ sāmye sthitaṁ manaḥ
nirdoṣaṁ hi samaṁ brahma tasmād brahmaṇi te sthitāḥ

Everything has been accomplished in this very life by one whose mind is set in equality. Such a person has realized the Supreme Being because the Supreme Being is flawless and impartial. (See also 18.55) (5.19)

To have a feeling of equality for everybody is the greatest worship of God (BP 7.08.10). Those who do not have such a feeling discriminate. Therefore, the victims of injustice and discrimination should feel sorry for the discriminator and pray to the Lord for a change of the discriminator's heart rather than get upset, angry, or vengeful.

न प्रहृष्येत् प्रियं प्राप्य नोद्विजेत् प्राप्य चाप्रियम् ।
स्थिरबुद्धिर् असंमूढो ब्रह्मविद् ब्रह्मणि स्थितः ।।२०।।

na prahṛṣyet priyaṁ prāpya nodvijet prāpya cā'priyam
sthirabuddhir asaṁmūḍho brahmavid brahmaṇi sthitaḥ

One who neither rejoices on obtaining what is pleasant nor grieves on obtaining the unpleasant, who has a steady mind, who is undeluded, and who is a knower of the Supreme Being — such a person eternally abides with the Supreme Being. (5.20)

बाह्यस्पर्शेष्व् असक्तात्मा विन्दत्यात्मनि यत् सुखम् ।
स ब्रह्मयोगयुक्तात्मा सुखम् अक्षयम् अश्नुते ।।२१।।

bāhyasparśeṣv asaktātmā vindatyā'tmani yat sukham
sa brahmayoga yuktātmā sukham akṣayam aśnute

Such a person who is in union with the Supreme Being becomes unattached to external sensual pleasures by discovering the joy of the Self through contemplation and enjoys transcendental bliss. (5.21)

ये हि संस्पर्शजा भोगा दुःखयोनय एव ते ।
आद्यन्तवन्तः कौन्तेय न तेषु रमते बुधः ।।२२।।

ye hi saṁsparśajā bhogā duḥkhayonaya eva te
ādy anta vantaḥ kaunteya na teṣu ramate budhaḥ

Sensual pleasures are, in fact, the source of misery and have a beginning and an end. Therefore, the wise, O Arjuna, do not rejoice in sensual pleasures. (See also 18.38) (5.22)

The wise constantly reflect on the futility of sensual pleasures that inevitably become the cause of misery; therefore, they do not become victims of sensual cravings.

शक्नोतीहैव यः सोढुं प्राक् शरीरविमोक्षणात् ।
कामक्रोधोद्भवं वेगं स युक्तः स सुखी नरः ।।२३।।
śaknotī'haiva yaḥ soḍhuṁ prāk śarīra vimokṣaṇāt
kāmakrodhodbhavaṁ vegaṁ sa yuktaḥ sa sukhī naraḥ

One who is able to withstand the impulses of lust and anger before death is a yogi and a happy person. (5.23)

योऽन्तः सुखोऽन्तरारामस् तथान्तर् ज्योतिर् एव यः ।
स योगी ब्रह्मनिर्वाणं ब्रह्मभूतोऽधिगच्छति ।।२४।।
yo'ntaḥ sukho'ntarārāmas tathā'ntarjyotir eva yaḥ
sa yogī brahmanirvāṇaṁ brahmabhūto'dhigacchati

One who finds happiness with the Supreme Being, who rejoices with the Supreme Being within, and who is illuminated by Self-knowledge — such a yogi attains Nirvana and goes to the Supreme Being. (5.24)

लभन्ते ब्रह्मनिर्वाणम् ऋषयः क्षीणकल्मषाः ।
छिन्नद्वैधा यतात्मानः सर्वभूतहिते रताः ।।२५।।
labhante brahmanirvāṇaṁ ṛṣayaḥ kṣīṇakalmaṣāḥ
chinnadvaidhā yatātmānaḥ sarvabhūtahite ratāḥ

Seers whose sins (or imperfections) are destroyed, whose doubts about the existence of the Universal Self have been dispelled by Self-knowledge, whose minds are disciplined, and who are engaged in the welfare of all beings, attain the Supreme Being. (5.25)

कामक्रोधवियुक्तानां यतीनां यतचेतसाम् ।
अभितो ब्रह्मनिर्वाणं वर्तते विदितात्मनाम् ॥२६॥

kāma krodha viyuktānāṁ yatīnāṁ yatacetasām
abhito brahmanirvāṇaṁ vartate viditā'tmanām

Those who are free from lust and anger, who have subdued the mind and senses, and who have realized the existence of the Self, easily attain Nirvana. (5.26)

THE THIRD PATH — THE PATH OF DEVOTIONAL MEDITATION AND CONTEMPLATION

स्पर्शान् कृत्वा बहिर् बाह्यांश् चक्षुश्चैवान्तरे भ्रुवोः ।
प्राणापानौ समौ कृत्वा नासाभ्यन्तरचारिणौ ॥२७॥

sparśān kṛtvā bahir bāhyāṁś cakṣuś cai'vā'ntre bhruvoḥ
prāṇāpānau samau kṛtvā nāsābhyantaracāriṇau

यतेन्द्रियमनोबुद्धिर् मुनिर् मोक्षपरायणः ।
विगतेच्छाभयक्रोधो यः सदा मुक्त एव सः ॥२८॥

yatendriya manobuddhir munir mokṣa parāyaṇaḥ
vigatecchā bhaya krodho yaḥ sadā mukta eva saḥ

A sage is, in truth, liberated by renouncing all sense enjoyments, fixing the eyes and the mind at an imaginary dot between the eye-brows, equalizing the breath moving through the nostrils by using yogic techniques, keeping the senses, mind, and intellect under control, having salvation as the prime goal, and by becoming free from lust, anger, and fear. (5.27-28)

The invisible astral channels of flow of energy in the human body are called Nadis. When the cosmic currents — flowing through Nadis in the astral spinal cord — are separated by the opening of the main Sushumna Nadi by the practice of yogic techniques, breath flows through both nostrils with equal pressure; the mind calms down; and the field is prepared for deep meditation leading to trance.

भोक्तारं यज्ञतपसां सर्वलोकमहेश्वरम् ।
सुहृदं सर्वभूतानां ज्ञात्वा मां शान्तिम् ऋच्छति ॥२९॥
bhoktāraṁ yajñatapasāṁ sarvaloka maheśvaram
suhṛdaṁ sarvabhūtānāṁ jñātvā māṁ śāntim ṛcchati

My devotee attains everlasting peace by knowing the Supreme Being as the enjoyer of sacrifices and austerities, as the great Lord of the entire universe, and as the friend of all beings. (5.29)

ॐ तत्सदिति श्रीमद्भगवद्गीतासूपनिषत्सु ब्रह्मविद्यायां योगशास्त्रे
श्रीकृष्णार्जुनसंवादे कर्मसंन्यासयोगो नाम पञ्चमोऽध्यायः ॥
OM tatsaditi śrīmadbhagavadgītāsūpaniṣatsu brahmavidyāyāṁ
yogaśāstre śrīkṛṣṇārjuna saṁvāde karmasaṁnyāsayogo
nāma pañcamo'dhyāyaḥ

Thus ends the fifth chapter named "Path of Renunciation" of the Upaniṣad of the Bhagavadgītā, the scripture of yoga, dealing with the science of the Absolute in the form of the dialogue between Śrīkṛṣṇa and Arjuna.

अथ षष्ठोऽध्यायः

CHAPTER 6

आत्मसंयमयोगः

PATH OF MEDITATION

श्रीभगवानुवाच
अनाश्रितः कर्मफलं कार्यं कर्म करोति यः ।
स संन्यासी च योगी च न निरग्निर् न चाक्रियः ।।१।।

śrī bhagavān uvāca
anāśritaḥ karma phalaṁ kāryaṁ karma karoti yaḥ
sa saṁnyāsī ca yogī ca na niragnir na cākriyaḥ

A KARMA-YOGI IS A RENUNCIANT

Lord Krishna said: One who performs the prescribed duty without seeking its fruit for personal enjoyment is both a renunciant and a KarmaYogi. One does not become a renunciant merely by not lighting the fire, and one does not become a yogi merely by abstaining from work. (6.01)

यं संन्यासम् इति प्राहुर् योगं तं विद्धि पाण्डव ।
न ह्य् असंन्यस्तसंकल्पो योगी भवति कश्चन ।।२।।

yaṁ saṁnyāsam iti prāhur yogaṁ taṁ viddhi pāṇḍava
na hy asaṁnyasta saṁkalpo yogī bhavati kaścana

O Arjuna, renunciation (Samnyasa) is the same as KarmaYoga because, no one becomes a KarmaYogi who has not renounced the selfish motive behind an action. (See also 5.01, 5.05, 6.01, and 18.02) (6.02)

A DEFINITION OF YOGA

आरुरुक्षोर् मुनेर् योगं कर्म कारणम् उच्यते ।
योगारूढस्य तस्यैव शमः कारणम् उच्यते ।।३।।

āruruksor muner yogaṁ karma kārṇam ucyate
yogārūḍhasya tasyaiva śamaḥ kāraṇam ucyate

यदा हि नेन्द्रियार्थेषु न कर्मस्व् अनुषज्जते ।
सर्वसंकल्पसंन्यासी योगारूढस् तदोच्यते ॥४॥

yadā hi nendriyārtheṣu na karmasv anuṣajjate
sarvasaṁkalpa saṁnyāsī yogārūḍhas tadocyate

For the wise, who seek to attain yoga of meditation or the equanimity of mind, KarmaYoga is said to be the means. For one who has attained yoga, equanimity becomes the means of Self-realization. A person is said to have attained yogic perfection when he or she has no desire for sensual pleasures or attachment to the fruits of work and has renounced all personal selfish motives. (6.03-04)

Yogic perfection can be achieved only when one does all activities for the pleasure of the Supreme Lord Krishna (Chimanbhai). KarmaYoga or unselfish work produces tranquility of mind. When one performs action as a matter of duty without any selfish motive, the mind is not disturbed by the fear of failure; it becomes tranquil, and one attains yogic perfection through meditation. The equanimity of mind necessary for Self-realization comes after giving up personal, selfish motives and desires. Selfishness is the root cause of other impure desires in the mind. The desireless mind becomes peaceful. Thus KarmaYoga is recommended to persons desiring success in yoga of meditation. Perfection in meditation results in control over the senses, bringing forth tranquility of mind that ultimately leads to God-realization.

MIND IS THE BEST FRIEND AS WELL AS THE WORST ENEMY

उद्धरेद् आत्मनात्मानं नात्मानम् अवसादयेत् ।
आत्मैव ह्यात्मनो बन्धुर् आत्मैव रिपुर् आत्मनः ॥५॥

uddhared ātmanā'tmānaṁ nā'tmānam avasādayet
ātmaiva hyā tmano bandhur ātmaiva ripur ātmanaḥ

बन्धुर् आत्मात्मनस् तस्य येनात्मैवात्मना जितः ।
अनात्मनस् तु शत्रुत्वे वर्तेतात्मैव शत्रुवत् ।।६।।

bandhur ātmā'tmanas tasya yenā'tmai'vā'tmanā jitaḥ
anātmanas tu śatrutve vartetā'tmai'va śatruvat

One must elevate — and not degrade — oneself by one's own mind. The mind alone is one's friend, as well as one's enemy. The mind is the friend of those who have control over it, and the mind acts like an enemy for those who do not control it. (6.05-06)

There is no enemy other than an uncontrolled mind in this world (BP 7.08.10). Therefore, one should first try to control and conquer this enemy by regular practice of meditation with a firm determination and effort. All spiritual practices are aimed towards the conquest of the mind. Guru Nanak said: "Master the mind, and you master the world." Sage Patanjali defines yoga as control over the activities (or the thought waves, Chitta Vritti) of mind and intellect (PYS 1.02). Firm control of the mind and senses is known as yoga (KaU 6.11). Control of the mind and senses is called austerity and yoga (MB 3.209.53). The purpose of meditation is to control the mind so that one can focus on God and live according to His instructions and will. The mind of a yogi is under control; a yogi is not under the control of the mind. Meditation is effortless control of the natural tendency of the mind to wander and tuning it with the Supreme. Yogi Bhajan says: A one-pointed, relaxed mind is the most powerful and creative mind — it can do anything.

The mind, indeed, is the cause of bondage as well as liberation of the living entity. The mind becomes the cause of bondage when controlled by modes of material Nature, and the same mind, when attached to the Supreme, becomes the cause of salvation (BP 3.25.15). The mind alone is the cause of salvation as well as bondage of human beings. The mind becomes the cause of bondage when controlled by sense objects, and it becomes the cause of salvation when controlled by the intellect (VP 6.07.28). Absolute control over mind and senses is a prerequisite for any spiritual practice for Self-realization. One who has not become the master of the senses cannot progress towards the goal of Self-realization. Therefore, after establishing control over the activities of the mind, one should take the mind away from the enjoyment of sensual pleasures and fix it on God. When the mind is disengaged from sense pleasures and engaged with God, sense impulses become ineffective because the senses obtain their power from the mind. The mind is the ruler of the other five senses. One who becomes master of the mind becomes master of all the senses.

जितात्मनः प्रशान्तस्य परमात्मा समाहितः ।
शीतोष्णसुखदुःखेषु तथा मानापमानयोः ॥७॥

jitātmanaḥ praśāntasya paramātmā samāhitaḥ
śītoṣṇasukhaduḥkheṣu tathā mānāpamānayoḥ

One who has control over the lower self — the mind and senses — is tranquil in heat and cold, in pleasure and pain, in honor and dishonor, and remains ever steadfast with the supreme Self. (6.07)

One can realize God only when the mind becomes tranquil and completely free from desires and dualities, such as pain and pleasure. However, people are rarely completely free from desires and duality. But one can become free from the bonds of desire and duality if one uses the mind and senses in the service of the Lord. They who master their mind get the spiritual wealth of knowledge and bliss. Self can only be realized when the lake of the mind becomes still, just as the reflection of the moon is seen in a lake when the water is still. (See also 2.70)

ज्ञानविज्ञानतृप्तात्मा कूटस्थो विजितेन्द्रियः ।
युक्त इत्युच्यते योगी समलोष्टाश्मकाञ्चनः ॥८॥

jñāna vijñāna tṛptātmā kūṭastho vijitendriyaḥ
yukta ity ucyate yogī sama loṣṭāśma kāñcanaḥ

A person is called yogi who has both Self-knowledge and Self-realization, who is tranquil, who has control over the mind and senses, and to whom a clod, a stone, and gold are the same. (6.08)

सुहृन्मित्रार्युदासीन-मध्यस्थद्वेष्यबन्धुषु ।
साधुष्व् अपि च पापेषु समबुद्धिर् विशिष्यते ॥९॥

suhṛn mitrār yudāsīna-madhyastha dveṣya bandhuṣu
sādhuṣv api ca pāpeṣu samabuddhir viśiṣyate

A person is considered superior who is impartial toward companions, friends, enemies, neutrals, arbiters, haters, relatives, saints, and sinners. (6.09)

TECHNIQUES OF MEDITATION

योगी युञ्जीत सततम् आत्मानं रहसि स्थितः ।
एकाकी यतचित्तात्मा निराशीर् अपरिग्रहः ॥१०॥

yogī yuñjīta satatam ātmānaṁ rahasi sthitaḥ
ekākī yatacittātmā nirāśīr aparigrahaḥ

A yogi, seated in solitude and alone, should constantly try to contemplate a mental picture (or just the majesty) of the Supreme Being after bringing the mind and senses under control and becoming free from desires and proprietorship. (6.10)

The place of meditation should have the serenity, solitude, and spiritual atmosphere of odor-free, noise-free, and light-free caves of the Himalayas. Massive, gorgeous buildings with exquisite marble figures of celestial controllers are not enough. These often come at the expense of spirituality and help religious commerce only.

The eight steps of meditation based on Patanjali's YogaSutras (PYS 2.29) are: (1) Moral conduct, (2) Spiritual practices, (3) Right posture and yogic exercises, (4) Yogic breathing, (5) Sense withdrawal, (6) Concentration, (7) Meditation, and (8) Trance or superconscious state of mind.

One must follow these eight steps, one by one, under proper guidance to make progress in meditation. Use of breathing and concentration techniques without necessary purification of the mind and without sublimation of feelings and desires by moral conduct and spiritual practices (See 16.24) may lead to a dangerous, neurotic state of mind. Patanjali says: The sitting posture for meditation should be stable, relaxed, and comfortable for the individual's physical body (PYS 2.46).

Yogic breathing is not the forcible — and often harmful — retention of breath in the lungs as is commonly misunderstood and wrongly practiced. Patanjali defines it as control of the Prana — the bioimpulses or the astral life forces — that cause the breathing process (PYS 2.49). It is a gradual process of bringing under control or slowing down — by using standard yogic techniques, such as yogic postures, breathing exercises, locks, and gestures — the bioimpulses that activate the motor and sensory nerves that regulate breathing, and over which we normally have no control.

When the body is supercharged by the huge reservoir of omnipresent cosmic current flowing through the medulla oblongata, the need for breathing is reduced or eliminated and the yogi reaches the breathless state of trance, the last milestone of the spiritual journey. The Upanishad says: No mortal ever lives by breathing oxygen in the air alone. Mortals depend on something else (KaU 5.05). Jesus said: One shall not live by bread (food, water, and air) alone, but by every word (or the cosmic energy) that comes out of the mouth of God (Matthew 4.04). The cord of breath ties the living entity (soul) to the body-mind complex. A yogi unties the soul from the body and ties it with the Supersoul during the breathless state of trance.

The withdrawal of the senses from the sense-objects is a major obstacle in the attainment of the goal of a yogi. When sense withdrawal has been accomplished, concentration, meditation, and

Samadhi become very easy to master. The mind should be controlled and trained to follow the intellect rather than let it be drawn towards and controlled by gross sense objects, such as hearing, touch, sight, taste, and smell. The mind is restless by nature. Watching the natural flow of breath coming in and going out, and alternate breathing help to make the mind steady.

The two most common techniques of sense withdrawal are these: (1) Focus your full attention on the point between the eyebrows. Perceive and expand a sphere of white, rotating light there, (2) Mentally chant a mantra or any holy name of the Lord as quickly as possible for a long time and let the mind get completely absorbed into the sound of mental chanting until you do not hear the ticking sound of a nearby clock. The speed and loudness of mental chanting should be increased with the restlessness of the mind, and vice versa.

Concentration on a particular part of a deity, on the sound of a mantra, on the flow of breath, on various energy centers in the body, on the mid-brows, on the tip of the nose, or on an imaginary crimson lotus inside the chest center, stills the mind and stops it from wandering.

शुचौ देशे प्रतिष्ठाप्य स्थिरम् आसनम् आत्मनः ।
नात्युच्छ्रितं नातिनीचं चैलाजिनकुशोत्तरम् ॥११॥

śucau deśe pratiṣṭhāpya sthiram āsanam ātmanaḥ
nā'tyucchritaṁ nā'tinīcaṁ cailājina kuśottaram

तत्रैकाग्रं मनः कृत्वा यतचित्तेन्द्रियक्रियः ।
उपविश्यासने युञ्ज्याद् योगमात्मविशुद्धये ॥१२॥

tatrai'kāgraṁ manaḥ kṛtvā yatacittendriyakriyaḥ
upaviśyā'sane yuñjyād yogam ātmaviśuddhaye

One should sit on his or her own firm seat that is neither too high nor too low, covered with grass, a deerskin, and a cloth, one over the other, in a clean spot. Sitting there in a comfortable position and concentrating the mind on God,

controlling the thoughts and the activities of the senses, one should practice meditation to purify the mind and senses. (6.11-12)

A yogi should contemplate any beautiful form of God until the form becomes ever present in the mind. Short meditation with full concentration is better than long meditation without concentration. Fixing the mind on a single object of contemplation for twelve (12) seconds, two and one-half (2.5) minutes, and half an hour is known as concentration, meditation, and trance, respectively. Meditation and trance are the spontaneous result of concentration. Meditation occurs when the mind stops oscillating off the point of concentration.

In the lower stage of trance, the mind becomes so centered on a particular part of the deity — such as the face or the feet — that it forgets everything. This is like a dream in a wakeful state where one remains aware of one's mind, thoughts, and the surroundings. In the higher stage of trance, the body becomes still and motionless, and the mind experiences various aspects of the Truth. The mind loses its individual identity and becomes one with the cosmic mind.

The superconscious state of mind is the highest stage of trance. In this state of mind, the normal human consciousness becomes connected to (or overpowered by) cosmic consciousness; one reaches a thoughtless, pulseless, and breathless state and does not feel anything except peace, joy, and supreme bliss. In the highest state of trance, the energy center (Chakra) on the top of the head opens up; the mind is merged into the infinite; and there is no mind or thought, but only the feeling of His transcendental existence, awareness, and bliss. A person who reaches this state is called a sage.

Attaining the blissful state of trance seems difficult for most people. Muniji gives a simple method. He says: When you are immersed in Him and His work is flowing through you, you become ever happy, ever joyful, and ever blissful.

समं कायशिरोग्रीवं धारयन्न् अचलं स्थिरः ।
संप्रेक्ष्य नासिकाग्रं स्वं दिशश्चानवलोकयन् ॥१३॥

samaṁ kāyaśirogrīvaṁ dhārayann acalaṁ sthiraḥ
saṁprekṣya nāsikāgraṁ svaṁ diśaś cā'navalokayan

प्रशान्तात्मा विगतभीर् ब्रह्मचारिव्रते स्थितः ।
मनः संयम्य मच्चित्तो युक्त आसीत मत्परः ॥१४॥

praśāntātmā vigatabhīr brahmacārivrate sthitaḥ
manaḥ saṁyamya maccitto yukta āsīta matparaḥ

One should sit by holding the waist, spine, chest, neck, and head erect, motionless and steady; fix the eyes and the mind steadily on the front of the nostril without looking around; make your mind serene and fearless; practice celibacy; have the mind under control; think of Me, and have Me as the supreme goal. (See also 4.29, 5.27, 8.10, and 8.12) (6.13-14)

Hariharananda suggests keeping pinpointed attention penetrating four inches deep between the eyebrows near the master gland — the pituitary. The Bible says: If your eyes are single, your whole body will (seem to) be full of light (Matthew 6.22). Fixing the gaze on the nose tip is one of the gestures of KriyaYoga recommended by Swami Sivananda to awaken the Kundalini power located at the base of the spine. After a little practice each day, the eyes will become accustomed and slightly convergent and see the two sides of the nose. As you gaze at the nose tip, concentrate on the movement of breath through the nostrils. After ten minutes, close your eyes and look into the dark space in front of your closed eyes. If you see a light, concentrate on it because this light can completely absorb your consciousness and lead you to trance according to yogic scriptures. The beginner should first practice fixing the gaze at the mid-brows, as mentioned in verse 5.27, or at the chest center, as hinted in verse 8.12, before learning to fix the gaze on the tip of the nose. The help of a teacher and use of a mantra is highly recommended.

Celibacy is necessary to still the mind and awaken the dormant Kundalini. Celibacy and certain breathing exercises are necessary to cleanse the subtle body. The subtle body is nourished by seminal and ovarian energy, just as the gross body needs food for nourishment. Sarada Ma warned her disciples not to be intimate with persons of the opposite gender even if God came in that form. The role of celibacy in spiritual life is overlooked in the West because it is not an easy task for most people. The individual should choose the right life partner for success in the spiritual journey if the practice of celibacy is not possible. It is very dangerous to force celibacy on disciples. The scripture says: Just as a King, protected by the castle walls, wins over the invincible enemy, similarly those who want victory over the mind and senses should try to subdue them by living as a householder (BP 5.01.18).

Sublimation of the sex impulse precedes enlightenment (AV 11.05.05). One sense organ, attached to its object, can drain the intellect, just as one hole in a water pot can empty the water (MS 2.99). One commits sin by engaging senses to sense objects and obtains yogic powers by controlling the senses (MS 2.93). Transmutation of the life force of procreative energy leads to yoga. One can transcend sex by beholding the presence of the divine in the body of all human beings and mentally bowing down to them.

युञ्जन्न् एवं सदात्मानं योगी नियतमानसः ।
शान्तिं निर्वाणपरमां मत्संस्थाम् अधिगच्छति ॥१५॥

yuñjann evaṁ sadā'tmānaṁ yogī niyatamānasaḥ
śāntiṁ nirvāṇaparamāṁ matsaṁsthām adhigacchati

Thus, by always practicing to keep the mind fixed on Me, the yogi whose mind is subdued attains peace of Nirvana and comes to Me. (6.15)

नात्यश्नतस् तु योगोऽस्ति न चैकान्तम् अनश्नतः ।
न चाति स्वप्नशीलस्य जाग्रतो नैव चार्जुन ॥१६॥

nā'tyaśnatas tu yogo'sti na cai'kāntam anaśnataḥ
na cāti svapnaśīlasya jāgrato nai'va ca'rjuna

This yoga is not possible, O Arjuna, for one who eats too much or who does not eat at all, who sleeps too much or too little. (6.16)

युक्ताहारविहारस्य युक्तचेष्टस्य कर्मसु ।
युक्तस्वप्नावबोधस्य योगो भवति दुःखहा ॥१७॥
yuktāhāra vihārasya yuktaceṣṭasya karmasu
yukta svapnāvabodhasya yogo bhavati duḥkhahā

The yoga of meditation destroys all sorrow for the one who is moderate in eating, recreation, working, sleeping, and waking. (6.17)

The Gita teaches that extremes should be avoided at all costs in all spheres of life. This moderation of the Gita was eulogized by Lord Buddha who called it the middle path, the right way, or the noble path. A healthy mind and body are required for successful performance of any spiritual practice. Therefore, it is required that a yogi should regulate his daily bodily functions, such as eating, sleeping, bathing, resting and recreation. Those who eat too much or too little may become sick or fragile. It is recommended to fill half of the stomach with food, one fourth with water, and leave the rest empty for air. If one sleeps more than six hours, one's lethargy, passion, and bile may increase. A yogi should avoid extreme indulgence in uncontrolled desires as well as the opposite extreme of yogic discipline — the torturing of the body and mind.

यदा विनियतं चित्तम् आत्मन्य् एवावतिष्ठते ।
निःस्पृहः सर्वकामेभ्यो युक्त इत्य् उच्यते तदा ॥१८॥
yadā viniyataṁ cittam ātmany evā'vatiṣṭhate
niḥspṛhaḥ sarvakāmebhyo yukta ity ucyate tadā

A person is said to have achieved yoga, union with the Self, when the perfectly disciplined mind becomes free from all desires and gets completely united with the Self in trance. (6.18)

यथा दीपो निवातस्थो नेङ्गते सोपमा स्मृता ।
योगिनो यतचित्तस्य युञ्जतो योगम् आत्मनः ॥१९॥
yathā dīpo nivātastho ne'ṅgate so'pamā smṛtā
yogino yatacittasya yuñjato yogam ātmanaḥ

A lamp in a spot sheltered by the Self from the wind of desires does not flicker. This simile is used for the subdued mind of a yogi practicing meditation on the Self. (6.19)

The sign of yogic perfection is that the mind remains always undisturbed like the flame of a lamp in a windless place.

यत्रोपरमते चित्तं निरुद्धं योगसेवया ।
यत्र चैवात्मनात्मानं पश्यन् आत्मनि तुष्यति ॥२०॥
yatro'paramate cittaṁ niruddhaṁ yogasevayā
yatra cai'vā'tmanā'tmānaṁ paśyann ātmani tuṣyati

When the mind disciplined by the practice of meditation becomes steady and quiet, one becomes content with the Self by beholding the Self with purified intellect. (6.20)

The self is present in all living beings as fire is present in wood. Friction makes the presence of fire in the wood visible to the eyes, similarly meditation makes the Self, residing in the body, perceivable (MB 12.210.42). A psychophysical transformation (or the superconscious state) of mind in trance is necessary for God-realization. Each of us has access to the superconscious mind that is not limited by time and space.

One cannot comprehend the Infinite by reason. Reason is powerless to grasp the nature of the beginningless Absolute. The highest faculty is not reasoning but intuition, the comprehension of knowledge coming from the Self and not from the fallible senses or reasoning. Self can be perceived only by the intuitive experience in the highest state of trance and by no other means. Yogananda said: Meditation can enlarge the magic cup of intuition to hold the ocean of infinite wisdom.

सुखम् आत्यन्तिकं यत् तद् बुद्धिग्राह्यम् अतीन्द्रियम्।
वेत्ति यत्र न चैवायं स्थितश् चलति तत्त्वतः ॥२१॥

sukham ātyantikaṁ yat tad buddhigrāhyam atīndriyam
vetti yatra na cai'vā'yaṁ sthitaś calati tattvataḥ

One feels infinite bliss that is perceivable only through the intellect, and is beyond reach of the senses. After realizing the Absolute Reality, one is never separated from it. (6.21)

यं लब्ध्वा चापरं लाभं मन्यते नाधिकं ततः ।
यस्मिन् स्थितो न दुःखेन गुरुणापि विचाल्यते ॥२२॥

yaṁ labdhvā ca'paraṁ lābhaṁ manyate nā'dhikaṁ tataḥ
yasmin sthito na duḥkhena guruṇā'pi vicālyate

After Self-realization (SR), one does not regard any other gain superior to SR. Established in SR, one is not moved even by the greatest calamity. (6.22)

तं विद्याद् दुःखसंयोग-वियोगं योगसंज्ञितम् ।
स निश्चयेन योक्तव्यो योगोऽनिर्विण्णचेतसा ॥२३॥

tam vidyād duḥkhasaṁyoga-viyogaṁ yogasaṁjñitam
sa niścayena yoktavyo yogo'nirviṇṇacetasā

The state of severance from union with sorrow is called yoga. This yoga should be practiced with firm determination, and without any mental reservation. (6.23)

Yoga is attained after long, constant, vigorous practice of meditation with firm faith (PYS 1.14).

संकल्पप्रभवान् कामांस् त्यक्त्वा सर्वान् अशेषतः ।
मनसैवेन्द्रियग्रामं विनियम्य समन्ततः ।।२४।।

saṁkalpa prabhavān kāmāṁs tyaktvā sarvān aśeṣataḥ
manasai've'ndriya grāmaṁ viniyamya samantataḥ

शनैः शनैर् उपरमेद् बुद्ध्या धृतिगृहीतया ।
आत्मसंस्थं मनः कृत्वा न किंचिद् अपि चिन्तयेत् ।।२५।।

śanaiḥ śanair uparamed buddhyā dhṛtigṛhītayā
ātmasaṁsthaṁ manaḥ kṛtvā na kiṁcid api cintayet

One gradually attains tranquility of mind by totally abandoning all selfish desires, completely restraining the senses by the intellect, and keeping the mind fully absorbed in the Self by means of a well-trained and purified intellect and thinking of nothing else. (6.24-25)

When the mind is freed with the help of spiritual practices from the impurities of lust and greed born out of the feeling of 'I, me, and my', it remains tranquil in material happiness and distress (BP 3.25.16).

यतो यतो निश्चरति मनश्चञ्चलम् अस्थिरम् ।
ततस् ततो नियम्यैतद् आत्मन्येव वशं नयेत् ।।२६।।

yato yato niścarati manaś cañcalam asthiram
tatas tato niyamyai'tad ātmany eva vaśaṁ nayet

Wherever this restless and unsteady mind wanders during meditation, one should just witness it under the watchful eye (or supervision and control) of the Self. (6.26)

The mind plays tricks to wander and roam in the world of sensuality. The meditator should keep the mind fixed on the Self by always pondering that one is the soul, not the body. Just watch and laugh at the wanderings of the mind and gently bring it back to the supervision of the Self.

The natural tendency of the mind is to wander. We know from personal experience that the mind is very difficult to control. To control the mind is an impossible task like controlling the wind. The human mind can only be subdued by a sincere practice of meditation and detachment (Gita 6.34-35). Most commentators, however, have stated that the mind or self should be brought back under the supervision of the Self when it starts to wander during meditation.

Atma is considered superior to the body, senses, mind, and the intellect. (Gita 3.42). Thus we can use the awareness of the Atma to subdue the mind. Swami Vishvas has developed a meditation technique based on a slightly different meaning, given above, of verse 6.26. This Method of meditation, based on the theory: Never let the mind wander unsupervised, is described below:

Assume the meditative posture given in verse 6.13. It is a very good practice, before starting any work, to invoke the grace of the personal god of your choice that you believe in. Lord Ganesha and the Guru should be also invoked by Hindus.

The main aim of meditation, or any spiritual practice, is to get oneself out of the outer world and its activities, start the journey within, and become an introvert. Always keep in mind that you are not the body nor the mind, but Self (Atma) that is separate and superior to the body-mind complex (BMC). Detach your Self from the BMC and make the Self a witness during meditation. Withdraw your mind from the outside world and fix your gaze at any one center of your choice (pituitary gland, the sixth Chakra, front of the nostrils, the heart center, or the naval center) where you feel most comfortable. Witness the activities of the mind without becoming judgmental — good or bad — about the thoughts coming to your mind. Just relax, take a joy ride in the back seat of the vehicle of mind, and watch the wanderings of mind in the thought-world. The mind will wander because this is its nature. It will not remain quiet in the beginning. Do not be in a hurry to slow down, pressure, control, or try to engage the mind in any other way, such as by chanting a mantra, concentrating on any object or thought.

Detach yourself completely from your mind and watch the play of Maya, the mind. Do not forget that your job is to see your (lower) self, the mind, with the (higher) Self, the Atma. Do not get attached or carried away by the thought waves (Vritti) of the mind; just witness or follow it. After serious and sincere practice, the mind will start slowing down when it finds out that it is being constantly watched and followed. Do not add anything to the process of witnessing the inner world of thought process (Chitta-vritti). Slowly, your power of concentration will increase; the mind will join the inward journey as a friend (Gita 6.05-06); and a state of bliss will radiate all around you. You will go beyond thought to the thoughtless world of Nirvikalp Samadhi. Practice this for half an hour in the morning and evening or at any other convenient, but fixed, time of your choice. The progress will depend on several factors beyond your control, but just persist without procrastination. Always conclude the meditation process with the triple sound vibration of Aum, and thank God.

WHO IS A YOGI

प्रशान्तमनसं ह्येनं योगिनं सुखम् उत्तमम् ।
उपैति शान्तरजसं ब्रह्मभूतम् अकल्मषम् ॥२७॥
praśāntamanasaṁ hyenaṁ yoginaṁ sukham uttamam
upaiti śānta rajasaṁ brahma bhūtam akalmaṣam

Supreme bliss comes to a Self-realized yogi whose mind is tranquil, whose desires are under control, and who is free from faults or sin. (6.27)

युञ्जन्न् एवं सदात्मानं योगी विगतकल्मषः ।
सुखेन ब्रह्मसंस्पर्शम् अत्यन्तं सुखम् अश्नुते ॥२८॥
yuñjann evaṁ sadā'tmānaṁ yogī vigata kalmaṣaḥ
sukhena brahma saṁsparśam atyantaṁ sukham aśnute

Such a sinless yogi, who constantly engages his or her mind and intellect with the Self, enjoys the eternal bliss of contact with the Self. (6.28)

Yogananda said: In the absence of inward joy, people turn to evil. Meditation on the God of bliss permeates us with goodness.

सर्वभूतस्थम् आत्मानं सर्वभूतानि चात्मनि ।
ईक्षते योगयुक्तात्मा सर्वत्र समदर्शनः ॥२९॥

sarvabhūtastham ātmānaṁ sarvabhūtāni cā'tmani
īkṣate yogayuktātmā sarvatra samadarśanaḥ

A yogi who is in union with the Supreme Being sees every being with an equal eye because of perceiving the omnipresent Supreme Being (or the Self) abiding in all beings and all beings abiding in the Supreme Being. (See also 4.35, 5.18) (6.29)

Perception of oneness of the Self in every being is the highest spiritual perfection. Sage Yajnavalkya said: A wife does not love her husband because of his or her satisfaction. She loves her husband because she feels the oneness of her soul with his soul. She is merged in her husband and becomes one with him (BrU 2.04.05). The foundation of Vedic marriage is based on this noble and solid rock of soul culture and is unbreakable. Trying to develop any meaningful human relationship without a firm understanding of the spiritual basis of all relationships is like trying to water the leaves of a tree rather than the root.

When one perceives one's own higher Self in all people and all people in one's own higher Self, then one does not hate or injure anybody (IsU 06). Eternal peace belongs to those who perceive God existing within everybody as Spirit (KaU 5.13). One should love others, including the enemy, because all are your own self. "Love your enemy and pray for those who persecute you" is not only one of the noblest teachings of the Bible, but is an elementary idea common to all paths leading to God. When one realizes that his or her very self has become everything, whom shall one hate or punish? One does not break the teeth that bite the tongue. When one perceives none other than one's own Lord abiding in the entire universe, with whom shall one fight? One should not only love the roses, but love the thorns also.

One who sees One in all and all in One, sees the One everywhere. To fully understand this and to experience the oneness of individual soul and the Supersoul, is the highest achievement and the only goal of human birth (BP 6.16.63). In the fullness of one's spiritual development, one finds that the Lord, who resides in one's own heart, resides in the hearts of all others — the rich, the poor, the Hindus, the Muslims, the Christians, the persecuted, the persecutor, the saint, and the sinner. Therefore, to hate a single person is to hate Him. This realization makes one a truly humble saint. One who realizes that the Supersoul is all-pervading and is none other than one's own individual self, bereft of all impurities collected over various incarnations, attains immortality and bliss.

यो मां पश्यति सर्वत्र सर्वं च मयि पश्यति ।
तस्याहं न प्रणश्यामि स च मे न प्रणश्यति ॥३०॥

yo māṁ paśyati sarvatra sarvaṁ ca mayi paśyati
tsyā'haṁ na praṇaśyāmi sa ca me na praṇaśyati

Those who perceive Me in everything, and behold everything in Me, are not separated from Me, and I am not separated from them. (6.30)

A Self-realized person sees Me in the entire universe and in oneself and sees the entire universe and oneself in Me. When one sees Me pervading everything, just as fire pervades wood, one is at once freed from delusion. One attains salvation when one sees oneself different from body, mind, and the modes of material Nature and non-different from Me (BP 3.09.31-33). The wise see their own higher Self present in the entire universe and the entire universe present in their own higher Self. True devotees never fear any condition of life, such as reincarnation, living in heaven or in hell, because they see God everywhere (BP 6.17.28). If you want to see, remember, and be with God at all times, then you must practice and learn to see God in everything and everywhere.

सर्वभूतस्थितं यो मां भजत्य् एकत्वम् आस्थितः ।
सर्वथा वर्तमानोऽपि स योगी मयि वर्तते ॥३१॥

sarvabhūta sthitaṁ yo māṁ bhajaty ekatvam āsthitaḥ
sarvathā vartamāno'pi sa yogī mayi vartate

The non-dualists, who adore Me abiding in all beings, abide in Me irrespective of their mode of living. (6.31)

आत्मौपम्येन सर्वत्र समं पश्यति योऽर्जुन ।
सुखं वा यदि वा दुःखं स योगी परमो मतः ॥३२॥

ātmaupamyena sarvatra samaṁ paśyati yo'rjuna
sukhaṁ vā yadi vā duḥkhaṁ sa yogī paramo mataḥ

The best yogi is one who regards every being like oneself and who can feel the pain and pleasures of others as one's own, O Arjuna. (6.32)

One should consider all creatures as one's own children (BP 7.14.09). This is one of the qualities of a true devotee. The sages consider all women their mother, other's wealth a clod, and all beings as their own self. Rare is a person whose heart melts by the fire of grief of others and who rejoices hearing the praise of others.

TWO METHODS TO SUBDUE THE RESTLESS MIND

अर्जुन उवाच
योऽयं योगस् त्वया प्रोक्तः साम्येन मधुसूदन ।
एतस्याहं न पश्यामि चञ्चलत्वात् स्थितिं स्थिराम् ॥३३॥

arjuna uvāca
yo'yaṁ yogas tvayā proktaḥ sāmyena madhusūdana
etasyā'haṁ na paśyāmi cañcalatvāt sthitiṁ sthirām

चञ्चलं हि मनः कृष्ण प्रमाथि बलवद् दृढम् ।
तस्याहं निग्रहं मन्ये वायोर् इव सुदुष्करम् ॥३४॥
cañcalaṁ hi manaḥ kṛṣṇa pramāthi balavad dṛḍham
tasyā'haṁ nigrahaṁ manye vāyor iva suduṣkaram

Arjuna said: O Krishna, You have said that the yoga of meditation is characterized by equanimity of mind, but due to restlessness of mind I do not perceive it as steady. Because the mind, indeed, is very unsteady, turbulent, powerful, and obstinate, O Krishna. I think restraining the mind is as difficult as restraining the wind. (6.33-34)

श्रीभगवानुवाच
असंशयं महाबाहो मनो दुर्निग्रहं चलम् ।
अभ्यासेन तु कौन्तेय वैराग्येण च गृह्यते ॥३५॥
śrī bhagavān uvāca
asaṁśayaṁ mahābāho mano durnigrahaṁ calam
abhyāsena tu kaunteya vairāgyeṇa ca gṛhyate

Lord Krishna said: Undoubtedly, O Arjuna, the mind is restless and difficult to restrain, but it is subdued by any constant vigorous spiritual practice — such as meditation — with perseverance, and by detachment, O Arjuna. (6.35)

Detachment is proportional to one's understanding of the baselessness of the world and its objects (MB 12.174.04). Contemplation without detachment is like jewels on the body without clothes (TR 2.177.02).

असंयतात्मना योगो दुष्प्राप इति मे मतिः ।
वश्यात्मना तु यतता शक्योऽवाप्तुम् उपायतः ॥३६॥

asaṁyatā'tmanā yogo duṣprāpa iti me matiḥ
vaśyā'tmanā tu yatatā śakyo'vāptum upāyataḥ

Yoga is difficult for one whose mind is not subdued. However, yoga is attainable by the person of subdued mind who strives through proper means. (6.36)

DESTINATION OF UNSUCCESSFUL YOGI

अर्जुन उवाच
अयतिः श्रद्धयोपेतो योगाच् चलितमानसः ।
अप्राप्य योगसंसिद्धिं कां गतिं कृष्ण गच्छति ।।३७।।

arjuna uvāca
ayatiḥ śraddhayopeto yogāc calitamānasaḥ
aprāpya yogasaṁsiddhiṁ kāṁ gatiṁ kṛṣṇa gacchati

Arjuna said: What is the destination of the faithful who deviate from the path of meditation and fail to attain yogic perfection due to an unsubdued mind, O Krishna? (6.37)

कच्चिन् नोभयविभ्रष्टश् छिन्नाभ्रम् इव नश्यति ।
अप्रतिष्ठो महाबाहो विमूढो ब्रह्मणः पथि ।।३८।।

kaccin no'bhayavibhraṣṭaś chinnābhram iva naśyati
apratiṣṭho mahābāho vimūḍho brahmaṇaḥ pathi

Do they not perish like a dispersing cloud, O Krishna, having lost both the heavenly and the worldly pleasures, supportless and bewildered on the path of Self-realization? (6.38)

एतन् मे संशयं कृष्ण छेत्तुम् अर्हस्य् अशेषतः ।
त्वदन्यः संशयस्यास्य छेत्ता न ह्य् उपपद्यते ।।३९।।

etan me saṁśayaṁ kṛṣṇa chettum arhasy aśeṣataḥ
tvadanyaḥ saṁśayasyā'sya chettā na hy upapadyate

O Krishna, only You are able to completely dispel this doubt of mine because there is none other than You who can dispel such a doubt. (See also 15.15) (6.39)

Arjuna asked a very good question. Because the mind is very difficult to control, it may not be possible to achieve perfection during one's lifetime. Does all the effort get wasted? The answer comes:

श्रीभगवानुवाच
पार्थ नैवेह नामुत्र विनाशस् तस्य विद्यते ।
न हि कल्याणकृत् कश्चिद् दुर्गतिं तात गच्छति ।।४०।।

śrī bhagavān uvāca
pārtha nai've'ha nā'mutra vināśas tasya vidyate
na hi kalyāṇakṛt kaścid durgatiṁ tāta gacchati

Lord Krishna said: Spiritual practice performed by a yogi never goes to waste either here or hereafter. A transcendentalist is never put to grief, My dear friend. (6.40)

प्राप्य पुण्यकृतां लोकान् उषित्वा शाश्वतीः समाः ।
शुचीनां श्रीमतां गेहे योगभ्रष्टोऽभिजायते ।।४१।।

prāpya puṇyakṛtāṁ lokān uṣitvā śāśvatīḥ samāḥ
śucīnāṁ śrīmatāṁ gehe yogabhraṣṭo'bhijāyate

अथवा योगिनाम् एव कुले भवति धीमताम् ।
एतद्धि दुर्लभतरं लोके जन्म यद् ईदृशम् ।।४२।।

athavā yogināṁ eva kule bhavati dhīmatām
etaddhi durlabhataraṁ loke janma yad īdṛśam

The less evolved unsuccessful yogi is reborn in the house of the pious and prosperous after attaining heaven and living there for many years. The highly evolved unsuccessful yogi does not go to heaven, but is born in a

spiritually advanced family. A birth like this is very difficult, indeed, to obtain in this world. (6.41-42)

तत्र तं बुद्धिसंयोगं लभते पौर्वदेहिकम् ।
यतते च ततो भूयः संसिद्धौ कुरुनन्दन ।।४३।।

tatra taṁ buddhi saṁyogaṁ labhate paurva dehikam
yatate ca tato bhūyaḥ saṁsiddhau kurunandana

The unsuccessful yogi regains the knowledge acquired in the previous life and strives again to achieve perfection, O Arjuna. (6.43)

पूर्वाभ्यासेन तेनैव ह्रियते ह्य् अवशोऽपि सः ।
जिज्ञासुर् अपि योगस्य शब्दब्रह्मातिवर्तते ।।४४।।

pūrvābhyāsena tenai'va hriyate hy avaśo'pi saḥ
jijñāsur api yogasya śabdabrahmā'tivartate

The unsuccessful yogi is instinctively carried towards God by virtue of the impressions of yogic practices of previous lives. Even the inquirer of yoga — union with God — surpasses those who perform Vedic rituals. (6.44)

प्रयत्नाद् यतमानस् तु योगी संशुद्धकिल्बिषः ।
अनेकजन्मसंसिद्धस् ततो याति परां गतिम् ।।४५।।

prayatnād yatamānas tu yogī saṁśuddhakilbiṣaḥ
aneka janma saṁsidhas tato yāti parāṁ gatim

The yogi who diligently strives becomes completely free from all imperfections after becoming gradually perfect through many incarnations and reaches the Supreme Abode. (6.45)

One must be very careful in spiritual life, or there is a possibility of being carried away by the powerful wind of bad association created by Maya, and one may abandon the spiritual path. One should never get discouraged. The unsuccessful yogi gets another chance by starting over from where he or she leaves off. The spiritual journey is long and slow, but no sincere effort is ever wasted. Normally it takes many, many births to reach the perfection of salvation. All living entities (souls) are eventually redeemed after they reach the zenith of spiritual evolution.

WHO IS THE BEST YOGI

तपस्विभ्योऽधिको योगी ज्ञानिभ्योऽपि मतोऽधिकः ।
कर्मिभ्यश् चाधिको योगी तस्माद् योगी भवार्जुन ।।४६।।

tapasvibhyo'dhiko yogī jñānibhyo'pi mato'dhikaḥ
karmibhyaś cādhiko yogī tasmād yogī bhavārjuna

The yogi is superior to the ascetics. The yogi is superior to the Vedic scholars. The yogi is superior to the ritualists. Therefore, O Arjuna, be a yogi. (6.46)

योगिनाम् अपि सर्वेषां मद्गतेनान्तरात्मना ।
श्रद्धावान् भजते यो मां स मे युक्ततमो मतः ।।४७।।

yoginām api sarveṣāṁ madgatenā'ntarātmanā
śraddhāvān bhajate yo māṁ sa me yuktatamo mataḥ

And I consider the yogi-devotee — who lovingly contemplates Me with supreme faith and whose mind is ever absorbed in Me— to be the best of all the yogis. (See also 12.02 and 18.66) (6.47)

Meditation or any other act becomes more powerful and efficient if it is done with knowledge, faith, and devotion to God. Meditation is a necessary condition but not a sufficient condition for spiritual progress. The mind should be kept ever absorbed in thoughts of God. The meditative mood is to be continued during other times through scriptural study, Self-analysis, and service. It is said that no single yoga alone is complete without the presence of other yogas. Just as the right combination of all ingredients is essential for preparation of a good meal, similarly, selfless service, chanting of Lord's name, meditation, study of scriptures, contemplation, and devotional love are essential for reaching the supreme goal. Some seekers prefer just to stick to one path. They should try all other major paths and see if a combination is better for them or not. Any path can become the right path if one has completely surrendered to God. The person who meditates with deep devotional love of God is called a yogi-devotee and is considered to be the best of all yogis.

Before one can purify one's psyche by a mantra or meditation, one has to reach a level whereby one's system of consciousness becomes sensitive to a mantra. This means one's mundane desires must be first fulfilled — or satisfied — by detachment, and one has practiced the first four steps of Patanjali's YogaSutra. It is just like cleaning jewelry first before gold-plating it.

ॐ तत्सदिति श्रीमद्भगवद्गीतासूपनिषत्सु ब्रह्मविद्यायां योगशास्त्रे
श्रीकृष्णार्जुनसंवादे आत्मसंयमयोगो नाम षष्ठोऽध्यायः ॥

OM tatsaditi śrīmadbhagavadgītāsūpaniṣatsu brahmavidyāyāṁ
yogaśāstre śrīkṛṣṇārjuna saṁvāde ātmasaṁyamayogo
nāma ṣaṣṭho'dhyāyaḥ

Thus ends the sixth chapter named "Path of Meditation" of the
Upaniṣad of the Bhagavadgītā, the scripture of yoga,
dealing with the science of the Absolute in the
form of the dialogue between
Śrīkṛṣṇa and Arjuna.

अथ सप्तमोऽध्यायः
CHAPTER 7
ज्ञानविज्ञानयोगः
SELF-KNOWLEDGE AND ENLIGHTENMENT

श्रीभगवानुवाच
मय्य् आसक्तमनाः पार्थ योगं युञ्जन् मदाश्रयः ।
असंशयं समग्रं मां यथा ज्ञास्यसि तच्छृणु ॥१॥

śrī bhagavān uvāca
mayy āsaktamanāḥ pārtha yogaṁ yuñjan madāśrayaḥ
asaṁśayaṁ samagraṁ māṁ yathā jñāsyasi tacchṛṇu

Lord Krishna said: O Arjuna, listen how you shall know Me fully without any doubt, with your mind absorbed in Me, taking refuge in Me and performing yogic practices. (7.01)

METAPHYSICAL KNOWLEDGE IS THE ULTIMATE KNOWLEDGE

ज्ञानं तेऽहं सविज्ञानम् इदं वक्ष्याम्य् अशेषतः ।
यज् ज्ञात्वा नेह भूयोऽन्यज् ज्ञातव्यम् अवशिष्यते ॥२॥

jñānaṁ te'haṁ savijñānam idaṁ vakṣyāmy aśeṣataḥ
yaj jñātvā neha bhūyo'nyaj jñātavyam avaśiṣyate

I shall impart to you both the transcendental knowledge and the transcendental experience or a vision, after knowing that nothing more remains to be known in this world. (7.02)

Those who have transcendental experience become perfect (RV 1.164.39). Everything becomes (as though) known when the Supreme Being is heard, reflected, meditated upon, seen, and known (BrU 4.05.06). The need to know all other things becomes irrelevant with the dawn of the knowledge of the Absolute, the

Supreme Spirit. All articles made of gold become known after knowing gold. Similarly, after knowing the Supreme Being (ParaBrahma), all other manifestations of the Eternal Being (Brahma) become known. Yogi Chimanbhai says: One who knows Lord Krishna as the Supreme Being (ParaBrahma), is considered to have known all, but one who knows everything, but does not know Krishna, does not know anything. The intent of the above verse is that knowledge of all other subjects remains incomplete without one's understanding of who am I?

SEEKERS ARE VERY FEW

मनुष्याणां सहस्रेषु कश्चिद् यतति सिद्धये ।
यतताम् अपि सिद्धानां कश्चिन् मां वेत्ति तत्त्वतः ।।३।।

manuṣyāṇāṁ sahasreṣu kaścid yatati siddhaye
yatatām api siddhānāṁ kaścin māṁ vetti tattvataḥ

Scarcely one out of thousands of persons strives for perfection of Self-realization. Scarcely one among those successful strivers truly understands Me. (7.03)

Many are called, but few are chosen (Matthew 22.14). Few are fortunate enough to obtain knowledge of, and devotion to, the Supreme Being.

DEFINITION OF SPIRIT AND MATTER

भूमिर् आपोऽनलो वायुः खं मनो बुद्धिर् एव च ।
अहंकार इतीयं मे भिन्ना प्रकृतिर् अष्टधा ।।४।।

bhūmir āpo'nalo vāyuḥ khaṁ mano buddhir eva ca
ahaṁkāra itīyaṁ me bhinnā prakṛtir aṣṭadhā

The mind, intellect, ego, ether, air, fire, water, and earth are the eightfold division of My material Nature. (See also 13.05) (7.04)

'Material Nature' is defined as the material cause or the material energy out of which everything is made. Material Nature is the original source of the material world, consisting of three modes of material Nature and eight basic elements out of which everything in the universe has evolved, according to Sankhya doctrine. Material Nature is one of the transformations of divine power (Maya) and is the material cause of creation of the entire universe. Matter is thus a part of Lord's illusory energy, Maya. Material Nature is also referred to as perishable, body, matter, Nature, Maya, field, creation, and manifest state. That which creates diversity as well as the diversity itself, and all that can be seen or known, including the universal mind, is called material Nature.

अपरेयम् इतस् त्व् अन्यां प्रकृतिं विद्धि मे पराम् ।
जीवभूतां महाबाहो ययेदं धार्यते जगत् ।।५।।

apareyam itas tv anyāṁ prakṛtiṁ viddhi me parām
jīvabhūtāṁ mahābāho yayedaṁ dhāryate jagat

Material Nature or matter is My lower Nature. My other higher Nature is the Spirit or consciousness by which this entire universe is sustained, O Arjuna. (7.05)

Two types of material Nature are described in verses 7.04 and 7.05. The eightfold material Nature described in verse 7.04 is called lower energy or material energy. This is commonly known as material Nature or Prakriti. It creates the material world with the help of consciousness (Cetanā). The other higher Nature mentioned in verse 7.05 is also called higher energy or the spiritual energy (Purusha). This is derived from consciousness, Self, Spirit, or Spiritual Being. Spirit is immutable; and material

Nature, born of Spirit, is mutable. Spirit observes, witnesses, enjoys as well as supervises material Nature.

The Supreme Spirit is the efficient cause of creation of the universe. The material Nature and Spirit are not two independent identities but the two aspects of the Supreme Spirit. The Supreme Spirit, Spirit, and material Nature are the same, yet different as the sun and its light and heat are the same as well as different.

The water and the fish that is born in and sustained by the water, are not one and the same. Similarly, the Spirit and the material Nature that is born out of Spirit, are not one and the same (MB 12.315.14). The spirit is also called soul when spirit enjoys the modes of material Nature by associating with the senses. The Spirit and soul are also different because Spirit sustains soul, but the wise perceive no difference between the two (BP 4.28.62).

Some of the terms — such as the Supreme Spirit, Spirit, material Nature, and soul — have different definitions in different doctrines and also take different meanings, depending on the context. In this rendering, the nonsectarian word 'God' stands for the one and only Lord of the universe — the Supreme Being — whom Hindus prefer to call by various personal names such as Rama, Krishna, Shiva, and Mother. Different terminology does confuse a reader who has to learn — preferably with the help of a teacher — full connotation, usage, and hierarchic relationships between these and various other expressions as one progresses on the path of spiritual journey.

SUPREME SPIRIT IS THE BASIS OF EVERYTHING

एतद्योनीनि भूतानि सर्वाणीत्य् उपधारय ।
अहं कृत्स्नस्य जगतः प्रभवः प्रलयस् तथा ।।६।।

etad yonīni bhūtāni sarvāṇī'ty upadhāraya
ahaṁ kṛtsnasya jagataḥ prabhavaḥ pralayas tathā

Know that all creatures have evolved from this twofold energy, and the Supreme Spirit is the source of the origin as well as the dissolution of the entire universe. (See also 13.26) (7.06)

मत्तः परतरं नान्यत् किंचिद् अस्ति धनंजय ।
मयि सर्वम् इदं प्रोतं सूत्रे मणिगणा इव ॥७॥

mattaḥ parataraṁ nā'nyat kiṁcid asti dhanaṁjaya
mayi sarvam idaṁ protaṁ sūtre maṇigaṇā iva

There is nothing higher than Me, the Supreme Being, O Arjuna. Everything in the universe is strung on Me like different jewels are strung on the thread of a necklace. (7.07)

One and the same Spirit is present in cows, horses, human beings, birds, and all other living beings just as the same thread is present in the necklace made of diamond, gold, pearl, or wood (MB 12.206.02-03). The entire creation is permeated by Him (YV 32.08).

रसोऽहम् अप्सु कौन्तेय प्रभास्मि शशिसूर्ययोः ।
प्रणवः सर्ववेदेषु शब्दः खे पौरुषं नृषु ॥८॥

raso'ham apsu kaunteya prabhā'smi śaśisūryayoḥ
praṇavaḥ sarva vedeṣu śabdaḥ khe pauruṣaṁ nṛṣu

पुण्यो गन्धः पृथिव्यां च तेजश्चास्मि विभावसौ ।
जीवनं सर्वभूतेषु तपश् चास्मि तपस्विषु ॥९॥

puṇyo gandhaḥ pṛthivyāṁ ca tejaś cā'smi vibhāvasau
jīvanaṁ sarva bhūteṣu tapaś cā'smi tapasviṣu

O Arjuna, I am the sapidity in the water, I am the radiance in the sun and the moon, the sacred syllable 'AUM' in all the Vedas, the sound in the ether, and potency in human beings. I am the sweet fragrance in the earth. I am the heat

in the fire, the life in all living beings, and the austerity in the ascetics. (7.08-09)

बीजं मां सर्वभूतानां विद्धि पार्थ सनातनम् ।
बुद्धिर् बुद्धिमताम् अस्मि तेजस् तेजस्विनाम् अहम् ॥१०॥

bījaṁ māṁ sarva bhūtānāṁ viddhi pārtha sanātanam
buddhir buddhimatām asmi tejas tejasvinām aham

बलं बलवतां चाहं कामरागविवर्जितम् ।
धर्माविरुद्धो भूतेषु कामोऽस्मि भरतर्षभ ॥११॥

balaṁ balavatāṁ cāhaṁ kāma rāga vivarjitam
dharmāviruddho bhūteṣu kāmo'smi bharatarṣabha

O Arjuna, know Me to be the eternal seed of all creatures. I am the intelligence of the intelligent and the brilliance of the brilliant. (See also 9.18 and 10.39). I am the strength of the strong who are devoid of selfish attachment. I am the lust or Cupid in human beings that is devoid of sense gratification and is in accord with Dharma (for the sacred purpose of procreation after marriage), O Arjuna. (7.10-11)

ये चैव सात्त्विका भावा राजसास् तामसाश्च ये ।
मत्त एवेति तान् विद्धि न त्व् अहं तेषु ते मयि ॥१२॥

ye caiva sāttvikā bhāvā rājasās tāmasāśca ye
matta eveti tān viddhi na tv ahaṁ teṣu te mayi

Know that three modes of material Nature — goodness, passion, and ignorance — also emanate indirectly from Me. I am neither dependent on, nor affected by, the modes of material Nature; but the modes of material Nature are dependent on Me. (See also 9.04 and 9.05) (7.12)

त्रिभिर् गुणमयैर् भावैर् एभिः सर्वम् इदं जगत् ।
मोहितं नाभिजानाति माम् एभ्यः परम् अव्ययम् ॥१३॥

tribhir guṇamayair bhāvair ebhiḥ sarvam idaṁ jagat
mohitaṁ nā'bhijānāti mām ebhyaḥ param avyayam

Human beings get deluded by various aspects of these three modes of material Nature; therefore, they do not know Me, who am eternal and above these modes. (7.13)

HOW TO OVERCOME THE DELUSIVE DIVINE POWER (MAYA)

दैवी ह्य् एषा गुणमयी मम माया दुरत्यया ।
माम् एव ये प्रपद्यन्ते मायाम् एतां तरन्ति ते ॥१४॥

daivī hy eṣā guṇamayī mama māyā duratyayā
mām eva ye prapadyante māyām etāṁ taranti te

This divine power of Mine called Maya, consisting of three modes of Nature, is very difficult to overcome. Only those who surrender unto Me easily pierce the veil of Maya and know the Absolute Reality. (See also 14.26, 15.19, and 18.66) (7.14)

When one fully dedicates one's life to the Supreme power and depends on Him under all circumstances, just as a small child depends on its parents, then Lord personally takes charge of such a devotee. And when He takes charge of you, there is no need to be afraid of anything or to depend on anybody else for anything — spiritual or material — in life.

WHO SEEKS GOD?

न मां दुष्कृतिनो मूढाः प्रपद्यन्ते नराधमाः ।
माययापहृतज्ञाना आसुरं भावम् आश्रिताः ॥१५॥

na māṁ duṣkṛtino mūḍhāḥ prapadyante narādhamāḥ
māyayā'pahṛtajñānā āsuraṁ bhāvam āśritāḥ

The evil doers, the ignorant, the lowest persons who are attached to demonic nature and whose power of discrimination has been taken away by divine illusive power (Maya), do not worship or seek Me. (7.15)

चतुर्विधा भजन्ते मां जनाः सुकृतिनोऽर्जुन ।
आर्तो जिज्ञासुर् अर्थार्थी ज्ञानी च भरतर्षभ ॥१६॥

caturvidhā bhajante māṁ janāḥ sukṛtino'rjuna
ārto jijñāsur arthārthī jñānī ca bharatarṣabha

Four types of virtuous ones worship or seek Me, O Arjuna. They are: the distressed, the seeker of Self-knowledge, the seeker of wealth, and the enlightened one who has experienced the Supreme Being. (7.16)

Whatever a person does is the product of desire. Nobody can ever do anything without the desire for it (MS 2.04). Desires cannot be completely wiped out. One should transmute the lower forms of selfish desires. Desire for salvation is a higher or noble form of desire. Desire for devotional love of God is regarded as the highest and the purest form of all human desires. It is said that advanced devotees do not even desire salvation from God. They long for loving devotional service to God, life after life.

The lower desires of devotees who approach Him for fulfillment become like roasted seeds that cannot sprout and grow into a big tree of desire. What really matters is the deep concentration of mind on God through feelings of devotion, love, fear, or even for material gain (BP 10.22.26).

तेषां ज्ञानी नित्ययुक्त एकभक्तिर् विशिष्यते ।
प्रियो हि ज्ञानिनोऽत्यर्थम् अहं स च मम प्रियः ॥१७॥

teṣāṁ jñānī nityayukta ekabhaktir viśiṣyate
priyo hi jñānino'tyartham ahaṁ sa ca mama priyaḥ

Among them the enlightened devotee, who is ever united with Me and whose devotion is single-minded, is the best because I am very dear to the enlightened and the enlightened is very dear to Me. (7.17)

Knowledge of God without devotion — the love of God — is a dry speculation, and devotion without knowledge of God is blind faith. The fruit of enlightenment grows on the tree of Self-knowledge only when the tree receives the water of pure devotion.

उदाराः सर्व एवैते ज्ञानी त्व् आत्मैव मे मतम् ।
आस्थितः स हि युक्तात्मा माम् एवानुत्तमां गतिम् ॥१८॥
udārāḥ sarva evaite jñānī tv ātmai'va me matam
āsthitaḥ sa hi yuktātmā mām evā'nuttamāṁ gatim

All these seekers are indeed noble, but I regard the enlightened devotee as My very Self because one who is steadfast becomes one with Me and abides in My supreme abode. (See also 9.29) (7.18)

बहूनां जन्मनाम् अन्ते ज्ञानवान् मां प्रपद्यते ।
वासुदेवः सर्वम् इति स महात्मा सुदुर्लभः ॥१९॥
bahūnāṁ janmanām ante jñānavān māṁ prapadyate
vāsudevaḥ sarvam iti sa mahātmā sudurlabhaḥ

After many births, the enlightened one resorts to Me by realizing that everything is, indeed, My manifestation. Such a great soul is very rare. (7.19)

All this is, of course, the Spirit because everything is born from, rests in, and merges into the Spirit (ChU 3.14.01). All this is Spirit. The Spirit is everywhere. All this universe is, indeed, Spirit (MuU 2.02.11). The Bible says: You are gods (John 10.34). The Vedas and Upanishads declare: (1) Consciousness is Spirit (AiU 3.03 in Rigveda). (2) I am Spirit (BrU 1.04.10 in Yajurveda). (3) You are Spirit (ChU 6.08.07 in Samaveda). (4) The Spirit is also called Atma (or Brahman, Brahm, Brahma) (MaU 02 in Atharvaveda). That which is One has become all these (RV 8.58.02). The entire creation and every order of reality are nothing but another form of divinity.

The male musk deer, after a vain search for the cause of the scent of the musk, at last will have to find the musk in himself. After God-realization, one sees that it is the Spirit of God (or Consciousness) that has become the universe and all living beings. Everything is consciousness. Creation is like countless waves appearing in the ocean of consciousness by the wind of divine power (Maya). Everything, including the primordial divine energy called Maya, is nothing but part and parcel of the Absolute.

कामैस् तैस्तैर् हृतज्ञानाः प्रपद्यन्तेऽन्यदेवताः ।
तं तं नियमम् आस्थाय प्रकृत्या नियताः स्वया ॥२०॥

kāmais taistair hṛtajñānāḥ prapadyante'nyadevatāḥ
taṁ taṁ niyamam āsthāya prakṛtyā niyatāḥ svayā

Persons whose discernment has been carried away by desires impelled by their Karmic impression, resort to celestial controllers and practice various religious rites for fulfillment of their material desires. (7.20)

WORSHIP OF DEITY IS ALSO WORSHIP OF GOD

यो यो यां यां तनुं भक्तः श्रद्धयार्चितुम् इच्छति ।
तस्य तस्याचलां श्रद्धां ताम् एव विदधाम्य् अहम् ॥२१॥

yo yo yāṁ yāṁ tanuṁ bhaktaḥ śraddhayā'rcitum icchati
tasya tasyā'calāṁ śraddhāṁ tām eva vidadhāmy ahaṁ

स तया श्रद्धया युक्तस् तस्याराधनम् ईहते ।
लभते च ततः कामान् मयैव विहितान् हि तान् ॥२२॥

sa tayā śraddhayā yuktas tasyā'rādhanam īhate
labhate ca tataḥ kāmān mayai'va vihitān hi tān

Whosoever desires to worship whatever deity — using any name, form, and method — with faith, I make their faith steady in that very deity. Endowed with steady faith, they worship that deity and obtain their wishes through that deity. Those wishes are, indeed, granted by Me. (7.21-22)

The power in the deities comes from the Supreme Lord as the aroma in the wind comes from the flower (BP 6.04.34). God is the bestower of fruits of work (BS 3.02.38). God fulfills all desires of His worshippers (BP 4.13.34). One should not look down upon any method of seeking God because all worship is worship of the same God. He fulfills all sincere and beneficial prayers of a devotee if He is worshipped with faith and love. The wise realize that all names and forms are His, whereas the ignorant play the game of holy war in the name of religion to seek personal gain at the cost of others.

It is said that whatever deity a person may worship, all his or her obeisance and prayers reach the Supreme Being just as all water that falls as rain eventually reaches the ocean. Whatever name and form of divinity one adores is worship of the same Supreme Being, and one gets the reward of deity-worship performed with faith. Desired results of worship are given indirectly by the Lord through one's favorite deity. Human beings live in the darkness of the prison cells of pairs of opposites. Deities are like icons or a medium that can open the window through which the Supreme may be perceived. However, the worship of deities without full understanding of the nature of the Supreme Being is considered to be in the mode of ignorance.

अन्तवत् तु फलं तेषां तद् भवत्य् अल्पमेधसाम् ।
देवान् देवयजो यान्ति मद्भक्ता यान्ति माम् अपि ।।२३।।

antavat tu phalaṁ teṣāṁ tad bhavaty alpamedhasām
devān devayajo yānti madbhaktā yānti mām api

Such material gains of these less intelligent human beings are temporary. The worshipers of celestial controllers go to celestial controllers, but My devotees certainly come to Me. (7.23)

Those who worship deities or celestial controllers are under the mode of passion; and those who practice other, much lower grades of worship, such as the worship of evil spirits, ghosts, black magic, and Tantra — also known as idolatry — to get progeny, fame, or to destroy their enemies are under the mode of ignorance. Lord Krishna advises against such lower grades of worship and recommends worship of the one and only Supreme Lord, using any one name and form. The devotees of Krishna may sometimes worship Krishna in other forms also. In Mahabharata, Lord Krishna Himself advised Arjuna to worship a much gentler mother form of God, known as Mother Durga, just before the start of the war for victory. This is like a child going to ask something from Mother instead of Father. The Lord is actually both mother and father of all creatures.

GOD CAN BE SEEN IN ANY DESIRED FORM OF WORSHIP

अव्यक्तं व्यक्तिम् आपन्नं मन्यन्ते माम् अबुद्धयः ।
परं भावम् अजानन्तो ममाव्ययम् अनुत्तमम् ।।२४।।

avyaktaṁ vyaktim āpannaṁ manyante mām abuddhayaḥ
paraṁ bhāvam ajānanto mamā'vyayam anuttamam

नाहं प्रकाशः सर्वस्य योगमायासमावृतः ।
मूढोऽयं नाभिजानाति लोको माम् अजम् अव्ययम् ।।२५।।

nā'haṁ prakāśaḥ sarvasya yogamāyāsamāvṛtaḥ
mūḍho'yaṁ nā'bhijānāti loko mām ajam avyayam

The ignorant ones — unable to completely understand My immutable, incomparable, incomprehensible, and transcendental form and existence — believe that I, the

Supreme Being, am formless and take forms or incarnate. I do not reveal Myself to the ignorant ones whose Self-knowledge is obscured by My divine power (Yoga Maya) and do not know My unborn, eternal, and transcendental form and personality (and consider Me formless). (See also 5.16) (7.24-25)

The Sanskrit word 'Avyakta' has been used in verses 2.25, 2.28, 7.24, 8.18, 8.20, 8.21, 9.04, 12.01, 12.03, 12.05, and 13.05. It takes different meanings according to the context. It is used in the sense of unmanifest, material Nature and also in the sense of Spirit. Supreme Being — the Absolute Consciousness — is higher than both unmanifest Nature and Spirit. 'Avyakta' does not mean formless; it means unmanifest or a transcendental form that is invisible to our physical eyes and cannot be comprehended by the human mind or described by words. Everything has a form. Nothing in the cosmos, including the Supreme Being, is formless. Every form is His form. Supreme Being has a transcendental form and Supreme Personality. He is eternal, without any origin and end. The invisible Absolute is the basis of the visible world.

The meaning of verse 7.24 also seems to contradict the common belief that Lord incarnates, as mentioned in verses 4.06-08, and 9.11. It is said here that the Supreme Being is ever unmanifest, and, as such, He never becomes manifest. In a true sense, the Supreme Being or Absolute does not incarnate. He actually never leaves His Supreme Abode! It is the intellect of the Supreme Being that does the work of creation, maintenance, incarnation, and destruction by using His innumerable powers. The deep meaning of this verse may be understood if one seriously studies the peace invocation of Ishopanishad that states: "The invisible is the Infinite, the visible too is infinite. From the Infinite, the infinite universes manifest. The Infinite (Absolute) remains Infinite or unchanged, even though infinite universes come out of it." People do not know the transcendental and imperishable nature of God and wrongly think that God also incarnates like an ordinary person. He does not incarnate, but manifests using His own divine potencies.

The transcendental Being is beyond the human conception of form and formless. Those who consider God formless are as wrong as those who say God has a form. The argument whether God is formless or has a form has nothing to do with our worship and spiritual practice. We can worship Him in any way or form that suits us. A name, form, and description of the imperceptible, all pervasive, and indescribable Lord has been given by saints and sages for cultivating the love of God in the hearts of common devotees. A name and a form are absolutely necessary for the purpose of worship and to nurture devotion — a deep love for God. God appears to a devotee in a form in order to make his or her faith firm. Therefore, it is necessary that one should respect all forms of God (or deity), but establish relationship with and worship one form only.

वेदाहं समतीतानि वर्तमानानि चार्जुन ।
भविष्याणि च भूतानि मां तु वेद न कश्चन ।।२६।।

vedā'haṁ samatītāni vartamānāni cā'rjuna
bhaviṣyāṇi ca bhūtāni māṁ tu veda na kaścana

I know, O Arjuna, the beings of the past, of the present, and those of the future, but no one really knows Me. (7.26)

इच्छाद्वेषसमुत्थेन द्वन्द्वमोहेन भारत ।
सर्वभूतानि संमोहं सर्गे यान्ति परंतप ।।२७।।

icchā dveṣa samutthena dvandva mohena bhārata
sarva bhūtāni saṁmohaṁ sarge yānti paraṁtapa

येषां त्व् अन्तगतं पापं जनानां पुण्यकर्मणाम् ।
ते द्वन्द्वमोहनिर्मुक्ता भजन्ते मां दृढव्रताः ।।२८।।

yeṣāṁ tv antagataṁ pāpaṁ janānāṁ puṇyakarmaṇām
te dvandva

All beings in this world are in utter ignorance due to the delusion of pairs of opposites born of likes and dislikes, O Arjuna. But the persons purified by unselfish deeds,

whose Karma has come to an end, become free from the delusion of pairs of opposites and worship Me with firm resolve. (7.27-28)

When the Karma of a person comes to an end, only then one can understand the transcendental science and develop love and devotion to God.

जरामरणमोक्षाय माम् आश्रित्य यतन्ति ये ।
ते ब्रह्म तद् विदुः कृत्स्नम् अध्यात्मं कर्म चाखिलम् ॥२९॥
jarā maraṇa mokṣāya mām āśritya yatanti ye
te brahma tad viduḥ kṛtsnam adhyātmaṁ karma cā'khilam

Those who strive for freedom from the cycles of birth, old age, and death — by taking refuge in Me — fully comprehend Brahman and the true nature and creative powers of Brahman. (7.29)

साधिभूताधिदैवं मां साधियज्ञं च ये विदुः ।
प्रयाणकालेऽपि च मां ते विदुर् युक्तचेतसः ॥३०॥
sādhibhūtā'dhidaivaṁ māṁ sādhiyajñaṁ ca ye viduḥ
prayāṇakāle'pi ca māṁ te vidur yuktacetasaḥ

The steadfast persons who know Me alone as the basis of all — mortal beings, Divine Beings, and the Eternal Being — even at the time of death, attain Me. (See also 8.04) (7.30)

Those who know God to be the governing principle of the whole creation and the underlying basis of all, are blessed.

ॐ तत्सदिति श्रीमद्भगवद्गीतासूपनिषत्सु ब्रह्मविद्यायां योगशास्त्रे
श्रीकृष्णार्जुनसंवादे ज्ञानविज्ञानयोगो
नाम सप्तमोऽध्यायः ॥

OM tatsaditi śrīmadbhagavadgītāsūpaniṣatsu brahmavidyāyāṁ
yogaśāstre śrīkṛṣṇārjuna saṁvāde jñānavijñānayogo
nāma saptamo'dhyāyaḥ

Thus ends the seventh chapter named "Self-knowledge and Enlightenment" of the Upaniṣad of the Bhagavadgītā, the scripture of yoga, dealing with the science of the Absolute in the form of the dialogue between Śrīkṛṣṇa and Arjuna.

अथ अष्टमोऽध्यायः
CHAPTER 8
अक्षरब्रह्मयोगः
THE ETERNAL BRAHMA

अर्जुन उवाच
किं तद् ब्रह्म किम् अध्यात्मं किं कर्म पुरुषोत्तम ।
अधिभूतं च किं प्रोक्तम् अधिदैवं किम् उच्यते ॥१॥

arjuna uvāca
kiṁ tad brahma kim adhyātmaṁ kiṁ karma puruṣottama
adhibhūtaṁ ca kiṁ proktam adhidaivaṁ kim ucyate

अधियज्ञः कथं कोऽत्र देहेऽस्मिन् मधुसूदन ।
प्रयाणकाले च कथं ज्ञेयोऽसि नियतात्मभिः ॥२॥

adhiyajñaḥ kathaṁ ko'tra dehe'smin madhusūdana
prayāṇakāle ca kathaṁ jñeyo'si niyatātmabhiḥ

Arjuna said: O Krishna, who is the Eternal Being or the Spirit? What is the nature of the Eternal Being? What is Karma? Who are the mortal beings? And who are Divine Beings? Who is the all pervading, Supreme Being and how does He dwell in the body? How can You, the Supreme Being, be remembered at the time of death by those who have control over their minds, O Krishna? (8.01-02)

DEFINITION OF SUPREME SPIRIT, SPIRIT, INDIVIDUAL SOUL, AND KARMA

श्रीभगवानुवाच
अक्षरं ब्रह्म परमं स्वभावोऽध्यात्मम् उच्यते ।
भूतभावोद्भवकरो विसर्गः कर्मसंज्ञितः ॥३॥

śrī bhagavān uvāca
akṣaraṁ brahma paramaṁ svabhāvo'dhyātmam ucyate
bhūtabhāvodbhavakaro visargaḥ karmasaṁjñitaḥ

Lord Krishna said: The eternal and immutable Spirit of the Supreme Being is called Eternal Being or the Spirit. The inherent powers of consciousness and expansion of Eternal Being are called the nature of Eternal Being. The creative power of Eternal Being that causes manifestation of the living entity is called Karma. (8.03)

Spirit is also called Eternal Spirit, Spiritual Being, Eternal Being, and God in English; and Brahm, or Eternal Brahm (Note: Brahm is also spelled as: Brahma, Brahman) in Sanskrit. Spirit is the cause of all causes. The word 'God' is generally used for both Spirit, and the Supreme Spirit (or the Supreme Being), the basis of Spirit. We have used the word 'Eternal Being' for Spirit; and 'Supreme Being', 'Absolute', and 'Krishna' for the Supreme Spirit in this rendering.

The subtle body consists of six sensory faculties, intellect, ego, and five vital forces called bioimpulses (Life forces, Prana). The individual soul (Jiva) is defined as the subtle body sustained by Spirit. The individual soul is enshrined in the physical body. The subtle body keeps the physical body active and alive by operating the organs of perception and action.

अधिभूतं क्षरो भावः पुरुषश्चाधिदैवतम् ।
अधियज्ञोऽहम् एवात्र देहे देहभृतां वर ।।४।।

adhibhūtaṁ kṣaro bhāvaḥ puruṣaś'cā'dhidaivatam
adhiyajño'ham evā'tra dehe dehabhṛtāṁ vara

Mortal beings, made up of the five basic elements, are changeable or temporal. Various expansions of the Supreme Being are called Divine Beings. I reside inside the physical bodies as the Divine Controller (Ishvara), O Arjuna. (8.04)

THEORY OF REINCARNATION AND KARMA

अन्तकाले च माम् एव स्मरन् मुक्त्वा कलेवरम् ।
यः प्रयाति स मद्भावं याति नास्त्य् अत्र संशयः ।।५।।

antakāle ca mām eva smaran muktvā kalevaram
yaḥ prayāti sa madbhāvaṁ yāti nā'sty atra saṁśayaḥ

One who remembers Me exclusively, even while leaving the body at the time of death, attains the Supreme Abode; there is no doubt about it. (8.05)

यं यं वापि स्मरन् भावं त्यजत्यन्ते कलेवरम् ।
तं तं एवैति कौन्तेय सदा तद्भावभावितः ॥६॥

yaṁ yaṁ vā'pi smaran bhāvaṁ tyajaty ante kalevaram
taṁ taṁ evaiti kaunteya sadā tadbhāvabhāvitaḥ

Whatever object one remembers as one leaves the body at the end of life, that object is attained. Thought of whatever object prevails during one's lifetime, one remembers only that object at the end of life and achieves it. (8.06)

One's destiny is determined by the predominant thought at the time of death. Even if one has practiced devotion and God-consciousness during one's lifetime, the thought of God may or may not come at the hour of death. Therefore, God-consciousness should be continued till death (BS 1.1.12). Sages continue their efforts in their successive lives, yet at the moment of death they may fail to remember God. One cannot expect to have good thoughts at the time of death if one has kept bad company. Keep the association of perfect devotees and avoid the company of worldly-minded people for success in spiritual life. Whatever thought one nurtures during life, the same thought comes at the time of death and determines one's future destiny. Therefore, life should be molded in such a way that one should be able to remember God at the time of death. People should practice God-consciousness in everyday life from very childhood by forming a habit of remembering God before taking any food, before going to bed, and before starting any work or study.

A SIMPLE METHOD OF GOD REALIZATION

तस्मात् सर्वेषु कालेषु माम् अनुस्मर युध्य च ।
मय्य् अर्पितमनोबुद्धिर् माम् एवैष्यस्य् असंशयम् ।।७।।

tasmāt sarveṣu kāleṣu mām anusmara yudhya ca
mayy arpitamanobuddhir mām evai'ṣyasy asaṁśayam

Therefore, always remember Me and do your duty. You shall certainly attain Me if your mind and intellect are ever focused on Me. (8.07)

The supreme purpose of life is to always remember a personal God one believes in; so that one can remember God at the time of death. To remember the absolute and impersonal God may not be possible for most human beings. A pure devotee is able to experience the ecstasy of Lord's personal presence within and reach His Supreme Abode by always remembering Him. Live in a state of constant spiritual awareness.

अभ्यासयोगयुक्तेन चेतसा नान्यगामिना ।
परमं पुरुषं दिव्यं याति पार्थानुचिन्तयन् ।।८।।

abhyāsayogayuktena cetasā nā'nyagāminā
paramaṁ puruṣaṁ divyaṁ yāti pārthā'nucintayan

By contemplating Me with an unwavering mind that is disciplined by the practice of meditation, one attains the Supreme Being, O Arjuna. (8.08)

One gets spiritual awakening and the vision of God by constantly thinking of God in meditation, silent repetition of the holy names of God, and contemplation. The endeavor of our whole life shapes our destiny. Spiritual practices are meant to keep the mind absorbed in His thoughts and fixed at His lotus feet. Ramakrishna said that when you desire anything, pray to the Mother aspect of God in a lonely place, with tears of sincerity in your eyes, and your wishes shall be fulfilled. He also said that it might be possible to attain Self-realization within three days. The more intensely one practices spiritual disciplines, the more quickly one attains perfection. The intensity of conviction and belief, combined with deep yearning, restlessness, intense longing, and persistence, determine the speed of spiritual progress. The real practice of HathaYoga is not only the yogic exercises taught in modern yoga centers, but also the consistence, persistence, and insistence in one's search for the Supreme Truth.

Self-realization is not a simple act but a process of gradual spiritual growth, starting with resolve, proceeding gradually to vow, divine grace, faith, and finally realization of Truth (YV 19.30). The Supreme Being is not realized through discourses, intellect, or learning. It is realized only when one sincerely longs for it with vigorous effort. Sincere craving brings divine grace that unveils the Supreme Being (MuU 3.02.03).

कविं पुराणम् अनुशासितारम्
अणोर् अणीयांसम् अनुस्मरेद् यः ।
सर्वस्य धातारम् अचिन्त्यरूपम्
आदित्यवर्णं तमसः परस्तात् ॥९॥

kavim̐ purāṇam anuśāsitāram
aṇor aṇīyām̐sam anusmared yaḥ
sarvasya dhātāram acintyarūpam
ādityavarṇam̐ tamasaḥ parastāt

प्रयाणकाले मनसाचलेन
भक्त्या युक्तो योगबलेन चैव ।
भ्रुवोर् मध्ये प्राणम् आवेश्य सम्यक्
स तं परं पुरुषम् उपैति दिव्यम् ॥१०॥

prayāṇakāle manasā'calena
bhaktyā yukto yogabalena cai'va
bhruvor madhye prāṇam āveśya samyak
sa tam̐ param̐ puruṣam upaiti divyam

One who meditates at the time of death with steadfast mind and devotion on the Supreme Being as the omniscient, the oldest, the controller, smaller than the smallest and bigger than the biggest, the sustainer of everything, the inconceivable, self-luminous like the sun, and transcendental (or beyond the material reality) by making the flow of bioimpulses (life forces, Prana) rise up to the middle of the eye brows by the power of yogic practices and holding there, attains Me, the Supreme Being. (See also verses 4.29, 5.27, 6.13) (8.09-10)

यद् अक्षरं वेदविदो वदन्ति
विशन्ति यद् यतयो वीतरागाः ।
यद् इच्छन्तो ब्रह्मचर्यं चरन्ति
तत् ते पदं संग्रहेण प्रवक्ष्ये ॥११॥

yad akṣaraṁ vedavido vadanti
viśanti yad yatayo vītarāgāḥ
yad icchanto brahmacaryaṁ caranti
tat te padaṁ saṁgraheṇa pravakṣye

Now I shall briefly explain the process to attain the Supreme Abode that the knowers of the Veda call immutable, into which the ascetics, freed from attachment, enter; and desiring which people lead a life of celibacy. (8.11)

ATTAIN SALVATION BY MEDITATING ON GOD AT THE TIME OF DEATH

सर्वद्वाराणि संयम्य मनो हृदि निरुध्य च ।
मूर्ध्न्य् आधायात्मनः प्राणम् आस्थितो योगधारणाम् ॥१२॥

sarvadvārāṇi saṁyamya mano hṛdi nirudhya ca
mūrdhny ādhāyā'tmanaḥ prāṇam āsthito yogadhāraṇām

ओम् इत्य् एकाक्षरं ब्रह्म व्याहरन् माम् अनुस्मरन् ।
यः प्रयाति त्यजन् देहं स याति परमां गतिम् ॥१३॥

om ity ekākṣaraṁ brahma vyāharan mām anusmaran
yaḥ prayāti tyajan dehaṁ sa yāti paramāṁ gatim

When one leaves the physical body, by controlling all the senses, focusing the mind on God and the bioimpulses (Life forces, Prana) in the cerebrum, engaged in yogic practice, meditating on Me, and uttering AUM— the sacred monosyllable cosmic sound power of the Spirit — one attains the Supreme Abode. (8.12-13)

Scriptural knowledge has its place, but it is through direct realization that the inner core can be reached and the outer shell discarded. Meditation is the way to inner realization and should be learnt, personally, from a competent teacher. Realization of the true nature of mind leads to meditation.

A simple technique of meditation is described here: (1) Wash your face, eyes, hands, and feet and sit in a clean, quiet, dark place, using any comfortable posture, with head, neck, and spine straight and vertical. No music or incense during meditation is recommended. The time and place of meditation should be fixed. Follow the good principles of living by thoughts, words, and deeds. Some yogic exercises are necessary. Midnight, morning, and evening are the best times to meditate for 15 to 25 minutes every day. (2) Remember any name or form of the personal god you believe in and ask His or Her blessings. (3) Close your eyes, tilt head slightly upward, and take 5 to 10 very slow and deep breaths. (4) Fix your gaze, mind, and feelings inside the chest center, the seat of the causal heart, and breathe slowly. Mentally chant 'So' as you breathe in and 'Hum' as you breathe out. Think as if breath itself is making these sounds 'So' and 'Hum' (I am That Spirit). Mentally visualize the breath going in and coming out through the nostrils. Be alert, and feel the sensation created by the breath in the body as you watch the breath. Do not try to control or lead your breathing; just watch your natural breathing. (5) Direct the will towards the thought of merging yourself into the infinite space of the air you are breathing. If your mind wanders away from following the breaths, start from step (4). Be regular, and persist without procrastination.

The sound of 'OM' or 'AUM' is a combination of three primary sounds: A, U, and M. It is the source of all sounds one can utter. Therefore, it is the fittest sound symbol of Spirit. It is also the primeval impulse that moves our five nerve centers that control bodily functions. Yogananda calls 'AUM' the sound of the vibration of the cosmic motor. The Bible says: In the beginning was the word (OM, Amen, Allah) and the word was with God, and the word was God (John 1.01). This cosmic sound vibration is heard by yogis as a sound, or a mixture of sounds, of various frequencies.

The Omnic meditation, mentioned here by Lord Krishna, is a very powerful, sacred technique used by saints and sages of all religions. Briefly, the Omnic method entails getting the mind permeated by a continuous, reverberating sound of AUM. When the mind gets absorbed in repeating this divine sound, the individual consciousness merges into the Cosmic Consciousness.

A simpler method of contemplation is given below by Lord Krishna for those who cannot follow the conventional path of meditation discussed above.

अनन्यचेताः सततं यो मां स्मरति नित्यशः ।
तस्याहं सुलभः पार्थ नित्ययुक्तस्य योगिनः ॥१४॥

ananyacetāḥ satataṁ yo māṁ smarati nityaśaḥ
tasyā'haṁ sulabhaḥ pārtha nityayuktasya yoginaḥ

I am easily attainable, O Arjuna, by that ever steadfast devotee who always thinks of Me and whose mind does not go elsewhere. (8.14)

It is not an easy task to always remember God. One must have a basis to remember God all the time. This basis could be an intense love of God or a passion to serve Him through the service of humanity.

माम् उपेत्य पुनर्जन्म दुःखालयम् अशाश्वतम् ।
नाप्नुवन्ति महात्मानः संसिद्धिं परमां गताः ॥१५॥
mām upetya punarjanma duḥkhālayam aśāśvatam
nāpnuvanti mahātmānaḥ saṁsiddhiṁ paramāṁ gatāḥ

After attaining Me, the great souls do not incur rebirth in this miserable transitory world because they have attained the highest perfection. (8.15)

Human birth is full of suffering. Even the saints, sages, and God in human form cannot escape the sufferings of the human body and mind. One has to learn to endure and work towards salvation.

आब्रह्मभुवनाल् लोकाः पुनरावर्तिनोऽर्जुन ।
माम् उपेत्य तु कौन्तेय पुनर्जन्म न विद्यते ॥१६॥
ā brahmabhuvanāl lokāḥ punarāvartino'rjuna
mām upetya tu kaunteya punarjanma na vidyate

The dwellers of all the worlds — up to and including the world of the Creator (Brahmā) — are subject to the miseries of repeated birth and death. But after attaining Me, O Arjuna, one does not take birth again. (See also 9.25) (8.16)

THE CREATION IS CYCLIC

सहस्रयुगपर्यन्तम् अहर् यद् ब्रह्मणो विदुः ।
रात्रिं युगसहस्रान्तां तेऽहोरात्रविदो जनाः ॥१७॥
sahasrayuga paryantam ahar yad brahmaṇo viduḥ
rātriṁ yugasahasrāntāṁ te'horātravido janāḥ

Those who know that the duration of creation lasts 4.32 billion years and that the duration of destruction also lasts 4.32 billion years, they are the knowers of the cycles of creation and destruction. (See also 9.07) (8.17)

अव्यक्ताद् व्यक्तयः सर्वाः प्रभवन्त्य् अहरागमे ।
रात्र्यागमे प्रलीयन्ते तत्रैवाव्यक्तसंज्ञके ॥१८॥

avyaktād vyaktayaḥ sarvāḥ prabhavanty aharāgame
rātryāgame pralīyante tatrai'vā'vyaktasaṁjñake

All manifestations come out of the subtle body of Brahmā during the creative cycle, and they merge into the same during the destructive cycle. (see also 9.07, 15.18) (8.18)

Thus, one complete creative cycle lasts 8.64 billion solar years. This consists of one day and one night of Brahmā, the Creator. The duration of partial dissolution, during which all heavenly planets, the earth, and the lower planets are annihilated and rest within Brahmā, is 4.32 billion years and is called Brahmā's night. Complete dissolution takes place at the end of Brahmā's (or creative cycle's) full life-span of 100 solar years, or 8.64 billion years x 30 x 12 x 100 = just over 311.04 trillion solar years called one Kalpa (See also BP 12.04.01-43), according to Vedic astrology. At this time, the complete material creation, including the modes of material Nature, enters into one of the four main, partial manifestations of the Absolute (See also 15.18) — called Avyakta Brahma or Adi Prakriti, the source and sink of the total material energy — and is annihilated. During the complete dissolution, everything is said to take rest in the abdomen of Avyakta Akshar Brahma (See verse 15.16) until the beginning of the next cycle of creation. In the second manifestation, Lord's energies enter into all the universes to create and support diversities. And in the third manifestation, the Absolute is diffused as the all-pervading supersoul in the universes and remains present within the atoms and every cell of everything — visible or invisible.

भूतग्रामः स एवायं भूत्वा भूत्वा प्रलीयते ।
रात्र्यागमेऽवशः पार्थ प्रभवत्य् अहरागमे ॥१९॥

bhūtagrāmaḥ sa evā'yaṁ bhūtvā bhūtvā pralīyate
rātryāgame'vaśaḥ pārtha prabhavaty aharāgame

The same multitude of beings comes into existence again and again at the arrival of the creative cycle and are annihilated, inevitably, at the arrival of the destructive cycle. (8.19)

According to the Vedas, creation is a beginningless and endless cycle, and there is no such thing as the first creation.

परस् तस्मात् तु भावोऽन्यो ऽव्यक्तोऽव्यक्तात् सनातनः ।
यः स सर्वेषु भूतेषु नश्यत्सु न विनश्यति ।।२०।।

paras tasmāt tu bhāvo'nyo 'vyakto'vyaktāt sanātanaḥ
yaḥ sa sarveṣu bhūteṣu naśyatsu na vinaśyati

अव्यक्तोऽक्षर इत्य् उक्तस् तम् आहुः परमां गतिम् ।
यं प्राप्य न निवर्तन्ते तद् धाम परमं मम ।।२१।।

avyakto'kṣara ity uktas tam āhuḥ paramāṁ gatim
yaṁ prāpya na nivartante tad dhāma paramaṁ mama

There is another eternal transcendental existence — higher than the changeable material Nature — called Eternal Being or Spirit that does not perish when all created beings perish. This is also called the Supreme Abode. Those who attain the Supreme Abode do not take birth again. (8.20-21)

TWO BASIC PATHS OF DEPARTURE FROM THE WORLD

पुरुषः स परः पार्थ भक्त्या लभ्यस् त्व् अनन्यया ।
यस्यान्तःस्थानि भूतानि येन सर्वम् इदं ततम् ।।२२।।

puruṣaḥ sa paraḥ pārtha bhaktyā labhyas tv ananyayā
yasyā'ntaḥsthāni bhūtāni yena sarvam idaṁ tatam

This Supreme Abode, O Arjuna, is attainable by unswerving devotion to Me, within which all beings exist

and by which the entire universe is pervaded. (See also 9.04 and 11.55) (8.22)

यत्र काले त्व् अनावृत्तिम् आवृत्तिं चैव योगिनः ।
प्रयाता यान्ति तं कालं वक्ष्यामि भरतर्षभ ॥२३॥

yatra kāle tv anāvṛttim āvṛttiṁ cai'va yoginaḥ
prayātā yānti taṁ kālaṁ vakṣyāmi bharatarṣabha

O Arjuna, now I shall describe different paths departing by which, after death, the yogis do or do not come back to the mortal or temporal world. (8.23)

Verses 8.23-26 are considered to be the most mysterious and misunderstood verses in the Gita. What appears to refer to the auspicious times of departure of the living entity during death in verses 8.24 and 8.25, actually refers to the presiding deities of various astral planes during gradual passage of the soul after death. This is made clear in verse 8.26. It should be noted that one's final destination and the corresponding path leading to the destination has to be earned and may have nothing to do, directly, with the time of death. Eligibility to tread the path, and not the time of departure, as is sometimes commonly misunderstood, determines the path of departure.

Lord explains in verses 8.24-25 that there are two goals in life which people seek. These two goals are achieved by two different paths guiding the two types of seekers to their destinations. One is called the path of no return (verse 8.24), and the other is the path of return (verse 8.25). These two paths are renamed in verse 8.26 as the path of light and the path of darkness, the path of Moksh and path of coming and going, the path of the seekers of spirituality and seekers of materialism, path of the light of knowledge and of darkness of ignorance.

अग्निर् ज्योतिर् अहः शुक्लः षण्मासा उत्तरायणम् ।
तत्र प्रयाता गच्छन्ति ब्रह्म ब्रह्मविदो जनाः ॥२४॥

agnir jyotir ahaḥ śuklaḥ ṣaṇmāsā uttarāyaṇam
tatra prayātā gacchanti brahma brahmavido janāḥ

Passing gradually after death, through celestial controllers of fire, light, daytime, the bright lunar fortnight, and the six months of the northern solstice of the sun, yogis who know the Self attain supreme abode (and do not come back to earth). (8.24)

The path of no return, described above, is also called the path of gods (Devayān), the path of light of Self-knowledge, the northern path, and the path of gradual liberation (Kram-mukti), the ascending path of evolution. This path is blocked for the ignorant and persons devoid of the necessary qualities such as austerity, abstinence, faith and knowledge. Those who have above-mentioned qualities will walk this path. It is also said that this path is closed during the six months of southern solstice of the sun as mentioned in verse 8.25.

Fire, light, day-time, the bright fortnight and the six months of the northern solstice of the sun indicate deities presided over by the Sun. It is said in the Upanishads (ChU 4.15.05, BrU 6.2.15) that those who qualify for the northern path after death reach the celestial ruler of flame, from there to the celestial ruler of the day, from there to the celestial ruler of the bright fortnight, from there to the celestial ruler of the six months during which the sun travels northwards, from there to Sun, and from there to lightening. Then a Superbeing, created from the mind of Brahmā, comes and leads them to the world of Brahmā. Becoming perfect at each stage, they stay in the world of Brahmā till the end of the cycle of creation; at the completion of which they merge in Brahman together with Brahmā. Having reached Brahman, they do not return back to worldly life again. This is also called Brahm-Nirvan.

धूमो रात्रिस् तथा कृष्णः षण्मासा दक्षिणायनम् ।
तत्र चान्द्रमसं ज्योतिर् योगी प्राप्य निवर्तते ।।२५।।

dhūmo rātris tathā kṛṣṇaḥ ṣaṇmāsā dakṣiṇāyanam
tatra cāndramasaṁ jyotir yogī prāpya nivartate

Passing gradually after death, through celestial controllers of smoke, night, the dark lunar fortnight, and the six months of southern solstice of the sun, the righteous person attains heaven and comes back to earth again. (8.25)

The destination of righteous persons, who work to enjoy the fruits of their labor, is described in the above verse. Those who leave the world after spending their lifetime in doing good and performing rituals and worship to enjoy the results so accrued, travel by the southern path. This path is also called the path of darkness of ignorance, the path of return, the path of ignorance, the path of ancestors, and the path of materialism. This path is presided over by the Moon god, representing the world of matter and sense enjoyment. Those who qualify for this path, after death, reach the celestial ruler of smoke, from there to the celestial ruler of the night, from there to the celestial ruler of the dark fortnight, from there to the celestial ruler of the six months during which the sun travels southwards, and from there to heaven. Such yogis return to the mortal world, after enjoying heavenly pleasures for a period of time, when the fruits of their virtuous deeds are exhausted.

शुक्लकृष्णे गती ह्येते जगतः शाश्वते मते ।
एकया यात्य् अनावृत्तिम् अन्ययावर्तते पुनः ॥२६॥
śuklakṛṣṇe gatī hy ete jagataḥ śāśvate mate
ekayā yāty anāvṛttim anyayā'vartate punaḥ

The path of light of spiritual practice and Self-knowledge and the path of darkness of materialism and ignorance are thought to be the world's two eternal paths. The former

leads to salvation, and the latter leads to rebirth as human beings. (8.26)

The path of transmigration may be included in the path of reincarnation, or it may be called the third path. The Upanishads describe this third path as the path of lower creatures, such as animals and insects. Unrighteous ones, who do not qualify for the two paths mentioned in verses 8.24 and 8.25, transmigrate into lower wombs, such as animals, birds, and insects (BrU 6.02.15-16). The immortal soul wanders endlessly through the ocean of transmigration, made up of 8.4 million different species of life on this planet. The good Lord, out of His sweet will or mercy and without any reason, bestows the precious gift of the human body that is like a raft to carry one across the ocean of transmigration (TR 7.43.02-04). Consider what we are is God's gift to us, and what we become is our gift to God. It is also said that human birth, faith in God, and the help of a real guru come only by His grace. Our present life provides the opportunity for preparation for the next life. According to the activities in this life, one can either get a promotion or salvation, a demotion or transmigration, or another chance for salvation by reincarnating as a human being.

To whatever object one's mind is set, to that goes one's subtle and causal bodies with Karma attached to it. Thus, a person who has no desire or whose desires have been satisfied or whose only object of desire is the Self, is merged in Brahman even in this very life. This is called Jeevan-Mukti or Nirvan.

KNOWLEDGE LEADS TO SALVATION

नैते सृती पार्थ जानन् योगी मुह्यति कश्चन ।
तस्मात् सर्वेषु कालेषु योगयुक्तो भवार्जुन ॥२७॥
nai'te sṛtī pārtha jānan yogī muhyati kaścana
tasmāt sarveṣu kāleṣu yogayukto bhavā'rjuna

Knowing these two paths, O Arjuna, a yogi is not bewildered at all. Therefore, one should be resolute in

attaining salvation — the goal of human birth — at all times. (8.27)

वेदेषु यज्ञेषु तपःसु चैव
दानेषु यत् पुण्यफलं प्रदिष्टम् ।
अत्येति तत् सर्वम् इदं विदित्वा
योगी परं स्थानम् उपैति चाद्यम् ॥२८॥

vedeṣu yajñeṣu tapaḥsu cai'va
dāneṣu yat puṇyaphalaṁ pradiṣṭam
atyeti tat sarvam idaṁ viditvā
yogī paraṁ sthānam upaiti cā'dyam

One who knows all this goes beyond getting the benefits of the study of the Vedas, performance of sacrifices, austerities, and charities; and attains salvation. (8.28)

ॐ तत्सदिति श्रीमद्भगवद्गीतासूपनिषत्सु ब्रह्मविद्यायां योगशास्त्रे
श्रीकृष्णार्जुनसंवादे अक्षरब्रह्मयोगो नाम अष्टमोऽध्यायः ॥

OM tatsaditi śrīmadbhagavadgītāsūpaniṣatsu brahmavidyāyāṁ
yogaśāstre śrīkṛṣṇārjuna saṁvāde akṣarabrahmayogo
nāma aṣtamo'dhyāyaḥ

Thus ends the eighth chapter named "The Eternal Brahma" of the Upaniṣad of the Bhagavadgītā, the scripture of yoga, dealing with the science of the Absolute in the form of the dialogue between Śrīkṛṣṇa and Arjuna.

अथ नवमोऽध्यायः
CHAPTER 9
राजविद्याराजगुह्ययोगः
SUPREME KNOWLEDGE AND THE BIG MYSTERY

श्रीभगवानुवाच
इदं तु ते गुह्यतमं प्रवक्ष्याम्य् अनसूयवे ।
ज्ञानं विज्ञानसहितं यज् ज्ञात्वा मोक्ष्यसेऽशुभात् ।।१।।
śrī bhagavān uvāca
idaṁ tu te guhyatamaṁ pravakṣyāmy anasūyave
jñānaṁ vijñānasahitaṁ yaj jñātvā mokṣyase'śubhāt

Lord Krishna said: Since you have faith in My words, I shall reveal to you the most profound, secret, transcendental knowledge, together with transcendental experience. Knowing this, you will be freed from the miseries of worldly existence. (9.01)

KNOWLEDGE OF THE NATURE OF THE SUPREME IS THE BIGGEST MYSTERY

राजविद्या राजगुह्यं पवित्रम् इदम् उत्तमम् ।
प्रत्यक्षावगमं धर्म्यं सुसुखं कर्तुम् अव्ययम् ।।२।।
rājavidyā rājaguhyaṁ pavitram idam uttamam
pratyakṣāvagamaṁ dharmyaṁ susukhaṁ kartum avyayam

This Self-knowledge is the king of all knowledge, is the most secret, is very sacred, can be perceived by instinct, conforms to righteousness (Dharma), is very easy to practice, and is timeless. (9.02)

अश्रद्दधानाः पुरुषा धर्मस्यास्य परंतप ।
अप्राप्य मां निवर्तन्ते मृत्युसंसारवर्त्मनि ॥३॥

aśraddadhānāḥ puruṣā dharmasyā'sya paraṁtapa
aprāpya māṁ nivartante mṛtyu saṁsāra vartmani

O Arjuna, those who have no faith in this knowledge do not attain Me and follow the cycles of birth and death. (9.03)

Everything is possible for the person who has faith in God (Mark 9.23). Faith in the Supreme power holds the key to unlock the gates of salvation.

मया ततम् इदं सर्वं जगद् अव्यक्तमूर्तिना ।
मत्स्थानि सर्वभूतानि न चाहं तेष्व् अवस्थितः ॥४॥

mayā tatam idaṁ sarvaṁ jagad avyakta mūrtinā
matsthāni sarva bhūtāni na cā'haṁ teṣv avasthitaḥ

This entire universe is an expansion of, or pervaded by, My Avyakta Brahma aspect. All beings depend on Me (like a gold chain depends on gold and milk products depend on milk). I do not depend on — or become affected by — them because I am the highest of all. (See also 7.12, 15.18) (9.04)

From a dualistic viewpoint, waves depend on the ocean; the ocean does not depend on the waves. But from a monist point of view, as stated in verse 9.05 below, the question of wave abiding in the ocean or the ocean abiding in the wave does not arise because there is no wave or ocean. It is water only. Similarly, everything is a manifestation of the Spirit only (Gita 7.19).

न च मत्स्थानि भूतानि पश्य मे योगम् ऐश्वरम् ।
भूतभृन् न च भूतस्थो ममात्मा भूतभावनः ॥५॥

na ca matsthāni bhūtāni paśya me yogam aiśvaram
bhūtabhṛn na ca bhūtastho mamā'tmā bhūtabhāvanaḥ

Look at the power of My divine mystery; in reality, I — the sustainer and Creator of all beings — do not depend on them, and they also do not depend on Me. (9.05) *(In fact, the gold-chain does not depend on gold; the gold-chain is nothing but gold. Also, matter and energy are different, as well as non-different).*

The wave is water, but the water is not wave. The water has become the vapor, the cloud, the rain, the ice, as well as the bubble, the lake, the river, the wave, and the ocean. These are nothing but names of different forms (or transformations) of water. From a monist viewpoint, there is no ocean, no wave, and no lake, but water only. However, a wave is a wave as long as it does not realize its true nature — that it is not a wave but water. When the wave realizes that it is water, the wave no longer remains a wave, but becomes water. Similarly, when one realizes that he or she is not this physical body — but the Eternal Being in the form of Spirit residing inside the physical body — one transcends physical body and immediately becomes one with the Spirit without undergoing any physical change. As a physical body, one is mortal, limited by a form, with color, gender, and temperament. But as a part of the Spirit, one is free, immortal, and limitless. This is called Nirvana, or salvation.

यथाकाशस्थितो नित्यं वायुः सर्वत्रगो महान् ।
तथा सर्वाणि भूतानि मत्स्थानीत्युपधारय ॥६॥
yathā'kāśasthito nityaṁ vāyuḥ sarvatrago mahān
tathā sarvāṇi bhūtāni matsthānī'ty upadhāraya

Perceive that all beings remain in Me — without any contact or without producing any effect — as the mighty wind, moving everywhere, eternally remains in space. (9.06)

Gross objects, such as planets and stars, remain in the subtle space without any visible connection at all. Similarly, the entire universe, including space itself, abides in the unified field called Consciousness. Time has no access to space; similarly, Consciousness is everlasting, indivisible, and unaffected by everything going on in its field, just as clouds do not make the sky wet.

THEORY OF EVOLUTION AND INVOLUTION

सर्वभूतानि कौन्तेय प्रकृतिं यान्ति मामिकाम् ।
कल्पक्षये पुनस् तानि कल्पादौ विसृजाम्य् अहम् ॥७॥
sarva bhūtāni kaunteya prakṛtiṁ yānti māmikām
kalpakṣaye punas tāni kalpādau visṛjāmy aham

All beings merge into My primary material Nature at the end of a cycle of just over 311 trillion solar years, O Arjuna, and I create them again at the beginning of the next cycle. (See also 8.17) (9.07)

As a spider spreads out the web from within, plays in it, and again draws the web into itself, similarly, the Eternal Being (or Spirit) creates the material world from itself, plays in it as living entity, and takes it into itself during complete dissolution (BP 11.09.21 and 12.04.01-43). All manifestations are born, sustained, and finally merge in Spirit as bubbles of water are born, sustained, and merge in water. Spirit manifests itself into the universe by using its own internal power without the help of any external agent. It is possible for one Spirit — by virtue of possessing diverse powers — to be transformed into multiplicity without any outside help. Spirit (or the Eternal Being) is thus both the efficient and the material cause of creation.

प्रकृतिं स्वाम् अवष्टभ्य विसृजामि पुनः पुनः ।
भूतग्रामम् इमं कृत्स्नम् अवशं प्रकृतेर् वशात् ॥८॥
prakṛtiṁ svām avaṣṭabhya visṛjāmi punaḥ punaḥ
bhūta grāmam imaṁ kṛtsnam avaśaṁ prakṛter vaśāt

I create the entire multitude of beings again and again with the help of My material Nature. These beings are under control of the modes of material Nature. (9.08)

न च मां तानि कर्माणि निबध्नन्ति धनंजय ।
उदासीनवद् आसीनम् असक्तं तेषु कर्मसु ॥९॥

na ca māṁ tāni karmāṅi nibadhnanti dhanaṁjaya
udāsīnavad āsīnam asaktaṁ teṣu karmasu

These acts of creation do not bind Me, O Arjuna, because I remain indifferent and unattached to those acts. (9.09)

मयाध्यक्षेण प्रकृतिः सूयते सचराचरम् ।
हेतुनानेन कौन्तेय जगद् विपरिवर्तते ॥१०॥

mayā'dhyakṣeṇa prakṛtiḥ sūyate sacarācaram
hetunā'nena kaunteya jagad viparivartate

The divine kinetic energy (Maya) — with the help of material Nature, Prakriti — creates all animate and inanimate objects under My supervision; thus, the creation keeps on going, O Arjuna. (See also 14.03) (9.10)

THE WAYS OF THE WISE AND OF THE IGNORANT ARE DIFFERENT

अवजानन्ति मां मूढा मानुषीं तनुम् आश्रितम् ।
परं भावम् अजानन्तो मम भूतमहेश्वरम् ॥११॥

avajānanti māṁ mūḍhā mānuṣīṁ tanum āśritam
paraṁ bhāvam ajānanto mama bhūta maheśvaram

मोघाशा मोघकर्माणो मोघज्ञाना विचेतसः ।
राक्षसीम् आसुरीं चैव प्रकृतिं मोहिनीं श्रिताः ॥१२॥

moghāśā moghakarmāṇo moghajñānā vicetasaḥ
rākṣasīm āsurīṁ cai'va prakṛtiṁ mohinīṁ śritāḥ

Ignorant persons despise Me when I appear in human form because they do not know My transcendental nature as the great Lord of all beings (and take Me for an ordinary human being), and because they have false hopes, false actions, false knowledge, and delusive (Tāmasika) qualities (See 16.04-18) of fiends and demons (they are unable to recognize Me). (9.11-12)

When Lord Krishna was here on this earth, in spite of accomplishing many transcendental and extraordinary feats, only a few people were able to recognize Him as an incarnation of the Supreme Being. Even a highly evolved soul, such as King Yudhishthira, was quite surprised to learn from sage Narada that his (King's) cousin brother, Krishna, is the Supreme Being in human form (BP 7.15.79). The moral is that the Supreme cannot be known without one's good Karma and His personal grace.

महात्मानस् तु मां पार्थ दैवीं प्रकृतिम् आश्रिताः ।
भजन्त्य् अनन्यमनसो ज्ञात्वा भूतादिम् अव्ययम् ॥१३॥
mahātmānas tu māṁ pārtha daivīṁ prakṛtim āśritāḥ
bhajanty ananya manaso jñātvā bhūtādim avyayam

But great souls, O Arjuna, who possess divine qualities (See 16.01-03), know Me as immutable, as the material and efficient cause of creation, and worship Me single-mindedly with loving devotion. (9.13)

सततं कीर्तयन्तो मां यतन्तश्च दृढव्रताः ।
नमस्यन्तश्च मां भक्त्या नित्ययुक्ता उपासते ॥१४॥
satataṁ kīrtayanto māṁ yatantaśca dṛḍha vratāḥ
namasyantaś ca māṁ bhaktyā nityayuktā upāsate

Persons of firm resolve worship Me with ever-steadfast devotion by always singing My glories, striving to attain Me, and prostrating before Me with devotion. (9.14)

ज्ञानयज्ञेन चाप्य् अन्ये यजन्तो माम् उपासते ।
एकत्वेन पृथक्त्वेन बहुधा विश्वतोमुखम् ॥१५॥

jñāna yajñena cāpy anye yajanto mām upāsate
ekatvena pṛthaktvena bahudhā viśvatomukham

Some worship Me by acquiring and propagating Self-knowledge. Others worship the infinite as one in all (or non-dual), as the master of all (or dual), and in various other ways. (9.15)

EVERYTHING IS A MANIFESTATION OF THE ABSOLUTE

अहं क्रतुर् अहं यज्ञः स्वधाहम् अहम् औषधम् ।
मन्त्रोऽहम् अहम् एवाज्यम् अहम् अग्निर् अहं हुतम् ॥१६॥

ahaṁ kratur ahaṁ yajñaḥ svadhā'ham aham auṣadham
mantro'ham aham evā'jyam aham agnir ahaṁ hutam

पिताहम् अस्य जगतो माता धाता पितामहः ।
वेद्यं पवित्रम् ओंकार ऋक् साम यजुर् एव च ॥१७॥

pitā'ham asya jagato mātā dhātā pitāmahaḥ
vedyaṁ pavitram oṁkāra ṛk sāma yajur eva ca

गतिर् भर्ता प्रभुः साक्षी निवासः शरणं सुहृत् ।
प्रभवः प्रलयः स्थानं निधानं बीजम् अव्ययम् ॥१८॥

gatir bhartā prabhuḥ sākṣī nivāsaḥ śaraṇaṁ suhṛt
prabhavaḥ pralayaḥ sthānaṁ nidhānaṁ bījam avyayam

I am the ritual, I am the sacrifice, I am the offering, I am the herb, I am the mantra, I am the clarified butter, I am the fire, and I am the oblation. (See also 4.24). I am the supporter of the universe, the father, the mother, and the grandfather. I am the object of knowledge, the sacred syllable 'AUM', and the Vedas. I am the goal, the supporter, the Lord, the witness, the abode, the refuge, the friend, the

origin, the dissolution, the foundation, the substratum, and the immutable seed. (See also 7.10 and 10.39) (9.16-18)

तपाम्य् अहम् अहं वर्षं निगृह्णाम्य् उत्सृजामि च ।
अमृतं चैव मृत्युश्च सद् असच् चाहम् अर्जुन ॥१९॥

tapāmy aham ahaṁ varṣaṁ nigṛhṇāmy utsṛjāmi ca
amṛtaṁ cai'va mṛtyuśca sad asac cā'ham arjuna

I give heat. I send, as well as withhold, the rain. I am immortality, as well as death. I am also both the eternal Absolute and the temporal, O Arjuna. (The Supreme Being has become everything. See also 13.12) (9.19)

ATTAIN SALVATION BY DEVOTIONAL LOVE

त्रैविद्या मां सोमपाः पूतपापा
यज्ञैर् इष्ट्वा स्वर्गतिं प्रार्थयन्ते ।
ते पुण्यम् आसाद्य सुरेन्द्रलोकम्
अश्नन्ति दिव्यान् दिवि देवभोगान् ॥२०॥

traividyā māṁ somapāḥ pūtapāpā
yajñair iṣṭvā svargatiṁ prārthayante
te puṇyam āsādya suredralokam
aśnanti divyān divi devabhogān

The doers of the rituals prescribed in the Vedas, the drinkers of the nectar of devotion, whose sins are cleansed, worship Me by doing good deeds for gaining heaven. As a result of their meritorious deeds, they go to heaven and enjoy celestial sense pleasures. (9.20)

ते तं भुक्त्वा स्वर्गलोकं विशालं
क्षीणे पुण्ये मर्त्यलोकं विशन्ति ।
एवं त्रयीधर्मम् अनुप्रपन्ना
गतागतं कामकामा लभन्ते ॥२१॥

te taṁ bhuktvā svargalokaṁ viśālaṁ
kṣīṇe puṇye martyalokaṁ viśanti
evaṁ trayīdharmam anuprapannā
gatāgataṁ kāmakāmā labhante

They again return to the mortal world — after enjoying the wide world of heavenly pleasures — upon exhaustion of the fruits of their good Karma. Thus, following the injunctions of the Vedas, persons working for the fruit of their actions take repeated births and deaths. (See also 8.25) (9.21)

अनन्याश् चिन्तयन्तो मां ये जनाः पर्युपासते ।
तेषां नित्याभियुक्तानां योगक्षेमं वहाम्य् अहम् ।।२२।।
ananyāś cintayanto māṁ ye janāḥ paryupāsate
teṣāṁ nityābhiyuktānāṁ yogakṣemaṁ vahāmy aham

I personally take care of both the spiritual and material welfare of those ever-steadfast devotees who always remember and adore Me with single-minded contemplation. (9.22)

Wealth and happiness automatically come to the righteous person, without that person asking for it, as the river automatically goes to the ocean (TR 1.293.02). Material wealth naturally comes to the virtuous person as river water naturally flows downstream (VP 1.11.24). Lord Rama said: I always take care of those who worship Me with unswerving devotion as a mother takes care of her child (TR 3.42.03). The worship of the Mother form of the Lord is encouraged for the seekers of health, wealth, and knowledge. One who always thinks of God is considered to be God-conscious, Krishna-conscious, or Self-realized. Lord personally takes charge of one who remembers Him single-mindedly. His nature is to reciprocate the love of His pure devotees by fulfilling their desires.

Father in the heaven knows all of what you need. Give first place to His Kingdom and what He requires. He will provide you everything (Matthew 6.32-33). Nothing is difficult to obtain when I am pleased, but a pure devotee whose mind is exclusively fixed upon Me does not ask anything, including salvation, but the opportunity to serve Me (BP 6.09.48). The Lord chooses much better things for you if you let Him be your guide by surrendering unto His will.

येऽप्य् अन्यदेवता भक्ता यजन्ते श्रद्धयान्विताः ।
तेऽपि माम् एव कौन्तेय यजन्त्य् अविधिपूर्वकम् ।।२३।।
ye'py anyadevatā bhaktā yajante śraddhayā'nvitāḥ
te'pi mām eva kaunteya yajanty avidhipūrvakam

O Arjuna, even those devotees who worship the deities with faith, they also worship Me, but in an improper way. (9.23)

There is only one Absolute; the wise call Him and worship Him by various names (RV 1.164.46). The worship of the divine as Mother is also found in the Vedas where the sage longs to be a child of the divine Mother (RV 7.81.04). The Absolute has also manifested as celestial controllers — for sustaining creation — who are one with many names and forms (RV 3.55.01). The Supreme Being is a woman, a man, a boy, a girl, and an old person. He exists in all forms (AV 10.08.27). All deities, male or female, are representations of one divine. He is One in many and many in One. One should not worship material objects in creation, such as family, friends, and possessions; but one can worship the creator in material objects because God is in all rocks. The Vedic principle of celestial controllers does not diversify the Unity, but unifies the diversity. Deities are just different names and forms, or symbolic representations, of the energies of nature.

The deity is a conduit through which the water of divine grace can be made to flow by the power of conviction —

expressed through worship and prayer — from the reservoir of infinite consciousness. However, the seedling of faith becomes the fruit tree of conviction only when it comes out of the ground of Self-knowledge and survives the frost of logic. We evoke the potential energy of cosmic forces by contemplating deities with faith. Faith really works. The power of faith in rituals or spiritual science works in the same manner as a placebo works by the power of faith in medical science. However, it is not very easy for intellectuals to develop a deep faith in the power of rituals. Joseph Campbell said: "The images of myth are reflections of the spiritual potentialities of everyone of us, and deities stimulate divine love."

All different types of worship reach One and the same Lord as waters of all different rivers reach the same ocean. External worship with the help of an image or a symbolic representation of God is necessary for beginners. It is very helpful to develop a personal relationship with a deity of one's choice who can be consulted and counted upon for help during moments of crisis in life. Those who are against deity worship do not understand that all-pervading God can also exist within a deity. Such persons limit His supremacy.

The ancient Vedic scriptures have authorized the deity form of worship of God because it cleanses the heart, mind, and the subtle and gross senses of the worshiper, and increases as well as sustains one's faith in God.

The next step is the chanting of hymns and the repetition (Japa) of divine names. The next stage is meditation. The vision of Spirit-consciousness, or beholding the Spirit manifested through every individual, is the highest spiritual development.

अहं हि सर्वयज्ञानां भोक्ता च प्रभुर् एव च ।
न तु माम् अभिजानन्ति तत्त्वेनातश् च्यवन्ति ते ॥२४॥

ahaṁ hi sarva yajñānāṁ bhoktā ca prabhur eva ca
na tu mām abhijānanti tattvenā'taś cyavanti te

Because I— the Supreme Being— alone am the enjoyer of all sacrificial services and Lord of the universe. But people do not know My true transcendental nature. Therefore, they fall into the repeated cycles of birth and death. (9.24)

यान्ति देवव्रता देवान् पितन् यान्ति पितृव्रताः ।
भूतानि यान्ति भूतेज्या यान्ति मद्याजिनोऽपि माम् ।।२५।।

yānti devavratā devān pitṝn yānti pitṛvratāḥ
bhūtāni yānti bhūtejyā yānti madyājino'pi mām

Worshippers of the celestial controllers go to the celestial controllers; the worshippers of the ancestors go to the ancestors; and the worshippers of the ghosts go to the ghosts; but My devotees come to Me, and are not born again. (See also 8.16) (9.25)

It is said that whatever one worships, that destination one attains; or one becomes what one regularly thinks of.

LORD ACCEPTS AND EATS THE OFFERING OF LOVE AND DEVOTION

पत्रं पुष्पं फलं तोयं यो मे भक्त्या प्रयच्छति ।
तद् अहं भक्त्युपहृतम् अश्नामि प्रयतात्मनः ।।२६।।

patraṁ puṣpaṁ phalaṁ toyaṁ yo me bhaktyā prayacchati
tad ahaṁ bhakty upahṛtam aśnāmi prayatātmanaḥ

Whosoever offers Me a leaf, a flower, a fruit, or water with devotion, I accept and eat the offering of devotion by the pure-hearted. (9.26)

The Lord is hungry for love and the feeling of devotion. A dedicated heart, not complicated rituals, is needed to please God and obtain His grace. One should consume food after offering it to God first. God eats the food offerings to please His devotees. The mind becomes purified when one eats food after offering it first to the Lord.

यत् करोषि यद् अश्नासि यज् जुहोषि ददासि यत् ।
यत् तपस्यसि कौन्तेय तत् कुरुष्व मदर्पणम् ।।२७।।

yat karoṣi yad aśnāsi yaj juhoṣi dadāsi yat
yat tapasyasi kaunteya tat kuruṣva mad arpaṇam

O Arjuna, whatever you do, whatever you eat, whatever you offer as oblation to the sacred fire, whatever charity you give, whatever austerity you perform — dedicate everything as an offering to Me. (See also 12.10, 18.46) (9.27)

It is neither necessary, nor sufficient that one should follow a certain routine, ritualistic offering of worship everyday to please God. Whatever one does per one's nature by body, mind, senses, thought, intellect, action, and speech, should be done with the thought that it is all for God only (BP 11.02.36). People have achieved liberation by performing only one type of devotional service, such as chanting, hearing, remembering, serving, meditating, renouncing, and surrendering. The love for fame is a fire that can destroy all yoga and austerity. The illusory power of divine kinetic energy (Maya) is formidable. It betrays everyone, including the yogis, unless one does everything for God.

शुभाशुभफलैर् एवं मोक्ष्यसे कर्मबन्धनैः ।
संन्यासयोगयुक्तात्मा विमुक्तो माम् उपैष्यसि ।।२८।।

śubhāśubhaphalair evaṁ mokṣyase karma bandhanaiḥ
saṁnyāsa yoga yuktātmā vimukto mām upaiṣyasi

You shall become free from the bondage — good and bad — of Karma and come to Me by this attitude of complete dedication to Me. (9.28)

समोऽहं सर्वभूतेषु न मे द्वेष्योऽस्ति न प्रियः ।
ये भजन्ति तु मां भक्त्या मयि ते तेषु चाप्य् अहम् ॥२९॥

samo'haṁ sarvabhūteṣu na me dveṣyo'sti na priyaḥ
ye bhajanti tu mām bhaktyā mayi te teṣu cāpy aham

The Self is present equally in all beings. There is no one hateful or dear to Me. But those who worship Me with love and devotion are very close to Me, and I am also very close to them. (See also 7.18) (9.29)

Lord Krishna says here that one should not be partial, but should treat a faithful or a helpful person better then others. Lord is neither merciless nor partial to anyone. Lord loves no one and hates no one, but does give special preference to His devotees. He said: My devotees do not know anything else but Me, and I do not know anyone else but them (BP 9.4.68). To protect His devotee is His nature. Lord goes out of way to help and fulfill the desires of His sincere devotees. He also reciprocates by always thinking of those devotees who always think of Him and saves such devotees from all calamities and major problems. The best path of perfection — suitable to the individual's nature — is shown to His sincere devotees.

I am with the Father, and the Father is with Me (John 10.38 and 14.11). Ask and it shall be given. Seek and you shall find (Matthew 7.07). God's grace is just for the asking. The doors of devotion are open to all, but the faithful and the dedicated ones who burn the incense of devotion in the temple of their heart become one with the Lord. A father loves all his children equally, but the child who is devoted to the father is more dear although he or she may not be very rich, intelligent, or powerful. Similarly, a devotee is very dear to the Lord. Lord does not give everything — such as both material and spiritual wealth — to everybody. One attains perfection — by the grace of God — through the practice of spiritual discipline. Both self-effort and grace are needed. According to the Vedas, the gods help only those who help themselves (RV 4.33.11). Yogananda said: God chooses those who choose Him.

The grace of God, like rays of the sun, is equally available to all, but due to free will one must open the window of the heart to let the sunshine come in. It is said that divinity is our birthright; however, self-effort in the right direction is also necessary to remove hindrances brought about by our own past deeds. The grace of God also comes expeditiously through our own efforts. It is also believed that divine grace and self-effort are one and the same. Self-effort promotes the process of God-realization as manure promotes growth of plants.

THERE IS NO UNFORGIVABLE SINNER

अपि चेत् सुदुराचारो भजते माम् अनन्यभाक् ।
साधुर् एव स मन्तव्यः सम्यग् व्यवसितो हि सः ॥३०॥

api cet sudurācāro bhajate mām ananyabhāk
sādhur eva sa mantavyaḥ samyag vyavasito hi saḥ

If even the most sinful person resolves to worship Me with single-minded, loving devotion, such a person must be regarded as a saint because of making the right resolution. (9.30)

There are no unforgivable sins or sinners. The fire of sincere repentance burns all sins. The Koran says: Those who believe in Allah and do right action, He will forgive their evil deeds (Surah 64.09). Yogananda used to say: A saint is the sinner who never gave up. Every saint had a past, and every sinner has a future. The Bible says: Everyone who believes in Him shall have eternal life (John 3.15). Acts of austerity, service, and charity, done without any selfish motive, can atone for sinful acts, as darkness vanishes after sunrise (MB 3.207.57). If a devotee keeps his or her mind focused on God, there will be no room for sinful desires to mature, and a sinful person soon becomes righteous as mentioned below:

क्षिप्रं भवति धर्मात्मा शश्वच्छान्तिं निगच्छति ।
कौन्तेय प्रतिजानीहि न मे भक्तः प्रणश्यति ।।३१।।

kṣipraṁ bhavati dharmātmā śaśvacchāntiṁ nigacchati
kaunteya pratijānīhi na me bhaktaḥ praṇaśyati

Such a person soon becomes righteous and attains everlasting peace. Be aware, O Arjuna, that My devotee never fails to reach the goal. (9.31)

PATH OF DEVOTIONAL LOVE IS EASIER

मां हि पार्थ व्यपाश्रित्य येऽपि स्युः पापयोनयः ।
स्त्रियो वैश्यास् तथा शूद्रास् तेऽपि यान्ति परां गतिम् ।।३२।।

māṁ hi pārtha vyapāśritya ye'pi syuḥ pāpayonayaḥ
striyo vaiśyās tathā śūdrās te'pi yānti parāṁ gatim

Anybody — including women, merchants, laborers, and the evil-minded — can attain the Supreme Abode by just surrendering unto My will with loving devotion, O Arjuna. (See also 18.66) (9.32)

A spiritual discipline should be commensurate with the faith, interest, and ability of the person. Some may be disqualified or not ready to receive the knowledge of the Supreme, but the path of devotion is open to all. No one is disqualified due to caste, creed, gender, or mental capacity to receive devotion. Most saints and sages consider the path of devotion the easiest and the best of all paths.

किं पुनर् ब्राह्मणाः पुण्या भक्ता राजर्षयस् तथा ।
अनित्यम् असुखं लोकम् इमं प्राप्य भजस्व माम् ।।३३।।

kiṁ punar brāhmaṇāḥ puṇyā bhaktā rājarṣayas tathā
anityam asukhaṁ lokam imaṁ prāpya bhajasva mām

Then it should be very easy for the wise and devout sages to attain the Supreme Being. Therefore, having obtained this joyless and transitory human life, one should always worship Me with loving devotion. (9.33)

The living entity, under the spell of illusory power of divine kinetic energy (Maya), goes through the repeated cycles of birth and death. The good Lord, out of His grace, gives to a living entity a human body that is very difficult to obtain. The human body, created in the image of God, is the jewel of creation and has the capacity to deliver the soul from the net of transmigration to higher levels of existence. All other forms of life on the earth, except human life, are devoid of higher intellect and discrimination.

As a tiger suddenly comes and takes away a lamb from the flock, similarly, death takes away a person unexpectedly. Therefore, spiritual discipline and righteous deeds should be performed without waiting for a proper time to come (MB 12.175.13). The goal and obligation of human birth are to seek Him. The search for God should not wait. One should continue this search parallel with other duties of life; otherwise, it may be too late. Lord Krishna concludes this chapter by giving practical ways to engage people in His devotional service below:

मन्मना भव मद्भक्तो मद्याजी मां नमस्कुरु ।
माम् एवैष्यसि युक्त्वैवम् आत्मानं मत्परायणः ।।३४।।
manmanā bhava madbhakto madyājī māṁ namaskuru
mām evai'ṣyasi yuktvai'vam ātmānaṁ matparāyaṇaḥ

Always think of Me, be devoted to Me, worship Me, and bow down to Me. Thus, uniting yourself with Me by setting Me as the supreme goal and the sole refuge, you shall certainly come to Me. (9.34)

ॐ तत्सदिति श्रीमद्भगवद्गीतासूपनिषत्सु ब्रह्मविद्यायां योगशास्त्रे
श्रीकृष्णार्जुनसंवादे राजविद्याराजगुह्ययोगो नाम नवमोऽध्यायः ॥

OM tatsaditi śrīmadbhagavadgītāsūpaniṣatsu brahmavidyāyāṁ
yogaśāstre śrīkṛṣṇārjuna saṁvāde rājavidyārājaguhyayogo
nāma navamo'dhyāyaḥ

Thus ends the ninth chapter named "Supreme Knowledge and the
Big Mystery" of the Upaniṣad of the Bhagavadgītā, the
scripture of yoga, dealing with the science of the
Absolute in the form of the dialogue
between Śrīkṛṣṇa and Arjuna.

अथ दशमोऽध्यायः
CHAPTER 10
विभूतियोगः
MANIFESTATION OF THE ABSOLUTE

श्रीभगवानुवाच
भूय एव महाबाहो शृणु मे परमं वचः ।
यत् तेऽहं प्रीयमाणाय वक्ष्यामि हितकाम्यया ॥१॥
śrī bhagavān uvāca
bhūya eva mahābāho śṛṇu me paramaṁ vacaḥ
yat te'haṁ prīyamāṇāya vakṣyāmi hitakāmyayā

Lord Krishna said: O Arjuna, listen once again to My supreme word that I shall speak to you, who are very dear to Me, for your welfare. (10.01)

GOD IS THE ORIGIN OF EVERYTHING

न मे विदुः सुरगणाः प्रभवं न महर्षयः ।
अहम् आदिर् हि देवानां महर्षीणां च सर्वशः ॥२॥
na me viduḥ suragaṇāḥ prabhavaṁ na maharṣayaḥ
aham ādir hi devānāṁ maharṣīṇāṁ ca sarvaśaḥ

Neither the celestial controllers nor the great sages know My origin because I am the origin of celestial controllers and great sages also. (10.02)

यो माम् अजम् अनादिं च वेत्ति लोकमहेश्वरम् ।
असंमूढः स मर्त्येषु सर्वपापैः प्रमुच्यते ॥३॥
yo mām ajam anādiṁ ca vetti lokamaheśvaram
asaṁmūḍhaḥ sa martyeṣu sarvapāpaiḥ pramucyate

One who knows Me as the unborn, the beginningless, and the Supreme Lord of the universe, is considered wise among mortals and becomes liberated from the bondage of Karma. (10.03)

बुद्धिर् ज्ञानम् असंमोहः क्षमा सत्यं दमः शमः ।
सुखं दुःखं भवोऽभावो भयं चाभयम् एव च ॥४॥

buddhir jñānam asaṁmohaḥ kṣamā satyaṁ damaḥ śamaḥ
sukhaṁ duḥkhaṁ bhavo'bhāvo bhayaṁ cā'bhayam eva ca

अहिंसा समता तुष्टिस् तपो दानं यशोऽयशः ।
भवन्ति भावा भूतानां मत्त एव पृथग्विधाः ॥५॥

ahiṁsā samatā tuṣṭis tapo dānaṁ yaśo'yaśaḥ
bhavanti bhāvā bhūtānāṁ matta eva pṛthagvidhāḥ

Discrimination, Self-knowledge, non-delusion, forgiveness, truthfulness, control over the mind and senses, tranquility, pleasure, pain, birth, death, fear, fearlessness, nonviolence, equanimity, contentment, austerity, charity, fame, ill fame — these diverse qualities in human beings arise from Me alone. (10.04-05)

If you forgive others, your Father in heaven will also forgive you (Matthew 6.14). Resist no evil with evil (Matthew 5.39). Love your enemies, and pray for those who mistreat you (Matthew 5.44). One should control anger toward the wrong-doer. The controlled anger itself punishes the wrong-doer if the wrong-doer does not ask forgiveness (MB 5.36.05). One who does wrong is destroyed by the same act of wrong doing if he or she does not ask forgiveness (MS 2.163). One who truly forgives trespassers is happy because the anger of the forgiver is exterminated. Progress in spiritual discipline is impeded if one's interpersonal relationship is full of hurt and negative feeling, even for a single living entity. Therefore, one must learn to forgive and to ask forgiveness.

Even virtue has its own vice. Forgiveness may often be construed as a sign of weakness; therefore, clemency is the strength of the strong and a virtue for the weak. A person should be forgiven if he or she has sincerely asked forgiveness, if it is the first offense, if the offense was not intentional, and if the offender has been helpful in the past. The tool of punishment may be used — without any feeling of revenge — to correct and teach intentional and repeated offenders.

महर्षयः सप्त पूर्वे चत्वारो मनवस् तथा ।
मद्भावा मानसा जाता येषां लोक इमाः प्रजाः ॥६॥
maharṣayaḥ sapta pūrve catvāro manavas tathā
madbhāvā mānasā jātā yeṣāṁ loka imāḥ prajāḥ

The great saints, sages, and all the creatures of the world were born from My potential energy. (10.06)

एतां विभूतिं योगं च मम यो वेत्ति तत्त्वतः ।
सोऽविकम्पेन योगेन युज्यते नात्र संशयः ॥७॥
etāṁ vibhūtiṁ yogaṁ ca mama yo vetti tattvataḥ
so'vikampena yogena yujyate nā'tra saṁśayaḥ

One who truly understands My manifestations and yogic powers, is united with Me by unswerving devotion. There is no doubt about it. (10.07)

अहं सर्वस्य प्रभवो मत्तः सर्वं प्रवर्तते ।
इति मत्वा भजन्ते मां बुधा भावसमन्विताः ॥८॥
ahaṁ sarvasya prabhavo mattaḥ sarvaṁ pravartate
iti matvā bhajante māṁ budhā bhāvasamanvitāḥ

I am the origin of all. Everything emanates from Me. The wise who understand this adore Me with love and devotion. (10.08)

That which is One has become this all (RV 8.58.02).

मच्चित्ता मद्गतप्राणा बोधयन्तः परस्परम् ।
कथयन्तश्च मां नित्यं तुष्यन्ति च रमन्ति च ॥९॥

maccittā madgataprāṇā bodhayantaḥ parasparam
kathayantaś ca māṁ nityaṁ tuṣyanti ca ramanti ca

My devotees remain ever content and delighted. Their minds remain absorbed in Me and their lives surrendered unto Me. They always enlighten each other by talking about Me. (10.09)

Devotees are the well wishers of everyone and help others to advance on the spiritual path.

LORD GIVES KNOWLEDGE TO HIS DEVOTEES

तेषां सततयुक्तानां भजतां प्रीतिपूर्वकम् ।
ददामि बुद्धियोगं तं येन माम् उपयान्ति ते ॥१०॥

teṣāṁ satata yuktānāṁ bhajatāṁ prītipūrvakam
dadāmi buddhi yogaṁ taṁ yena mām upayānti te

I give the powers of analysis and reasoning to understand the metaphysical science — to those who are ever united with Me and lovingly adore Me — by which they come to Me. (10.10)

We are given powers of analysis and reasoning (Viveka) that can be used to understand the metaphysical science or Self-knowledge. Those who receive Him and believe in Him, He makes them come to the Father in heaven (John 1.12). Whosoever shall not receive the kingdom of God as a little child shall not enter therein (Luke 18.17).

तेषाम् एवानुकम्पार्थम् अहम् अज्ञानजं तमः ।
नाशयाम्य् आत्मभावस्थो ज्ञानदीपेन भास्वता ॥११॥

teṣām evānukampārtham aham ajñānajaṁ tamaḥ
nāśayāmy ātmabhāvastho jñānadīpena bhāsvatā

I, who dwell within their inner psyche as consciousness, destroy the darkness born of ignorance by the shining lamp of transcendental knowledge as an act of compassion for them. (10.11)

All other forms of Krishna can be achieved by different means of worship, but Krishna Himself can be achieved only by devotion and exclusive love (Chimanbhai). The lamp of spiritual knowledge and God-realization can be easily ignited by the intense spark of devotion, but never by intellect and logic alone.

अर्जुन उवाच
परं ब्रह्म परं धाम पवित्रं परमं भवान् ।
पुरुषं शाश्वतं दिव्यम् आदिदेवम् अजं विभुम् ।।१२।।
arjuna uvāca
paraṁ brahma paraṁ dhāma pavitraṁ paramaṁ bhavān
puruṣaṁ śāśvataṁ divyam ādidevam ajaṁ vibhum

आहुस् त्वाम् ऋषयः सर्वे देवर्षिर् नारदस् तथा ।
असितो देवलो व्यासः स्वयं चैव ब्रवीषि मे ।।१३।।
āhus tvām ṛṣayaḥ sarve devarṣir nāradas tathā
asito devalo vyāsaḥ svayaṁ caiva bravīṣi me

Arjuna said: You are the Supreme Being, the Supreme Abode, the Supreme Purifier, the Eternal Being, the primal God, the unborn, and the omnipresent. All saints and sages have thus acclaimed You, and now You Yourself are telling me that. (10.12-13)

NOBODY CAN KNOW THE REAL NATURE OF REALITY

सर्वम् एतद् ऋतं मन्ये यन् मां वदसि केशव ।
न हि ते भगवन् व्यक्तिं विदुर् देवा न दानवाः ।।१४।।

sarvam etad ṛtaṁ manye yan māṁ vadasi keśava
na hi te bhagavan vyaktiṁ vidur devā na dānavāḥ

O Krishna, I believe all that You have told me to be true. O Lord, neither the celestial controllers nor the demons fully understand Your real nature. (See also 4.06) (10.14)

स्वयम् एवात्मनात्मानं वेत्थ त्वं पुरुषोत्तम ।
भूतभावन भूतेश देवदेव जगत्पते ॥१५॥

svayam evā'tmanā'tmānaṁ vettha tvaṁ puruṣottama
bhūtabhāvana bhūteśa devadeva jagatpate

O Creator and Lord of all beings, God of all celestial rulers, the Supreme person, and Lord of the universe, You alone know Yourself by Yourself. (10.15)

The Vedas left the final question of the origin of ultimate Reality unanswered by stating that nobody knows the ultimate source from where this creation has come. Sages went further by stating that perhaps even He does not know (RV 10.129.06-07). One who says that I know God does not know; one who knows the Truth says that I do not know. God is the unknown to a person of true knowledge; only the ignorant claim to know God (KeU 2.01-03). The ultimate source of cosmic energy is and will remain a big mystery. Any specific description of God, including a description of heaven and hell, is nothing but a mental speculation.

वक्तुम् अर्हस्य् अशेषेण दिव्या ह्य् आत्मविभूतयः ।
याभिर् विभूतिभिर् लोकान् इमांस् त्वं व्याप्य तिष्ठसि ॥१६॥

vaktum arhasy aśeṣeṇa divyā hy ātmavibhūtayaḥ
yābhir vibhūtibhir lokān imāṁs tvaṁ vyāpya tiṣṭhasi

Therefore, You alone are able to fully describe Your own divine glories or the manifestations by which You exist pervading all the universes. (10.16)

कथं विद्याम् अहं योगिंस् त्वां सदा परिचिन्तयन् ।
केषु केषु च भावेषु चिन्त्योऽसि भगवन् मया ॥१७॥

katham vidyām aham yogiṁs tvāṁ sadā paricintayan
keṣu keṣu ca bhāveṣu cintyo'si bhagavan mayā

How may I know You, O Lord, constantly contemplating on You? In what form of manifestation are You to be thought of by me, O Lord? (10.17)

विस्तरेणात्मनो योगं विभूतिं च जनार्दन ।
भूयः कथय तृप्तिर् हि शृण्वतो नास्ति मेऽमृतम् ॥१८॥

vistareṇā'tmano yogaṁ vibhūtiṁ ca janārdana
bhūyaḥ kathaya tṛptir hi śṛṇvato nāsti me'mṛtam

O Lord, explain to me again, in detail, Your yogic power and glory because I am not satiated by hearing Your nectar-like words. (10.18)

EVERYTHING IS A MANIFESTATION OF THE ABSOLUTE

श्रीभगवानुवाच
हन्त ते कथयिष्यामि दिव्या ह्य् आत्मविभूतयः ।
प्राधान्यतः कुरुश्रेष्ठ नास्त्य् अन्तो विस्तरस्य मे ॥१९॥

śrī bhagavān uvāca
hanta te kathayiṣyāmi divyā hy ātmavibhūtayaḥ
prādhānyataḥ kuruśreṣṭha nā'sty anto vistarasya me

Lord Krishna said: O Arjuna, now I shall explain to you My prominent divine manifestations because My manifestations are endless. (10.19)

अहम् आत्मा गुडाकेश सर्वभूताशयस्थितः ।
अहम् आदिश्च मध्यं च भूतानाम् अन्त एव च ॥२०॥

aham ātmā guḍākeśa sarvabhūtāśayasthitaḥ
aham ādiśca madhyaṁ ca bhūtānām anta eva ca

O Arjuna, I am the Supreme Spirit (or Supersoul) abiding in the inner psyche of all beings as soul (Atma). I am also the creator, maintainer, and destroyer — or the beginning, the middle, and the end — of all beings. (10.20)

Spirit has no origin and is a property of the Supreme Being, just as sunlight is a property of the sun (BS 2.03.17). The Supreme Being and Spirit are like sun and sunlight, different as well as non-different (BS 3.02.28). Within living beings, Spirit is the controller. Spirit is different from the physical body, just as fire is different from wood.

The senses, mind, and intellect cannot know Spirit or universal consciousness because the senses, mind, and intellect get their power to function from Spirit alone (KeU 1.06). Spirit supplies power and supports the senses, just as air burns and supports fire (MB 12.203.03). Spirit is the basis and support behind every form of power, movement, intellect, and life in this universe. It is the power by which one sees, hears, smells, thinks, loves, hates, and desires objects.

आदित्यानाम् अहं विष्णुर् ज्योतिषां रविर् अंशुमान् ।
मरीचिर् मरुताम् अस्मि नक्षत्राणाम् अहं शशी ।।२१।।
ādityānām ahaṁ viṣṇur jyotiṣāṁ ravir aṁśumān
marīcir marutām asmi nakṣatrāṇām ahaṁ śaśī

I am the sustainer. I am the radiant sun among the luminaries; I am the controller of wind; I am the moon among the stars. (10.21)

वेदानां सामवेदोऽस्मि देवानाम् अस्मि वासवः ।
इन्द्रियाणां मनश्चास्मि भूतानाम् अस्मि चेतना ।।२२।।
vedānāṁ sāmavedo'smi devānām asmi vāsavaḥ
indriyāṇāṁ manaś cā'smi bhūtānām asmi cetanā

I am the Vedas. I am the celestial rulers. I am the mind among the senses; I am the consciousness in living beings. (10.22)

रुद्राणां शंकरश् चास्मि वित्तेशो यक्षरक्षसाम् ।
वसूनां पावकश् चास्मि मेरुः शिखरिणाम् अहम् ।।२३।।
rudrāṇāṁ śaṁkaraś cā'smi vitteśo yakṣarakṣasām
vasūnāṁ pāvakaś cā'smi meruḥ śikhariṇām aham

I am Lord Shiva. I am the god of wealth; I am the god of fire and the mountains. (10.23)

पुरोधसां च मुख्यं मां विद्धि पार्थ बृहस्पतिम् ।
सेनानीनाम् अहं स्कन्दः सरसाम् अस्मि सागरः ।।२४।।
purodhasāṁ ca mukhyaṁ māṁ viddhi pārtha bṛhaspatim
senānīnām ahaṁ skandaḥ sarasām asmi sāgaraḥ

I am the priest and the army general of the celestial controllers, O Arjuna. I am the ocean among the bodies of water. (10.24)

महर्षीणां भृगुर् अहं गिराम् अस्म्य् एकम् अक्षरम् ।
यज्ञानां जपयज्ञोऽस्मि स्थावराणां हिमालयः ।।२५।।
maharṣīṇāṁ bhṛgur ahaṁ girām asmy ekam akṣaram
yajñānāṁ japayajño'smi sthāvarāṇāṁ himālayaḥ

I am the great sage, Bhrigu. I am the monosyllable cosmic sound 'AUM' among words; I am the silent repetition of mantra (Japa) among the spiritual disciplines, and I am the Himalaya among the mountains. (10.25)

A constant chanting of a mantra or any holy name of God is considered by saints and sages of all religions to be the easiest and most powerful method of Self-realization in the present age. The practice of this spiritual discipline with faith will drive sound vibrations into the deeper layers of mind where it works like a damper in preventing the rise of waves of negative thoughts and ideas, leading the way to inner awakening in due course of time. Meditation is the extended and higher stage of this process. One must first practice this before going into transcendental meditation. Swami Harihar says: There should be no desire to gain any worldly objects in exchange for the repetition of the divine name. The spiritual force of the divine name should not be applied even for the destruction of sin. It should be resorted to for divine realization only.

The form of the Lord cannot be known nor comprehended by the human mind without a name. If one chants or meditates on the name without seeing the form, the form flashes on the screen of the mind as an object of love. A great saint said: Place the lamp of the name of the Lord near the door of your tongue if you want the light both inside and outside. The name of God is greater than both impersonal and personal aspects of God because the power of the name has control over both aspects of God. It is said that the best of all spiritual efforts is to always remember and repeat the name of God.

A BRIEF DESCRIPTION OF DIVINE MANIFESTATIONS

अश्वत्थः सर्ववृक्षाणां देवर्षीणां च नारदः ।
गन्धर्वाणां चित्ररथः सिद्धानां कपिलो मुनिः ।।२६।।

aṣvatthaḥ sarvavṛkṣāṇāṁ devarṣīṇāṁ ca nāradaḥ
gandharvāṇāṁ citrarathaḥ siddhānāṁ kapilo muniḥ

I am the holy fig tree among the trees, Narada among the sages, and I am all other celestial rulers. (10.26)

उच्चैःश्रवसम् अश्वानां विद्धि माम् अमृतोद्भवम् ।
ऐरावतं गजेन्द्राणां नराणां च नराधिपम् ।।२७।।

uccaiḥśravasam aśvānāṁ biddhi mām amṛtodbhavam
airāvataṁ gajendrāṇāṁ narāṇāṁ ca narādhipam

आयुधानाम् अहं वज्रं धेनूनाम् अस्मि कामधुक् ।
प्रजनश् चास्मि कन्दर्पः सर्पाणाम् अस्मि वासुकिः ॥२८॥

āyudhānām ahaṁ vajraṁ dhenūnām asmi kāmadhuk
prajanaś cāsmi kandarpaḥ sarpāṇām asmi vāsukiḥ

Know Me as the celestial animals among the animals and the King among men. I am the thunderbolt among weapons, and I am Cupid for procreation. (10.27-28)

अनन्तश् चास्मि नागानां वरुणो यादसाम् अहम् ।
पितणाम् अर्यमा चास्मि यमः संयमताम् अहम् ॥२९॥

anantaś cāsmi nāgānāṁ varuṇo yādasām aham
pitṝṇām aryamā cāsmi yamaḥ saṁyamatām aham

प्रह्लादश् चास्मि दैत्यानां कालः कलयताम् अहम् ।
मृगाणां च मृगेन्द्रोऽहं वैनतेयश्च पक्षिणाम् ॥३०॥

prahlādaś cāsmi daityānāṁ kālaḥ kalayatām aham
mṛgāṇāṁ ca mṛgendro'haṁ vainateyaṣca pakṣiṇām

I am the water-god and the manes. I am the controller of death. I am the time or death among the healers, lion among the beasts, and the king of birds among birds. (10.29-30)

पवनः पवताम् अस्मि रामः शस्त्रभृताम् अहम् ।
झषाणां मकरश् चास्मि स्रोतसाम् अस्मि जाह्नवी ॥३१॥

pavanaḥ pavatām asmi rāmaḥ śastrabhṛtām aham
jhaṣāṇāṁ makaraś cāsmi srotasām asmi jāhnavī

I am the wind among the purifiers and Lord Rama among the warriors. I am the crocodile among the fishes and the holy Gangaa river among the rivers. (10.31)

सर्गाणाम् आदिर् अन्तश्च मध्यं चैवाहम् अर्जुन ।
अध्यात्मविद्या विद्यानां वादः प्रवदताम् अहम् ॥३२॥

sargāṇām ādir antaśca madhyaṁ cai'vā'ham arjuna
adhyātmavidyā vidyānāṁ vādaḥ pravadatām aham

I am the beginning, the middle, and the end of all creation, O Arjuna. Among knowledge I am knowledge of the supreme Self. I am logic of the logician. (10.32)

अक्षराणाम् अकारोऽस्मि द्वन्द्वः सामासिकस्य च ।
अहम् एवाक्षयः कालो धाताहं विश्वतोमुखः ॥३३॥

akṣarāṇām akāro'smi dvandvaḥ sāmāsikasya ca
aham evā'kṣayaḥ kālo dhātā'haṁ viśvatomukhaḥ

I am the letter 'A' among the alphabets. I am the dual compound among the compound words. I am endless time. I am the sustainer, and I am omniscient. (10.33)

मृत्युः सर्वहरश्चाहम् उद्भवश्च भविष्यताम् ।
कीर्तिः श्रीर् वाक् च नारीणां स्मृतिर् मेधा धृतिः क्षमा ॥३४॥

mṛtyuḥ sarvaharaś cā'ham udbhavaśca bhaviṣyatām
kīrtiḥ śrīr vāk ca nārīṇāṁ smṛtir medhā dhṛtiḥ kṣamā

I am the all-devouring death and also the origin of future beings. I am the seven goddesses or guardian angels presiding over the seven qualities — fame, prosperity, speech, memory, intellect, resolve, and forgiveness. (10.34)

बृहत्साम तथा साम्नां गायत्री छन्दसाम् अहम् ।
मासानां मार्गशीर्षोऽहम् ऋतूनां कुसुमाकरः ॥३५॥

bṛhatsāma tathā sāmnāṁ gāyatrī chandasām aham
māsānāṁ mārgaśīrṣo'ham ṛtūnāṁ kusumākaraḥ

I am the Vedic and other hymns. I am the mantras; I am November-December among the months, I am spring among the seasons. (10.35)

द्यूतं छलयताम् अस्मि तेजस् तेजस्विनाम् अहम् ।
जयोऽस्मि व्यवसायोऽस्मि सत्त्वं सत्त्ववताम् अहम् ॥३६॥

dyūtaṁ chalayatām asmi tejas tejasvinām aham
jayo'smi vyavasāyo'smi sattvaṁ sattvavatām aham

I am gambling of the cheats, splendor of the splendid, victory of the victorious, resolution of the resolute, and goodness of the good. (10.36)

Both good and bad are the product of divine power (Maya). Maya creates a multitude of merits and demerits that have no real existence. The wise do not attach too much importance to it. One should develop good qualities and get rid of bad ones. After enlightenment, both good and bad, virtue and vice, are transcended, just as darkness vanishes after the sunrise. Vice and virtue are not two things, but one, the difference being only the degree of manifestation. It is true that God also dwells in the most sinful beings, but it is not proper to hate them or associate with them. Gandhi said: Hate the sin and not the sinner.

One should view the marvelous cosmic drama, full of pairs of opposites in life, with ever-joyous heart because there is no good or evil, only different masks of the cosmic actor. The scriptures denounce the idea of growing rich by unfair means, such as gambling, gifts, and bribes. They recommend honest labor, sweat of the brow, such as cultivating a cornfield, that is good for society as well as the individual (RV 10.34.13).

वृष्णीनां वासुदेवोऽस्मि पाण्डवानां धनंजयः ।
मुनीनाम् अप्य् अहं व्यासः कवीनाम् उशना कविः ॥३७॥

vṛṣṇīnāṁ vāsudevo'smi pāṇḍavānāṁ danaṁjayaḥ
munīnām apy ahaṁ vyāsaḥ kavīnām uśanā kaviḥ

दण्डो दमयताम् अस्मि नीतिर् अस्मि जिगीषताम् ।
मौनं चैवास्मि गुह्यानां ज्ञानं ज्ञानवताम् अहम् ॥३८॥

daṇḍo damayatām asmi nītir asmi jigīṣatām
maunaṁ cai'vā'smi guhyānāṁ jñānaṁ jñānavatām aham

I am Krishna, Vyasa, Arjuna, and the power of rulers, the statesmanship of the seekers of victory. I am silence among secrets and Self-knowledge of the knowledgeable. (10.37-38)

यच् चापि सर्वभूतानां बीजं तद् अहम् अर्जुन ।
न तद् अस्ति विना यत् स्यान् मया भूतं चराचरम् ॥३९॥

yac cā'pi sarvabhūtānāṁ bījaṁ tad aham arjuna
na tad asti vinā yat syān mayā bhūtaṁ carācaram

I am the origin of all beings, O Arjuna. There is nothing, animate or inanimate, that can exist without Me. (See also 7.10 and 9.18) (10.39)

A big tree — with many branches, leaves, flowers, fruits, and seeds — remains inside a tiny seed in unmanifest form and becomes manifest again and again into a tree. The tree again becomes unmanifest into the seed. Similarly, all manifestations remain in the Absolute in unmanifest form and become manifest during creation and unmanifest during dissolution again and again. The fruit remains hidden in the seed and the seed in the fruit; similarly, God is in human beings and human beings in God.

MANIFEST CREATION IS A VERY SMALL FRACTION OF THE ABSOLUTE

नान्तोऽस्ति मम दिव्यानां विभूतीनां परंतप ।
एष तूद्देशतः प्रोक्तो विभूतेर् विस्तरो मया ॥४०॥

nā'nto'sti mama divyānāṁ vibhūtīnāṁ paraṁtapa
eṣa tū'ddeśataḥ prokto vibhūter vistaro mayā

There is no end of My divine manifestations, O Arjuna. This is only a brief description by Me of the extent of My divine manifestations. (10.40)

The variety in the universe, from the highest celestial controllers to the smallest insects and even the inert dust, is nothing but a manifestation of One and the same Absolute.

यद् यद् विभूतिमत् सत्त्वं श्रीमद् ऊर्जितम् एव वा ।
तत् तद् एवावगच्छ त्वं मम तेजोऽंशसंभवम् ।।४१।।
yad yad vibhūtimat sattvaṁ śrīmad ūrjitam eva vā
tat tad evā'vagaccha tvaṁ mama tejoṁ'śa saṁbhavam

Whatever is endowed with glory, brilliance, and power — know that to be a manifestation of a very small fraction of My splendor. (10.41)

Through the word, His cosmic sound vibration, God made all things; not one thing in creation was made without His cosmic energy (John 1.03). This cosmic manifestation is non-separate from the Absolute just as sunshine is not separate from the sun (BP 4.31.16). The entire creation is a partial revelation and part and parcel of the Infinite. The divine manifests its glory through creation. The beauty and splendor of the visible universe are only a small fraction of His glory.

अथवा बहुनैतेन किं ज्ञातेन तवार्जुन ।
विष्टभ्याहम् इदं कृत्स्नम् एकांशेन स्थितो जगत् ।।४२।।
athavā bahunai'tena kiṁ jñātena tavā'rjuna
viṣṭabhyā'ham idaṁ kṛtsnam ekāṁśena sthito jagat

What is the need for this detailed knowledge, O Arjuna? I continually support the entire universe by a very small fraction of My divine power. (10.42)

Quantitatively, manifest creation is a very small fraction of the Absolute. The universe reflects the divine splendor for human beings to see the invisible Lord. One should learn to perceive God, not only as a person or vision, but also through His splendor as manifested in the universe and through His laws that govern and control nature and life. He is existence, goodness, and beauty.

ॐ तत्सदिति श्रीमद्भगवद्गीतासूपनिषत्सु ब्रह्मविद्यायां योगशास्त्रे
श्रीकृष्णार्जुनसंवादे विभूतियोगो नाम दशमोऽध्यायः ॥
OM tatsaditi śrīmadbhagavadgītāsūpaniṣatsu brahmavidyāyāṁ
yogaśāstre śrīkṛṣṇārjuna saṁvāde vibhūtiyogo
nāma daśamo'dhyāyaḥ

Thus ends the tenth chapter named "Manifestation of the Absolute" of the Upaniṣad of the Bhagavadgītā, the scripture of yoga, dealing with the science of the Absolute in the form of the dialogue between Śrīkṛṣṇa and Arjuna.

अथ एकादशोऽध्यायः
CHAPTER 11
विश्वरूपदर्शनयोगः
VISION OF THE COSMIC FORM

अर्जुन उवाच
मदनुग्रहाय परमं गुह्यम् अध्यात्मसंज्ञितम् ।
यत् त्वयोक्तं वचस् तेन मोहोऽयं विगतो मम ।।१।।
arjuna uvāca
madanugrahāya paramaṁ guhyam adhyātma saṁjñitam
yat tvayo'ktaṁ vacas tena moho'yaṁ vigato mama

Arjuna said: My illusion is dispelled by the profound words of wisdom You spoke out of compassion for me about the supreme secret of the Self. (11.01)

भवाप्ययौ हि भूतानां श्रुतौ विस्तरशो मया ।
त्वत्तः कमलपत्राक्ष माहात्म्यम् अपि चाव्ययम् ।।२।।
bhavāpyayau hi bhūtānāṁ śrutau vistaraśo mayā
tvattaḥ kamalapatrākṣa māhātmyam api cā'vyayam

O Krishna, I have heard from You in detail about the origin and dissolution of beings and Your immutable glory. (11.02)

VISION OF GOD IS THE ULTIMATE AIM OF A SEEKER

एवम् एतद् यथात्थ त्वम् आत्मानं परमेश्वर ।
द्रष्टुम् इच्छामि ते रूपम् ऐश्वरं पुरुषोत्तम ।।३।।
evam etad yathā'ttha tvam ātmānaṁ parameśvara
draṣṭum icchāmi te rūpam aiśvaraṁ puruṣottama

O Lord, You are as You have said; yet I wish to see Your divine cosmic form, O Supreme Being. (11.03)

मन्यसे यदि तच् छक्यं मया द्रष्टुम् इति प्रभो ।
योगेश्वर ततो मे त्वं दर्शयात्मानम् अव्ययम् ।।४।।

manyase yadi tac chakyaṁ mayā draṣṭum iti prabho
yogeśvara tato me tvaṁ darśayā'tmānam avyayam

O Lord, if You think it is possible for me to see Your universal form, then, O Lord of the yogis, show me Your transcendental form. (11.04)

There is no way to know God before experiencing Him. Faith in God rests on a shaky ground without a psychic vision of the object of devotion. All our spiritual discipline is aimed at this vision. The vision is essential to overcome the last bit of emotional impurity and any lingering doubt in the mind of the seeker because, to a human mind, seeing is believing. Therefore, Arjuna, like any other devotee, longs to see the transcendental form of the Lord.

श्रीभगवानुवाच
पश्य मे पार्थ रूपाणि शतशोऽथ सहस्रशः ।
नानाविधानि दिव्यानि नानावर्णाकृतीनि च ।।५।।

śrī bhagavān uvāca
paśya me pārtha rūpāṇi śataśo'tha sahasraśaḥ
nānāvidhāni divyāni nānāvarṇā'kṛtīni ca

पश्यादित्यान् वसून् रुद्रान् अश्विनौ मरुतस् तथा ।
बहून्य् अदृष्टपूर्वाणि पश्याश्चर्याणि भारत ।।६।।

paśyā'dityān vasūn rudrān aśvinau marutas tathā
bahūny adṛṣṭapūrvāṇi paśyā'ścaryāṇi bhārata

इहैकस्थं जगत् कृत्स्नं पश्याद्य सचराचरम् ।
मम देहे गुडाकेश यच् चान्यद् द्रष्टुम् इच्छसि ।।७।।

ihai'kastham jagat kṛtsnaṁ paśyā'dya sacarācaram
mama dehe guḍākeśa yac cā'nyad draṣṭum icchasi

Lord Krishna said: O Arjuna, behold My hundreds and thousands of multifarious divine forms of different colors and shapes. Behold all the celestial beings and many wonders never seen before. Also behold the entire creation — animate, inanimate, and whatever else you would like to see — all at one place in My body. (11.05-07)

न तु मां शक्यसे द्रष्टुम् अनेनैव स्वचक्षुषा ।
दिव्यं ददामि ते चक्षुः पश्य मे योगम् ऐश्वरम् ॥८॥

na tu māṁ śakyase draṣṭum anenaiva svacakṣuṣā
divyaṁ dadāmi te cakṣuḥ paśya me yogam aiśvaram

But you are not able to see Me with your physical eye; therefore, I give you the divine eye to see My majestic power and glory. (11.08)

No one can see Him with the physical eye. His transcendental form is beyond our field of vision. He is revealed through the faculty of intuition of the intellect that, residing within the inner psyche, controls the mind. Those who know Him become immortal (KaU 6.09). We, like color blinds, are not able to see the full range of cosmic color and light with human eyes. The divine vision, which is a gift of God, is needed to see the beauty and glory of the Supreme Personality of Godhead.

LORD SHOWS HIS COSMIC FORM TO ARJUNA

संजय उवाच
एवम् उक्त्वा ततो राजन् महायोगेश्वरो हरिः ।
दर्शयामास पार्थाय परमं रूपम् ऐश्वरम् ॥९॥

saṁjaya uvāca
evam uktvā tato rājan mahāyogeśvaro hariḥ
darśayāmāsa pārthāya paramaṁ rūpam aiśvaram

Sanjaya said: O King, having said this, Lord Krishna, the great Lord of the mystic power of yoga, revealed His supreme majestic form to Arjuna. (11.09)

अनेकवक्त्रनयनम् अनेकाद्भुतदर्शनम् ।
अनेकदिव्याभरणं दिव्यानेकोद्यतायुधम् ॥१०॥

aneka vaktra nayanam anekādbhuta darśanam
aneka divyābharaṇaṁ divyānekodyatāyudham

दिव्यमाल्याम्बरधरं दिव्यगन्धानुलेपनम् ।
सर्वाश्चर्यमयं देवम् अनन्तं विश्वतोमुखम् ॥११॥

divya mālyāmbara dharaṁ divya gandhānulepanam
sarvāścaryamayaṁ devam anantaṁ viśvatomukham

Arjuna saw the Universal Form of the Lord with many mouths and eyes, and many marvelous visions with numerous divine ornaments, holding many divine weapons, wearing divine garlands and apparel, anointed with celestial perfumes and ointments, full of all wonders — the limitless God with faces on all sides. (11.10-11)

दिवि सूर्यसहस्रस्य भवेद् युगपद् उत्थिता ।
यदि भाः सदृशी सा स्याद् भासस् तस्य महात्मनः ॥१२॥

divi sūrya sahasrasya bhaved yugapad utthitā
yadi bhāḥ sadṛśī sā syād bhāsas tasya mahātmanaḥ

If the splendor of thousands of suns were to blaze forth all at once in the sky, even that would not resemble the splendor of that exalted being. (11.12)

He came to tell about the light. This was the real light, the light that comes into the world and sustains everything (John

1.09). O Lord, not even a million suns could match You (RV 8.70.05). Robert Oppenheimer spoke this verse as he witnessed the explosion of the first atom bomb.

तत्रैकस्थं जगत् कृत्स्नं प्रविभक्तम् अनेकधा ।
अपश्यद् देवदेवस्य शरीरे पाण्डवस् तदा ॥१३॥
tatrai'kasthaṁ jagat kṛtsnaṁ pravibhaktam anekadhā
apaśyad devadevasya śarīre pāṇḍavas tadā

Arjuna saw the entire universe, divided in many ways, but standing as all in One and One in all in the transcendental body of Krishna, the Lord of celestial rulers. (See also 13.16, and 18.20) (11.13)

ONE MAY NOT BE PREPARED TO SEE THE LORD

ततः स विस्मयाविष्टो हृष्टरोमा धनंजयः ।
प्रणम्य शिरसा देवं कृताञ्जलिर् अभाषत ॥१४॥
tataḥ sa vismayāviṣṭo hṛṣṭaromā dhanaṁjayaḥ
praṇamya śirasā devaṁ kṛtāñjalir abhāṣata

Having seen the cosmic form of the Lord, Arjuna was filled with wonder and his hairs standing on end, bowed his head to the Lord and prayed with folded hands. (11.14)

अर्जुन उवाच
पश्यामि देवांस् तव देव देहे
सर्वांस् तथा भूतविशेषसंघान् ।
ब्रह्माणम् ईशं कमलासनस्थम्
ऋषींश्च सर्वान् उरगांश्च दिव्यान् ॥१५॥
arjuna uvāca
paśyāmi devāṁs tava deva dehe
sarvāṁs tathā bhūta viśeṣa saṁghān

brahmāṇam īśaṁ kamalāsanasthaṁ
ṛṣīṁśca sarvān uragāṁśca divyān

Arjuna said: O Lord, I see in Your body all supernatural controllers, and multitudes of beings, sages, and celestials. (11.15)

अनेकबाहूदरवक्त्रनेत्रं
पश्यामि त्वां सर्वतोऽनन्तरूपम् ।
नान्तं न मध्यं न पुनस् तवादिं
पश्यामि विश्वेश्वर विश्वरूप ॥१६॥

aneka bāhūdara vaktra netraṁ
paśyāmi tvāṁ sarvato'nantarūpam
nā'ntaṁ na madhyaṁ na punas tavā'diṁ
paśyāmi viśveśvara viśvarūpa

O Lord of the universe, I see You everywhere with infinite forms, with many arms, stomachs, faces, and eyes. O Universal Form, I see neither your beginning nor the middle nor the end. (11.16)

The Self is omnipresent, all pervading, beginningless and endless.

किरीटिनं गदिनं चक्रिणं च
तेजोराशिं सर्वतो दीप्तिमन्तम् ।
पश्यामि त्वां दुर्निरीक्ष्यं समन्ताद्
दीप्तानलार्कद्युतिम् अप्रमेयम् ॥१७॥

kirīṭinaṁ gadinaṁ cakriṇaṁ ca
tejorāśiṁ sarvato dīptimantam
paśyāmi tvāṁ durnirīkṣyaṁ samantād
dīptānalārkadyutim aprameyam

I see You with Your crown, club, discus, and massive radiance, difficult to behold, shining all around like the immeasurable brilliance and blazing fire of the sun. (11.17)

त्वम् अक्षरं परमं वेदितव्यं
त्वम् अस्य विश्वस्य परं निधानम् ।
त्वम् अव्ययः शाश्वतधर्मगोप्ता
सनातनस् त्वं पुरुषो मतो मे ॥१८॥

tvam akṣaraṁ paramaṁ veditavyaṁ
tvam asya viśvasya paraṁ nidhānam
tvam avyayaḥ śāśvata dharma goptā
sanātanas tvaṁ puruṣo mato me

I believe You are the Supreme Being to be realized. You are the ultimate resort of the universe. You are the Spirit and protector of the eternal order (Dharma). (11.18)

अनादिमध्यान्तम् अनन्तवीर्यम्
अनन्तबाहुं शशिसूर्यनेत्रम् ।
पश्यामि त्वां दीप्तहुताशवक्त्रं
स्वतेजसा विश्वम् इदं तपन्तम् ॥१९॥

anādi madhyāntam ananta vīryam
ananta bāhuṁ śaśisūrya netram
paśyāmi tvāṁ dīpta hutāśa vaktraṁ
svatejasā viśvam idaṁ tapantam

I see You with infinite power, without beginning, middle, or end; with many arms; with the sun and the moon as Your eyes; with Your mouth as a blazing fire, scorching all the universe with Your radiance. (11.19)

द्यावापृथिव्योर् इदम् अन्तरं हि
व्याप्तं त्वयैकेन दिशश्च सर्वाः ।
दृष्ट्वाद्भुतं रूपम् उग्रं तवेदं
लोकत्रयं प्रव्यथितं महात्मन् ॥२०॥

dyāvāpṛthivyor idam antaraṁ hi
vyāptaṁ tvayai'kena diśaśca sarvāḥ
dṛṣtvā 'dbhutaṁ rūpam ugraṁ tave'daṁ
lokatrayaṁ pravyathitaṁ mahātman

O Lord, You pervade the entire space between heaven and earth in all directions. Seeing Your marvelous and terrible form, the three worlds are tre mbling with fear. (11.20)

अमी हि त्वां सुरसंघा विशन्ति
केचिद् भीताः प्राञ्जलयो गृणन्ति ।
स्वस्तीत्य् उक्त्वा महर्षिसिद्धसंघाः
स्तुवन्ति त्वां स्तुतिभिः पुष्कलाभिः ॥२१॥

amī hi tvāṁ surasaṁghā viśanti
kecid bhītāḥ prāñjalayo gṛṇanti
svastī'ty uktvā maharṣi sidhasaṁghāḥ
stuvanti tvāṁ stutibhiḥ puṣkalābhiḥ

Hosts of supernatural rulers enter into You. Some with folded hands sing Your names and glories in fear. A multitude of perfected beings hail and adore You with abundant praises. (11.21)

रुद्रादित्या वसवो ये च साध्या
विश्वेऽश्विनौ मरुतश् चोष्मपाश्च ।
गन्धर्वयक्षासुरसिद्धसंघा
वीक्षन्ते त्वां विस्मिताश् चैव सर्वे ॥२२॥

rudrādityā vasavo ye ca sādhyā
viśve 'śvinau marutaś co'ṣmapāś ca
gandharva yakṣāsura siddha saṁghā
vīkṣante tvāṁ vismitāś cai'va sarve

रूपं महत् ते बहुवक्त्रनेत्रं
महाबाहो बहुबाहूरुपादम् ।
बहूदरं बहुदंष्ट्राकरालं
दृष्ट्वा लोकाः प्रव्यथितास् तथाऽहम् ।।२३।।

rūpaṁ mahat te bahu vaktra netraṁ
mahābāho bahu bāhū rupādam
bahūdaraṁ bahu daṁṣṭrākarālaṁ
dṛṣṭvā lokāḥ pravyathitās tathā 'ham

All the celestial beings gaze at You in amazement. Seeing your infinite form with many mouths, eyes, arms, thighs, feet, stomachs, and many fearful tusks, the worlds are trembling with fear, and so do I, O mighty Lord. (11.22-23)

ARJUNA IS FRIGHTENED TO SEE THE COSMIC FORM

नभःस्पृशं दीप्तम् अनेकवर्णं
व्यात्ताननं दीप्तविशालनेत्रम् ।
दृष्ट्वा हि त्वां प्रव्यथितान्तरात्मा
धृतिं न विन्दामि शमं च विष्णो ।।२४।।

nabhaḥ spṛśaṁ dīptam aneka varṇaṁ
vyāttānanaṁ dīpta viśāla netram
dṛṣṭvā hi tvāṁ pravyathitā 'ntarātmā
dhṛtiṁ na vindāmi śamaṁ ca viṣṇo

I am frightened and find neither peace nor courage, O Krishna, after seeing Your effulgent and colorful form touching the sky and Your wide open mouth with large shining eyes. (11.24)

दंष्ट्राकरालानि च ते मुखानि
दृष्ट्वैव कालानलसन्निभानि ।
दिशो न जाने न लभे च शर्म
प्रसीद देवेश जगन्निवास ।।२५।।

daṁṣṭrākarālāni ca te mukhāni
dṛṣṭvai'va kālānala sannibhāni
diśo na jāne na labhe ca śarma
prasīda deveśa jagannivāsa

I lose my sense of direction and find no comfort after seeing Your mouths with fearful tusks glowing like fires of cosmic dissolution. Have mercy on me, O Lord of celestial rulers, and refuge of the universe! (11.25)

अमी च त्वां धृतराष्ट्रस्य पुत्राः
सर्वे सहैवावनिपालसंघैः ।
भीष्मो द्रोणः सूतपुत्रस् तथासौ
सहास्मदीयैर् अपि योधमुख्यैः ।।२६।।

amī ca tvāṁ dhṛtarāṣṭrasya putrāḥ
sarve sahai'vā'vanipālasaṁghaiḥ
bhīṣmo droṇaḥ sūtaputras tathā'sau
sahā'smadīyair api yodhamukhyaiḥ

वक्त्राणि ते त्वरमाणा विशन्ति
दंष्ट्राकरालानि भयानकानि ।
केचिद् विलग्ना दशनान्तरेषु
संदृश्यन्ते चूर्णितैर् उत्तमाङ्गैः ।।२७।।

vaktrāṇi te tvaramāṇā viśanti
daṁṣṭrākarālāni bhayānakāni
kecid vilagnā daśanāntareṣu
saṁdṛśyante cūrṇitair uttamāṅgaiḥ

All my cousin brothers, along with the hosts of other kings and warriors of the other side, together with chief warriors on our side, are also quickly entering into Your fearful mouths with terrible tusks. Some are seen caught in between the tusks with their heads crushed. (11.26-27)

यथा नदीनां बहवोऽम्बुवेगाः
समुद्रम् एवाभिमुखा द्रवन्ति ।
तथा तवामी नरलोकवीरा
विशन्ति वक्त्राण्य् अभिविज्वलन्ति ॥२८॥

yathā nadīnāṁ bahavo 'mbuvegāḥ
samudram evā'bhimukhā dravanti
tathā tavā'mī naralokavīrā
viśanti vaktrāṇy abhivijvalanti

These warriors of the mortal world are entering Your blazing mouths as many torrents of rivers enter into the ocean. (11.28)

यथा प्रदीप्तं ज्वलनं पतङ्गा
विशन्ति नाशाय समृद्धवेगाः ।
तथैव नाशाय विशन्ति लोकास्
तवापि वक्त्राणि समृद्धवेगाः ॥२९॥

yathā pradīptaṁ jvalanaṁ pataṅgā
viśanti nāśāya samṛdhavegāḥ
tathai'va nāśāya viśanti lokās
tavā'pi vaktrāṇi samṛdhavegāḥ

All these people are rapidly rushing into Your mouths for destruction as moths rush with great speed into the blazing flame for destruction. (11.29)

लेलिह्यसे ग्रसमानः समन्ताल्
लोकान् समग्रान् वदनैर् ज्वलद्भिः ।
तेजोभिर् आपूर्य जगत् समग्रं
भासस् तवोग्राः प्रतपन्ति विष्णो ॥३०॥

lelihyase grasamānaḥ samantāl
lokān samagrān vadanair jvaladbhiḥ
tejobhir āpūrya jagat samagraṁ
bhāsas tavo'grāḥ pratapanti viṣṇo

You are licking up all the worlds with Your flaming mouths, swallowing them from all sides. Your powerful radiance is filling the entire universe with effulgence and burning it, O Krishna. (11.30)

आख्याहि मे को भवान् उग्ररूपो
नमोऽस्तु ते देववर प्रसीद ।
विज्ञातुम् इच्छामि भवन्तम् आद्यं
न हि प्रजानामि तव प्रवृत्तिम् ।।३१।।

ākhyāhi me ko bhavān ugrarūpo
namo 'stu te devavara prasīda
vijñātum icchāmi bhavantam ādyaṁ
na hi prajānāmi tava pravṛttim

Tell me, who are You in such a fierce form? My salutations to You, O best of all celestial rulers. Be merciful! I wish to understand You, O primal Being, because I do not know Your mission. (11.31)

LORD DESCRIBES HIS POWERS

श्रीभगवानुवाच
कालोऽस्मि लोकक्षयकृत् प्रवृद्धो
लोकान् समाहर्तुम् इह प्रवृत्तः ।
ऋतेऽपि त्वां न भविष्यन्ति सर्वे
येऽवस्थिताः प्रत्यनीकेषु योधाः ।।३२।।

śrī bhagavān uvāca
kālo 'smi lokakṣayakṛt pravṛdho
lokān samāhartum iha pravṛttaḥ
ṛte 'pi tvāṁ na bhavisyanti sarve
ye 'vasthitāḥ pratyanīkeṣu yodhāḥ

Lord Krishna said: I am death, the mighty destroyer of the world. I have come here to destroy all these people. Even without your participation in the war, all the warriors standing arrayed in the opposing armies shall cease to exist. (11.32)

तस्मात् त्वम् उत्तिष्ठ यशो लभस्व
जित्वा शत्रून् भुङ्क्ष्व राज्यं समृद्धम् ।
मयैवैते निहताः पूर्वम् एव
निमित्तमात्रं भव सव्यसाचिन् ॥३३॥

tasmāt tvam uttiṣṭha yaśo labhasva
jitvā śatrūn bhuṅkṣva rājyaṁ samṛdham
mayai'vai'te nihatāḥ pūrvam eva
nimittamātraṁ bhava savyasācin

Therefore, get up and attain glory. Conquer your enemies, and enjoy a prosperous kingdom. I have already destroyed all these warriors. You are merely My instrument, O Arjuna. (11.33)

This is My battle, not yours. I use you, O Arjuna, only as an instrument. I do everything through your body. One must remember at all times that all battles are His, not ours. The Koran also says: You are but an instrument, and Allah is in charge of all things. (Surah 11.12). The will and power of God do everything. No one can do anything without His power and will. It is God only who makes one restless for material life or spiritual life. Those who are not Self-realized mistakenly take their will as God's will and do wrong things.

द्रोणं च भीष्मं च जयद्रथं च
कर्णं तथान्यान् अपि योधवीरान् ।
मया हतांस् त्वं जहि मा व्यथिष्ठा
युध्यस्व जेतासि रणे सपत्नान् ॥३४॥

droṇaṁ ca bhīṣmaṁ ca jayadrathaṁ ca
karṇaṁ tathā'nyān api yodhavīrān
mayā hatāṁs tvaṁ jahi mā vyathiṣṭhā
yudhyasva jetāsi raṇe sapatnān

Kill all these great warriors, who are already killed by Me. Do not fear. You will certainly conquer the enemies in the battle; therefore, fight! (11.34)

ARJUNA'S PRAYERS TO THE COSMIC FORM

संजय उवाच
एतच् छ्रुत्वा वचनं केशवस्य
कृताञ्जलिर् वेपमानः किरीटी ।
नमस्कृत्वा भूय एवाह कृष्णं
सगद्गदं भीतभीतः प्रणम्य ॥३५॥

saṁjaya uvāca
etac chrutvā vacanaṁ keśavasya
kṛtāñjalir vepamānaḥ kirīṭī
namaskṛtvā bhūya evāha kṛṣṇaṁ
sagadgadaṁ bhītabhītaḥ praṇamya

Sanjaya said: Having heard these words of Krishna, the crowned Arjuna, trembling with folded hands, prostrated with fear, spoke to Krishna in a choked voice. (11.35)

अर्जुन उवाच
स्थाने हृषीकेश तव प्रकीर्त्या
जगत् प्रहृष्यत्य् अनुरज्यते च ।
रक्षांसि भीतानि दिशो द्रवन्ति
सर्वे नमस्यन्ति च सिद्धसंघाः ॥३६॥

arjuna uvāca
sthāne hṛṣikeśa tava prakīrtyā
jagat prahṛṣyaty anurajyate ca
rakṣāṁsi bhītāni diśo dravanti
sarve namasyanti ca siddhasaṁghāḥ

Arjuna said: Rightly, O Krishna, the world delights and rejoices in glorifying You. Terrified demons flee in all directions. The hosts of sages bow to You in adoration. (11.36)

कस्माच् च ते न नमेरन् महात्मन्
गरीयसे ब्रह्मणोऽप्य् आदिकर्त्रे ।
अनन्त देवेश जगन्निवास
त्वम् अक्षरं सद् असत् तत्परं यत् ॥३७॥

kasmāc ca te na nameran mahātman
garīyase brahmaṇo 'py ādikartre
ananta deveśa jagannivāsa
tvam akṣaraṁ sad asat tatparaṁ yat

Why should they not, O great soul, bow to You — the original Creator — who is even greater than Brahmaa, the creator of material worlds? O infinite Lord, O God of all celestial rulers, O abode of the universe, You are both Eternal and Temporal, and the Supreme Being that is beyond Eternal and Temporal. (See also 9.19, and 13.12 for a commentary) (11.37)

त्वम् आदिदेवः पुरुषः पुराणस्
त्वम् अस्य विश्वस्य परं निधानम् ।
वेत्तासि वेद्यं च परं च धाम
त्वया ततं विश्वम् अनन्तरूप ॥३८॥

tvam ādidevaḥ puruṣaḥ purāṇas
tvam asya viśvasya paraṁ nidhānam
vettāsi vedyaṁ ca paraṁ ca dhāma
tvayā tataṁ viśvam anantarūpa

You are the primal God, the most ancient Person. You are the ultimate resort of the entire universe. You are the knower, the object of knowledge, and the Supreme Abode. O Lord of the infinite form, You pervade the entire universe. (11.38)

वायुर् यमोऽग्निर् वरुणः शशाङ्कः
प्रजापतिस् त्वं प्रपितामहश्च ।
नमो नमस्तेऽस्तु सहस्रकृत्वः
पुनश्च भूयोऽपि नमो नमस्ते ॥३९॥

vāyur yamo 'agnir varuṇaḥ śaśāṅkaḥ
prajāpatis tvaṁ prapitāmahaś ca
namo namaste 'stu sahasrakṛtvaḥ
punaśca bhūyo 'pi namo namaste

You are the fire, the wind, the water god, the moon god, the Creator (Brahmā), as well as the father of the Creator (Brahmā), and the controller of death. Salutations to You a thousand times, and again and again salutations to You. (11.39)

नमः पुरस्ताद् अथ पृष्ठतस् ते
नमोऽस्तु ते सर्वत एव सर्व ।
अनन्तवीर्यामितविक्रमस् त्वं
सर्वं समाप्नोषि ततोऽसि सर्वः ॥४०॥

namaḥ purastād atha pṛṣṭhatas te
namo 'stu te sarvata eva sarva
ananta vīryāmita vikramas tvaṁ
sarvaṁ samāpnoṣi tato 'si sarvaḥ

My salutations to You from front and from behind. O Lord, my obeisance to You from all sides. You are infinite valor and boundless might. You pervade everything, and, therefore, You are everywhere and in everything. (11.40)

सखेति मत्वा प्रसभं यद् उक्तं
हे कृष्ण हे यादव हे सखेति ।
अजानता महिमानं तवेदं
मया प्रमादात् प्रणयेन वापि ।।४१।।
sakheti matvā prasabhaṁ yad uktaṁ
he kṛṣṇa he yādava he sakheti
ajānatā mahimānaṁ tave'daṁ
myā pramādāt praṇayena vāpi

Considering You merely as a friend and not knowing Your greatness, I have inadvertently addressed You as O Krishna, O Yadava, and O friend merely out of affection or carelessness. (11.41)

यच् चावहासार्थम् असत्कृतोऽसि
विहारशय्यासनभोजनेषु ।
एकोऽथवाप्य् अच्युत तत्समक्षं
तत् क्षामये त्वाम् अहम् अप्रमेयम् ।।४२।।
yac cā'vahāsārtham asatkṛto 'si
vihāra śayyāsana bhojaneṣu
eko 'thavāpy acyuta tat samakṣaṁ
tat kṣāmaye tvām aham aprameyam

In whatever way I may have insulted You in jokes while playing, reposing in bed, sitting, or at meals; when alone or in front of others, O Krishna, the immeasurable One, I implore You for forgiveness. (11.42)

पितासि लोकस्य चराचरस्य
त्वम् अस्य पूज्यश्च गुरुर् गरीयान् ।
न त्वत्समोऽस्त्य् अभ्यधिकः कुतोऽन्यो
लोकत्रयेऽप्य् अप्रतिमप्रभाव ॥४३॥

pitā'si lokasya carācarasya
tvam asya pūjyaśca gurur garīyān
na tvatsamo 'sty abhyadhikaḥ kuto 'nyo
lokatraye 'py apratima prabhāva

You are the father of this animate and inanimate world and the greatest guru to be worshipped. No one is even equal to You in the three worlds; how can there be one greater than You, O Being of incomparable glory? (11.43)

तस्मात् प्रणम्य प्रणिधाय कायं
प्रसादये त्वाम् अहम् ईशम् ईड्यम् ।
पितेव पुत्रस्य सखेव सख्युः
प्रियः प्रियायार्हसि देव सोढुम् ॥४४॥

tasmāt praṇamya praṇidhāya kāyaṁ
prasādaye tvām aham īśam īḍyam
piteva putrasya sakheva sakhyuḥ
priyaḥ priyāyā'rhasi deva soḍhum

Therefore, O adorable Lord, I seek Your mercy by bowing down and prostrating my body before You. Bear with me as a father to his son, as a friend to a friend, and as a husband to his wife, O Lord. (11.44)

अदृष्टपूर्वं हृषितोऽस्मि दृष्ट्वा
भयेन च प्रव्यथितं मनो मे ।
तद् एव मे दर्शय देव रूपं
प्रसीद देवेश जगन्निवास ॥४५॥

adṛṣṭapūrvaṁ hṛṣito 'smi dṛṣṭvā
bhayena ca pravyathitaṁ mano me
tad eva me darśaya deva rūpaṁ
prasīda deveśa jagannivāsa

Beholding that which has never been seen before delights me, and yet my mind is tormented with fear. Therefore, O God of celestial rulers, the refuge of the universe, have mercy on me and show me your four-armed form. (11.45)

ONE MAY SEE GOD IN ANY FORM OF ONE'S CHOICE

किरीटिनं गदिनं चक्रहस्तम्
इच्छामि त्वां द्रष्टुम् अहं तथैव ।
तेनैव रूपेण चतुर्भुजेन
सहस्रबाहो भव विश्वमूर्ते ॥४६॥

kirītinaṁ gadinaṁ cakrahastam
icchāmi tvāṁ draṣṭum ahaṁ tathai'va
tenai'va rūpeṇa caturbhujena
sahasrabāho bhava viśvamūrte

I wish to see You with a crown, holding mace and discus in Your hand. Therefore, O Lord, with thousand arms and universal form, please appear in the four-armed form. (11.46)

श्रीभगवानुवाच
मया प्रसन्नेन तवार्जुनेदं
रूपं परं दर्शितम् आत्मयोगात् ।
तेजोमयं विश्वम् अनन्तम् आद्यं
यन् मे त्वदन्येन न दृष्टपूर्वम् ॥४७॥

śrī bhagavān uvāca
mayā prasannena tavā'rjune'daṁ
rūpaṁ paraṁ darṣitam ātmayogāt
tejomayaṁ viśvam anantam ādyaṁ
yan me tvadanyena na dṛṣṭapūrvam

Lord Krishna said: O Arjuna, being pleased with you I have shown you, through My own yogic powers, My particular supreme, shining, universal, infinite, and primal form that has never been seen before by anyone other than you. (11.47)

न वेदयज्ञाध्ययनैर् न दानैर्
न च क्रियाभिर् न तपोभिर् उग्रैः ।
एवंरूपः शक्य अहं नृलोके
द्रष्टुं त्वदन्येन कुरुप्रवीर ।।४८।।

na vedayajñādhyayanair na dānair
na ca kriyābhir na tapobhir ugraiḥ
evaṁrūpaḥ śakya ahaṁ nṛloke
draṣṭuṁ tvadanyena kurupravīra

O Arjuna, neither by study of the Vedas nor by sacrifice nor by charity nor by rituals nor by severe austerities can I be seen in this cosmic form by any one other than you in this human world. (11.48)

LORD SHOWS ARJUNA HIS FOUR-ARMED AND THE HUMAN FORM

मा ते व्यथा मा च विमूढभावो
दृष्ट्वा रूपं घोरम् ईदृङ्ममेदम् ।
व्यपेतभीः प्रीतमनाः पुनस् त्वं
तद् एव मे रूपम् इदं प्रपश्य ।।४९।।

mā te vyathā mā ca vimūḍhabhāvo
dṛṣṭvā rūpaṁ ghoram īdṛṅ mame'dam
vyapetabhīḥ prītamanāḥ punas tvaṁ
tad eva me rūpam idaṁ prapaśya

Do not be perturbed and confused by seeing such a terrible form of Mine as this. With fearless and cheerful mind, now behold My four-armed form. (11.49)

संजय उवाच
इत्य् अर्जुनं वासुदेवस् तथोक्त्वा
स्वकं रूपं दर्शयामास भूयः ।
आश्वासयामास च भीतम् एनं
भूत्वा पुनः सौम्यवपुर् महात्मा ।।५०।।
saṁjaya uvāca
ity arjunaṁ vāsudevas tatho'ktvā
svakaṁ rūpaṁ darśayāmāsa bhūyaḥ
āśvāsayāmāsa ca bhītam enaṁ
bhūtvā punaḥ saumyavapur mahātmā

Sanjaya said: After speaking like this to Arjuna, Krishna revealed His four-armed form. And then assuming His pleasant human form, Lord Krishna, the Great One, consoled Arjuna, who was terrified. (11.50)

अर्जुन उवाच
दृष्ट्वेदं मानुषं रूपं तव सौम्यं जनार्दन ।
इदानीम् अस्मि संवृत्तः सचेताः प्रकृतिं गतः ।।५१।।
arjuna uvāca
dṛṣṭve'daṁ mānuṣaṁ rūpaṁ tava saumyaṁ janārdana
idānīm asmi saṁvṛttaḥ sacetāḥ prakṛtiṁ gataḥ

Arjuna said: O Krishna, seeing this lovely human form of Yours, I have now become tranquil and normal again. (11.51)

LORD CAN BE SEEN BY DEVOTIONAL LOVE

श्रीभगवानुवाच
सुदुर्दर्शम् इदं रूपं दृष्टवानसि यन् मम ।
देवा अप्य् अस्य रूपस्य नित्यं दर्शनकाङ्क्षिणः ।।५२।।

śrī bhagavān uvāca
sudurdarśam idaṁ rūpaṁ dṛṣṭavānasi yan mama
devā apy asya rūpasya nityaṁ darśana kāṅkṣiṇaḥ

Lord Krishna said: This four-armed form of Mine that you have seen is very difficult, indeed, to see. Even celestial controllers are ever longing to see this form. (11.52)

नाहं वेदैर् न तपसा न दानेन न चेज्यया ।
शक्य एवंविधो द्रष्टुं दृष्टवानसि मां यथा ।।५३।।

nā'haṁ vedair na tapasā na dānena na ce'jyayā
śakya evaṁvidho draṣṭuṁ dṛṣṭavānasi māṁ yathā

This four-armed form of Mine that you have just seen cannot be seen even by study of the Vedas or by austerity or by acts of charity or by the performance of rituals. (11.53)

No one attains the almighty Lord by good works alone (RV 8.70.03, AV 20.92.18). The omnipresent form of the Lord cannot be perceived by organs, but by the eyes of intuition and faith. The vision and yogic powers are the special gift and grace of God that may be granted, even without asking, when one is found fit by the Lord to use them in His service. According to Saint Ramdas, all visions of lights and forms have to be transcended before realization of the ultimate Truth. Yogic powers may become a hindrance on the path of spiritual journey.

भक्त्या त्व् अनन्यया शक्य अहम् एवंविधोऽर्जुन ।
ज्ञातुं द्रष्टुं च तत्त्वेन प्रवेष्टुं च परंतप ।।५४।।

bhaktyā tv ananyayā śakya aham evaṁvidho'rjuna
jñātuṁ draṣṭuṁ ca tattvena praveṣṭuṁ ca paraṁtapa

However, through single-minded devotion alone, I can be seen in this form, can be known in essence, and also can be reached, O Arjuna. (11.54)

मत्कर्मकृन् मत्परमो मद्भक्तः सङ्गवर्जितः ।
निर्वैरः सर्वभूतेषु यः स माम् एति पाण्डव ॥५५॥
matkarmakṛn matparamo madbhaktaḥ saṅgavarjitaḥ
nirvairaḥ sarvabhūteṣu yaḥ sa mām eti pāṇḍava

One who dedicates all works to Me and to whom I am the supreme goal, who is my devotee, who has no attachment or selfish desires, and who is free from malice toward any creature — reaches Me, O Arjuna. (See also 8.22) (11.55)

ॐ तत्सदिति श्रीमद्भगवद्गीतासूपनिषत्सु ब्रह्मविद्यायां योगशास्त्रे
श्रीकृष्णार्जुनसंवादे विश्वरूपदर्शनयोगो नाम एकादशोऽध्यायः ॥
OM tatsaditi śrīmadbhagavadgītāsūpaniṣatsu brahmavidyāyāṁ
yogaśāstre śrīkṛṣṇārjuna saṁvāde viśvarūpadarśanayogo
nāma ekādaśo'dhyāyaḥ

Thus ends the eleventh chapter named "Vision of the Cosmic Form" of the Upaniṣad of the Bhagavadgītā, the scripture of yoga, dealing with the science of the Absolute in the form of the dialogue between Śrīkṛṣṇa and Arjuna.

अथ द्वादशोऽध्यायः
CHAPTER 12
भक्तियोगः
PATH OF DEVOTION

SHOULD ONE WORSHIP A PERSONAL OR AN IMPERSONAL GOD?

अर्जुन उवाच
एवं सततयुक्ता ये भक्तास् त्वां पर्युपासते ।
ये चाप्य् अक्षरम् अव्यक्तं तेषां के योगवित्तमाः ॥१॥

arjuna uvāca
evaṁ satata yuktā ye bhaktās tvāṁ paryupāsate
ye cāpy akṣaram avyaktaṁ teṣāṁ ke yogavittamāḥ

Arjuna asked: Which of these has the best knowledge of yoga — those ever-steadfast devotees who worship Your personal aspect, or those who worship Your impersonal aspect, the formless Absolute? (12.01)

Lord Krishna explained the superiority of the path of spiritual knowledge in the fourth chapter (4.33, and 4.34). He explained the importance of worship of the formless Supreme (or Self) in verses 5.24-25, 6.24-28, and 8.11-13. He also emphasized the worship of God with form or Krishna in 7.16-18, 9.34, and 11.54-55. It was thus natural for Arjuna to ask which path is better for most people in general.

श्रीभगवानुवाच
मय्य् आवेश्य मनो ये मां नित्ययुक्ता उपासते ।
श्रद्धया परयोपेतास् ते मे युक्ततमा मताः ॥२॥

śrī bhagavān uvāca
mayy āveśya mano ye māṁ nityayuktā upāsate
śraddhayā parayopetās te me yuktatamā matāḥ

Lord Krishna said: I consider the best yogis to be those ever steadfast devotees who worship with supreme faith by fixing their mind on Me as their personal God. (See also 6.47) (12.02)

Devotion is defined as the highest love for God (SBS 02). True devotion is motiveless intense love of God to attain Him (NBS 02). Real devotion is seeking God's grace and serving with love to please Him. Thus, devotion is doing one's duty as an offering to the Lord with love of God in one's heart. It is also said that devotion is granted by the grace of God. A loving relationship with God is easily developed through a personal God. The faithful followers of the path of devotion to the personal God in human form such as Rama, Krishna, Moses, Buddha, Christ, and Muhammad are considered the best. The Bible says: I am the way; no one goes to Father except through me (John 14.06). Some saints consider devotion superior to Self-knowledge (SBS 05).

All spiritual practices are useless in the absence of devotion, the deep love of God. The pearl of Self-knowledge is born on the nucleus of faith and devotion only. Saint Ramanuja said that those who worship the manifest reach their goal sooner and with less difficulty. Love of God and all His creatures is the essence of all religion. Jesus also said: You shall love the Lord with all your heart, with all your soul, and with all your mind; and you shall love everybody as yourself (Matthew 22.37-39).

ये त्व् अक्षरम् अनिर्देश्यम् अव्यक्तं पर्युपासते ।
सर्वत्रगम् अचिन्त्यं च कूटस्थम् अचलं ध्रुवम् ।।३।।

ye tv akṣaram anirdeśyam avyaktaṁ paryupāsate
sarvatragam acintyaṁ ca kūṭastham acalaṁ dhruvam

संनियम्येन्द्रियग्रामं सर्वत्र समबुद्धयः ।
ते प्राप्नुवन्ति माम् एव सर्वभूतहिते रताः ।।४।।

saṁniyamye'ndriyagrāmaṁ sarvatra samabuddhayaḥ
te prāpnuvanti mām eva sarvabhūta hite ratāḥ

They also attain Me who worship the unchangeable, the inexplicable, the invisible, the omnipresent, the inconceivable, the unchanging, the immovable, and the formless — My impersonal aspect — restraining all the senses, even-minded under all circumstances, engaged in the welfare of all creatures. (12.03-04)

A person who is competent to worship the formless aspect of God must have a complete mastery over the senses, be tranquil under all circumstances, and be engaged in the welfare of all creatures. The path of personalism allows one to relish the name, form, and pastimes of the Lord as they happened when He manifested on the earth. The path of impersonalism is dry, full of difficulties, and advancement on this path is very slow as discussed in the next verse.

REASONS FOR WORSHIPPING A PERSONAL FORM OF GOD

क्लेशोऽधिकतरस् तेषाम् अव्यक्तासक्तचेतसाम् ।
अव्यक्ता हि गतिर् दुःखं देहवद्भिर् अवाप्यते ।।५।।

kleśo'dhikataras teṣām avyaktāsaktacetasām
avyaktā hi gatir duḥkhaṁ dehavadbhir avāpyate

Self-realization is more difficult for those who fix their mind on the impersonal, unmanifest, and formless Absolute because comprehension of the unmanifest by embodied beings is attained with great difficulty. (12.05)

One must be free from body-feeling and be established in feeling the existence of the Self alone if one wants to succeed in worship of formless Absolute. One becomes free from the bodily conception of life when one is fully purified and acts solely for the Supreme Lord. Attainment of such a state is not possible for the average human being, but only for advanced souls. Therefore, the natural course for the ordinary seeker is to worship God with a form. Thus the method of worship depends on the individual. One should find out for oneself which method suits one best. It is quite fruitless to ask a child to worship a formless God, whereas a sage sees God in every form and does not need a statue or even a picture of God for worship.

Loving contemplation and deity worship of a personal God is a necessary first step for realization of the impersonal Absolute. It is also said that devotion to the personal aspect of God leads one to the transcendental aspect. God is not only an extra cosmic, all-powerful Being, but the very Self in all beings. The worship of God as a person in the form of one's personal favorite deity stimulates divine love that rouses Self-consciousness and experience of unity in due course of time. God, the transcendent, is revealed in one's pure inner psyche after the loving contemplation of God, the immanent.

There is no real difference between the two paths — the path of devotion to a personal God and the path of Self-knowledge of the impersonal God — in their higher reaches. In the highest stage of realization they merge and become one. Other sages also consider the path of devotion easier for most people, particularly for beginners. According to Tulasidasa, the path of Self-knowledge is difficult to comprehend, to explain, and to follow. It is also very easy to fall down from the path of knowledge or retreat to the lower sensual plane of consciousness (TR 7.118.00). In the next two verses, the Lord says that the path of devotion is not only easier, but also faster than the path of knowledge.

The personal and the impersonal, the physical form and the transcendental form, are the two sides of the coin of ultimate Reality. Ramakrishna said: "Image worship is necessary in the beginning, but not afterwards, just as a scaffolding is necessary during the construction of a building." A person must learn to fix thoughts and mind first on a personal God with a form and then, after succeeding therein, fix them upon the transcendental form. The highest liberation is possible only by realization of God as the very Self in all beings, (BS 4.3.15, ShU 3.07) and it comes only through maturity of devotion to the personal God and His grace. This realization is the second (or spiritual) birth, or the second coming of Christ. Jesus said: The Kingdom of the Father is spread upon the earth, and people do not see. Another great saint said: It is like a fish in the water remaining thirsty and searching for water.

According to ancient scriptures, any spiritual practice becomes more powerful when it is done with knowledge, faith, and contemplation of a personal deity (ChU 1.01.10). Ascetic practice, prayer, charity, penance, performance of sacrifice, vows, and other religious observances fail to evoke Lord's compassion to the same degree as unalloyed devotion does. The magnet of devotion easily attracts the Lord (TR 6.117.00).

ये तु सर्वाणि कर्माणि मयि संन्यस्य मत्पराः ।
अनन्येनैव योगेन मां ध्यायन्त उपासते ॥६॥

ye tu sarvāṇi karmāṇi mayi saṁnyasya matparāḥ
ananyenaiva yogena māṁ dhyāyanta upāsate

तेषाम् अहं समुद्धर्ता मृत्युसंसारसागरात् ।
भवामि नचिरात् पार्थ मय्य् आवेशितचेतसाम् ॥७॥

teṣām ahaṁ samuddhartā mṛtyu saṁsāra sāgarāt
bhavāmi nacirāt pārtha mayy āveśita cetasām

But for those who worship Me with unswerving devotion as their personal God, whose thoughts are set on My personal form, who offer all actions to Me, intent on Me as the Supreme, and meditate on Me — I swiftly become their savior from the world that is the ocean of death and transmigration, O Arjuna. (12.06-07)

One can easily cross the ocean of transmigration with the help of the boat of unswerving love and devotion to a personal God with form (TR 7.122.00). The following verses explain four different methods of worship of God with or without the help of a form of God or deity.

FOUR PATHS TO GOD

People are born different. Anybody who prescribes one method for all is certainly deluded because there is no panacea. A single method or system cannot meet the spiritual needs of all. Hinduism, with its many branches and sub-branches, offers a very wide choice of spiritual practices to suit persons in any stage of spiritual development. All paths lead to salvation because they all culminate in devotion — the intense love of God.

मय्येव मन आधत्स्व मयि बुद्धिं निवेशय ।
निवसिष्यसि मय्येव अत ऊर्ध्वं न संशयः ॥८॥

mayyeva mana ādhatsva mayi buddhiṁ niveśaya
nivasiṣyasi mayyeva ata ūrdhvaṁ na saṁśayaḥ

Therefore, focus your mind on Me and let your intellect dwell upon Me alone through meditation and contemplation. Thereafter, you shall certainly attain Me. (12.08)

This is the path of meditation (See Chapter 6 for more details) for the contemplative mind. Thinking of a chosen form of God all the time is different from worshipping that form, but both practices are the same in quality and effect. In other words, contemplation is also a form of worship.

अथ चित्तं समाधातुं न शक्नोषि मयि स्थिरम् ।
अभ्यासयोगेन ततो माम् इच्छाप्तुं धनंजय ॥९॥

atha cittaṁ samādhātuṁ na śaknoṣi mayi sthiram
abhyāsa yogena tato mām icchāptuṁ dhanaṁjaya

If you are unable to focus your mind steadily on Me, then long to attain Me by practice of any other spiritual discipline, such as a ritual, or deity worship that suits you. (12.09)

This is the path of ritual, prayer, and devotional worship recommended for people who are emotional, have more faith but less reasoning and intellect (See also 9.32). Constantly contemplate and concentrate your mind on God, using symbols or mental pictures of a personal God as an aid to develop devotion.

अभ्यासेऽप्य् असमर्थोऽसि मत्कर्मपरमो भव ।
मदर्थम् अपि कर्माणि कुर्वन् सिद्धिम् अवाप्स्यसि ॥१०॥

abhyāse'py asamartho'si matkarmaparamo bhava
madartham api karmāṇi kurvan siddhim avāpsyasi

If you are unable even to do any spiritual discipline, then dedicate all your work to Me, or do your duty just for Me. You shall attain perfection by doing your prescribed duty for Me — without any selfish motive — just as an instrument to serve and please Me. (12.10)

This is the path of transcendental knowledge or renunciation, acquired through contemplation and scriptural study for people who have realized the truth that we are only divine instruments. (See also 9.27, 18.46). Lord Himself guides every endeavor of the person who works for the good of humanity, and success comes to a person who dedicates his or her life to the service of God.

अथैतद् अप्य् अशक्तोऽसि कर्तुं मद्योगम् आश्रितः ।
सर्वकर्मफलत्यागं ततः कुरु यतात्मवान् ॥११॥

athaitad apy aśakto'si kartuṁ madyogam āśritaḥ
sarva karmaphala tyāgaṁ tataḥ kuru yatātmavān

If you are unable to dedicate your work to Me, then just surrender unto My will and renounce the attachment to, and the anxiety for, the fruits of all work by learning to accept all results with equanimity as God's grace. (12.11)

This is the path of KarmaYoga, the selfless service to humanity, discussed in Chapter 3, for householders who cannot renounce worldly activity and work full-time for God, as discussed in verse 12.10, above. The main thrust of verses 12.08-11 is that one must establish some relationship with the Lord — such as the progenitor, father, mother, beloved, child, savior, guru, master, helper, guest, friend, and even an enemy.

KarmaYoga, or the renunciation of the selfish attachment to fruits of work, is not a method of last resort — as it may appear from verse 12.11. It is explained in the following verse.

KARMA-YOGA IS THE BEST WAY TO START WITH

श्रेयो हि ज्ञानम् अभ्यासाज् ज्ञानाद् ध्यानं विशिष्यते ।
ध्यानात् कर्मफलत्यागस् त्यागाच् छान्तिर् अनन्तरम् ॥१२॥

śreyo hī jñānam abhyāsāj jñānād dhyānaṁ viśiṣyate
dhyānāt karmaphala tyāgas tyāgāc chāntir anantaram

The transcendental knowledge of scriptures is better than mere ritualistic practice; meditation is better than scriptural knowledge; renunciation of selfish attachment to the fruits of work (KarmaYoga) is better than meditation because peace immediately follows renunciation of selfish motives. (See more on renunciation in 18.02, and 18.09) (12.12)

When one's knowledge of God increases, all Karma is gradually eliminated because one who is situated in knowledge thinks he or she is not the doer but an instrument working at the pleasure of the creator. Such an action in God-consciousness becomes devotion — free from any Karmic bondage. Thus, there is no sharp demarcation between the paths of selfless service, spiritual knowledge, and devotion.

THE ATTRIBUTES OF A DEVOTEE

अद्वेष्टा सर्वभूतानां मैत्रः करुण एव च ।
निर्ममो निरहंकारः समदुःखसुखः क्षमी ।।१३।।

advesṭā sarva bhūtānāṁ maitraḥ karuṇa eva ca
nirmamo nirahaṁkāraḥ samaduḥkhasukhaḥ kṣamī

संतुष्टः सततं योगी यतात्मा दृढनिश्चयः ।
मय्य् अर्पितमनोबुद्धिर् यो मद्भक्तः स मे प्रियः ।।१४।।

saṁtuṣṭaḥ satataṁ yogī yatātmā dṛḍhaniścayaḥ
mayy arpita manobuddhir yo madbhaktaḥ sa me priyaḥ

One is dear to Me who does not hate any creature, who is friendly and compassionate, who is free from the notion of 'I' and 'my', who is even-minded in pain and pleasure, who is forgiving, who is ever content, who has subdued the mind, whose resolve is firm, whose mind and intellect are engaged in dwelling upon Me, and who is devoted to Me. (12.13-14)

To attain oneness with God, one has to become perfect like Him by cultivating moral virtues. The Bible also says: Try to perfect yourself, just as your Father in the heaven is perfect (Matthew 5.48). Saint Tulasidasa said: O Lord, anyone on whom You shower Your favor becomes an ocean of perfection. The monstrous squad of lust, anger, greed, infatuation, and pride haunts the mind so long as the Lord does not abide in the inner psyche. Virtues and discipline are two sure means of devotion. A list of forty (40) virtues and values is given in verses 12.13-12.19 by describing the qualities of an ideal devotee, or a Self-realized person. All these noble qualities become manifest in a devotee.

यस्मान् नोद्विजते लोको लोकान् नोद्विजते च यः ।
हर्षामर्षभयोद्वेगैर् मुक्तो यः स च मे प्रियः ।।१५।।

yasmān nodvijate loko lokān nodvijate ca yaḥ
harṣāmarṣabhayodvegair mukto yaḥ sa ca me priyaḥ

One is also dear to Me who does not agitate others and who is not agitated by them, who is free from joy, envy, fear, and anxiety. (12.15)

अनपेक्षः शुचिर् दक्ष उदासीनो गतव्यथः ।
सर्वारम्भपरित्यागी यो मद्भक्तः स मे प्रियः ॥१६॥
anapekṣaḥ śucir dakṣa udāsīno gatavyathaḥ
sarvārambha parityāgī yo madbhaktaḥ sa me priyaḥ

One who is desireless, pure, wise, impartial, and free from anxiety; who has renounced the doership in all undertakings — such a devotee is dear to Me. (12.16)

यो न हृष्यति न द्वेष्टि न शोचति न काङ्क्षति ।
शुभाशुभपरित्यागी भक्तिमान् यः स मे प्रियः ॥१७॥
yo na hṛṣyati na dveṣṭi na śocati na kāṅkṣati
śubhāśubha parityāgī bhaktimān yaḥ sa me priyaḥ

One who neither rejoices nor grieves, neither likes nor dislikes, has renounced both the good and the evil, and is full of devotion — is also dear to Me. (12.17)

समः शत्रौ च मित्रे च तथा मानापमानयोः ।
शीतोष्णसुखदुःखेषु समः सङ्गविवर्जितः ॥१८॥
samaḥ śatrau ca mitre ca tathā mānāpamānayoḥ
śītoṣṇa sukha duḥkheṣu samaḥ saṅgavivarjitaḥ

तुल्यनिन्दास्तुतिर् मौनी संतुष्टो येन केनचित् ।
अनिकेतः स्थिरमतिर् भक्तिमान् मे प्रियो नरः ॥१९॥
tulya nindā stutir maunī saṁtuṣṭo yena kenacit
aniketaḥ sthiramatir bhaktimān me priyo naraḥ

One who remains the same towards friend or foe, in honor or disgrace, in heat or cold, in pleasure or pain; who is free from attachment; who is indifferent to censure or praise;

who is quiet, and content with whatever one has, unattached to a place, a country, or a house; who is tranquil, and full of devotion — that person is dear to Me. (12.18-19)

It is said that divine Controllers with their exalted qualities, such as the knowledge of God, wisdom, renunciation, detachment, and equanimity, always reside in the inner psyche of a pure devotee. Thus, perfect devotees who have renounced affinity for the world and its objects and have love for God are rewarded by the Lord with divine qualities discussed above and elsewhere in the Gita, and are dear to the Lord. But what about those who are imperfect, but trying sincerely for perfection? The answer comes in the next verse.

ONE SHOULD SINCERELY STRIVE TO DEVELOP DIVINE QUALITIES

ये तु धर्म्यामृतम् इदं यथोक्तं पर्युपासते ।
श्रद्दधाना मत्परमा भक्तास् तेऽतीव मे प्रियाः ।।२०।।

ye tu dharmyāmṛtam idaṁ yathoktaṁ paryupāsate
śraddadhānā matparamā bhaktās te'tīva me priyāḥ

But those faithful devotees are very dear to Me who set Me as their supreme goal and follow — or just sincerely strive to develop — the above mentioned nectar of (forty) moral values. (12.20)

One may not have all the virtues, but a sincere effort to develop virtues is most appreciated by the Lord. Thus the striver is very dear to the Lord. The upper-class devotees do not desire anything, including salvation from the Lord, except for one boon: devotion to the lotus feet of a personal God, birth after birth (TR 2.204.00). Lower class devotees use God as a servant to fulfill their material demands and desires. The development of unswerving love and devotion to the lotus feet of the Lord is the ultimate aim of all spiritual discipline and meritorious deeds, as well as the goal of human birth. A true devotee considers oneself the servant, the Lord as the master, and the entire creation as His body.

The path of devotion is a better path for most people, but devotion does not develop without a combination of personal effort, faith, and the grace of God. Nine techniques for cultivating devotion — an intense love for God as a personal Being — based on Tulasi Ramayana (TR 3.34.04-3.35.03), are: (1) The company of the holy and wise, (2) Hearing and reading the glories and stories of Lord's incarnations and His activities of creation, preservation and dissolution as given in the religious scriptures, (3) Seva or serving God through service to the needy, the saints, and society, (4) Congregational chanting and singing of the glories of God, (5) Repeating the Lord's name and mantra with firm faith, (6) Discipline, control over the six senses, and detachment, (7) Seeing your personal God everywhere and in everything, (8) Contentment and lack of greed as well as overlooking others' faults, and (9) Simplicity, lack of anger, jealousy, and hatred. The best thing a person should do is develop love of God. Lord Rama said that one needs to follow any one of the above methods with faith to develop love of God and become a devotee.

Good company of saints and sages is a very powerful tool for God-realization. It is said that friendship, discussions, dealings, and marriage should be with equals or those who are better than oneself, not with persons of lower level of intellect (MB 5.13.117). A person is known by the company he or she keeps. According to most saints and sages, the path of devotion is very simple and easy to perform. One can begin by simply chanting a personal mantra or any holy name of God. There is no restriction on the correct time or place for chanting the holy name of God. The process of devotional service consists of one or more of the following practices: hearing discourses, chanting the holy name of God, remembering and contemplating God, worshipping Him, praying to Him, serving God and humanity, and surrendering to His will.

The four inter-connected paths of yoga discussed in the first twelve chapters of the Gita may be summarized as follows:

The practice of KarmaYoga leads to purification of the mind from the stain of selfishness that paves the way for knowledge of God to be revealed. Knowledge develops into devotional love of God. Constant thinking of God, the object of our love due to devotion, is called meditation and contemplation that eventually lead to enlightenment and salvation.

IS THERE ONLY ONE RIGHT WAY TO GOD?

Lord Krishna has been talking about both manifest and unmanifest aspects of God in the previous chapters. Arjuna's question has been answered in great detail in this chapter, but people still argue that one method of worship or certain religious practices are better than others. Such persons only understand half the truth. In our opinion, it is quite clear that the method of worship depends on the nature of the individual. The person or the person's guru should find out which path will be most suitable for the individual, depending on the person's temperament. To force his or her own method of worship on people is the greatest disservice a guru can do to disciples. Introverts should worship a personal God, whereas extroverts may contemplate the impersonal aspect. The important thing is to develop faith in and love of God. God has the power to manifest before a devotee in any form, regardless of the devotee's chosen form of worship.

What has worked for one may not work for all, so what makes you think your method is universal? There was no need for the Lord to discuss different paths of yoga if there was one path for all. If the chosen path of spiritual discipline does not give one peace or God-realization, then it must be understood that one is not practicing correctly or the path is not right for the individual.

ॐ तत्सदिति श्रीमद्भगवद्गीतासूपनिषत्सु ब्रह्मविद्यायां योगशास्त्रे
श्रीकृष्णार्जुनसंवादे भक्तियोगो नाम द्वादशोऽध्यायः ॥

OM tatsaditi śrīmadbhagavadgītāsūpaniṣatsu brahmavidyāyāṁ
yogaśāstre śrīkṛṣṇārjuna saṁvāde bkaktiyogo
nāma dvādaśo'dhyāyaḥ

Thus ends the twelfth chapter named "Path of Devotion" of the
Upaniṣad of the Bhagavadgītā, the scripture of yoga,
dealing with the science of the Absolute in the
form of the dialogue between
Śrīkṛṣṇa and Arjuna.

अथ त्रयोदशोऽध्यायः

CHAPTER 13

क्षेत्रक्षेत्रज्ञविभागयोगः

CREATION AND THE CREATOR

THEORY OF CREATION

श्रीभगवानुवाच
इदं शरीरं कौन्तेय क्षेत्रम् इत्य् अभिधीयते ।
एतद् यो वेत्ति तं प्राहुः क्षेत्रज्ञ इति तद्विदः ॥१॥
śrī bhagavān uvāca
idaṁ śarīraṁ kaunteya kṣetram ity abhidhīyate
etad yo vetti taṁ prāhuḥ kṣetrajña iti tadvidaḥ

Lord Krishna said: O Arjuna, this physical body, the miniature universe, may be called the field or creation. One who knows the creation is called the Creator (or the Spirit, Atma, God, Ishvara) by the seers of truth. (13.01)

Whatever is here in the body is also there in the cosmos; whatever is there, the same is here (KaU 4.10). The human body, the microcosm, is a replica of the universe, the macrocosm. The body is called the field of activities for the soul. The body or creation is different from the soul or the Creator. To experience this difference is the metaphysical knowledge.

क्षेत्रज्ञं चापि मां विद्धि सर्वक्षेत्रेषु भारत ।
क्षेत्रक्षेत्रज्ञयोर् ज्ञानं यत् तज् ज्ञानं मतं मम ॥२॥
kṣetrajñaṁ cā'pi māṁ viddhi sarvakṣetreṣu bhārata
kṣetra kṣetrajñayor jñānaṁ yat taj jñānaṁ mataṁ mama

O Arjuna, know Me to be the Creator of all the creation. I consider the true understanding of both the Creator and the creation to be transcendental knowledge. (13.02)

The body (or creation) and Spirit (or the Creator) are distinct from one another. Yet, the ignorant are not able to distinguish between them. That knowledge is the true knowledge by which one is able to make a clear distinction between body and Spirit. Body is called the field (or the medium) of activities for the Spirit. The human body is the medium by which the individual soul enjoys the material world, gets entangled, and in the end attains liberation. The soul inside the body knows all the activities of its own body; it is, therefore, called the knower of the field of activities. The Supersoul knows all the bodies, whereas the individual soul knows only his own body. When one clearly understands the difference between the body, the individual soul inside the body, and the Supersoul, one is said to have real knowledge.

तत् क्षेत्रं यच् च यादृक् च यद्विकारि यतश्च यत् ।
स च यो यत्प्रभावश्च तत् समासेन मे शृणु ॥३॥

tat kṣetraṁ yac ca yādṛk ca yadvikāri yataśca yat
sa ca yo yat prabhāvaśca tat samāsena me śṛṇu

What creation is, what it is like, what its transformations are, where the source of creation is, who that Creator is, and what His powers are— hear all these from Me in brief. (13.03)

ऋषिभिर् बहुधा गीतं छन्दोभिर् विविधैः पृथक् ।
ब्रह्मसूत्रपदैश्चैव हेतुमद्भिर् विनिश्चितैः ॥४॥

ṛṣibhir bahudhā gītaṁ chandobhir vividhaiḥ pṛthak
brahmasūtrapadaiś cai'va hetumadbhir viniścitaiḥ

The seers have separately described the creation and the Creator in different ways in the Vedic hymns and also in the conclusive and convincing verses of other scriptures. (13.04)

The Gita also expounds on the truths of other scriptures. All scriptures, as well as saints and sages of all religions, draw the water of truth from the same ocean of Spirit. Their accent varies with the need of the individual and the society at the time.

महाभूतान्य् अहंकारो बुद्धिर् अव्यक्तम् एव च ।
इन्द्रियाणि दशैकं च पञ्च चेन्द्रियगोचराः ॥५॥

mahābhūtāny ahaṁkāro buddhir avyaktam eva ca
indriyāṇi daśai'kaṁ ca pañca ce'ndriyagocarāḥ

इच्छा द्वेषः सुखं दुःखं संघातश्चेतना धृतिः ।
एतत् क्षेत्रं समासेन सविकारम् उदाहृतम् ॥६॥

icchā dveṣaḥ sukhaṁ duḥkhaṁ saṁghātaś cetanā dhṛtiḥ
etat kṣetraṁ samāsena savikāram udāhṛtam

The primary material Nature, the cosmic intellect, 'I' consciousness or ego, five basic elements, ten organs, mind, five sense objects, and desire, hatred, pleasure, pain, the physical body, consciousness, and resolve — thus the entire field has been briefly described with its transformations. (See also 7.04) (13.05-06)

According to Sankhya doctrine (BP 3.26.10-18, 11.22.10-16), Spirit undergoes twenty-five basic transformations in the following order: Spiritual Being (Purusha, Chetanā, Ishvara) and the following twenty-four transformations of Total Energy (Prakriti, Mahat): Mind, Intellect, Consciousness (Chitta), and the conception of individuality (ego); the five basic elements, or raw ingredients, in subtle and gross form (ether or subtle substance, air, fire, water, and earth); the five sense objects (sound, touch, sight, taste, and smell); the five sense organs (ear, skin, eye, tongue, and nose); and the five organs of action (mouth, hand, leg, anus, and urethra).

The Supreme Intellect is known by various names, based on functions performed in the body. It is called mind when it feels and thinks, intellect when it reasons, thought waves (Chitta Vriti) when it does the act of remembering and wandering from one thought to another, and ego when it has the feeling of doership and individuality. The subtle senses consist of all four — mind, intellect, thought waves, and ego. It is the Karmic footprints that actually make the final decision with the help of mind and intellect. When the cosmic power does the functions of the body, it is called the bioimpulse (Vital life forces, Prāna). The Supreme Spirit or Consciousness manifests Itself as both energy and matter. Matter and energy are nothing but condensed forms of Consciousness. According to Einstein, mind and matter are both energies (Prāna). Ramana Maharshi said: The mind is a form of energy. It manifests itself as the world.

THE FOURFOLD NOBLE TRUTH AS MEANS OF NIRVANA

अमानित्वम् अदम्भित्वम् अहिंसा क्षान्तिर् आर्जवम् ।
आचार्योपासनं शौचं स्थैर्यम् आत्मविनिग्रहः ॥७॥

amānitvam adambhitvam ahiṁsā kṣāntir ārjavam
ācāryopāsanaṁ śaucaṁ sthairyam ātmavinigrahaḥ

इन्द्रियार्थेषु वैराग्यम् अनहंकार एव च ।
जन्ममृत्युजराव्याधि-दुःखदोषानुदर्शनम् ॥८॥

indriyārtheṣu vairāgyam anahaṁkāra eva ca
janma mṛtyu jarā vyādhi-duḥkha doṣānudarśanam

Humility, modesty, nonviolence, forgiveness, honesty, service to guru, purity of thought, word, and deed, steadfastness, self-control, aversion for sense objects, absence of ego, constant reflection on the pain and suffering inherent in birth, old age, disease, and death; (13.07-08)

Verse 13.08 of the Gita formed the foundation of Buddhism. The constant contemplation and understanding of agony and suffering inherent in birth, old age, disease, and death are called the understanding of the Fourfold Noble Truth in Buddhism. A clear understanding of this truth is necessary before starting the spiritual journey. A disgust and discontent for the meaninglessness and unreality of the world and its objects become a necessary prelude to the spiritual journey. As birds seek the shelter of a tree when tired, similarly, human beings seek the divine shelter after discovering the frustrations and joylessness of material existence.

असक्तिर् अनभिष्वङ्गः पुत्रदारगृहादिषु ।
नित्यं च समचित्तत्वम् इष्टानिष्टोपपत्तिषु ।।९।।

asaktir anabhiṣvaṅgaḥ putra dāra gṛhādiṣu
nityaṁ ca samacittatvam iṣṭā'niṣṭopapattiṣu

मयि चानन्ययोगेन भक्तिर् अव्यभिचारिणी ।
विविक्तदेशसेवित्वम् अरतिर् जनसंसदि ।।१०।।

mayi cā'nanyayogena bhaktir avyabhicāriṇī
vivikta deśa sevitvam aratir janasaṁsadi

अध्यात्मज्ञाननित्यत्वं तत्त्वज्ञानार्थदर्शनम् ।
एतज् ज्ञानम् इति प्रोक्तम् अज्ञानं यद् अतोऽन्यथा ।।११।।

adhyātma jñāna nityatvaṁ tattva jñānārtha darśanam
etaj jñānam iti proktam ajñānaṁ yad ato'nyathā

Detachment with family members, home, etc.; unfailing equanimity upon attainment of the desirable and the undesirable and unswerving devotion to Me through single-minded contemplation; taste for solitude; distaste for social gatherings and gossips; steadfastness in acquiring the knowledge of the Self; and seeing the omnipresent Supreme Being everywhere — this is said to be knowledge. That which is contrary to this is ignorance. (13.09-11)

Cultivating the virtues described in verses 13.07-11 will enable one to perceive the body as different from the Self. Thus, one will attain Self-knowledge. Therefore, these virtues are called knowledge. Those who do not possess these virtues cannot get the true knowledge of the Self and will remain in the darkness of body-consciousness or ignorance.

When one becomes firmly convinced that God alone is everything — father, mother, brother, friend, enemy, sustainer, destroyer, and refuge — and there is nothing higher than Him to attain, and one has no thought of any other object, one is said to have developed unswerving devotion to the Lord through single-minded contemplation. In this state of mind, the seeker and the sought-after become qualitatively one and the same.

THE SUPREME CAN BE DESCRIBED BY PARABLES, AND NOT IN ANY OTHER WAY

ज्ञेयं यत् तत् प्रवक्ष्यामि यज् ज्ञात्वाऽमृतम् अश्नुते ।
अनादिमत् परं ब्रह्म न सत् तन् नासद् उच्यते ॥१२॥
jñeyaṁ yat tat pravakṣyāmi yaj jñātvā'mṛtam aśnute
anādimat paraṁ brahma na sat tan nā'sad ucyate

I shall fully describe the Supreme Being — the object of knowledge. By knowing this one attains immortality. The beginningless Supreme Being is said to be neither eternal nor temporal. (See also 9.19, 11.37, and 15.18) (13.12)

In the beginning there was neither Eternal Being (Sat, Brahma) nor temporal (Asat, Divine Beings, Devas) — no sky, no air, neither day nor night. There was nothing whatsoever other than the Absolute Supreme Being (RV 10.129.01, AiU 1.01). The Absolute is beyond both Divine Beings (celestial controllers, Devas) and the Eternal Being (Spirit) (Verse 15.18). Therefore, He is neither temporal nor eternal. The Supreme Being or the Absolute is also both temporal and eternal (Verse 9.19) and beyond temporal and eternal (Verses 11.37, 15.18) because He is everywhere, in everything, and also beyond everything. Therefore, the Absolute is all three — neither temporal nor eternal, beyond both temporal and eternal, as well as both temporal and eternal — at the same time.

सर्वतःपाणिपादं तत् सर्वतोऽक्षिशिरोमुखम् ।
सर्वतःश्रुतिमल् लोके सर्वम् आवृत्य तिष्ठति ॥१३॥

sarvataḥ pāṇipādaṁ tat sarvato'kṣiśiromukham
sarvataḥ śrutimal loke sarvam āvṛtya tiṣṭhati

The Supreme Being has His hands, feet, eyes, head, mouth, and ears everywhere because He is all-pervading and omnipresent. (13.13)

सर्वेन्द्रियगुणाभासं सर्वेन्द्रियविवर्जितम् ।
असक्तं सर्वभृच् चैव निर्गुणं गुणभोक्तृ च ॥१४॥
sarvendriya guṇābhāsaṁ sarvendriya vivarjitam
asaktaṁ sarvabhṛc cai'va nirguṇaṁ guṇabhoktṛ ca

He is the perceiver of all sense objects without the physical sense organs; unattached, and yet the sustainer of all; devoid of the three modes of material Nature, and yet the enjoyer of the modes of material Nature by becoming the living entity. (13.14)

Self walks without legs, hears without ears, performs many actions without hands, smells without a nose, sees without eyes, speaks without a mouth, and enjoys all tastes without a tongue. All His actions are so marvelous that one finds His greatness utterly beyond description (TR 1.117.03-04). The Supreme Being may be described only by parables and paradoxes and in no other way. (See also ShU 3.19). Self expands Himself as the living entity to enjoy three modes of material Nature.

God does not possess a body like an ordinary being. All His senses are transcendental, or out of this world. His potencies are multifarious. Any one of His senses can perform the action of any other sense. All His deeds are automatically performed as a natural consequence.

बहिर् अन्तश्च भूतानाम् अचरं चरम् एव च ।
सूक्ष्मत्वात् तद् अविज्ञेयं दूरस्थं चान्तिके च तत् ॥१५॥
bahir antaśca bhūtānām acaraṁ caram eva ca
sūkṣmatvāt tad avijñeyaṁ dūrasthaṁ cā'ntike ca tat

He is inside as well as outside all beings, animate and inanimate. He is incomprehensible because of His subtlety. And because of His omnipresence, He is very near — residing in one's inner psyche — as well as far away in the Supreme Abode. (13.15)

अविभक्तं च भूतेषु विभक्तम् इव च स्थितम् ।
भूतभर्तृ च तज् ज्ञेयं ग्रसिष्णु प्रभविष्णु च ॥१६॥
avibhaktaṁ ca bhūteṣu vibhaktam iva ca sthitam
bhūta bhartṛ ca taj jñeyaṁ grasiṣṇu prabhaviṣṇu ca

He is undivided, yet appears to exist as if divided in living beings. He is the object of knowledge and appears as the Creator (Brahmā), Sustainer (Vishnu), and Destroyer (Shankara) of all beings. (See also 11.13, and 18.20) (13.16)

One planet earth appears divided into so many countries; one country appears divided into several states; one state appears divided into counties, and so on; similarly, one Reality appears as many. These are apparent divisions because they have the same order of reality. The term God is used for the Generator, Operator, and Destroyer aspects of Self.

ज्योतिषाम् अपि तज् ज्योतिस् तमसः परम् उच्यते ।
ज्ञानं ज्ञेयं ज्ञानगम्यं हृदि सर्वस्य विष्ठितम् ॥१७॥
jyotiṣām api taj jyotis tamasaḥ param ucyate
jñānaṁ jñeyaṁ jñānagamyaṁ hṛdi sarvasya viṣṭhitam

The Supreme Being is the source of all lights. He is said to be beyond darkness of ignorance. He is Self-knowledge, the object of Self-knowledge, and seated in the inner psyche as consciousness (or Ishvara in verse 18.61) of all beings, He is to be realized by Self-knowledge. (13.17)

I am the light of knowledge of the world. Whoever follows me will have the light of life and will never walk in the darkness of ignorance (John 8.12). One who knows the Almighty as much more radiant than the sun and beyond the darkness of material reality, transcends death. There is no other way (YV 31.18, SV 3.08). The Supreme is beyond the reach of senses and mind. It cannot be described or defined by words. Different means of attaining the Supreme continue below:

इति क्षेत्रं तथा ज्ञानं ज्ञेयं चोक्तं समासतः ।
मद्भक्त एतद् विज्ञाय मद्भावायोपपद्यते ।।१८।।
iti kṣetraṁ tathā jñānaṁ jñeyaṁ co'ktaṁ samāsataḥ
madbhakta etad vijñāya madbhāvāyo'papadyate

Thus, I have briefly described creation, as well as Self-knowledge and the object of Self-knowledge. Understanding this, My devotee attains My Supreme Abode. (13.18)

SUPREME SPIRIT, SPIRIT, MATERIAL NATURE, AND THE INDIVIDUAL SOULS

प्रकृतिं पुरुषं चैव विद्ध्य् अनादी उभाव् अपि ।
विकारांश्च गुणांश्चैव विद्धि प्रकृतिसंभवान् ।।१९।।
prakṛtiṁ puruṣaṁ caiva viddhy anādī ubhāv api
vikārāṁśca guṇāṁś caiva viddhi prakṛtisaṁbhavān

कार्यकरणकर्तृत्वे हेतुः प्रकृतिर् उच्यते ।
पुरुषः सुखदुःखानां भोक्तृत्वे हेतुर् उच्यते ।।२०।।
kārya karaṇa kartṛtve hetuḥ prakṛtir ucyate
puruṣaḥ sukhaduḥkhānāṁ bhoktṛtve hetur ucyate

Know that both the material Nature and the Spiritual Being are beginningless. All manifestations and three dispositions of mind and matter, called modes or Gunas, are born of material Nature. Material Nature is said to be the cause of production of the physical body and organs

of perception and action. Spirit (or Consciousness) in the individual soul is said to be the cause of experiencing pleasure and pain. (13.19-20)

पुरुषः प्रकृतिस्थो हि भुङ्क्ते प्रकृतिजान् गुणान् ।
कारणं गुणसङ्गोऽस्य सदसद्योनिजन्मसु ॥२१॥

puruṣaḥ prakṛtistho hi bhuṅkte prakṛtijān guṇān
kāraṇaṁ guṇa saṅgo'sya sad asad yoni janmasu

Spiritual Being (by becoming jeeva) enjoys three modes of material Nature by associating with the material Nature. Attachment to the three modes of material Nature (due to ignorance caused by previous Karma) is the cause of birth of the living entity in good and evil wombs. (13.21)

Spirit is unaffected by material Nature just as the sun's reflection in water is unaffected by the properties of water. Spirit, because of His nature, associates with the six sensory faculties and ego of material Nature and becomes attached, forgets His real nature, performs good and evil deeds, loses independence, and transmigrates as a living entity (individual soul, Jiva) (BP 3.27.01-03). The living entity does not know the divine illusory energy (Maya), as well as the supreme controller and its own real nature. The individual soul is a reflection of the sun of Spirit in the water pot of human body.

उपद्रष्टानुमन्ता च भर्ता भोक्ता महेश्वरः ।
परमात्मेति चाप्य् उक्तो देहेऽस्मिन् पुरुषः परः ॥२२॥

upadraṣṭā'numantā ca bhartā bhoktā maheśvaraḥ
paramātmeti cāpy ukto dehe'smin puruṣaḥ paraḥ

The Spirit in the body is the witness, the guide, the supporter, the enjoyer, the controller of all events, and also the Supreme Self. (13.22)

Two aspects of Eternal Being — the divine Controller and the controlled (living entity, individual soul) — make their nest and reside on the same tree (the inner psyche of the body) as a part of the cosmic drama. Virtue and vice are its glorious flowers; pains and pleasures of sense gratification are its sweet and sour fruits. The living entities are like beautiful birds of various hues. No two birds are the same. Creation is just beautiful. And the Creator must be inconceivably beautiful. The living entity, due to ignorance, becomes captivated by the fruits of the tree and gets attached to material Nature, eats these fruits and becomes subject to bondage and liberation, whereas the divine controller sits on the tree, watches, and guides the living entity. The divine Controller, being unattached to material Nature, remains free as a witness and a guide (BP 11.11.06, See also RV 1.164.20, AV 9.09.20, MuU 3.01.01, ShU 4.06). The divine Controller remains unaffected and unattached to the modes of material Nature just as a lotus leaf remains unaffected by water.

Spirit is sentient, and material Nature is insentient. Material Nature, with the help of Spirit, produces five bioimpulses (Life forces, Prana) and the three modes. Spirit, residing as the divine Controller in the physical body that is a house with nine gates and made of twenty-four elements of material Nature, enjoys sense objects by associating with the modes of material Nature. Spirit forgets its real nature under the influence of divine illusory energy (Maya), feels pain and pleasure, does good and evil deeds, incurs the bondage of works done by free will due to ignorance, and seeks salvation. When the living entity renounces sense objects and rises above the modes of material Nature, it attains salvation.

The mind, endowed with infinite power, creates a body to reside in and fulfill its latent desires. The living entity becomes willingly entangled — and suffers like a silkworm entangled in its own cocoon — and it cannot get out. The living entity becomes bound by its own Karma and transmigrates. All actions, good or bad, produce bondage if performed with ego. Good actions are the golden shackles, and bad ones are the iron shackles. Both are fetters. The golden shackle is not a bracelet.

The living entity is like a farmer who has been given a plot of land that is the body. The farmer should take the weeds of lust, anger, and greed out of the land, cultivate it with the plow of intense desire for the love of God, and fertilize it with the firm faith in the power and omnipresence of God. Depending on the intensity of the desire and the degree of faith, the seedling of devotion will come out in due course of time. This seedling must be consistently and continually irrigated with the water of meditation on the chosen form of one's personal God. The forgetfulness of living entity's real nature disappears with the blooming of the flowers of Self-knowledge and detachment. The flowers bear the fruits of Self-realization and vision of God, leading to the freedom from transmigration of Jeeva, the individual soul, by the grace of Ishvara, the supreme controller.

य एवं वेत्ति पुरुषं प्रकृतिं च गुणैः सह ।
सर्वथा वर्तमानोऽपि न स भूयोऽभिजायते ।।२३।।

ya evaṁ vetti puruṣaṁ prakṛtiṁ ca guṇaiḥ saha
sarvathā vartamāno'pi na sa bhūyo'bhijāyate

They who truly understand Spirit and material Nature with its three modes are not born again, regardless of their way of life. (13.23)

ध्यानेनात्मनि पश्यन्ति केचिद् आत्मानमात्मना ।
अन्ये सांख्येन योगेन कर्मयोगेन चापरे ।।२४।।

dhyānenā'tmani paśyanti kecid ātmānam ātmanā
anye sāṁkhyena yogena karmayogena cā'pare

Some perceive the Supersoul in their inner psyche through mind and intellect that have been purified either by meditation or by metaphysical knowledge or by selfless service. (13.24)

FAITH AND DEVOTION CAN ALSO LEAD TO NIRVANA

अन्ये त्व् एवम् अजानन्तः श्रुत्वान्येभ्य उपासते ।
तेऽपि चातितरन्त्य् एव मृत्युं श्रुतिपरायणाः ॥२५॥

anye tv evam ajānantaḥ śrutvā'nyebhya upāsate
te'pi cā'titaranty eva mṛtyuṁ śrutiparāyaṇāḥ

Others, however, do not know the yogas of meditation, knowledge, and selfless service; but they perform deity worship with firm faith and loving devotion, as mentioned in the scriptures by the saints and sages. They also transcend death by virtue of their firm faith in what they have heard. (13.25)

Blessed are they that have not understood, yet have believed (John 20.29). If you believe, you will receive whatever you ask for (Matthew 21.22). It is not necessary to completely understand God to obtain His grace, to love Him, and to attain Him. Any spiritual practice done without faith is an exercise in futility. Our intellect stands in the way as an obstruction to faith.

यावत् संजायते किंचित् सत्त्वं स्थावरजङ्गमम् ।
क्षेत्रक्षेत्रज्ञसंयोगात् तद् विद्धि भरतर्षभ ॥२६॥

yāvat saṁjāyate kiṁcit sattvaṁ sthāvara jaṅgamam
kṣetrakṣetrajña saṁyogāt tad viddhi bharatarṣabha

Whatever is born — animate or inanimate — know them to be born from the union of Spirit and matter, O Arjuna. (See also 7.06) (13.26)

समं सर्वेषु भूतेषु तिष्ठन्तं परमेश्वरम् ।
विनश्यत्स्व् अविनश्यन्तं यः पश्यति स पश्यति ॥२७॥

samaṁ sarveṣu bhūteṣu tiṣṭhantaṁ parameśvaram
vinaśyatsv avinaśyantaṁ yaḥ paśyati sa paśyati

One who sees the one and the same Supreme Lord dwelling as Spirit (or Ishvara) equally within all mortal beings, truly sees. (13.27)

समं पश्यन् हि सर्वत्र समवस्थितम् ईश्वरम् ।
न हिनस्त्य् आत्मनात्मानं ततो याति परां गतिम् ।।२८।।

samaṁ paśyan hi sarvatra samavasthitam īśvaram
na hinasty ātmanā'tmānaṁ tato yāti parāṁ gatim

When one beholds One and the same Ishvara existing equally in every being, one does not harm anybody because one considers everything as one's own self, and thereupon attains the Supreme Abode. (13.28)

प्रकृत्यैव च कर्माणि क्रियमाणानि सर्वशः ।
यः पश्यति तथात्मानम् अकर्तारं स पश्यति ।।२९।।

prakṛtyai'va ca karmāṇi kriyamāṇāni sarvaśaḥ
yaḥ paśyati tathā'tmānam akartāraṁ sa paśyati

One who perceives that all works are done by the powers of material Nature, truly understands and does not consider oneself as the doer. (See also 3.27, 5.09, and 14.19) (13.29)

यदा भूतपृथग्भावम् एकस्थम् अनुपश्यति ।
तत एव च विस्तारं ब्रह्म संपद्यते तदा ।।३०।।

yadā bhūtapṛthagbhāvam ekastham anupaśyati
tata eva ca vistāraṁ brahma saṁpadyate tadā

The moment one discovers the diverse variety of beings and their different ideas abiding in One and coming out from That alone, one attains the Supreme Being. (13.30)

ATTRIBUTES OF THE SPIRIT (BRAHMA)

अनादित्वान् निर्गुणत्वात् परमात्मायम् अव्ययः ।
शरीरस्थोऽपि कौन्तेय न करोति न लिप्यते ॥३१॥

anāditvān nirguṇatvāt paramātmā'yam avyayaḥ
śarīrastho'pi kaunteya na karoti na lipyate

Because of being beginningless and unaffectable by the three modes of material Nature, the eternal Supersoul — even though dwelling in the body as a living entity — neither does anything nor becomes tainted by Karma, O Arjuna. (13.31)

The eternal Supersoul is called attributeless because He does not have the three attributes of material Nature. The word 'attributeless' has been commonly misunderstood as formless. Attributeless refers only to the absence of material form and attributes known to the human mind. The Lord has an incomparable personality and transcendental qualities.

यथा सर्वगतं सौक्ष्म्याद् आकाशं नोपलिप्यते ।
सर्वत्रावस्थितो देहे तथात्मा नोपलिप्यते ॥३२॥

yathā sarvagataṁ saukṣmyād ākāśaṁ no'palipyate
sarvatrā'vasthito dehe tathā'tmā no'palipyate

Just as the all-pervading space is not tainted because of its subtlety, similarly, the Spirit abiding in all bodies is not tainted. (13.32)

Spirit is present everywhere. It is present inside the body, outside the body, as well as all over the body. Actually, Spirit is inside and outside of everything that exists in creation.

यथा प्रकाशयत्य् एकः कृत्स्नं लोकम् इमं रविः ।
क्षेत्रं क्षेत्री तथा कृत्स्नं प्रकाशयति भारत ॥३३॥

yathā prakāśayaty ekaḥ kṛtsnaṁ lokam imaṁ raviḥ
kṣetraṁ kṣetrī tathā kṛtsnaṁ prakāśayati bhārata

Just as one sun illuminates the entire world, similarly, Spirit gives life to the entire creation, O Arjuna. (13.33)

According to Shankara, one sees the creation but not the Creator behind the creation due to ignorance, just as a person in the darkness of night sees the snake and not the rope that sustains the false notion of a snake. If any object other than Spirit appears to exist, it is unreal like a mirage, a dream, or the existence of a snake in the rope. The absolute monism that negates all manifestation as a dream world is not the whole truth. According to the Vedas, God is both transcendent and immanent in one. The illustration of the world as a dream is a metaphor meant only to illustrate certain points and should not be stretched too far or taken literally. If the world is a dream, it is a very beautiful dream, indeed, of the cosmic dreamer who must also be extraordinarily beautiful.

क्षेत्रक्षेत्रज्ञयोर् एवम् अन्तरं ज्ञानचक्षुषा ।
भूतप्रकृतिमोक्षं च ये विदुर् यान्ति ते परम् ॥३४॥

kṣetra kṣetrajñayor evam antaraṁ jñāna cakṣuṣā
bhūtaprakṛti mokṣaṁ ca ye vidur yānti te param

They attain the Supreme, who perceive — with the eye of Self-knowledge — the difference between creation (or the body) and the Creator (or the Spirit), as well as know the techniques of liberation (See verses 13.24-13.25) of the living entity from the trap of divine illusory energy, Maya. (13.34)

Spirit emits its power (Maya) as the sun emits light, fire emits heat, and the moon gives cooling rays (DB 7.32.05). Maya is the inexplicable divine power of Spirit that does not exist apart from Spirit, the possessor of power. Maya has the power of creation. Maya also deludes the living entity by making it identify with a body, enjoy three modes of material Nature, and forget its real nature as Spirit, the basis of the entire visible and invisible universe. Creation is just a partial revelation of the power of Spirit and is called unreal like a dream world because it is subject to change and destruction. The clay is real, but the pot is unreal because the clay exists before the pot is created, while the pot exists, and after the pot is destroyed.

Creation is a natural effortless projection of the powers of Spirit and is therefore purposeless (MuU 1.01.07). The creative activity of the Lord is a mere pastime of the divine power (Maya) without any purpose or motive (BS 2.01.33). It is nothing but an apparent natural modification of His infinite limitless energy (E) into matter (m) and vice versa ($E=mc^2$ of Einstein) done as a mere pastime. Creation, an effect, is related to the Creator, the cause, as a piece of cloth is related to cotton. In the case of the cloth, however, the weaver is not sitting in every thread of the cloth, but in creation the efficient and material causes are one and the same, a divine mystery indeed! Everything in the universe is connected with everything else. Creation is not a mechanical or engineering construction. It is the supreme, spiritual phenomena revealing divine splendor. Creation is made by the Lord, of the Lord, and for the Lord. The Creator and creation is different as well as the same.

ॐ तत्सदिति श्रीमद्भगवद्गीतासूपनिषत्सु ब्रह्मविद्यायां योगशास्त्रे
श्रीकृष्णार्जुनसंवादे क्षेत्रक्षेत्रज्ञविभागयोगो नाम त्रयोदशोऽध्यायः ॥

OM tatsaditi śrīmadbhagavadgītāsūpaniṣatsu brahmavidyāyāṁ
yogaśāstre śrīkṛṣṇārjuna saṁvāde kṣetrakṣetrajñavibhāga
yogo nāma trayodaśo'dhyāyaḥ

Thus ends the thirteenth chapter named "Creation and the Creator" of the Upaniṣad of the Bhagavadgītā, the scripture of yoga, dealing with the science of the Absolute in the form of the dialogue between Śrīkṛṣṇa and Arjuna.

अथ चतुर्दशोऽध्यायः

CHAPTER 14

गुणत्रयविभागयोगः

THREE MODES OF MATERIAL NATURE

श्रीभगवानुवाच
परं भूयः प्रवक्ष्यामि ज्ञानानां ज्ञानम् उत्तमम् ।
यज् ज्ञात्वा मुनयः सर्वे परां सिद्धिम् इतो गताः ॥१॥
śrī bhagavān uvāca
paraṁ bhūyaḥ pravakṣyāmi jñānānāṁ jñānam uttamam
yaj jñātvā munayaḥ sarve parāṁ siddhim ito gatāḥ

Lord Krishna said: I shall further explain to you the supreme knowledge, the best of all knowledge, knowing this all the sages have attained salvation. (14.01)

इदं ज्ञानम् उपाश्रित्य मम साधर्म्यम् आगताः ।
सर्गेऽपि नोपजायन्ते प्रलये न व्यथन्ति च ॥२॥
idaṁ jñānam upāśritya mama sādharmyam āgatāḥ
sarge'pi no'pajāyante pralaye na vyathanti ca

Those who have taken refuge in this transcendental knowledge attain unity with Me and are neither born at the time of creation nor afflicted at the time of dissolution. (14.02)

ALL BEINGS ARE BORN FROM THE UNION OF SPIRIT AND MATTER

मम योनिर् महद् ब्रह्म तस्मिन् गर्भं दधाम्य् अहम् ।
संभवः सर्वभूतानां ततो भवति भारत ॥३॥
mama yonir mahad brahma tasmin garbhaṁ dadhāmy aham
saṁbhavaḥ sarva bhūtānāṁ tato bhavati bhārata

My material Nature is the womb of creation wherein I place the seed of Consciousness from which all beings are born, O Arjuna. (See also 9.10) (14.03)

Material Nature, a product of divine kinetic energy (Maya), is the origin of the entire universe. Material Nature creates living beings when the seed of Spirit is sown in it for germination.

सर्वयोनिषु कौन्तेय मूर्तयः संभवन्ति याः ।
तासां ब्रह्म महद् योनिर् अहं बीजप्रदः पिता ॥४॥

sarva yoniṣu kaunteya mūrtayaḥ saṁbhavanti yāḥ
tāsāṁ brahma mahad yonir aham bījapradaḥ pitā

Whatever forms are produced in all different wombs, O Arjuna, the material Nature is their body-giving cosmic mother; and the Spirit or Consciousness is the life-giving father. (14.04)

HOW THREE MODES OF MATERIAL NATURE BIND THE SPIRIT SOUL TO THE BODY

सत्त्वं रजस् तम इति गुणाः प्रकृतिसंभवाः ।
निबध्नन्ति महाबाहो देहे देहिनम् अव्ययम् ॥५॥

sattvaṁ rajas tama iti guṇāḥ prakṛti saṁbhavāḥ
nibadhnanti mahābāho dehe dehinam avyayam

Goodness, activity or passion, and inertia or ignorance — these three modes (or ropes) of material Nature fetter the eternal individual soul to the body, O Arjuna. (14.05)

तत्र सत्त्वं निर्मलत्वात् प्रकाशकम् अनामयम् ।
सुखसङ्गेन बध्नाति ज्ञानसङ्गेन चानघ ॥६॥

tatra sattvaṁ nirmalatvāt prakāśakam anāmayam
sukha saṅgena badhnāti jñāna saṅgena cā'nagha

Of these, the mode of goodness is illuminating and good because it is pure. The mode of goodness fetters the living entity by attachment to happiness and knowledge, O sinless Arjuna. (14.06)

रजो रागात्मकं विद्धि तृष्णासङ्गसमुद्भवम् ।
तन् निबध्नाति कौन्तेय कर्मसङ्गेन देहिनम् ॥७॥

rajo rāgātmakaṁ viddhi tṛṣṇāsaṅga samudbhavam
tan nibadhnāti kaunteya karma saṅgena dehinam

Arjuna, know that the mode of passion is characterized by intense craving for sense gratification and is the source of material desire and attachment. The mode of passion binds the living entity by attachment to the fruits of work. (14.07)

तमस् त्व् अज्ञानजं विद्धि मोहनं सर्वदेहिनाम् ।
प्रमादालस्यनिद्राभिस् तन् निबध्नाति भारत ॥८॥

tamas tv ajñānajaṁ viddhi mohanaṁ sarvadehinām
pramādālasya nidrābhis tan nibadhnāti bhārata

Know, O Arjuna, that the mode of ignorance— the deluder of the living entity — is born of inertia. The mode of ignorance binds the living entity by carelessness, laziness, and excessive sleep. (14.08)

सत्त्वं सुखे सञ्जयति रजः कर्मणि भारत ।
ज्ञानम् आवृत्य तु तमः प्रमादे सञ्जयत्य् उत ॥९॥

sattvaṁ sukhe sañjayati rajaḥ karmaṇi bhārata
jñānam ābṛtya tu tamaḥ pramāde sañjayaty uta

O Arjuna, the mode of goodness attaches one to happiness of learning and knowing the Spirit; the mode of

passion attaches to action; and the mode of ignorance attaches to negligence by covering Self-knowledge. (14.09)

The mode of goodness keeps one away from sinful acts and leads one to Self-knowledge and happiness, but not to salvation. The mode of passion creates strong Karmic bonds and takes the individual further away from liberation. Such persons know right and wrong actions based on religious principles, but are unable to follow them because of strong impulses of lust. The mode of passion obscures real knowledge of Self and causes one to experience both the pain and pleasure of this worldly life. Such persons are very much attached to wealth, power, prestige, sensual pleasure, and are very selfish and greedy. In the mode of ignorance, one is unable to recognize the real goal of life, is unable to distinguish between right and wrong action, and remains attached to sinful and forbidden activities. Such a person is lazy, violent, lacks intellect, and has no interest in spiritual knowledge.

CHARACTERISTICS OF THREE MODES OF NATURE

रजस् तमश् चाभिभूय सत्त्वं भवति भारत ।
रजः सत्त्वं तमश्चैव तमः सत्त्वं रजस् तथा ॥१०॥

rajas tamaś cā'bhibhūya sattvaṁ bhavati bhārata
rajaḥ sattvaṁ tamaścaiva tamaḥ sattvaṁ rajas tathā

Goodness prevails by suppressing passion and ignorance; passion prevails by suppressing goodness and ignorance; and ignorance prevails by suppressing goodness and passion, O Arjuna. (14.10)

सर्वद्वारेषु देहेऽस्मिन् प्रकाश उपजायते ।
ज्ञानं यदा तदा विद्याद् विवृद्धं सत्त्वम् इत्य् उत ॥११॥

sarvadvāreṣu dehe'smin prakāśa upajāyate
jñānaṁ yadā tadā vidyād vivṛddhaṁ sattvam ity uta

When the light of Self-knowledge illuminates all the senses in the body, then it should be known that goodness is predominant. (14.11)

The sense organs (nose, tongue, eye, skin, ear, mind, and intellect) are called the gateway to Self-knowledge in the body. The mind and intellect get into the mode of goodness and become receptive to Self-knowledge when senses are purified by selfless service, discipline, and spiritual practice. It is also said in verse 14.17 that the rise of Self-knowledge takes place when one's mind gets firmly established in the mode of goodness. As objects are seen very clearly in the light, similarly, one perceives and thinks in the right perspective, and the senses shun whatever is improper. There is no attraction in the mind for sensual pleasures when the senses are illumined by the dawning of the light of Self-knowledge.

लोभः प्रवृत्तिर् आरम्भः कर्मणाम् अशमः स्पृहा ।
रजस्य् एतानि जायन्ते विवृद्धे भरतर्षभ ॥१२॥
lobhaḥ pravṛttir ārambhaḥ karmaṇām aśamaḥ spṛhā
rajasy etāni jāyante vivṛddhe bharatarṣabha

O Arjuna, when passion is predominant, greed, activity, undertaking of selfish work, restlessness, and excitement arise. (14.12)

अप्रकाशोऽप्रवृत्तिश्च प्रमादो मोह एव च ।
तमस्य् एतानि जायन्ते विवृद्धे कुरुनन्दन ॥१३॥
aprakāśo'pravṛttiśca pramādo moha eva ca
tamasy etāni jāyante vivṛddhe kurunandana

O Arjuna, when inertia is predominant, ignorance, inactivity, carelessness, and delusion arise. (14.13)

A particular mode of Nature becomes dominant in the present life due to one's past Karma. The three modes fuel the vehicles of transmigration that carry one's baggage of Karma, as discussed in the following verses.

THREE MODES ARE ALSO THE VEHICLES OF TRANSMIGRATION FOR THE INDIVIDUAL SOUL

यदा सत्त्वे प्रवृद्धे तु प्रलयं याति देहभृत् ।
तदोत्तमविदां लोकान् अमलान् प्रतिपद्यते ॥१४॥

yadā sattve pravṛddhe tu pralayaṁ yāti dehabhṛt
tado'ttamavidāṁ lokān amalān pratipadyate

One who dies when goodness dominates goes to heaven — the pure world of knowers of the Supreme. (14.14)

रजसि प्रलयं गत्वा कर्मसङ्गिषु जायते ।
तथा प्रलीनस् तमसि मूढयोनिषु जायते ॥१५॥

rajasi pralayaṁ gatvā karmasaṅgiṣu jāyate
tathā pralīnas tamasi mūḍhayoniṣu jāyate

One who dies when passion dominates is reborn attached to action (or the utilitarian). One who dies in ignorance is reborn as a lower creature. (14.15)

कर्मणः सुकृतस्याहुः सात्त्विकं निर्मलं फलम् ।
रजसस् तु फलं दुःखम् अज्ञानं तमसः फलम् ॥१६॥

karmaṇaḥ sukṛtasyā'huḥ sāttvikaṁ nirmalaṁ phalam
rajasas tu phalaṁ duḥkham ajñānaṁ tamasaḥ phalam

The fruit of good action is said to be beneficial and pure; the fruit of passionate action is pain; and the fruit of ignorant action is laziness. (14.16)

सत्त्वात् सञ्जायते ज्ञानं रजसो लोभ एव च ।
प्रमादमोहौ तमसो भवतोऽज्ञानम् एव च ॥१७॥

sattvāt sañjāyate jñānaṁ rajaso lobha eva ca
pramādamohau tamaso bhavato'jñānam eva ca

Self-knowledge arises from the mode of goodness; greed arises from the mode of passion; and negligence, delusion, and slowness of mind arise from the mode of ignorance. (14.17)

ऊर्ध्वं गच्छन्ति सत्त्वस्था मध्ये तिष्ठन्ति राजसाः ।
जघन्यगुणवृत्तिस्था अधो गच्छन्ति तामसाः ॥१८॥
ūrdhvaṁ gacchanti sattvasthā madhye tiṣṭhanti rājasāḥ
jaghanya guṇa vṛttisthā adho gacchanti tāmasāḥ

They who are established in goodness go to heaven; passionate persons are reborn in the mortal world; and the insipid ones, abiding in the mode of ignorance, go to lower planets of hell, or take birth as lower creatures (depending on the degree of their ignorance). (14.18)

ATTAIN NIRVANA AFTER TRANSCENDING THE THREE MODES OF MATERIAL NATURE

नान्यं गुणेभ्यः कर्तारं यदा द्रष्टानुपश्यति ।
गुणेभ्यश्च परं वेत्ति मद्भावं सोऽधिगच्छति ॥१९॥
nā'nyaṁ guṇebhyaḥ kartāraṁ yadā draṣṭā'nupaśyati
guṇebhyaśca paraṁ vetti madbhāvaṁ so'dhigacchati

When visionaries perceive no doer other than the three modes of material Nature (Gunas) and know the Supreme, which is above and beyond these modes, then they attain Nirvana or salvation. (See also 3.27, 5.09, and 13.29) (14.19)

Karmic laws bind one who does not believe that the Lord controls everything and who considers oneself the doer, enjoyer, and owner (BP 6.12.12). The power of doing all actions, good or bad, proceeds from God, but we are ultimately responsible for our actions because we also have the power to reason. God has given us the power to do work; however, we are free to use the power in the right or wrong way and become liberated or bound.

The good Lord gives one only the faculties to act; He is not liable for one's actions. It is up to the individual to decide how to act. This decision is controlled by the modes of material Nature and is governed by one's past Karma. Those who understand this properly know how to act and do not blame God for their misfortunes or feel jealous of others' fortune.

Due to ignorance created by illusory energy (Maya), one considers oneself the doer and consequently becomes bound by Karma and undergoes transmigration (BP 11.11.10). Whenever one asserts or even thinks of oneself as doing things, one assumes the role of a doer, becomes accountable for the action (Karma), and gets caught in the intricate Karmic net of transmigration.

गुणान् एतान् अतीत्य त्रीन् देही देहसमुद्भवान् ।
जन्ममृत्युजरादुःखैर् विमुक्तोऽमृतम् अश्नुते ।।२०।।

guṇān etān atītya trīn dehī deha samudbhavān
janma mṛtyu jarā duḥkhair vimukto'mṛtam aśnute

When one rises above, or transcends the three modes of material Nature that originate in the body, one attains immortality or salvation and is freed from the pains of birth, old age, and death. (14.20)

THE PROCESS OF RISING ABOVE THE THREE MODES

अर्जुन उवाच
कैर् लिङ्गैस् त्रीन् गुणान् एतान् अतीतो भवति प्रभो ।
किमाचारः कथं चैतांस् त्रीन् गुणान् अतिवर्तते ।।२१।।

arjuna uvāca
kair liṅgais trīn guṇān etān atīto bhavati prabho
kimācāraḥ kathaṁ cai'tāṁs trīn guṇān ativartate

Arjuna said: What are the marks of those who have transcended the three modes of material Nature, and what is their conduct? How does one transcend these three modes of material Nature, O Lord Krishna? (14.21)

श्रीभगवानुवाच
प्रकाशं च प्रवृत्तिं च मोहम् एव च पाण्डव ।
न द्वेष्टि संप्रवृत्तानि न निवृत्तानि काङ्क्षति ॥२२॥
śrī bhagavān uvāca
prakāśaṁ ca pravṛttiṁ ca moham eva ca pāṇḍava
na dveṣṭi saṁpravṛttāni na nivṛttāni kāṅkṣati

उदासीनवद् आसीनो गुणैर् यो न विचाल्यते ।
गुणा वर्तन्त इत्य् एव योऽवतिष्ठति नेङ्गते ॥२३॥
udāsīnavad āsīno guṇair yo na vicālyate
guṇā vartanta ity eva yo'vatiṣṭhati ne'ṅgate

Lord Krishna said: One transcends the modes of material Nature who neither hates the presence of enlightenment, activity, and delusion nor desires them when they are absent; who remains like a witness without being affected by the modes of material Nature; who stays firmly attached to the Lord without wavering — thinking that only the modes of material Nature are operating. (14.22-23)

समदुःखसुखः स्वस्थः समलोष्टाश्मकाञ्चनः ।
तुल्यप्रियाप्रियो धीरस् तुल्यनिन्दात्मसंस्तुतिः ॥२४॥
sama duḥkha sukhaḥ svasthaḥ sama loṣṭāśma kāñcanaḥ
tulyapriyāpriyo dhīras tulyanindātmasaṁstutiḥ

मानापमानयोस् तुल्यस् तुल्यो मित्रारिपक्षयोः ।
सर्वारम्भपरित्यागी गुणातीतः स उच्यते ॥२५॥
mānāpamānayos tulyas tulyo mitrāripakṣayoḥ
sarvārambhaparityāgī guṇātītaḥ sa ucyate

And one who depends on the Lord and is indifferent to pain and pleasure; to whom a clod, a stone, and gold are alike and to whom the dear and the unfriendly are alike; who is of firm mind; who is calm in censure and in praise and indifferent to honor and disgrace; who is impartial to friend and foe; and who has renounced the sense of doership — is said to have transcended the modes of material nature. (14.24-25)

Guru Nanak said: One who obeys the will of God with pleasure is free and wise. Gold and stone, pain and pleasure are alike only for such a person.

BONDS OF THREE MODES CAN BE CUT BY DEVOTIONAL LOVE

मां च योऽव्यभिचारेण भक्तियोगेन सेवते ।
स गुणान् समतीत्यैतान् ब्रह्मभूयाय कल्पते ।।२६।।

māṁ ca yo'vyabhicāreṇa bhaktiyogena sevate
sa guṇān samatītyai'tān brahmabhūyāya kalpate

One who serves Me with love and unswerving devotion transcends the three modes of material Nature and becomes fit for Nirvana. (See also 7.14 and 15.19) (14.26)

Unswerving devotion is defined as the loving devotion in which one does not depend on any other person, but only God for everything.

The mode of goodness is the topmost rung of the ladder leading to the Truth, but it is not the Truth as such. The three modes of material Nature have to be transcended, step by step. First, one has to overcome the modes of ignorance and passion and become established in the mode of goodness by developing certain values and following certain disciplines. Then one becomes ready to surmount the dualities of good and bad, pain and pleasure, and to rise to the higher transcendental plane by going beyond the highest mode — the mode of goodness.

Spiritual practices and vegetarian food raise the mind from the modes of ignorance and passion to the transcendental plane of bliss where pairs of opposites disappear. The mode of goodness is the natural result of profound thought generated by firm understanding of metaphysics. Anybody can easily cross the ocean of illusion (Maya), consisting of three modes of material Nature, by the boat of firm faith, devotion, and exclusive love for God. There is no other way to transcend the three modes of material Nature and attain salvation. It is also said that anyone situated in any one of the three modes of material nature can come up to the transcendental plane by the grace of a genuine and empowered guru.

ब्रह्मणो हि प्रतिष्ठाहम् अमृतस्याव्ययस्य च ।
शाश्वतस्य च धर्मस्य सुखस्यैकान्तिकस्य च ।।२७।।
brahmaṇo hi pratiṣṭhā'ham amṛtasyā'vyayasya ca
śāśvatasya ca dharmasya sukhasyai'kāntikasya ca

Because I am the source of the immortal Spirit (Brahma), of everlasting cosmic order (Dharma), and of the absolute bliss. (14.27)

The Supreme Being is the source or the basis of Spirit. Spirit is one of the expansions of the Supreme Being. It is Spirit (of the Supreme Being) that performs the entire cosmic drama and sustains everything. Therefore, Spirit is also called the Supreme Being or the Lord.

It is very significant that Lord Krishna never used such words as "worship the Supreme God," or "the Absolute is the basis of everything." In this verse and elsewhere in the Gita, Lord Krishna declares that He is the Supreme Spirit. Krishna means different things to different people. Some commentators consider Krishna other than God; others call Him a "Hindu God." To others Krishna is a politician, a teacher, a divine lover, and a diplomat. To devotees, Krishna is the incarnation of the Absolute and the object of love. Readers would do well just to understand and use

Krishna's teachings in their daily lives without getting confused about who was Krishna.

ॐ तत्सदिति श्रीमद्भगवद्गीतासूपनिषत्सु ब्रह्मविद्यायां योगशास्त्रे
श्रीकृष्णार्जुनसंवादे गुणत्रयविभागयोगो नाम चतुर्दशोऽध्यायः ॥
OM tatsaditi śrīmadbhagavadgītāsūpaniṣatsu brahmavidyāyāṁ
yogaśāstre śrīkṛṣṇārjuna saṁvāde guṇatrayavibhāga
yogo nāma caturdaśo'dhyāyaḥ

Thus ends the fourteenth chapter named "Three Modes of Material Nature" of the Upaniṣad of the Bhagavadgītā, the scripture of yoga, dealing with the science of the Absolute in the form of the dialogue between Śrīkṛṣṇa and Arjuna.

अथ पञ्चदशोऽध्यायः
CHAPTER 15
पुरुषोत्तमयोगः
THE SUPREME BEING

CREATION IS LIKE A TREE CREATED BY THE POWERS OF MAYA

श्रीभगवानुवाच
ऊर्ध्वमूलम् अधःशाखम् अश्वत्थं प्राहुर् अव्ययम् ।
छन्दांसि यस्य पर्णानि यस् तं वेद स वेदवित् ॥१॥

śrī bhagavān uvāca
ūrdhvamūlam adhaḥśākham aśvatthaṁ prāhur avyayam
chandāṁsi yasya parṇāni yas taṁ veda sa vedavit

Lord Krishna said: The universe (or human body) may be compared to an eternal tree that has its origin (or root) in the Supreme Being and its branches below in the cosmos. The Vedic hymns are the leaves of this tree. One who understands this tree is a knower of the Vedas. (15.01)

अधश्चोर्ध्वं प्रसृतास् तस्य शाखा
गुणप्रवृद्धा विषयप्रवालाः।
अधश्च मूलान्य् अनुसंततानि
कर्मानुबन्धीनि मनुष्यलोके ॥२॥

adhaśco'rdhvaṁ prasṛtās tasya śākhā
guṇapravṛddhā viṣayapravālāḥ
adhaśca mūlāny anusaṁtatāni
karmānubandhīni manuṣyaloke

The branches of this eternal tree are spread all over the cosmos. The tree is nourished by the energy of material Nature; sense pleasures are its sprouts; and its roots of

ego and desires stretch below in the human world, causing Karmic bondage. (15.02)

The human body, a microcosmic universe or world, may be also compared to a beginningless and endless tree. Karma is the seed; the countless desires are its roots; five basic elements are its main branches; and the ten organs of perception and action are its sub-branches. Three modes of material Nature provide the nourishment, and sense pleasures are its sprouts. This tree is ever changing, but eternal, without beginning and end. Just as the leaves protect the tree, so the rituals protect and perpetuate this tree. One who truly understands this marvelous tree, its origin (or root), its nature and working, is a knower of the Vedas in a true sense.

HOW TO CUT THE TREE OF ATTACHMENT AND ATTAIN SALVATION BY TAKING REFUGE IN GOD

न रूपम् अस्येह तथोपलभ्यते
नान्तो न चादिर् न च संप्रतिष्ठा ।
अश्वत्थम् एनं सुविरूढमूलम्
असङ्गशस्त्रेण दृढेन छित्त्वा ॥३॥

na rūpam asye'ha tatho'palabhyate
nā'nto na cā'dir na ca saṁpratiṣṭhā
aśvattham enaṁ suvirūḍhamūlam
asaṅgaśastreṇa dṛḍhena chittvā

ततः पदं तत् परिमार्गितव्यं
यस्मिन् गता न निवर्तन्ति भूयः ।
तम् एव चाद्यं पुरुषं प्रपद्ये
यतः प्रवृत्तिः प्रसृता पुराणी ॥४॥

tataḥ padaṁ tat parimārgitavyaṁ
yasmin gatā na nivartanti bhūyaḥ
tam eva cā'dyaṁ puruṣaṁ prapadye
yataḥ pravṛtti prasṛtā purāṇi

The beginning, the end, or the real form of this tree is not perceptible on earth. Having cut the firm roots — the desires — of this tree by the mighty ax of Self-knowledge and detachment, one should seek that Supreme Abode, reaching which one does not come back to the mortal world again. One should be always thinking: I take refuge in that very primal person from which this primal manifestation comes forth. (15.03-04)

Creation is cyclic, without beginning and end. It is ever changing and has no permanent existence or real form. One must sharpen the ax of metaphysical knowledge and detachment over the stone of spiritual practice, cut the feeling of separateness between the living entity and the Lord, cheerfully participate in the drama of life made up of passing shadows of joys and sorrows, and live in this world completely free from ego and desires. When the attachments are severed, an attitude of sacred dispassion takes place, which is the prerequisite for spiritual progress.

निर्मानमोहा जितसङ्गदोषा
अध्यात्मनित्या विनिवृत्तकामाः ।
द्वन्द्वैर् विमुक्ताः सुखदुःखसंज्ञैर्
गच्छन्त्य् अमूढाः पदम् अव्ययं तत् ।।५।।

nirmānamohā jitasaṅgadoṣā
adhyātmanityā vinivṛttakāmāḥ
dvandvair vimuktāḥ sukhaduḥkhasaṁjñair
gacchanty amūḍhāḥ padam avyayaṁ tat

That eternal goal is reached by the wise who are free from pride and delusion, who have conquered the evil of attachment, who constantly dwell in the Supreme Being with all lust completely stilled, and who are free from dualities of pleasure and pain. (15.05)

न तद् भासयते सूर्यो न शशाङ्को न पावकः ।
यद् गत्वा न निवर्तन्ते तद् धाम परमं मम ।।६।।

na tad bhāsayate sūryo na śaśāṅko na pāvakaḥ
yad gatvā na nivartante tad dhāma paramaṁ mama

The sun does not illumine My Supreme Abode, nor does the moon, nor the fire. Having reached there, people attain permanent liberation (Mukti) and do not come back to this temporal world. (See also 13.17 and 15.12, and KaU 5.15, ShU 6.14, MuU 2.02.10) (15.06)

The Supreme Being is self-luminous, not illumined by any other source. He illumines the sun and the moon as a luminous lamp illumines other objects (DB 7.32.14). The Supreme Being existed before the sun, moon, and fire came into existence during creation, and it will exist even after everything gets dissolved into unmanifest Nature during complete dissolution.

THE EMBODIED SOUL IS THE ENJOYER

ममैवांशो जीवलोके जीवभूतः सनातनः ।
मनः षष्ठानीन्द्रियाणि प्रकृतिस्थानि कर्षति ।।७।।

mamai'vā'ṁśo jīvaloke jīvabhūtaḥ sanātanaḥ
manaḥ ṣaṣṭhānī'ndriyāṇi prakṛtisthāni karṣati

The eternal individual soul (Jiva, Jivatma) in the body of living beings is, indeed, My integral part. It associates with the six sensory faculties of perception — including the mind — and activates them. (15.07)

In essence, Spirit is called Eternal Being or 'Brahman' in Sanskrit. Spirit is the true nature of the Supreme Being (ParaBrahm), and therefore is also called the integral part of the Supreme Being. The same Spirit is called individual soul, living entity, Jiva, soul, and Jivatma in the bodies of living beings. The difference between Spirit and the individual soul is due to the limiting adjuncts — the body and mind — similar to the illusion that the enclosed pot space is different from unlimited space.

शरीरं यद् अवाप्नोति यच् चाप्य् उत्क्रामतीश्वरः ।
गृहीत्वैतानि संयाति वायुर् गन्धान् इवाशयात् ॥८॥

śarīraṁ yad avāpnoti yac cāpy utkrāmatī'śvaraḥ
gṛhītvai'tāni saṁyāti vāyur gandhān ivā'śayāt

Just as the air takes aroma away from the flower; similarly, the individual soul takes the six sensory faculties from the physical body it casts off during death to the new physical body it acquires in reincarnation. (See also 2.13) (15.08)

The individual soul takes the subtle body — six sensory faculties of perception, intellect, ego, and five vital forces — from one physical body to another after death, as the wind takes dust from one place to another. The wind is neither affected nor unaffected by association with dust; similarly, the individual soul is neither affected nor unaffected by association with the body (MB 12.211.13-14). Physical bodies are limited in space and time, but invisible subtle bodies are unlimited and all pervading. The subtle body carries the individual's good and bad Karma to the next life till all Karma is exhausted. When all trace of desires is eradicated after the dawn of Self-knowledge, the physical body seems not to exist any more and the conception of subtle body is firmed up in the mind. The astral body is an exact duplicate of the physical body. The beings in the astral world are more advanced in art, technology, and culture. They take up physical bodies to improve and enhance the physical world. Hariharananda Giri says: One may not perceive, conceive, and realize God if one does not seek the invisible subtle body.

During a wakeful state, the physical body, mind, intellect, and ego are active. In a dream state, the individual soul temporarily creates a dream world and wanders in it with a dream body without leaving the physical body. In deep sleep, the individual soul completely rests in the Eternal Being (Spirit) without being bothered by mind and intellect. Supreme Being, the Universal Consciousness, watches us as a witness during all the three states — wakeful, dream, and deep sleep. The living entity leaves one physical body and takes another body after death. The living entity becomes bound or lost, then tries to be liberated by discovering its real nature. Reincarnation allows the living entity to change its vehicle, the physical body, during the long and difficult spiritual journey to the Supreme Being. The individual soul acquires different physical bodies till all Karma is exhausted; after that, the goal of attaining the Supreme Being is reached.

It is said that Spiritual Being wears the veil of illusion, becomes an individual soul, and takes human and other forms just to perform the cosmic drama in which the writer, producer, director, all the players, as well as the audience are the same. Lord performs, plays, and enjoys His own creation. Our problems will disappear if we keep in mind that we are just playing a role and never take things very personally. In order to see the cosmic player, we must detach our mind from the play. Science deals with the knowledge of the cosmic play; spirituality deals with the knowledge of the cosmic Player as partially understood by the player.

श्रोत्रं चक्षुः स्पर्शनं च रसनं घ्राणम् एव च ।
अधिष्ठाय मनश्चायं विषयान् उपसेवते ।।९।।

śrotraṁ cakṣuḥ sparśanaṁ ca rasanaṁ ghrāṇam eva ca
adhiṣṭhāya manaścā'yaṁ viṣayān upasevate

उत्क्रामन्तं स्थितं वापि भुञ्जानं वा गुणान्वितम् ।
विमूढा नानुपश्यन्ति पश्यन्ति ज्ञानचक्षुषः ।।१०।।

utkrāmantaṁ sthitaṁ vā'pi bhuñjānaṁ vā guṇānvitam
vimūḍhā nā'nupaśyanti paśyanti jñāna cakṣuṣaḥ

The living entity enjoys sense pleasures using six sensory faculties of hearing, touch, sight, taste, smell, and mind. The ignorant cannot perceive the living entity departing from the body nor staying in the body and enjoying sense pleasures by associating with the material body. But those who have the eye of Self-knowledge can see it. (15.09-10)

Senses lose their taste for material enjoyment when they develop a higher taste for the nectar of spiritual bliss. The attainment of spiritual bliss is the real fulfillment of one's desire for sense gratification. A purified soul will refrain from doing wrong things that arise from residual, subtle desires for sensual pleasures.

यतन्तो योगिनश्चैनं पश्यन्त्य् आत्मन्य् अवस्थितम् ।
यतन्तोऽप्य् अकृतात्मानो नैनं पश्यन्त्य् अचेतसः ॥११॥
yatanto yoginaścai'naṁ paśyanty ātmany avasthitam
yatanto'py akṛtā'tmāno nai'naṁ paśyanty acetasaḥ

The yogis, striving for perfection, behold the living entity abiding in their inner psyche as consciousness, but the ignorant whose inner psyche is not pure, even though striving, cannot perceive Him. (15.11)

SPIRIT IS THE ESSENCE OF EVERYTHING

यद् आदित्यगतं तेजो जगद् भासयतेऽखिलम् ।
यच् चन्द्रमसि यच् चाग्नौ तत् तेजो विद्धि मामकम् ॥१२॥
yad ādityagataṁ tejo jagad bhāsayate'khilam
yac candramasi yac cā'gnau tat tejo viddhi māmakam

Know that light energy to be Mine that comes from the sun and illumines the whole world and is in the moon and in fire. (See also 13.17 and 15.06) (15.12).

The light of the sun is a reflection of His radiance (RV 10.07.03). The knowers of the Supreme Being visualize everywhere — in themselves, in every human being, and in the whole universe — that supreme cluster of light which is the source of the visible world and which shines like the all-pervading daylight (ChU 3.17.07). The world and its objects are only pictures made of shadows and light, cast on a cosmic movie screen

(Yogananda). The Koran says: Allah is the light of the heavens and the earth (Surah 24.35).

The holy eternal light has the shape of a huge shining cluster of bright light energy. It is the light of the Supreme Being that is in the eternal light and in all the luminaries of the galaxies, such as the sun, the moon, and the stars. It is His light that is in wood, lamps, candles, and is the energy in all living beings. His light is behind all lights and the source of all energy in the universe. Without the power of the Supreme Being, fire is unable to burn a blade of grass. This light of the Supreme Being cannot be realized and seen unless one has completely stilled and strengthened the mind, purified the intellect, and developed the power of will and visualization. One must also be strong enough to bear the mental shock generated while experiencing the light of all lights in trance.

Just as the complete spectrum of sunlight is not visible to the human eye without a prism, similarly, we cannot see the light of the Supreme Being without the grace of God and scriptural reading. The yogis who have tuned-in their consciousness with the supreme consciousness can see the eternal light in trance. The entire universe is sustained by the energy of the Supreme Being and reflects His glory.

गाम् आविश्य च भूतानि धारयाम्य् अहम् ओजसा ।
पुष्णामि चौषधीः सर्वाः सोमो भूत्वा रसात्मकः ।।१३।।
gām āviśya ca bhūtāni dhārayāmy aham ojasā
puṣṇāmi cau'ṣadhīḥ sarvāḥ somo bhūtvā rasātmakaḥ

Entering the earth, I support all beings with My energy. Becoming the sap-giving moon, I nourish all the plants. (15.13)

अहं वैश्वानरो भूत्वा प्राणिनां देहम् आश्रितः ।
प्राणापानसमायुक्तः पचाम्य् अन्नं चतुर्विधम् ।।१४।।
ahaṁ vaiśvānaro bhūtvā prāṇināṁ deham āśritaḥ
prāṇāpānasamāyuktaḥ pacāmy annaṁ caturvidham

Becoming the digestive fire, I remain in the body of all living beings. Uniting with vital breaths or bioimpulses, I digest all types of food. (15.14)

सर्वस्य चाहं हृदि संनिविष्टो
मत्तः स्मृतिर् ज्ञानम् अपोहनं च ।
वेदैश्च सर्वैर् अहम् एव वेद्यो
वेदान्तकृद् वेदविद् एव चाहम् ॥१५॥

sarvasya cā'haṁ hṛdi saṁniviṣṭo
mattaḥ smṛtir jñānam apohanaṁ ca
vedaiśca sarvair aham eva vedyo
vedāntakṛd vedavid eva cā'ham

And I am seated in the inner psyche of all beings. Memory, Self-knowledge, and removal of doubts and wrong notions about God come from Me. I am, in truth, that which is to be known by the study of all the Vedas. I am, indeed, the author as well as the student of the Vedas. (See also 6.39) (15.15)

The Supreme Being is the source of all scriptures (BS 1.01.03). The Lord resides in the inner psyche (or the causal heart) as the consciousness of all beings — not in the physical heart of the body as commonly misunderstood.

WHAT ARE THE SUPREME SPIRIT, SPIRIT AND THE INDIVIDUAL SOUL?

द्वाव् इमौ पुरुषौ लोके क्षरश्चाक्षर एव च ।
क्षरः सर्वाणि भूतानि कूटस्थोऽक्षर उच्यते ॥१६॥

dvāv imau puruṣau loke kṣaraścā'kṣara eva ca
kṣaraḥ sarvāṇi bhūtāni kūtastho'kṣara ucyate

There are two entities in the cosmos: The changeable Divine Beings, and the unchangeable Eternal Being

(Spirit). All created beings are subject to change, but the Spirit does not change. (15.16)

Two aspects of divine manifestation — Divine Beings and the Eternal Being (Spirit) — are described here. The entire creation — including Lord Brahmā (the creative force), all celestial controllers, fourteen planetary spheres, down to a blade of grass — is the expansion of Divine Beings. Spirit is the Consciousness, the cause of all causes, from which Divine Beings, material Nature, and countless cosmos take birth, by which they are sustained, and into which they become dissolved again and again. Divine Beings and Spirit are called creation and the Creator, respectively, in verses 13.01-02, and Womb and seed-giving Father in verses 14.03-04. The Supreme Being is beyond both Divine Beings and Spirit, and is called the Absolute Reality in the scriptures and in the following verses:

उत्तमः पुरुषस् त्व् अन्यः परमात्मेत्य् उदाहृतः ।
यो लोकत्रयम् आविश्य बिभर्त्य् अव्यय ईश्वरः ॥१७॥

uttamaḥ puruṣas tv anyaḥ paramātme'ty udāhṛtaḥ
yo lokatrayam āviśya bibharty avyaya īśvaraḥ

The Supreme Being is beyond both the Temporal Divine Beings and the Eternal Being. He is also called the Absolute Reality that sustains both the Temporal and the Eternal by pervading everything. (15.17)

यस्मात् क्षरम् अतीतोऽहम् अक्षराद् अपि चोत्तमः ।
अतोऽस्मि लोके वेदे च प्रथितः पुरुषोत्तमः ॥१८॥

yasmāt kṣaram atīto'ham akṣarād api co'ttamaḥ
ato'smi loke vede ca prathitaḥ puruṣottamaḥ

Because I, the Supreme Being, am beyond both the Temporal (Divine) Beings and the Eternal Being, therefore I am known in this world and in the scriptures as the Supreme Being (Absolute Reality, Truth, Supersoul) (15.18)

Basically, there are two different aspects (or levels of existence) — Temporal Beings (also called Divine Souls, Divine Beings, Temporal Divine Beings, Deva, celestial forces, guardian angels), and the Eternal Being (Spirit, Atma, Brahm) — of One and the same Absolute Reality known as the Supreme Being. The invisible, unchanging, and immutable entity is called Eternal Being. The Temporal Divine Beings are the expansions of the Eternal Being in the material world. The entire creation is ever-changing and mutable and is also called temporal. Both Temporal and Eternal Beings are expansions of the Supreme Being. The Supreme Being — the basis of both Temporal and Eternal — is the highest or the Absolute, who is referred to by various names. The personal aspect of the Absolute is called by names, such as Krishna, Mother, Father, and Allah. According to our scriptures, no one, except ParaBrahma Paramatma, has their own power or consciousness. Everyone, including the Eternal Being (Akshar Brahma), receives power from the Absolute, Lord Krishna.

DESCENT OF THE SUPREME BEING

Note: The following explanation is **only** for advanced readers who have studied Gita for several years and are familiar with some Sanskrit terms. Readers should also visit our website:

http://www.gita-society.com/section2/genesis.jpg

for a diagram showing this hierarchy of cosmic control that will make the following explanations more clear.

In Vedic cosmology, the cosmic space (Akāsha) is divided into five major zones: **1. Chidākāsha, 2. Sadākāsha, 3. Paramākāsha, 4. Brahmāndākāsha, and 5. Ghatākāsha.** The **Supreme Being (1)** resides in ParamaDhāma (Supreme Abode, Gita 15.06), located in **Chidākāsha**, the uppermost space. ShriKrishna is known here as Paramātmā, Supreme Being, Supersoul, ParaBrahma, Purushottama, Saccidānanda, Absolute, Father, the Supreme Personality of Godhead and by various other names.

(2) Akshar Brahma (Eternal Being or Atmā) is the expansion of the **SAT** (or existence) nature of Supreme Being in Sadākāsha, as explained in Gita 10.42 and 14.27. Akshara Brahma, mentioned in Gita 8.03 and 15.16, has three major expansions (Pāda or natures). They are: **(2a) Sat, (2b) Chitta or Sabal Brahma,** and **(2c) Ananda or Keval Brahma.** Sat nature is also called Atmā or Parameshvara. Chitta nature has various other names, such as Chaitanya Braham, Consciousness, ParamaShiva, cosmic intellect, and Parātmā. Ananda, the blissful energy of Keval Brahma, is also called YogaMāyā (Gita 4.06, 7.25).

(2b) Chitta and **(2c)** Ananda natures combine to give rise to the fourth Pāda, the **Avyakta Brahma** or **(3) Avyakta Akshara Brahma** in Paramākāsha. This is known by various names such as the inexplicable Brahma, Avyakta, Adi Purusha, Adi Prakriti, Pradhān, Sarva Kārana Kāranam (cause of all causes). Avyakta Brahma, a small fraction of the Absolute, expands into infinite cosmos, as mentioned in Gita 8.18 and 10.41. Paramākāsh is also the abode of major powers of YogaMāyā, such as: power to veil the real nature of things (Avaran Shakti), power to place obstructions (Vikshep Shakti), powers to multiply and become many (Vigrah Shakti), powers of cosmic intellect, knowledge, and action, and power of converting energy into matter and vice versa.

Lord Krishna is known as **Golokinātha** in Paramākāsha. Golokinātha (or Avyakta Brahma) has two major expansions: **(3a) PranavaBrahma (or BrahmaShiva) and (3b)** Māyā **Brahma. PranavaBrahma** expands into **(3a.1) Omkāra (or Nādashiva). Omkāra** expands into **(3a.1a) AUM** (or **Shiva)** (Gita 10.25). **PranavaBrahma** also gives rise to **(3a.2) Gāyatri** (Gita 10.35) which is the abode of the **Vedas** (Gita 7.08).

(3b) Māyā**Brahma** is a reflection of **(2c)** YogaMāyā in Paramākāsha. It undergoes further successive transformations as: MahāMāyā, KālaMāyā and **(3b.**1) Māyā (Gita 7.14).

The creative power of Māyā creates **Brahmāndākāsha** by a small fraction (Residual Energy) of her power. A Golden Egg or **HiranyaGarbha (4)** is also created by Māyā Devi in

Brahmāndākāsh. AdiNārāyana (or **Adi Purusha, Shambhu, MahāDeva**) and **MahāDevi** (or **Mother Nature/Ambā**) remain in an inactive (YogaNidrā) state for over 311 trillion years (verse 9.07) in the Golden Egg until the cosmic sound vibration (or a big bang) of **AUM** activates the Golden Egg giving rise to **(4a) Purusha** (also known as **Kshara Purusha, Nārāyana, MahāVishnu**, Gita 7.05, 15.16) and **(4b) Prakriti** (also known as **Nature**, Gita 7.04). MahāVishnu creates infinite Cosmic Eggs (Brahmāndas) by His breathing power. Nature has three Gunas or modes (see Chapter 14). The combination of these three Gunas of Nature is called **(4b.1)** the Cosmic Mind (Mahatatattva, Tannamātrā or **Mahat**).

In Ghatākāsha (or Vishnu Loka), **Nārāyana/MahāVishnu** of Brahmāndākāsha appears as **(5) Lord Vishnu** where he is also called **Kshirodak Vishnu**, and he further expands his role as **(5b) Brahmā** and **(5c) Shankara**. Brahmā creates seven heavens, seven lower planets (Pātāls), Jambu islands, earth, and other hellish planets. During partial dissolution (Gita 8.17), the entire creation of Brahmā rests in the abdomen of Kshirodak Vishnu. Nārāyana also expands as **Niranjan Deva** and **Ishvara**. **Niranjan Deva** activates the cosmic mind **(4b.1)** and creates **(5d) five basic elements** (earth, water, fire, air, subtle space, also see Gita 7.04) that are further transformed into a body mass (Pind) made up of **twenty four elements** (See Gita 13.06 for more details), out of which physical bodies of living beings, **Jīva**, on the earth are created when the **Supreme Lord Krishna** puts His seed of life force (see verses 7.10, 10.39, and 14.04) into the body mass (Pind) and resides in the inner psyche of all beings as **Ishvara** (see Gita verses 15.07 and 18.61). Jīva transmigrates into 8.4 million species of life on the earth as long as it remains in bodily concept due to the veil of ignorance created by Māyā. Jīva attains salvation when, by virtue of one's good Karma, one obtains the grace of God, Gita, or a SadGuru, and truly realizes that he or she is not this physical body or a doer; but Atmā, a divine instrument and an integral part and parcel of the Supreme Being.

Everything in Brahmāndākāsha and Ghatākāsha is called Kshara or temporal. Everything in Sadākāsha and Paramākāsha, is called Akshara or eternal. The Supreme Being is beyond both temporal and eternal as stated in verse 15.18.

यो माम् एवम् असंमूढो जानाति पुरुषोत्तमम् ।
स सर्वविद् भजति मां सर्वभावेन भारत ।।१९।।

yo māṁ evam asaṁmūḍho jānāti puruṣottamam
sa sarvavid bhajati māṁ sarvabhāvena bhārata

The wise, who truly understand Me as the Supreme Being, know everything and worship Me wholeheartedly, O Arjuna. (See also 7.14, 14.26, and 18.66) (15.19)

इति गुह्यतमं शास्त्रम् इदम् उक्तं मयाऽनघ ।
एतद् बुद्ध्वा बुद्धिमान् स्यात् कृतकृत्यश्च भारत ।।२०।।

iti guhyatamaṁ śāstram idam uktaṁ mayā'nagha
etad buddhvā buddhimān syāt kṛtakṛtyaśca bhārata

Thus, I have explained this most secret transcendental science of the Absolute. Having understood this, one becomes enlightened, one's all duties are accomplished, and the goal of human life is achieved, O Arjuna. (15.20)

ॐ तत्सदिति श्रीमद्भगवद्गीतासूपनिषत्सु ब्रह्मविद्यायां योगशास्त्रे
श्रीकृष्णार्जुनसंवादे पुरुषोत्तमयोगो नाम पञ्चदशोऽध्यायः ।।

OM tatsaditi śrīmadbhagavadgītāsūpaniṣatsu brahmavidyāyāṁ
yogaśāstre śrīkṛṣṇārjuna saṁvāde puruṣottamayogo
nāma pañcadaśo'dhyāyaḥ

Thus ends the fifteenth chapter named "The Supreme Being" of the Upaniṣad of the Bhagavadgītā, the scripture of yoga, dealing with the science of the Absolute in the form of the dialogue between Śrīkṛṣṇa and Arjuna.

अथ षोडशोऽध्यायः
CHAPTER 16
दैवासुरसंपद्विभागयोगः
DIVINE AND THE DEMONIC QUALITIES

MAJOR DIVINE QUALITIES THAT SHOULD BE CULTIVATED FOR SALVATION

श्रीभगवानुवाच
अभयं सत्त्वसंशुद्धिर् ज्ञानयोगव्यवस्थितिः ।
दानं दमश्च यज्ञश्च स्वाध्यायस् तप आर्जवम् ॥१॥
śrī bhagavān uvāca
abhayaṁ sattvasaṁśuddhir jñānayoga vyavasthitiḥ
dānaṁ damaśca yajñaśca svādhyāyas tapa ārjavam

अहिंसा सत्यम् अक्रोधस् त्यागः शान्तिर् अपैशुनम् ।
दया भूतेष्व् अलोलुप्त्वं मार्दवं ह्रीर् अचापलम् ॥२॥
ahiṁsā satyam akrodhas tyāgaḥ śāntir apaiśunam
dayā bhūteṣv aloluptvaṁ mārdavaṁ hrīr acāpalam

तेजः क्षमा धृतिः शौचम् अद्रोहो नातिमानिता ।
भवन्ति संपदं दैवीम् अभिजातस्य भारत ॥३॥
tejaḥ kṣamā dhṛtiḥ śaucam adroho nā'timānitā
bhavanti saṁpadaṁ daivīm abhijātasya bhārata

Lord Krishna said: Fearlessness, purity of the inner psyche, perseverance in the yoga of Self-knowledge, charity, sense-restraint, sacrifice, study of the scriptures, austerity, honesty; nonviolence, truthfulness, absence of anger, renunciation, equanimity, abstinence from malicious talk, compassion for all creatures, freedom from greed, gentleness, modesty, absence of fickleness, splendor, forgiveness, fortitude, cleanliness, absence of malice, and absence of pride — these are some of the

qualities of those endowed with divine virtues, O Arjuna. (16.01-03)

One must not condemn anybody and commend one self (MB 3.207.50). We should treat others in the same manner as we would like ourselves to be treated (MB 12.167.09). A person of demonic nature needs to be dealt with and controlled differently than a person of divine nature (MB 12.109.30). No one is perfect. People do things because they don't know any better, so we should not censure them. We all pay the price for those who act out of ignorance. Speaking ill of others is the most heinous sin. Do not see others' faults; improve your own shortcomings until you yourself become enlightened.

One should not talk about, listen to, or even think about the faults and shortcomings of others. When we think about the defects of others, our own minds become polluted. Nothing is gained by finding fault with others; therefore, find your own faults and correct them. To love the unlovable, to be kind to the unkind, and to be gracious to the ungracious is really divine. It is said that we will have to account for how we treat others.

Values may also create problems if one forgets that people have different values; my values will be different from yours. A conflict of values between individuals ruins relationships. In practice, sometimes two values of the same person also conflict. For example, if telling a lie saves a valuable life, one should not tell the truth. One should not be blindly attached to values because a value is not absolute. We should neither sneer at any ideal nor judge others by our own standards because basic unity in variety is the plan of the creator.

All kinds of people make up this world. You want to change others so that you can be free, but it never works that way. If you accept others totally and unconditionally, only then you are free. People are what they are because they have their own backgrounds, and they cannot be otherwise (Swami Dayananda). You can love your spouse and not like the way he or she acts. Your enemy might become your friend if you allow him or her to be who he or she is. If you want to make an enemy, try to change someone. People will change only when it becomes more difficult to suffer than to change. No one is in a position to disqualify another's way of life, thinking, or ideas. Evolution on the ladder of perfection is a slow and difficult process. It is not an easy task to get rid of Karmic impressions of the past, but one must try. Changes come by one's own effort and when the season of the grace of God comes, not a day before. Also, the manifestation of primordial energy, consciousness, is different in different beings. Therefore, seek reconciliation with everything in the universe, and everything will become your friend. Ramakrishna said: When divinity dawns, the human weaknesses vanish of their own accord just as the petals drop off when the flower develops into the fruit.

Mortals are helplessly tied like cattle by the rope of latent desires born of their Karmic footprints. This rope can be cut only if we use the God-given knife of intellect that animals do not have. A tiger is controlled by the instinct to kill and is helpless in this regard. Human beings are endowed with intellect and power to reason by which they can slowly and steadily cut the rope. We fail to use our power of reasoning and intellect due to ignorance. One's enemy is none other than the other side of oneself. Sometimes intellect is taken away by the trick of divine illusory energy (Maya) before the dawn of fate-born adversity. One must use intellect, the precious divine gift to human beings, to analyze the situation. There is no other way to get out of the vicious circle of Maya.

No one can hurt one who does not do violence to others by thought, word, or deed (VP 1.19.05). Even violent animals do not harm those who practice nonviolence by thought, word, and deed (MB 12.175.27). One who does not do violence to any creature, gets what one wishes and becomes successful in all spiritual disciplines without too much effort (MS 5.47).

The higher form of life uses the lower form of life as food for sustenance (MB 12.15.20). It is impossible to practice nonviolence — or any other value — in an absolute sense. Even farming operations involve violence to insects and earthworms.

Practicing nonviolence towards all creatures is meant for our own evolution on the ladder of perfection. A minimal amount of necessary violence in the day-to-day practical life is required. Determination of minimum vio lence is, of course, very subjective. Violence should never be used in service of a personal grudge. It may be used to defend the weak or to uphold Dharma (order and justice).

दम्भो दर्पोऽभिमानश्च क्रोधः पारुष्यम् एव च ।
अज्ञानं चाभिजातस्य पार्थ संपदम् आसुरीम् ॥४॥
dambho darpo'bhimānaśca krodhaḥ pāruṣyam eva ca
ajñānaṁ cā'bhijātasya pārtha saṁpadam āsurīm

DEMONIC QUALITIES THAT SHOULD BE GIVEN UP BEFORE SPIRITUAL JOURNEY CAN BEGIN

O Arjuna, the marks of those who are born with demonic qualities are: hypocrisy, arrogance, pride, anger, harshness, and ignorance. (16.04)

It is the universal practice to return the favor — in one way or another — to those who have been helpful to you (VR 5.01.113). An ungrateful person is the worst person. One must abandon such a person (MB 12.168.26). There is no atonement for ungratefulness in this world (MB 12.172.25). It is said that even carnivores do not eat the flesh of an ungrateful person (MB 5.36.42). One must feel and express genuine gratitude if one accepts something from another person.

दैवी संपद् विमोक्षाय निबन्धायासुरी मता ।
मा शुचः संपदं दैवीम् अभिजातोऽसि पाण्डव ॥५॥
daivī saṁpad vimokṣāya nibandhāyā'surī matā
mā śucaḥ saṁpadaṁ daivīm abhijāto'si pāṇḍava

Divine qualities lead to salvation, the demonic qualities are said to be for bondage. Do not grieve, O Arjuna — you are born with divine qualities. (16.05)

Habits of sinful activity are very difficult to get rid of; therefore, one should always avoid sinful acts and practice good deeds (MB 3.209.41). Fundamental morality is the backbone of spiritual life. Self-knowledge without moral virtues is as incomplete as food without salt.

THERE ARE ONLY TWO TYPES OF HUMAN BEINGS — THE WISE AND THE IGNORANT

द्वौ भूतसर्गौ लोकेऽस्मिन् दैव आसुर एव च ।
दैवो विस्तरशः प्रोक्त आसुरं पार्थ मे शृणु ।।६।।

dvau bhūtasargau loke'smin daiva āsura eva ca
daivo vistaraśaḥ prokta āsuraṁ pārtha me śṛṇu

There are only two types (or castes) of human beings in this world: The divine, or the wise; and the demonic, or the ignorant. The divine has been described at length; now hear from Me about the demonic, O Arjuna. (16.06)

Self-knowledge manifests as divine qualities, and ignorance manifests as demonic qualities. Those who are in tune with the cosmic plan have divine qualities; those who are out of tune with the divine plan possess demonic qualities. Those who acted piously in their past lives are born with divine qualities, and those who were sinful in previous life are born with demonic qualities.

प्रवृत्तिं च निवृत्तिं च जना न विदुर् आसुराः ।
न शौचं नापि चाचारो न सत्यं तेषु विद्यते ।।७।।

pravṛttim ca nivṛttiṁ ca janā na vidur āsurāḥ
na śaucaṁ nā'pi cā'cāro na satyaṁ teṣu vidyate

Persons of demonic nature do not know what to do and what not to do. They have neither purity nor good conduct nor truthfulness. (16.07)

असत्यम् अप्रतिष्ठं ते जगद् आहुर् अनीश्वरम् ।
अपरस्परसंभूतं किम् अन्यत् कामहैतुकम् ॥८॥

asatyam apratiṣṭhaṁ te jagad āhur anīśvaram
aparasparasaṁbhūtaṁ kim anyat kāmahaitukam

They say: The world is unreal, without a substratum, without a God, and without an order. Sexual union of man and woman alone and nothing else causes the world. (16.08)

एतां दृष्टिम् अवष्टभ्य नष्टात्मानोऽल्पबुद्धयः ।
प्रभवन्त्य् उग्रकर्माणः क्षयाय जगतोऽहिताः ॥९॥

etāṁ dṛṣṭim avaṣṭabhya naṣṭā'tmāno'lpabuddhayaḥ
prabhavanty ugrakarmāṇaḥ kṣayāya jagato'hitāḥ

Adhering to these (and other) twisted, diabolic views, these degraded souls — with small intellect and cruel deeds — are born as enemies for the destruction of the world. (16.09)

कामम् आश्रित्य दुष्पूरं दम्भमानमदान्विताः ।
मोहाद् गृहीत्वाऽसद्ग्राहान् प्रवर्तन्तेऽशुचिव्रताः ॥१०॥

kāmam āśritya duṣpūraṁ dambhamānamadānvitāḥ
mohād gṛhītvā'sadgrāhān pravartante'śucivratāḥ

Filled with insatiable desires, hypocrisy, pride, and arrogance; holding wrong views due to delusion, they act with impure motives. (16.10)

चिन्ताम् अपरिमेयां च प्रलयान्ताम् उपाश्रिताः ।
कामोपभोगपरमा एतावद् इति निश्चिताः ॥११॥

cintām aparimeyāṁ ca pralayāntām upāśritāḥ
kāmopabhogaparamā etāvad iti niścitāḥ

आशापाशशतैर् बद्धाः कामक्रोधपरायणाः ।
ईहन्ते कामभोगार्थम् अन्यायेनार्थसञ्चयान् ॥१२॥

āśāpāśaśatair baddhāḥ kāmakrodhaparāyaṇāḥ
īhante kāmabhogārtham anyāyenā'rthasañcayān

Obsessed with endless anxiety lasting until death, considering sense gratification their highest aim, and convinced that sense pleasure is everything, bound by hundreds of ties of desire and enslaved by lust and anger, they strive to obtain wealth by unlawful means to fulfill sensual pleasures. They think: (16.11-12)

इदम् अद्य मया लब्धम् इमं प्राप्स्ये मनोरथम् ।
इदम् अस्तीदम् अपि मे भविष्यति पुनर् धनम् ॥१३॥

idam adya mayā labdham imaṁ prāpsye manoratham
idam astī'dam api me bhaviṣyati punar dhanam

This has been gained by me today; I shall fulfill this desire; I have this much wealth and will have more wealth in the future; (16.13)

असौ मया हतः शत्रुर् हनिष्ये चापरान् अपि ।
ईश्वरोऽहम् अहं भोगी सिद्धोऽहं बलवान् सुखी ॥१४॥

asau mayā hataḥ śatrur haniṣye cā'parān api
īśvaro'ham ahaṁ bhogī siddho'haṁ balavān sukhī

That enemy has been slain by me, and I shall slay others also. I am the Lord. I am the enjoyer. I am successful, powerful, and happy; (16.14)

आढ्योऽभिजनवान् अस्मि कोऽन्योऽस्ति सदृशो मया ।
यक्ष्ये दास्यामि मोदिष्य इत्य् अज्ञानविमोहिताः ॥१५॥

āḍhyo'bhijanavān asmi ko'nyo'sti sadṛśo mayā
yakṣye dāsyāmi modiṣya ity ajñānavimohitāḥ

अनेकचित्तविभ्रान्ता मोहजालसमावृताः ।
प्रसक्ताः कामभोगेषु पतन्ति नरकेऽशुचौ ॥१६॥

anekacittavibhrāntā mohajālasamāvṛtāḥ
prasaktāḥ kāmabhogeṣu patanti narake'śucau

I am rich and born in a noble family. Who is equal to me? I shall perform sacrifice, I shall give charity, and I shall rejoice. Thus they are deluded by ignorance, bewildered by many fancies, entangled in the net of delusion, addicted to the enjoyment of sensual pleasures, they fall into a foul hell. (16.15-16)

आत्मसंभाविताः स्तब्धा धनमानमदान्विताः ।
यजन्ते नामयज्ञैस् ते दम्भेनाविधिपूर्वकम् ॥१७॥

ātmasaṁbhāvitāḥ stabdhā dhanamānamadānvitāḥ
yajante nāmayajñais te dambhenā'vidhipūrvakam

Self-conceited, stubborn, filled with pride and intoxication of wealth, they perform service only in name for show, not according to scriptural injunction. (16.17)

अहंकारं बलं दर्पं कामं क्रोधं च संश्रिताः ।
माम् आत्मपरदेहेषु प्रद्विषन्तोऽभ्यसूयकाः ॥१८॥

ahaṁkāraṁ balaṁ darpaṁ kāmaṁ krodhaṁ ca saṁśritāḥ
mām ātmaparadeheṣu pradviṣanto'bhyasūyakāḥ

These malicious people cling to egoism, power, arrogance, lust, and anger; and they deny My presence in their own body and in others' bodies. (16.18)

SUFFERING IS THE DESTINY OF THE IGNORANT

तान् अहं द्विषतः क्रूरान् संसारेषु नराधमान् ।
क्षिपाम्य् अजस्रम् अशुभान् आसुरीष्व् एव योनिषु ॥१९॥
tān ahaṁ dviṣataḥ krūrān saṁsāreṣu narādhamān
kṣipāmy ajasram aśubhān āsurīṣv eva yoniṣu

I hurl these haters, these cruel, sinful, and mean people, into the cycles of death and birth in the womb of demons (or degraded parents) again and again, according to their Karma. (16.19)

आसुरीं योनिम् आपन्ना मूढा जन्मनि जन्मनि ।
माम् अप्राप्यैव कौन्तेय ततो यान्त्य् अधमां गतिम् ॥२०॥
āsurīṁ yonim āpannā mūḍhā janmani janmani
mām aprāpyai'va kaunteya tato yānty adhamāṁ gatim

O Arjuna, entering the wombs of demons, birth after birth, the deluded ones sink to the lowest level without ever attaining Me (until their minds turn Godward by My causeless mercy). (16.20)

A never-ending war between good and evil forces is going on in each person's life. One takes birth to learn to purge the demonic qualities that block the gateway to God-realization. God appears only after the devil within us is completely subjugated. Spirit does not have any of the three qualities of material Nature. These qualities belong to body and mind only. Scriptures say: The divine, illusory energy (Maya) creates a multitude of pairs of opposites, such as good and evil, loss and gain, pleasure and pain, hope and despair, compassion and apathy, generosity and greed, perseverance and laziness, courage and cowardice, love and hatred, merits and demerits, and divine and demonic qualities. They have no real existence whatsoever. Therefore, it is wise not to note any merit or demerit in people (BP 11.19.45, TR 7.41.00).

LUST, ANGER, AND GREED ARE THE THREE GATES TO HELL

त्रिविधं नरकस्येदं द्वारं नाशनम् आत्मनः ।
कामः क्रोधस् तथा लोभस् तस्माद् एतत् त्रयं त्यजेत् ॥२१॥

trividhaṁ narakasye'daṁ dvāraṁ nāśanam ātmanaḥ
kāmaḥ krodhas tathā lobhas tasmād etat trayaṁ tyajet

Lust, anger, and greed are the three gates of hell leading to the downfall (or bondage) of the individual. Therefore, one must learn to give up these three. (16.21)

The Upanishad says: A golden gate (of lust, anger, greed, illusion, delusion, and attachment) blocks the passage to God (IsU 15). This gate can be opened by concerted, individual effort only. Lust, anger, and greed were created to control the entry of human beings to heaven and to lead them to the gates of hell. Lust, anger, and greed evaporate from the mind only after discovering that there is no 'I' and 'my'. Uncontrolled greed for material possessions of modern civilization may destroy the possessor by destroying the natural environment, the very support of life and civilization.

Selfish desire or lust is the root of all evil. Mundane desires are also the origin of all demonic qualities. These demonic or negative qualities, such as anger, greed, attachment, pride, jealousy, hatred, and fraud, are born out of desire and are also called sin. Desire, when fulfilled, brings more desires, thereby breeding greed. Unfulfilled desires cause anger. Anger is a temporary insanity. People do sinful acts when they are angry. They who act in haste under the spell of anger, repent afterwards. Ignorance of metaphysics is responsible for lust; therefore, lust can be removed only by acquiring Self-knowledge. Lust also obscures Self-knowledge as a cloud covers the sun. One must learn to control desires with contentment, and anger with forgiveness. They who have overcome desires have really conquered the world and live a peaceful, healthy, and happy life.

एतैर् विमुक्तः कौन्तेय तमोद्वारैस् त्रिभिर् नरः ।
आचरत्य् आत्मनः श्रेयस् ततो याति परां गतिम् ।।२२।।
etair vimuktaḥ kaunteya tamodvārais tribhir naraḥ
ācaraty ātmanaḥ śreyas tato yāti parāṁ gatim

One who is liberated from these three gates of hell, O Arjuna, does what is best and consequently reaches Me. (16.22)

Lust, anger, and greed are the commanders of the army of illusion (Maya) that must be defeated before salvation is possible. The best way to become free from demonic qualities is to follow any one of the paths discussed in the Gita, as well as other scriptural injunctions.

ONE MUST FOLLOW THE SCRIPTURAL INJUNCTIONS

यः शास्त्रविधिम् उत्सृज्य वर्तते कामकारतः ।
न स सिद्धिम् अवाप्नोति न सुखं न परां गतिम् ।।२३।।
yaḥ śāstravidhim utsṛjya vartate kāmakārataḥ
na sa siddhim avāpnoti na sukhaṁ na parāṁ gatim

One who acts under the influence of desires, disobeying scriptural injunctions, neither attains perfection nor happiness, nor the Supreme Abode. (16.23)

The world becomes full of sweetness and beauty for those who live their life according to the law of the scriptures (RV 1.90.06). A scripture is the blueprint for society. It deals with every aspect of life and lays down the ground rules for proper development of all men, women, and children. For example, Manu said: Women must be honored and adorned. Where women are honored, there celestial controllers dwell pleased. Women must always be loved and protected from the temptation of evil-minded men. A woman's father protects her in childhood; her husband protects her in youth; and her sons protect her in old age (MS

3.56). Fortitude, righteousness (Dharma), friends, and spouse — these four are tested only during adversity. To be devoted — in thought, word, and deed — to each other should be the only religion, the only vow, and the only duty of a husband and wife (TR 3.04.05). The Bible says: Men ought to love their wives as their own bodies, and the wife should respect her husband. Respect, and submit yourselves one to another in the fear of God (Ephesians 5.21-33). However, men and women have differing roles to play in the cosmic drama; therefore, their needs and temperament are different.

One must not find fault or criticize any scripture because the scripture is the foundation stone of righteousness (Dharma) and social order. One can get name, fame, peace, and salvation by just following the scriptures (MS 2.09). The study of scriptures keeps the mind absorbed in high thoughts and is a spiritual discipline by itself. One is delivered by the practice of the truth of the scriptures and not by mere lip service. Guru Nanak said: One who preaches to others but does not practice the same, shall take birth again and again.

Let God, Gita, and Guru show us the way to enlightenment. People cannot be saved from the spell of divine, illusory power (Maya) just by using their own wisdom. They must follow a scripture with faith, especially in this age when it is difficult to find a true guru. Adherence to the high teachings of the scriptures will ward off all evil and bring about good. If a bridge is built, even an ant can easily cross the river, no matter how big a river is. Similarly, the scripture is the bridge to cross over the river of Maya. Therefore, one should always follow the guidance of a person who is well versed in the scriptures, as stated by the Lord in the following verse:

तस्माच् छास्त्रं प्रमाणं ते कार्याकार्यव्यवस्थितौ ।
ज्ञात्वा शास्त्रविधानोक्तं कर्म कर्तुम् इहार्हसि ॥२४॥

tasmāc chāstraṁ pramāṇaṁ te kāryākāryavyavasthitau
jñātvā śāstravidhānoktaṁ karma kartum ihā'rhasi

Therefore, let the scripture be your guide in determining what should be done and what should not be done. You should perform your duty following the scriptural injunction. (16.24)

The Ten Commandments of Hinduism according to sage Patanjali (PYS 2.30-2.32), are: (1) Nonviolence, (2) Truthfulness, (3) Non-stealing, (4) Celibacy or sense control, (5) Non-greed, (6) Purity of thought, word, and deed, (7) Contentment, (8) Austerity or renuncia tion, (9) Study of scriptures, and (10) Surrendering to God with faithful loving devotion.

Compare these with the ten basic teachings of the Bible: (1) Thou shall not kill; (2) Do not lie; (3) Do not steal; (4) Do not commit adultery; (5) Do not covet; (6) Do not divorce your wife; (7) Do for others what you want them to do for you; (8) If anyone slaps you on the right cheek, turn the other cheek; (9) Love your neighbor as yourself; and (10) Love the Lord with all thy heart.

The Eightfold Noble Path of Buddhism is: Right view, right thought, right speech, right deeds, right livelihood, right effort, right resolve, and right meditation. Abstinence from all evil, performance of good acts, and purification of the mind is the doctrine of Buddha.

The five cardinal principles of Islam are: (1) Faith in God, His message, and His messengers; (2) Meditation and prayer on the glory, greatness, and the message of God for spiritual growth; (3) Helping others by giving charity; (4) Austerity for self-purification by fasting in the month of Ramadan; and (5) Pilgrimage to the holy places.

All great masters have given us Truth revealed by the Supreme. Krishna taught us to feel spiritual oneness by seeing divinity in each and everyone. Buddha taught us to purify ourselves and have compassion for all creatures. Christ asked us to love all beings as we love ourselves. Muhammad taught us to submit to the will of God and act like His instruments.

In some religions, however, only the members of one's own sect are considered favorites of God, and others are considered infidels. The Vedas teach not only mere religious tolerance but the acceptance of all other religions and prophets as analogous to one's own. The Vedas say: Let noble thoughts come to us from everywhere (RV 1.89.01). The dignity and welfare of humanity lie in the unity of races and religion (Swami Harihar). True knowledge of religion breaks down all barriers, including the barriers between faiths (Gandhi). Any religion that creates walls of conflict and hatred among people in the name of God is not a religion, but selfish politics in disguise. We have no right to criticize any religion, sect, or cult in any way. Differences in human interpretation of scriptures — the transcendent voice — are due to taking the literal meaning, prejudice, ignorance, taking lines out of context, as well as distortion, misinterpretation, and interpolation with personal selfish motives.

ॐ तत्सदिति श्रीमद्भगवद्गीतासूपनिषत्सु ब्रह्मविद्यायां योगशास्त्रे
श्रीकृष्णार्जुनसंवादे दैवासुरसंपद्विभागयोगो नाम षोडशोऽध्यायः ॥

OM tatsaditi śrīmadbhagavadgītāsūpaniṣatsu
brahmavidyāyāṁ yogaśāstre śrīkṛṣṇārjuna saṁvāde
daivāsurasaṁpadvibhāgayogo
nāma ṣoḍaśo'dhyāyaḥ

Thus ends the sixteenth chapter named "Divine and the Demonic Qualities" of the Upaniṣad of the Bhagavadgītā, the scripture of yoga, dealing with the science of the Absolute in the form of the dialogue between Śrīkṛṣṇa and Arjuna.

अथ सप्तदशोऽध्यायः
CHAPTER 17
श्रद्धात्रयविभागयोगः
THREEFOLD FAITH

अर्जुन उवाच
ये शास्त्रविधिम् उत्सृज्य यजन्ते श्रद्धयान्विताः ।
तेषां निष्ठा तु का कृष्ण सत्त्वम् आहो रजस् तमः ॥१॥
arjuna uvāca
ye śāstravidhim utsṛjya yajante śraddhayā'nvitāḥ
teṣāṁ niṣṭhā tu kā kṛṣṇa sattvam āho rajas tamaḥ

Arjuna said: What is the mode of devotion of those who perform spiritual practices with faith but without following the scriptural injunctions, O Krishna? Is it in the mode of goodness, passion, or ignorance? (17.01)

THREE TYPES OF FAITH

श्रीभगवानुवाच
त्रिविधा भवति श्रद्धा देहिनां सा स्वभावजा ।
सात्त्विकी राजसी चैव तामसी चेति तां शृणु ॥२॥
śrī bhagavān uvāca
trividhā bhavati śraddhā dehināṁ sā svabhāvajā
sāttvikī rājasī cai'va tāmasī ce'ti tāṁ śṛṇu

Lord Krishna said: The natural faith of embodied beings is of three kinds: Goodness, passion, and ignorance. Now hear about these from Me. (17.02)

सत्त्वानुरूपा सर्वस्य श्रद्धा भवति भारत ।
श्रद्धामयोऽयं पुरुषो यो यच्छ्रद्धः स एव सः ॥३॥

sattvānurūpā sarvasya śraddhā bhavati bhārata
śraddhāmayo'yaṁ puruṣo yo yacchraddhaḥ sa eva saḥ

O Arjuna, the faith of each is in accordance with one's own natural disposition that is governed by Karmic impressions. One is known by one's faith. One can become whatever one wants to be if one constantly contemplates the object of desire with faith. (17.03)

One can attain success in any endeavor if one perseveres with firm determination (MB 12.153.116). Whatever a person of purified mind desires, is obtained (MuU 3.01.10). The doer of good acts becomes good, and the doer of evil becomes evil. One becomes virtuous by virtuous deeds and vicious by vicious acts (BrU 4.04.05). One becomes what one constantly and intensely thinks of, irrespective of reasons, such as reverence, fear, jealousy, love, or even hatred (BP 11.09.22). You always get what you look for — consciously or unconsciously. The thought produces action; action soon becomes habits and habit leads to success in any endeavor when it becomes passion. Become passionate about what you want to achieve, and you will achieve it. Passion brings out the dormant forces within us.

We are the products of our own thoughts and desires, and we are our own architects. Thoughts create our destiny. We become what we think. There is a tremendous power in our thoughts to draw on the negative or positive energies around us. Where there is a will, there is a way. We should harbor noble thoughts because thoughts precede deeds. Thoughts control our physical, mental, financial, as well as spiritual well-being. Never allow any negative thought or doubt to enter. We have such a great power at our disposal, yet the irony is that we fail to use it. If you do not have what you want, you are not committed to it one hundred percent. You are the cause of everything that happens to you. You should not expect life's very best if you are not giving your very best. Success is achieved by a series of well planned steps taken slowly and persistently. Stephen Covey says: "The best way to predict your future is to create it." Every great achievement was once considered impossible. Never underestimate the potential and power of the human mind and spirit. Many books have been written and motivational programs developed for the practical application of the power of this single mantra of the Gita.

यजन्ते सात्त्विका देवान् यक्षरक्षांसि राजसाः ।
प्रेतान् भूतगणांश् चान्ये यजन्ते तामसा जनाः ॥४॥
yajante sāttvikā devān yakṣarakṣāṁsi rājasāḥ
pretān bhūtagaṇāṁś ca'nye yajante tāmasā janāḥ

Persons in the mode of goodness worship celestial controllers; those in the mode of passion worship supernatural rulers and demons; and those in the mode of ignorance worship ghosts and spirits. (17.04)

अशास्त्रविहितं घोरं तप्यन्ते ये तपो जनाः ।
दम्भाहंकारसंयुक्ताः कामरागबलान्विताः ॥५॥
aśāstravihitaṁ ghoraṁ tapyante ye tapo janāḥ
dambhāhaṁkāra saṁyuktāḥ kāma rāga balānvitāḥ

कर्षयन्तः शरीरस्थं भूतग्रामम् अचेतसः ।
मां चैवान्तःशरीरस्थं तान् विद्ध्य् आसुरनिश्चयान् ॥६॥
karṣayantaḥ śarīrasthaṁ bhūtagrāmam acetasaḥ
māṁ cai'vā'ntaḥśarīrasthaṁ tān viddhy āsuraniścayān

Ignorant persons of demonic nature are those who practice severe austerities without following the prescription of the scriptures, who are full of hypocrisy and egotism, who are impelled by the force of desire and attachment, and who senselessly torture the elements in their body and also Me who dwells within the body. (17.05-06)

THREE TYPES OF FOOD

आहारस् त्व् अपि सर्वस्य त्रिविधो भवति प्रियः ।
यज्ञस् तपस् तथा दानं तेषां भेदम् इमं शृणु ॥७॥

āhāras tv api sarvasya trividho bhavati priyaḥ
yajñas tapas tathā dānaṁ teṣāṁ bhedam imaṁ śṛṇu

The food preferred by all of us is also of three types. So are the sacrifice, austerity, and charity. Now hear the distinction between them. (17.07)

आयुःसत्त्वबलारोग्य-सुखप्रीतिविवर्धनाः ।
रस्याः स्निग्धाः स्थिरा हृद्या आहाराः सात्त्विकप्रियाः ॥८॥

āyuḥ sattva balārogya-sukha prīti vivardhanāḥ
rasyāḥ snigdhāḥ sthirā hṛdyā āhārāḥ sāttvikapriyāḥ

The foods that promote longevity, virtue, strength, health, happiness, and joy are juicy, smooth, substantial, and nutritious. Persons in the mode of goodness like such foods. (17.08)

One should eat good food for protecting and sustaining life as a patient takes medicine for protection from disease (MB 12.212.14). Whatever a person eats, his or her personal deity eats the same (VR 2.104.15, See also Gita 8.24). (Because) I am Thou, and Thou art I (BS 3.3.37). The food we eat becomes divided into three constituents. The grossest part turns into feces; the medium component becomes flesh, blood, marrow, and bone. Semen, the subtlest part, rises upward and nourishes the brain and subtle organs of the body by uniting with the vital force (ChU 6.05.01-6.06.02). Food is called the root of the body-tree. A healthy body and mind are the prerequisites for success in spiritual life. The mind will be healthy if the body is healthy. Persons in the mode of goodness like vegetarian foods. One can also become a noble person by taking vegetarian food because one becomes what one eats.

कट्वम्ललवणात्युष्ण-तीक्ष्णरूक्षविदाहिनः ।
आहारा राजसस्येष्टा दुःखशोकामयप्रदाः ॥९॥
katvamla lavaṇātyuṣṇa-tīkṣṇa rūkṣa vidāhinaḥ
āhārā rājasasye'ṣṭā duḥkha śokāmaya pradāḥ

People in the mode of passion like foods that are very bitter, sour, salty, hot, pungent, dry, and burning, and cause pain, grief, and disease. (17.09)

यातयामं गतरसं पूति पर्युषितं च यत्
उच्छिष्टम् अपि चामेध्यं भोजनं तामसप्रियम् ॥१०॥
yātayāmaṁ gatarasaṁ pūti paryuṣitaṁ ca yat
ucchiṣṭam api cā'medhyaṁ bhojanaṁ tāmasapriyam

People in the mode of ignorance like foods that are stale, tasteless, putrid, rotten, refuses, and impure (such as meat and alcohol). (17.10)

Purity of mind comes from purity of food. Truth is revealed to a pure mind. One becomes free from all bondage after knowing the Truth (ChU 7.26.02). Gambling, intoxication, illicit sexual relationships, and meat-eating are a natural, negative tendency of human beings, but abstaining from these four activities is really divine. One must avoid these four pillars of sin (BP 1.17.38). Abstaining from meat-eating is equivalent to performing one hundred holy sacrifices (MS 5.53-56).

THREE TYPES OF SACRIFICES

अफलाकाङ्क्षिभिर् यज्ञो विधिदृष्टो य इज्यते ।
यष्टव्यम् एवेति मनः समाधाय स सात्त्विकः ॥११॥
aphalākāṅkṣibhir yajño vidhidṛṣṭo ya ijyate
yaṣṭavyam eve'ti manaḥ samādhāya sa sāttvikaḥ

Sacrifice, enjoined by the scriptures and performed without the desire for the fruit, with a firm belief and conviction that it is a duty, is in the mode of goodness. (17.11)

अभिसन्धाय तु फलं दम्भार्थम् अपि चैव यत् ।
इज्यते भरतश्रेष्ठ तं यज्ञं विद्धि राजसम् ।।१२।।

abhisandhāya tu phalaṁ dambhārtham api cai'va yat
ijyate bharataśreṣṭha taṁ yajñaṁ viddhi rājasam

Sacrifice that is performed only for show and aiming for fruit, is in the mode of passion, O Arjuna. (17.12)

विधिहीनम् असृष्टान्नं मन्त्रहीनम् अदक्षिणम् ।
श्रद्धाविरहितं यज्ञं तामसं परिचक्षते ।।१३।।

vidhihīnam asṛṣṭānnaṁ mantrahīnam adakṣiṇam
śraddhāvirahitaṁ yajñaṁ tāmasaṁ paricakṣate

Sacrifice that is performed without following the scripture, in which no food is distributed, which is devoid of mantra, faith, and gift, is said to be in the mode of ignorance. (17.13)

A spiritual discipline or sacrifice is incomplete without a mantra, and a mantra is incomplete without a spiritual discipline (DB 7.35.60).

AUSTERITY OF THOUGHT, WORD, AND DEED

देवद्विजगुरुप्राज्ञ-पूजनं शौचम् आर्जवम् ।
ब्रह्मचर्यम् अहिंसा च शारीरं तप उच्यते ।।१४।।

deva dvija guru prājña-pūjanaṁ śaucam ārjavam
brahmacaryam ahiṁsā ca śārīraṁ tapa ucyate

The worship of celestial controllers, the priest, the guru, and the wise; purity, honesty, celibacy, and nonviolence— these are said to be the austerity of deed. (17.14)

अनुद्वेगकरं वाक्यं सत्यं प्रियहितं च यत् ।
स्वाध्यायाभ्यसनं चैव वाङ्मयं तप उच्यते ॥१५॥

anudvegakaraṁ vākyaṁ satyaṁ priyahitaṁ ca yat
svādhyāyā'bhyasanaṁ cai'va vāṅmayaṁ tapa ucyate

Speech that is non-offensive, truthful, pleasant, beneficial, and is used for the regular reading aloud of scriptures is called the austerity of word. (17.15)

The path of truth is the path of spiritual progress. The Upanishad says: Only the truthful wins, not the untruthful. Truth is the divine path by which the sages, who are free from desires, ascend to the Supreme Abode (MuU 3.01.06). To be truthful is desirable. To speak what is beneficial is better than speaking truth. That which brings the greatest benefit to a person is the real truth (MB 12.329.13). The real truth is that which produces the maximum benefit to people. That which harms a person in any way is untrue and wrong — although it may appear to be true at the first sight (MB 3.209.04). One may lie to protect the truth, but must not speak the truth for the protection of a lie.

A wise person should speak the truth if it is beneficial and keep quiet if it is harmful. One must speak the beneficial truth whether it is pleasant or unpleasant. Non-beneficial pleasant speech, such as flattery, should be avoided (VP 3.12.44). A pleasant speech is beneficial to all. One who speaks pleasantly wins the heart of all and is liked by everybody (MB 12.84.04). The wound inflicted by harsh words is very difficult to heal. The wise should never inflict such wounds on others (MB 5.34.80). Sweetness of speech and calmness of mind are the marks of a true yogi (Swami Atmananda Giri). One may lie — if it becomes absolutely necessary — to protect life, property, and righteousness (Dharma); during courtship; and for getting married (MB

12.109.19). Husband and wife should try to improve and help develop each other with tender loving care as a cow purifies her calf by licking. Their words to each other should be sweet, as if dipped in honey (AV 3.30.01-02).

Truth is the root of all noble virtues. One should present the bitter pill of truth with a sugar coating of pleasantness. Be truthful in a pleasant manner, but do not deviate from truth for the sake of pleasantness. Use candor with courtesy and avoid flattery. Speech should always be beneficial, truthful, and sweet. According to the Bible: It is not what goes into a person's mouth that makes one unclean; rather, what comes out of it (Matthew 15.11). Speech is the verbal reflection of one's personality, thinking, and mind; therefore, we should prefer silence to almost anything negative. Abstinence from harmful speech is very important.

मनःप्रसादः सौम्यत्वं मौनम् आत्मविनिग्रहः ।
भावसंशुद्धिर् इत्य् एतत् तपो मानसम् उच्यते ॥१६॥

manaḥprasādaḥ saumyatvaṁ maunam ātmavinigrahaḥ
bhāvasaṁśuddhir ity etat tapo mānasam ucyate

The austerity of thought includes serenity of mind, gentleness, equanimity, self-control, and the purity of thought. (17.16)

THREE TYPES OF AUSTERITY

श्रद्धया परया तप्तं तपस् तत् त्रिविधं नरैः ।
अफलाकाङ्क्षिभिर् युक्तैः सात्त्विकं परिचक्षते ॥१७॥

śraddhayā parayā taptaṁ tapas tat trividhaṁ naraiḥ
aphalākāṅkṣibhir yuktaiḥ sāttvikaṁ paricakṣate

The above mentioned threefold austerity (of thought, word, and deed) practiced by yogis with supreme faith, without a

desire for the fruit, is said to be in the mode of goodness. (17.17)

Nonviolence, truthfulness, forgiveness, kindness, and control of mind and senses are considered austerity by the wise (MB 12.79.18). There cannot be purity of word and deed without purity of thought.

सत्कारमानपूजार्थं तपो दम्भेन चैव यत् ।
क्रियते तद् इह प्रोक्तं राजसं चलम् अध्रुवम् ॥१८॥
satkāra māna pūjārthaṁ tapo dambhena cai'va yat
kriyate tad iha proktaṁ rājasaṁ calam adhruvam

Austerity that is performed for gaining respect, honor, reverence, and for the sake of show, yielding an uncertain and temporary result, is said to be in the mode of passion. (17.18)

मूढग्राहेणात्मनो यत् पीडया क्रियते तपः ।
परस्योत्सादनार्थं वा तत् तामसम् उदाहृतम् ॥१९॥
mūḍhagrāheṇā'tmano yat pīḍayā kriyate tapaḥ
parasyo'tsādanārthaṁ vā tat tāmasam udāhṛtam

Austerity performed with foolish stubbornness or with self-torture or for harming others, is said to be in the mode of ignorance. (17.19)

THREE TYPES OF CHARITY

दातव्यम् इति यद् दानं दीयतेऽनुपकारिणे ।
देशे काले च पात्रे च तद् दानं सात्त्विकं स्मृतम् ॥२०॥
dātavyam iti yad dānaṁ dīyate'nupakāriṇe
deśe kāle ca pātre ca tad dānaṁ sāttvikaṁ smṛtam

Charity that is given at the right place and time as a matter of duty, to a deserving candidate who does nothing in return, is considered to be in the mode of goodness. (17.20)

Charity in the mode of goodness is the best purifying, beneficial, and righteous act. It equally benefits both the giver and the receiver (MB 13.120.16). If you give a charity or gift, watch yourself closely for ulterior motives; don't look for anything in return. One never does anything for others, but for one's own benefit. Even charitable works done for others are really done for one's own good (MB 12.292.01). It is the giver, not the receiver, who is blessed. Yogiraj Mumtaz Ali says: When you serve a less fortunate person in any way — material or spiritual — you are not doing him or her a favor. In fact, one who receives your help does you a favor by accepting what you give, thereby helping you to evolve and move closer to the divine, blissful being, who in reality is within all.

Charity taken unnecessarily — compelled by greed for name or fame — does great harm to the recipient. Improper charity harms both the giver and the taker (MS 4.186). Give anything you can — love, knowledge, help, service, prayer, food, but look for no return. Love — the cheapest charity — holds the key to enter His Kingdom. Charity is not only the best, but also the only use of wealth. However, all genuine requests for charity should be handled with delicate care and diplomacy because charity denied may create a negative feeling that is harmful.

Charity has no value if the money is earned by wrongful means (MB 5.39.66). To obtain wealth for meritorious or charitable deeds using wrong means is like soiling one's dress and then washing it. Not to soil the dress in the first place is better than washing the dress after soiling (MB 3.02.49). You cannot accomplish a worthy end with unworthy means. Ends and means are absolutely inseparable (Stephen Covey). It is not possible to help everybody by giving material goods and money. To pray for the physical and spiritual welfare of others in trouble or need — including ones not on your favorite list — is called mental charity.

यत् तु प्रत्युपकारार्थं फलम् उद्दिश्य वा पुनः।
दीयते च परिक्लिष्टं तद् दानं राजसं स्मृतम् ।।२१।।

yat tu pratyupakārārthaṁ phalam uddiśya vā punaḥ
dīyate ca parikliṣṭaṁ tad dānaṁ rājasaṁ smṛtam

Charity that is given unwillingly or to get something in return or looking for some fruit, is said to be in the mode of passion. (17.21)

Jesus said: When you give something to a needy person, do not make a big show of it, but when you help a needy person, do it in such a way that even your closest friend will not know about it (Matthew 6.02-03). Charity given anonymously is the best charity. To give charity to an unworthy person or cause and not to give to a worthy person, are both wrong and worse than giving no charity. Charity that is obtained without asking for it, is the best; charity that is obtained upon asking is the second best; and charity given unwillingly should be avoided.

अदेशकाले यद् दानम् अपात्रेभ्यश्च दीयते ।
असत्कृतम् अवज्ञातं तत् तामसम् उदाहृतम् ।।२२।।

adeśakāle yad dānam apātrebhyaś ca dīyate
asatkṛtam avajñātaṁ tat tāmasam udāhṛtam

Charity that is given at a wrong place and time to unworthy persons or without paying respect to the receiver or with ridicule, is said to be in the mode of ignorance. (17.22)

Be considerate and compassionate to those less fortunate than you. Charity should be given without humiliating the receiver. Charity given by humiliating the receiver destroys the giver (VR 1.13.33). One should always remember that God is both the giver and the receiver.

THREEFOLD ASPECT OF GOD

ॐ तत् सद् इति निर्देशो ब्रह्मणस् त्रिविधः स्मृतः ।
ब्राह्मणास् तेन वेदाश्च यज्ञाश्च विहिताः पुरा ।।२३।।
auṁ tat sad iti nirdeśo brahmaṇas trividhaḥ smṛtaḥ
brāhmaṇās tena vedāśca yajñāśca vihitāḥ purā

ParaBrahma alone is all three — AUM (OM) TAT SAT — aspects of Reality. Persons with divine qualities, the Vedas, and sacrifice (or selfless service) were created by ParaBrahma in the ancient time. (17.23)

तस्माद् ओम् इत्य् उदाहृत्य यज्ञदानतपःक्रियाः ।
प्रवर्तन्ते विधानोक्ताः सततं ब्रह्मवादिनाम् ।।२४।।
tasmād om ity udāhṛtya yajña dāna tapaḥ kriyāḥ
pravartante vidhānoktāḥ satataṁ brahmavādinām

Therefore, acts of sacrifice, charity, and austerity prescribed in the scriptures are always commenced by uttering any one of the many names of God (such as AUM, Amen, or Allah) by the knowers of the Supreme. (17.24)

तद् इत्य् अनभिसंधाय फलं यज्ञतपःक्रियाः ।
दानक्रियाश्च विविधाः क्रियन्ते मोक्षकाङ्क्षिभिः ।।२५।।
tad ity anabhisaṁdhāya phalaṁ yajña tapaḥ kriyāḥ
dāna kriyāś ca vividhāḥ kriyante mokṣakāṅkṣibhiḥ

The seekers of salvation perform various types of sacrifice, charity, and austerity by uttering: He is all or 'TAT' without seeking a reward. (17.25)

सद्भावे साधुभावे च सद् इत्य् एतत् प्रयुज्यते ।
प्रशस्ते कर्मणि तथा सच्छब्दः पार्थ युज्यते ।।२६।।
sadbhāve sādhubhāve ca sad ity etat prayujyate
praśaste karmaṇi tathā sacchabdaḥ pārtha yujyate

The word 'SAT or Truth' is used in the sense of Reality and goodness. The word 'SAT' is also used for an auspicious act, O Arjuna. (17.26)

यज्ञे तपसि दाने च स्थितिः सद् इति चोच्यते ।
कर्म चैव तदर्थीयं सद् इत्य् एवाभिधीयते ॥२७॥

yajñe tapasi dāne ca sthitiḥ sad iti co'cyate
karma cai'va tadarthīyaṁ sad ity evā'bhidhīyate

Faith in sacrifice, charity, and austerity is also called Truth. Selfless service for the sake of the Supreme is verily termed as 'SAT'. (17.27)

अश्रद्धया हुतं दत्तं तपस् तप्तं कृतं च यत् ।
असद् इत्य् उच्यते पार्थ न च तत् प्रेत्य नो इह ॥२८॥

aśraddhayā hutaṁ dattaṁ tapas taptaṁ kṛtaṁ ca yat
asad ity ucyate pārtha na ca tat pretya no iha

Whatever is done without faith — whether it is sacrifice, charity, austerity, or any other act — is useless. It has no value here or hereafter, O Arjuna. (17.28)

ॐ तत्सदिति श्रीमद्भगवद्गीतासूपनिषत्सु ब्रह्मविद्यायां योगशास्त्रे
श्रीकृष्णार्जुनसंवादे श्रद्धात्रयविभागयोगो नाम सप्तदशोऽध्यायः ॥

OM tatsaditi śrīmadbhagavadgītāsūpaniṣatsu brahmavidyāyāṁ
yogaśāstre śrīkṛṣṇārjuna saṁvāde śraddhātrayavibhāgayogo
nāma saptadaśo'dhyāyaḥ

Thus ends the seventeenth chapter named "Threefold Faith" of the Upaniṣad of the Bhagavadgītā, the scripture of yoga, dealing with the science of the Absolute in the form of the dialogue between Śrīkṛṣṇa and Arjuna.

अथ अष्टादशोऽध्यायः
CHAPTER 18
मोक्षसंन्यासयोगः
NIRVANA THROUGH RENUNCIATION

अर्जुन उवाच
संन्यासस्य महाबाहो तत्त्वम् इच्छामि वेदितुम् ।
त्यागस्य च हृषीकेश पृथक् केशिनिषूदन ॥१॥

arjuna uvāca
saṁnyāsasya mahābāho tattvam icchāmi veditum
tyāgasya ca hṛṣīkeśa pṛthak keśiniṣūdana

Arjuna said: I wish to know the nature of renunciation (Samnyāsa) and sacrifice (Tyāga), and the difference between the two, O Lord Krishna. (18.01)

DEFINITION OF RENUNCIATION AND SACRIFICE

श्रीभगवानुवाच
काम्यानां कर्मणां न्यासं संन्यासं कवयो विदुः ।
सर्वकर्मफलत्यागं प्राहुस् त्यागं विचक्षणाः ॥२॥

śrī bhagavān uvāca
kāmyānāṁ karmaṇāṁ nyāsaṁ saṁnyāsaṁ kavayo viduḥ
sarva karma phala tyāgaṁ prāhus tyāgaṁ vicakṣaṇāḥ

Lord Krishna said: The sages define renunciation (Saṁnyāsa) as abstaining from all desire-ridden work. The wise define sacrifice (Tyāga) as the sacrifice of, and the freedom from, a selfish attachment to the fruits of all work. (See also 5.01, 5.05, and 6.01) (18.02)

We have used the word 'renunciation' for Samnyāsa, and 'sacrifice' for Tyāga in this rendering. A renunciant (Samnyāsi) does not own anything. A true renunciant works for others and lives for — not on — others. Samnyāsa means complete renunciation of doership, ownership, and personal selfish motive behind an action, whereas Tyāga means renunciation of the selfish attachment to the fruits of all work, or working just for God. A person who does sacrificial services (Seva) for God is called Tyāgi or a KarmaYogi. Thus a Tyāgi who thinks that he or she is doing all works just to please God will always remember Him. Therefore, it is mentioned in verse 12.12 that Tyāga is the best spiritual practice. The words 'Samnyāsa' and 'Tyāga' are used interchangeably in the Gita because there is no real difference between the two (See verses 5.04, 5.05, 6.01, and 6.02). According to the Gita, Samnyāsa does not mean living in the forest or any other secluded place outside society. Samnyāsa is a state of mind that is completely detached from the outcome or the fruits of work.

Everybody desires peace of mind, but that is only possible for one who works for God without being attached to results and dedicates the results of all work to God. This is not necessarily the same as offering all one's material wealth and possessions to one's guru as propagated by some sects.

त्याज्यं दोषवद् इत्य् एके कर्म प्राहुर् मनीषिणः ।
यज्ञदानतपःकर्म न त्याज्यम् इति चापरे ।।३।।

tyājyaṁ doṣavad ity eke karma prāhur manīṣiṇaḥ
yajña dāna tapaḥ karma na tyājyam iti cā'pare

Some philosophers say that all work is full of faults and should be given up, while others say that acts of sacrifice, charity, and austerity should not be abandoned. (18.03)

निश्चयं शृणु मे तत्र त्यागे भरतसत्तम ।
त्यागो हि पुरुषव्याघ्र त्रिविधः संप्रकीर्तितः ।।४।।

niścayaṁ śṛṇu me tatra tyāge bharata sattama
tyāgo hi puruṣa vyāghra trividhaḥ saṁprakīrtitaḥ

O Arjuna, listen to My conclusion about sacrifice. Sacrifice is said to be of three types. (18.04)

यज्ञदानतपःकर्म न त्याज्यं कार्यम् एव तत् ।
यज्ञो दानं तपश्चैव पावनानि मनीषिणाम् ।।५।।

yajña dāna tapaḥ karma na tyājyaṁ kāryam eva tat
yajño dānaṁ tapaś cai'va pāvanāni manīṣiṇām

Acts of service, charity, and austerity should not be abandoned, but should be performed because service, charity, and austerity are the purifiers of the wise. (18.05)

एतान्य् अपि तु कर्माणि सङ्गं त्यक्त्वा फलानि च ।
कर्तव्यानीति मे पार्थ निश्चितं मतम् उत्तमम् ।।६।।

etāny api tu karmāṇi saṅgaṁ tyaktvā phalāni ca
kartavyānī'ti me pārtha niścitaṁ matam uttamam

Even these obligatory works should be performed without attachment to the fruits. This is My definite supreme advice, O Arjuna. (18.06)

THREE TYPES OF SACRIFICE

नियतस्य तु संन्यासः कर्मणो नोपपद्यते ।
मोहात् तस्य परित्यागस् तामसः परिकीर्तितः ।।७।।

niyatasya tu saṁnyāsaḥ karmaṇo no'papadyate
mohāt tasya parityāgas tāmasaḥ parikīrtitaḥ

Giving up one's duty is not proper. The abandonment of obligatory work is due to delusion and is declared to be in the mode of ignorance. (18.07)

दुःखम् इत्येव यत् कर्म कायक्लेशभयात् त्यजेत् ।
स कृत्वा राजसं त्यागं नैव त्यागफलं लभेत् ।।८।।

duḥkham ity eva yat karma kāyakleśa bhayāt tyajet
sa kṛtvā rājasaṁ tyāgaṁ nai'va tyāgaphalaṁ labhet

One who abandons duty merely because it is difficult or because of fear of bodily affliction, does not get the benefits of sacrifice by performing such a sacrifice in the mode of passion. (18.08)

कार्यम् इत्येव यत् कर्म नियतं क्रियतेऽर्जुन ।
सङ्गं त्यक्त्वा फलं चैव स त्यागः सात्त्विको मतः ।।९।।

kāryam ity eva yat karma niyataṁ kriyate'rjuna
saṅgaṁ tyaktvā phalaṁ cai'va sa tyāgaḥ sāttviko mataḥ

Obligatory work performed as duty, renouncing selfish attachment to the fruit, is alone to be regarded as sacrifice in the mode of goodness, O Arjuna. (18.09)

Renunciation of attachment to sensual pleasures is the real sacrifice (Tyāga). The perfection of Tyāga comes only after a person becomes free from the clutches of attachments and aversions (MB 12.162.17). There is no eye better than the eye of Self-knowledge, no austerity better than truth, no pain greater than attachment, and no pleasure greater than Tyāga (MB 12.175.35). One cannot become happy without Tyāga; one cannot become fearless without Tyāga; and one cannot attain God without Tyāga (MB 12.176.22). Even the bliss of trance should not be enjoyed just for the sake of enjoyment. The Gita recommends renunciation while living in the world — not renunciation of the world as commonly misinterpreted.

Christ said: If you want perfection, give away everything you have, and then follow Me (Matthew 19.21). No one can serve two masters. You cannot serve both God and mammon — the material desires (Matthew 6.24, Luke 16.13). Christ did not hesitate to sacrifice his own life for the noble teachings. Lord Rama gave up His kingdom and even His wife for the establishment of righteousness (Dharma). Give up attachment and attain perfection by renunciation is the message of the Vedas and the Upanishads. Selfless service or 'Tyāga' is the essence of the Gita as given in this last chapter. A person who is Tyāgi cannot commit sin and is released from the cycles of transmigration. One can cross the ocean of transmigration and reach the shores of salvation in this very life by the boat of Tyāga.

The Nine Types of Renunciation leading to salvation, based on the teachings of the Gita, are: (1) Renunciation of actions forbidden by the scriptures (16.23-24), (2) Renunciation of lust, anger, greed, fear, likes and dislikes, and jealousy (3.34, 16.21); (3) Spurning of procrastination in the search of Truth (12.09), (4) Giving up feeling pride in one's knowledge, detachment, devotion, wealth, and charitable deeds (15.05, 16.01-04); (5) Rejection of selfish motives and attachment to the fruits of all works (2.51, 3.09, 4.20, 6.10), (6) Renunciation of the feeling of doership in all undertakings (12.13, 18.53), (7) Giving up thoughts of using the Lord to fulfill selfish, material desires (2.43, 7.16); (8) Spurning attachments to material objects, such as a house, wealth, position, and power (12.19, 13.09); and (9) Sacrifice of wealth, prestige, and even life for a noble cause and protection of righteousness (Dharma) (2.32, 4.28).

न द्वेष्ट्य् अकुशलं कर्म कुशले नानुषज्जते ।
त्यागी सत्त्वसमाविष्टो मेधावी छिन्नसंशयः ॥१०॥

na dveṣṭy akuśalaṁ karma kuśale nā'nuṣajjate
tyāgī sattvasamāviṣṭo medhāvī chinnasaṁśayaḥ

One who neither hates a disagreeable work, nor is attached to an agreeable work, is considered a renunciant (Tyāgi), imbued with the mode of goodness, intelligent, and free from all doubts about the Supreme Being. (18.10)

न हि देहभृता शक्यं त्यक्तुं कर्माण्य् अशेषतः ।
यस् तु कर्मफलत्यागी स त्यागीत्य् अभिधीयते ॥११॥

na hi dehabhṛtā śakyaṁ tyaktuṁ karmāṇy aśeṣataḥ
yas tu karmaphala tyāgī sa tyāgī'ty abhidhīyate

Human beings cannot completely abstain from work. Therefore, one who completely renounces selfish attachment to the fruits of all work is considered a renunciant. (18.11)

अनिष्टम् इष्टं मिश्रं च त्रिविधं कर्मणः फलम् ।
भवत्य् अत्यागिनां प्रेत्य न तु संन्यासिनां क्वचित् ।।१२।।

anişṭam iṣṭaṁ miśraṁ ca trividhaṁ karmaṇaḥ phalam
bhavaty atyāgināṁ pretya na tu saṁnyāsināṁ kvacit

The threefold fruit of works — desirable, undesirable, and mixed — accrues after death to one who is not a renunciant (Tyāgi), but never to a Tyāgi. (18.12)

FIVE CAUSES OF ANY ACTION

पञ्चैतानि महाबाहो कारणानि निबोध मे ।
सांख्ये कृतान्ते प्रोक्तानि सिद्धये सर्वकर्मणाम् ।।१३।।

pañcai'tāni mahābāho kāraṇāni nibodha me
sāṁkhye kṛtānte proktāni siddhaye sarvakarmaṇām

अधिष्ठानं तथा कर्ता करणं च पृथग्विधम् ।
विविधाश्च पृथक्चेष्टा दैवं चैवात्र पञ्चमम् ।।१४।।

adhiṣṭhānaṁ tathā kartā karaṇaṁ ca pṛthagvidham
vividhāś ca pṛthakceṣṭā daivaṁ cai'vā'tra pañcamam

Learn from Me, O Arjuna, the five causes, as described in the Sankhya doctrine, for the accomplishment of all actions. They are: the physical body, the seat of Karma; the modes of material Nature, the doer; the eleven organs of perception and action, the instruments; various life forces; and the fifth, the presiding deities of the eleven organs. (18.13-14)

शरीरवाङ्मनोभिर् यत् कर्म प्रारभते नरः ।
न्याय्यं वा विपरीतं वा पञ्चैते तस्य हेतवः ॥१५॥

śarīravāṅmanobhir yat karma prārabhate naraḥ
nyāyyaṁ vā viparītaṁ vā pañcai'te tasya hetavaḥ

These are the five causes of whatever action, whether right or wrong, one performs by thought, word, and deed. (18.15)

तत्रैवं सति कर्तारम् आत्मानं केवलं तु यः ।
पश्यत्य् अकृतबुद्धित्वान् न स पश्यति दुर्मतिः ॥१६॥

tatrai'vaṁ sati kartāram ātmānaṁ kevalaṁ tu yaḥ
paśyaty akṛta buddhitvān na sa paśyati durmatiḥ

Therefore, the one who considers one's body or the Spirit (Atma, soul) as the sole agent, do not understand, due to imperfect knowledge. (18.16)

यस्य नाहंकृतो भावो बुद्धिर् यस्य न लिप्यते ।
हत्वापि स इमाँल् लोकान् न हन्ति न निबध्यते ॥१७॥

yasya nā'haṁkṛto bhāvo buddhir yasya na lipyate
hatvā'pi sa imāṁl lokān na hanti na nibadhyate

One who is free from the notion of doership and whose intellect is not polluted by the desire to reap the fruit — even after slaying these people — neither slays nor is bound by the act of killing. (18.17)

Those who are free from the notion of doership, free from likes and dislikes of their work, and detached from the fruits of work become free from Karmic reactions even for the act of killing.

ज्ञानं ज्ञेयं परिज्ञाता त्रिविधा कर्मचोदना ।
करणं कर्म कर्तेति त्रिविधः कर्मसंग्रहः ॥१८॥

jñānaṁ jñeyaṁ parijñātā trividhā karmacodanā
karaṇaṁ karma karte'ti trividhaḥ karmasaṁgrahaḥ

The subject, the object, and the knowledge of the object are the threefold driving force to an action. The eleven organs, the act, and the agent or the modes of material Nature are the three components of action. (18.18)

THREE TYPES OF KNOWLEDGE

ज्ञानं कर्म च कर्ता च त्रिधैव गुणभेदतः ।
प्रोच्यते गुणसंख्याने यथावच् छृणु तान्य् अपि ॥१९॥
jñānaṁ karma ca kartā ca tridhai'va guṇabhedataḥ
procyate guṇasaṁkhyāne yathāvac chṛṇu tāny api

Self-knowledge, action, and agent are said to be of three types, according to Sankhya doctrine. Hear duly about these also. (18.19)

सर्वभूतेषु येनैकं भावम् अव्ययम् ईक्षते ।
अविभक्तं विभक्तेषु तज् ज्ञानं विद्धि सात्त्विकम् ॥२०॥
sarvabūteṣu yenai'kaṁ bhāvam avyayam īkṣate
avibhaktaṁ vibhakteṣu taj jñānaṁ vidhhi sāttvikam

The knowledge by which one sees one and the same immutable, undivided divinity in all creatures — such knowledge is in the mode of goodness. (See also 11.13, and 13.16) (18.20)

पृथक्त्वेन तु यज् ज्ञानं नानाभावान् पृथग्विधान् ।
वेत्ति सर्वेषु भूतेषु तज् ज्ञानं विद्धि राजसम् ॥२१॥
pṛthaktvena tu yaj jñānaṁ nānābhāvān pṛthagvidhān
vetti sarveṣu bhūteṣu taj jñānaṁ viddhi rājasam

The knowledge by which one sees each individual as different and separate from one another — such knowledge is in the mode of passion. (18.21)

यत् तु कृत्स्नवद् एकस्मिन् कार्ये सक्तम् अहैतुकम् ।
अतत्त्वार्थवद् अल्पं च तत् तामसम् उदाहृतम् ।।२२।।
yat tu kṛtsnavad ekasmin kārye saktam ahaitukam
atattvārthavad alpaṁ ca tat tāmasam udāhṛtam

The irrational, baseless, and worthless knowledge by which one clings to one single effect, such as the body, as if it is everything — such knowledge is in the mode of darkness of ignorance (18.22)

THREE TYPES OF ACTION

नियतं सङ्गरहितम् अरागद्वेषतः कृतम् ।
अफलप्रेप्सुना कर्म यत् तत् सात्त्विकम् उच्यते ।।२३।।
niyataṁ saṅgarahitam arāgadveṣataḥ kṛtam
aphalaprepsunā karma yat tat sāttvikam ucyate

Obligatory duty performed without likes and dislikes and without selfish motives and attachment to the fruit, is in the mode of goodness. (18.23)

यत् तु कामेप्सुना कर्म साहंकारेण वा पुनः ।
क्रियते बहुलायासं तद् राजसम् उदाहृतम् ।।२४।।
yat tu kāmepsunā karma sāhaṁkāreṇa vā punaḥ
kriyate bahulāyāsaṁ tad rājasam udāhṛtam

Action performed with ego, with selfish motives, and with too much effort, is in the mode of passion. (18.24)

अनुबन्धं क्षयं हिंसाम् अनवेक्ष्य च पौरुषम् ।
मोहाद् आरभ्यते कर्म यत् तत् तामसम् उच्यते ।।२५।।

anubandhaṁ kṣayaṁ hiṁsām anavekṣya ca pauruṣam
mohād ārabhyate karma yat tat tāmasam ucyate

Action that is undertaken because of delusion, disregarding consequences, loss, injury to others, as well as one's own ability, is in the mode of ignorance. (18.25)

THREE TYPES OF AGENT

मुक्तसङ्गोऽनहंवादी धृत्युत्साहसमन्वितः ।
सिद्ध्यसिद्ध्योर् निर्विकारः कर्ता सात्त्विक उच्यते ॥२६॥

muktasaṅgo'nahaṁvādī dhṛtyutsāha samanvitaḥ
siddhyasiddhyor nirvikāraḥ kartā sāttvika ucyate

The agent who is free from attachment, is non-egotistic, endowed with resolve and enthusiasm, and unperturbed in success or failure is called good. (18.26)

रागी कर्मफलप्रेप्सुर् लुब्धो हिंसात्मकोऽशुचिः ।
हर्षशोकान्वितः कर्ता राजसः परिकीर्तितः ॥२७॥

rāgī karmaphalaprepsur lubdho hiṁsātmako'śuciḥ
harṣaśokānvitaḥ kartā rājasaḥ parikīrtitaḥ

The agent who is impassioned, who desires the fruits of work, who is greedy, violent, impure, and affected by joy and sorrow, is called passionate. (18.27)

अयुक्तः प्राकृतः स्तब्धः शठो नैष्कृतिकोऽलसः ।
विषादी दीर्घसूत्री च कर्ता तामस उच्यते ॥२८॥

ayuktaḥ prākṛtaḥ stabdhaḥ śaṭho naiṣkṛtiko'lasaḥ
viṣādī dīrghasūtrī ca kartā tāmasa ucyate

The agent who is undisciplined, vulgar, stubborn, wicked, malicious, lazy, depressed, and procrastinating is called ignorant. (18.28)

THREE TYPES OF INTELLECT

बुद्धेर् भेदं धृतेश् चैव गुणतस् त्रिविधं शृणु ।
प्रोच्यमानम् अशेषेण पृथक्त्वेन धनंजय ।।२९।।

buddher bhedaṁ dhṛteś cai'va guṇatas trividhaṁ śṛṇu
procyamānam aśeṣeṇa pṛthaktvena dhanaṁjaya

Now hear Me explain, fully and separately, the threefold division of intellect and resolve, based on modes of material Nature, O Arjuna. (18.29)

प्रवृत्तिं च निवृत्तिं च कार्याकार्ये भयाभये ।
बन्धं मोक्षं च या वेत्ति बुद्धिः सा पार्थ सात्त्विकी ।।३०।।

pravṛttiṁ ca nivṛttiṁ ca kāryākārye bhayābhaye
bandhaṁ mokṣaṁ ca yā vetti buddhiḥ sā pārtha sāttvikī

O Arjuna, that intellect is in the mode of goodness which understands the path of work and the path of renunciation, right and wrong action, fear and fearlessness, bondage and liberation. (18.30)

यया धर्मम् अधर्मं च कार्यं चाकार्यम् एव च ।
अयथावत् प्रजानाति बुद्धिः सा पार्थ राजसी ।।३१।।

yayā dharmam adharmaṁ ca kāryaṁ cā'kāryam eva ca
ayathāvat prajānāti buddhiḥ sā pārtha rājasī

That intellect is in the mode of passion which cannot distinguish between righteousness (Dharma) and unrighteousness (Adharma), and right and wrong action, O Arjuna. (18.31)

अधर्मं धर्मम् इति या मन्यते तमसावृता ।
सर्वार्थान् विपरीतांश्च बुद्धिः सा पार्थ तामसी ॥३२॥

adharmaṁ dharmam iti yā manyate tamasā'vṛtā
sarvārthān viparītāṁś ca buddhiḥ sā pārtha tāmasī

That intellect is in the mode of ignorance which accepts unrighteousness (Adharma) as righteousness (Dharma) and thinks everything to be that which it is not, O Arjuna. (18.32)

THREE TYPES OF RESOLVE, AND THE FOUR GOALS OF HUMAN LIFE

धृत्या यया धारयते मनःप्राणेन्द्रियक्रियाः ।
योगेनाव्यभिचारिण्या धृतिः सा पार्थ सात्त्विकी ॥३३॥

dhṛtyā yayā dhārayate manaḥ prāṇendriya kriyāḥ
yogenā'vyabhicāriṇyā dhṛtiḥ sā pārtha sāttvikī

That resolve is in the mode of goodness by which one manipulates the functions of the mind, Prana (Life forces, bioimpulses) and senses for God-realization only, O Arjuna. (18.33)

यया तु धर्मकामार्थान् धृत्या धारयतेऽर्जुन ।
प्रसङ्गेन फलाकाङ्क्षी धृतिः सा पार्थ राजसी ॥३४॥

yayā tu dharma kāmārthān dhṛtyā dhārayate'rjuna
prasaṅgena phalākāṅkṣī dhṛtiḥ sā pārtha rājasī

That resolve is in the mode of passion by which one, craving for the fruits of work, clings to duty, wealth, and pleasure with great attachment, O Arjuna. (18.34)

Doing one's duty, earning wealth, material enjoyment, and attaining salvation are the four noble goals of human life for the householder in the Vedic tradition. Lord Rama said: One who is engaged only in sense gratification, abandoning duty and earning wealth, soon gets into trouble (VR 2.53.13). One who uses duty, earning wealth, and enjoying sensual pleasure in a balanced manner without any one of the three being harmed by the other two attains salvation (MB 9.60.22). A person completely involved in acquiring and preserving material wealth and possessions has no time for Self-realization (MB 12.07.41). One can obtain all four noble goals by devotion to the Lord (VP 1.18.24). One should first follow Dharma by doing one's duty righteously. Then one should earn money and make economic progress, fulfill all noble material and spiritual desires with the money earned, and progress towards salvation, the only noble goal of human birth.

As human beings are always afraid of death, a rich person is always afraid of the tax collector, thieves, relatives, and natural disasters (MB 3.02.39). There is great pain in accumulating, protecting, and losing wealth. The desire for wealth accumulation is never satisfied; therefore, the wise consider contentment as the supreme pleasure (MB 3.02.46). People are never satisfied with wealth and material possessions (KaU 1.27). One should always remember that we are just the trustees of all wealth and possessions.

यया स्वप्नं भयं शोकं विषादं मदम् एव च ।
न विमुञ्चति दुर्मेधा धृतिः सा पार्थ तामसी ।।३५।।

yayā svapnaṁ bhayaṁ śokaṁ viṣādaṁ madam eva ca
na vimuñcati durmedhā dhṛtiḥ sā pārtha tāmasī

That resolve is in the mode of ignorance by which a dull person does not give up sleep, fear, grief, despair, and carelessness, O Arjuna. (18.35)

THREE TYPES OF PLEASURE

सुखं त्व् इदानीं त्रिविधं शृणु मे भरतर्षभ ।
अभ्यासाद् रमते यत्र दुःखान्तं च निगच्छति ।।३६।।

sukhaṁ tv idānīṁ trividhaṁ śṛṇu me bharatarṣabha
abhyāsād ramate yatra duḥkhāntaṁ ca nigacchati

And now hear from Me, O Arjuna, about the threefold pleasure. The pleasure that one enjoys from spiritual practice results in cessation of all sorrows. (18.36)

यत् तद् अग्रे विषम् इव परिणामेऽमृतोपमम् ।
तत् सुखं सात्त्विकं प्रोक्तम् आत्मबुद्धिप्रसादजम् ॥३७॥
yat tad agre viṣam iva pariṇāme'mṛtopamam
tat sukhaṁ sāttvikaṁ proktam ātmabuddhi prasādajam

The pleasure that appears as poison in the beginning, but is like nectar in the end, comes by the grace of Self-knowledge and is in the mode of goodness. (18.37)

One who enjoys the ocean of the nectar of devotion has no use for the sensual pleasures that are like water of a pond (BP 6.12.22). The river of material joy dries up quickly after the rainy season if there is no perennial source of spiritual water. Material objects are like straws to a Self-realized person.

विषयेन्द्रियसंयोगाद् यत् तद् अग्रेऽमृतोपमम् ।
परिणामे विषम् इव तत् सुखं राजसं स्मृतम् ॥३८॥
viṣayendriyasaṁyogād yat tad agre'mṛtopamam
pariṇāme viṣam iva tat sukhaṁ rājasaṁ smṛtam

Sensual pleasures that appear as nectar in the beginning, but become poison in the end, are in the mode of passion. (See also 5.22) (18.38)

Two paths — the beneficial spiritual path and the pleasant path of sensual pleasure — are open to us. The wise choose the former while the ignorant chooses the latter (KaU 2.02). Sensual pleasures wear out the vigor of the senses and bring diseases in the end (KaU 1.26). Sensual pleasure is not the object of precious human birth. Even heavenly enjoyment is temporary and ends in sorrow. Those who are attached to sensual delights are like fools who choose poison in exchange for the nectar of devotion (TR 7.43.01). The ignorant ones, due to delusion, do not think that they are taking poison while drinking it. They only know after the result, and then it is too late (VR 7.15.19). It is the natural tendency of the senses to go easily toward external sensual pleasures as water flows downstream. Regrets follow the fulfillment of all sensual and material desires.

Worldly pleasure is like a mirage in the desert. Thirsty persons reckon it as water until they come to drink it and find nothing. Worldly happiness is temporary and flickering, whereas happiness derived from spiritual life is permanent and continuous. Ramakrishna said: One does not feel intensely restless for God until all worldly desires are satisfied. Manu is of the opinion that it may be easier to control the senses after enjoying sense pleasure and discovering its uselessness and harmfulness (MS 2.96). Desirelessness comes easily after most of our desires are fulfilled. A person may be healthy and wealthy but still unhappy without a taste of spiritual pleasure. A spiritually mature person does not miss worldly pleasures.

यद् अग्रे चानुबन्धे च सुखं मोहनम् आत्मनः ।
निद्रालस्यप्रमादोत्थं तत् तामसम् उदाहृतम् ॥३९॥
yad agre cā'nubandhe ca sukhaṁ mohanam ātmanaḥ
nidrālasya pramādotthaṁ tat tāmasam udāhṛtam

Pleasure that confuses a person in the beginning and in the end as a result of sleep, laziness, and carelessness, is in the mode of ignorance. (18.39)

न तद् अस्ति पृथिव्यां वा दिवि देवेषु वा पुनः ।
सत्त्वं प्रकृतिजैर् मुक्तं यद् एभिः स्यात् त्रिभिर् गुणैः ॥४०॥
na tad asti pṛthivyāṁ vā divi deveṣu vā punaḥ
sattvaṁ prakṛtijair muktaṁ yad ebhiḥ syāt tribhir guṇaiḥ

There is no being, either on the earth or among the celestial controllers in the heaven, who can remain free from these three modes of material Nature. (18.40)

DIVISION OF LABOR IS BASED ON ONE'S ABILITY

ब्राह्मणक्षत्रियविशां शूद्राणां च परंतप ।
कर्माणि प्रविभक्तानि स्वभावप्रभवैर् गुणैः ॥४१॥

brāhmaṇa kṣatriya viśāṁ śūdrāṇāṁ ca paraṁtapa
karmāṇi pravibhaktāni svabhāva prabhavair guṇaiḥ

The division of human labor into four catagories is also based on the qualities inherent in peoples' nature or their make up. (See also 4.13) (18.41)

In the ancient Vedic system, activities of human beings were categorized into four social orders, based on the three modes of material Nature. These four orders are often mistaken for the caste system of modern times in India and elsewhere that is based on birth only. These four, universal, social orders of human society, as described by Lord Krishna, relate to persons' nature, quality, and work, not their birth. Those who were dominated by the mode of goodness and were peaceful and self-controlled were called Brāhmans. Those who were controlled by passion and preferred to engage in administration and protective services were labeled Kshatriyas. Those under the mixed modes of passion and ignorance, engaged in farming and trades, were called Vaishyas. Those mostly in the lowest mode of ignorance were called Shudras, and their nature was to serve the other three social orders.

The Vedas compare human society with a person whose four main limbs represent the four broad types of work and workers in society. The Vedas also state that their words are for all mankind, for all people (YV 26.02). There are only two types (or castes) of people — the decent and the indecent (Gita 16.06).

शमो दमस् तपः शौचं क्षान्तिर् आर्जवम् एव च ।
ज्ञानं विज्ञानम् आस्तिक्यं ब्रह्मकर्म स्वभावजम् ॥४२॥
śamo damas tapaḥ śaucaṁ kṣāntir ārjavam eva ca
jñānaṁ vijñānam āstikyaṁ brahmakarma svabhāvajam

Intellectuals who have serenity, self-control, austerity, purity, patience, honesty, transcendental knowledge, transcendental experience, and belief in God are labeled as intellectuals (Brāhmans). (18.42)

An intellectual is one who has the above-mentioned qualities (MB 3.180.21). Anybody may be called 'intellectual' if he or she possesses the divine gift of Self-knowledge (RV 10.125.05, AV 4.30.03). Intellectualism is an acquirement — a quality or state of mind — rather than a caste or creed. The illuminated ones who know the Absolute Truth and are in touch with the Supreme Being are the real Brāhmans and are next to God. All are born equal, but can become superior or inferior by deeds only.

Whenever a sector of any society gives predominance to caste, creed, race, religion, color, gender, or place of birth over the ability of an individual, the seeds of that society's downfall and inefficiency are planted and begin to grow. The devil of discrimination knows no national boundaries. It is unfortunately practiced by ignorant persons all over the world in one form or another. It is a human temptation and a manifestation of a superiority complex. The wise should try to overcome all types and shades of bias. All are the children of God, equal in His eyes, and should be treated as such. A person, for the progress of society, must be judged by his or her ability — not by any other standard.

शौर्यं तेजो धृतिर् दाक्ष्यं युद्धे चाप्य् अपलायनम् ।
दानम् ईश्वरभावश्च क्षात्रं कर्म स्वभावजम् ॥४३॥
śauryaṁ tejo dhṛtir dākṣyaṁ yuddhe cā'py apalāyanam
dānam īśvarabhāvaś ca kṣātraṁ karma svabhāvajam

Those having the qualities of heroism, vigor, firmness, dexterity, steadfastness in battle, charity, and administrative skills are called leaders or protectors (Kshatriyas). (18.43)

The ideal protector possesses uncompromising, unrelenting opposition to evil-doers in society. The duty (Dharma) of a protector is to fight all unrighteousness (Adharma) and injustice in society.

कृषिगौरक्ष्यवाणिज्यं वैश्यकर्म स्वभावजम् ।
परिचर्यात्मकं कर्म शूद्रस्यापि स्वभावजम् ।।४४।।

kṛṣi gaurakṣya vāṇijyaṁ vaiśyakarma svabhāvajam
paricaryātmakaṁ karma śūdrasyā'pi svabhāvajam

Those who are good at cultivation, cattle rearing, business, trade, finance, and industry are known as business men (Vaishyas). Those who are very good in service and labor are classed as workers (Shudras). (18.44)

A Shudra is a person who is ignorant of spiritual knowledge and identifies with the material body due to ignorance. According to Lord Krishna, these four designations or types are not determined by birth. A Shudra-type person may be born in any family. The results of one's previous activities or Karma return as one's nature and habits.

People are either born with certain qualities or develop them through training and effort. One who does not have the requisite qualities of the four social orders of society, cannot be categorized improperly by virtue of birth or position only.

ATTAINMENT OF SALVATION THROUGH DUTY, DISCIPLINE, AND DEVOTION

स्वे स्वे कर्मण्य् अभिरतः संसिद्धिं लभते नरः ।
स्वकर्मनिरतः सिद्धिं यथा विन्दति तच् छृणु ।।४५।।

sve sve karmaṇya abhirataḥ saṁsiddhiṁ labhate naraḥ
svakarmaniratah siddhiṁ yathā vindati tac chṛṇu

One can attain the highest perfection by devotion to one's natural work. Listen to Me how one attains perfection while engaged in one's natural work. (18.45)

यतः प्रवृत्तिर् भूतानां येन सर्वम् इदं ततम् ।
स्वकर्मणा तम् अभ्यर्च्य सिद्धिं विन्दति मानवः ।।४६।।

yataḥ pravṛttir bhūtānāṁ yena sarvam idaṁ tatam
svakarmaṇā tam abhyarcya siddhiṁ vindati mānavaḥ

One attains perfection by worshipping the Supreme Being — from whom all beings originate and by whom all this universe is pervaded — through performance of one's natural duty dedicated to Him. (See also 9.27, 12.10) (18.46)

श्रेयान् स्वधर्मो विगुणः परधर्मात् स्वनुष्ठितात् ।
स्वभावनियतं कर्म कुर्वन् नाप्नोति किल्बिषम् ।।४७।।

śreyān svadharmo viguṇaḥ paradharmāt svanuṣṭhitāt
svabhāvaniyataṁ karma kurvan nā'pnoti kilbiṣam

One's inferior natural work is better than superior unnatural work, even though well performed. One who does the work ordained by one's inherent nature, incurs no sin (or Karmic reaction). (See also 3.35, 5.10, 18.07, 18.09, 18.17, 18.23) (18.47)

Obligatory or natural work that is not forbidden by the scriptures, and is done without selfish attachment to the fruits and without the notion of doership, is sinless.

सहजं कर्म कौन्तेय सदोषम् अपि न त्यजेत् ।
सर्वारम्भा हि दोषेण धूमेनाग्निर् इवावृताः ।।४८।।

sahajaṁ karma kaunteya sadoṣam api na tyajet
sarvārambhā hi doṣeṇa dhūmenā'gnir ivā'vṛtāḥ

One's natural work, even though defective, should not be abandoned because all undertakings are enveloped by defects as fire is covered by smoke, O Arjuna. (18.48)

Nothing in this world has only good or only bad qualities. There is no perfect undertaking. All ventures have both good and bad aspects (MB 12.15.50). It is not what you do — but how you do it — that is important. Work becomes worship when done with an attitude of adoration of the Lord.

असक्तबुद्धिः सर्वत्र जितात्मा विगतस्पृहः ।
नैष्कर्म्यसिद्धिं परमां संन्यासेनाधिगच्छति ।।४९।।

asaktabuddhiḥ sarvatra jitātmā vigataspṛhaḥ
naiṣkarmyasiddhiṁ paramāṁ saṁnyāsenā'dhigacchati

The person whose mind is always free from selfish attachment, who has subdued the mind and senses, and who is free from desires, attains the supreme perfection of freedom from the bondage of Karma by renouncing selfish attachment to the fruits of work. (18.49)

सिद्धिं प्राप्तो यथा ब्रह्म तथाप्नोति निबोध मे ।
समासेनैव कौन्तेय निष्ठा ज्ञानस्य या परा ।।५०।।

siddhiṁ prāpto yathā brahma tathā'pnoti nibodha me
samāsenai'va kaunteya niṣṭhā jñānasya yā parā

Learn from Me briefly, O Arjuna, how one who has attained such perfection, or the freedom from the bondage of Karma, attains Supreme Being, the goal of transcendental knowledge. (18.50)

बुद्ध्या विशुद्धया युक्तो धृत्यात्मानं नियम्य च ।
शब्दादीन् विषयांस् त्यक्त्वा रागद्वेषौ व्युदस्य च ।।५१।।

buddhyā viśuddhayā yukto dhṛtyā'tmānaṁ niyamya ca
śabdādīn viṣayāṁs tyaktvā rāgadveṣau vyudasya ca

विविक्तसेवी लघ्वाशी यतवाक्कायमानसः ।
ध्यानयोगपरो नित्यं वैराग्यं समुपाश्रितः ॥५२॥

viviktasevī laghvāśī yatavākkāyamānasaḥ
dhyānayogaparo nityaṁ vairāgyaṁ samupāśritaḥ

अहंकारं बलं दर्पं कामं क्रोधं परिग्रहम् ।
विमुच्य निर्ममः शान्तो ब्रह्मभूयाय कल्पते ॥५३॥

ahaṁkāraṁ balaṁ darpaṁ kāmaṁ krodhaṁ parigraham
vimucya nirmamaḥ śānto brahmabhūyāya kalpate

Endowed with purified intellect; subduing the mind with firm resolve; turning away from sound and other objects of the senses; giving up likes and dislikes; living in solitude; eating lightly; controlling the mind, speech, and organs of action; ever absorbed in yoga of meditation; taking refuge in detachment; and relinquishing egotism, violence, pride, lust, anger, and proprietorship — one becomes peaceful, free from the notion of 'I, me, and my', and fit for attaining oneness with the Supreme Being. (18.51-53)

When the torch of meditation fuses Selfless service, Self-knowledge, and devotional love during the thoughtless state of trance, the rays of enlightenment radiate, divine communion is perfected, the fog of ignorance disappears, and all material and sensual desires evaporate from the mind.

ब्रह्मभूतः प्रसन्नात्मा न शोचति न काङ्क्षति ।
समः सर्वेषु भूतेषु मद्भक्तिं लभते पराम् ॥५४॥

brahmabhūtaḥ prasannātmā na śocati na kāṅkṣati
samaḥ sarveṣu bhūteṣu madbhaktiṁ labhate parām

Absorbed in the Supreme Being, the serene one neither grieves nor desires. Becoming impartial to all beings, one obtains the highest devotional love for God. (18.54)

भक्त्या माम् अभिजानाति यावान् यश् चास्मि तत्त्वतः ।
ततो माम् तत्त्वतो ज्ञात्वा विशते तदनन्तरम् ॥५५॥

bhaktyā mām abhijānāti yāvān yaś cā'smi tattvataḥ
tato mām tattvato jñātvā viśate tadanantaram

By devotion one truly understands what and who I am in essence. Having known Me in essence, one immediately merges with Me. (See also 5.19) (18.55)

There is no doubt God can be known only through faith and unswerving devotion (BP 11.14.21). There are numerous spiritual practices — not just one — prescribed in the scriptures to get that faith and unswerving devotion. Knowledge and devotion are one and the same like a tree and its seed. The entire process of spirituality gets started by the spark of grace that comes only as faith, and not by any other method.

Delusion of Maya prevents people from knowing and seeing God. As one cannot see the ever-existing salt in ocean water with the eye, but can taste it by the tongue, similarly, the Self can be realized only by faith and devotion, not by logic and reasoning. God may be realized not only by meditation and Self-knowledge, but also through ecstatic personal love and intense devotion to one's personal deity.

Only they know You to whom You make Yourself known; the moment one knows You, one becomes one with You (TR 2.126.02). The knower of the Spirit becomes like Spirit (BrU 1.04.10, MuU 3.02.09). The Kingdom of God is within you (Luke 17.21). No one can enter the Kingdom of God unless one is born again (by realizing that one is not this body, but Spirit behind the body) (John 3.03). Whoever does not receive the Kingdom of God like a child, will never go there (Mark 10.15). The Father and I are one (John 10.30). To truly understand God is to love Him and become one with Him. Liberation or Mukti is a state of mind.

सर्वकर्माण्य् अपि सदा कुर्वाणो मद्व्यपाश्रयः ।
मत्प्रसादाद् अवाप्नोति शाश्वतं पदम् अव्ययम् ।।५६।।

sarvakarmāṇy api sadā kurvāṇo madvyapāśrayaḥ
matprasādād avāpnoti śāśvataṁ padam avyayam

A KarmaYogi devotee attains the eternal immutable abode by My grace— even while doing all duties— just by taking refuge in Me (by dedicating all action to Me with loving devotion). (18.56)

चेतसा सर्वकर्माणि मयि संन्यस्य मत्परः ।
बुद्धियोगम् उपाश्रित्य मच्चित्तः सततं भव ।।५७।।

cetasā sarvakarmāṇi mayi saṁnyasya matparaḥ
buddhiyogam upāśritya maccittaḥ satataṁ bhava

Sincerely offer all actions to Me; set Me as your supreme goal, and completely depend on Me. Always fix your mind on Me and resort to KarmaYoga. (18.57)

Everything we use or eat should be first offered to the Lord, the giver of all things, before we put it to our own use. This includes — but is not limited to — food, a new dress, a new car, a new house, and a new baby. Offering everything to the Lord is the highest form of worship that one has to learn and practice every day. According to Swami Chidanand Saraswati (Muniji) this verse means to have His name in your heart and on your lips, and to have His work in your hands.

KarmaYoga saves one from being entangled in the wheels of transmigration and leads to liberation. KarmaYoga is recommended even for one who does not believe in God, who has no knowledge of God, who has no faith and devotion, and consequently cannot follow any other spiritual path.

मच्चित्तः सर्वदुर्गाणि मत्प्रसादात् तरिष्यसि ।
अथ चेत् त्वम् अहंकारान् न श्रोष्यसि विनङ्क्ष्यसि ॥५८॥

maccittaḥ sarvadurgāṇi matprasādāt tariṣyasi
atha cet tvam ahaṁkārān na śroṣyasi vinaṅkṣyasi

You shall overcome all difficulties by My grace when your mind becomes fixed on Me. But if you do not listen to Me due to ego, you shall perish. (18.58)

KARMIC BONDAGE AND THE FREE WILL

यद् अहंकारम् आश्रित्य न योत्स्य इति मन्यसे ।
मिथ्यैष व्यवसायस् ते प्रकृतिस् त्वां नियोक्ष्यति ॥५९॥

yad ahaṁkāram āśritya na yotsya iti manyase
mithyai'ṣa vyavasāyas te prakṛtis tvāṁ niyokṣyati

If due to ego you think: I shall not fight, your resolve is vain because your own nature will compel you to fight. (18.59)

स्वभावजेन कौन्तेय निबद्धः स्वेन कर्मणा ।
कर्तुं नेच्छसि यन् मोहात् करिष्यस्य् अवशोऽपि तत् ॥६०॥

svabhāvajena kaunteya nibaddhaḥ svena karmaṇā
kartuṁ ne'cchasi yan mohāt kariṣyasy avaśo'pi tat

O Arjuna, you are controlled by your own nature-born Karmic impressions. Therefore, you shall do — even against your will — what you do not wish to do out of delusion. (18.60)

The mind often knows right and wrong, but it runs after evil — reluctantly — by the force of Karmic footprints. The wise should always keep this in mind before finding fault with others.

WE BECOME THE PUPPETS OF OUR OWN FREEWILL

To satisfy the free will of the ignorant, overwhelmed by the three modes of material Nature, the good Lord creates an environment conducive for engaging in unwanted actions. Our free will is like the very limited freedom of a dog on a leash. As a facilitator, God reciprocates with everyone according to their desires and allows them to fulfill desires generated by free will. Lord uses His illusory kinetic energy called Maya to engage the living entities in good and bad acts according to their desires and their previously accumulated good and bad Karma.

ईश्वरः सर्वभूतानां हृद्देशेऽर्जुन तिष्ठति ।
भ्रामयन् सर्वभूतानि यन्त्रारूढानि मायया ।।६१।।

īśvaraḥ sarvabhūtānāṁ hṛddeśe'rjuna tiṣṭhati
bhrāmayan sarvabhūtāni yantrārūḍhāni māyayā

The Supreme Lord — abiding in the inner psyche of all beings, O Arjuna — causes them to work out their Karma by His power of Maya like a puppet mounted on a machine. (18.61)

The Supreme Controller (Ishvara) is the reflection of the Supreme Spirit in the body. The Supreme Lord organizes, controls, supervises, and directs everything in the universe. Jiva is like a puppet (of Karma) mounted on a body which is the vehicle of transmigration. The word revolve (or evolve) refers to working out of one's Karma. Thus we become the puppet of our own Karma created by our free will.

The Lord has made Karmic laws as the controller of all living beings. Therefore, one must learn to gladly endure all that fate imposes by taking refuge in Him and following the commandments (TR 2.218.02). Vedas declare that the Lord, using Karma, makes us dance as a juggler would make his monkey dance (TR 4.6.12). Without the laws of Karma, the scriptural injunctions, prohibitions, as well as self-effort, would have no value at all. Karma is the eternal justice and the eternal law. As a result of the working of eternal justice, there can be no escape from the consequences of our deeds. We become the product of our own past thinking and action. Therefore, we must think and act wisely at the present moment, using the scriptures as a guide.

The doctrine of Karma and reincarnation is also found in the following two verses of the Koran: Allah is He who created you and then sustained you, then causes you to die, then gives life to you again (Surah 30.40). He may reward those who believe and do good works. No one is able to escape His law of consequences (Surah 30.45). People cannot escape from the consequences of their deeds, for as we sow, so we reap. Cause and effect cannot be separated because the effect exists in the cause as the fruit exists in the seed. Good and evil deeds follow us continually like our shadows.

The Bible also says: Whosoever shedeth man's blood, by man shall his blood be shed (Genesis 9.06). It is believed that all references to Karma and reincarnation were taken out of the Bible during the second century with the noble aim of encouraging people to strive hard for perfection during this very life. Those who believe in reincarnation must avoid laziness and procrastination, stress intense spiritual discipline, and try their best to get Self-realization in this very life as if there were no reincarnation. Live as though this is your last day on this earth. One cannot achieve anything through laziness and procrastination.

One cannot take wealth, fame, and power from here to hereafter; but one can convert these into good or bad Karma and carry it to the next life. Even death cannot touch one's Karma. Those who have acted very piously in the past life achieve fame in this life without much endeavor.

तम् एव शरणं गच्छ सर्वभावेन भारत ।
तत्प्रसादात् परां शान्तिं स्थानं प्राप्स्यसि शाश्वतम् ।।६२।।

tam eva śaraṇaṁ gaccha sarva bhāvena bhārata
tatprasādāt parāṁ śāntiṁ sthānaṁ prāpsyasi śāśvatam

Seek refuge in the Supreme Lord alone, with loving devotion, O Arjuna. By His grace you shall attain supreme peace and the Eternal Abode. (18.62)

इति ते ज्ञानम् आख्यातं गुह्याद् गुह्यतरं मया ।
विमृश्यैतद् अशेषेण यथेच्छसि तथा कुरु ॥६३॥

iti te jñānam ākhyātaṁ guhyād guhyataraṁ mayā
vimṛśyai'tad aśeṣeṇa yathe'cchasi tathā kuru

Thus, I have explained the knowledge that is more secret than the secret. After fully reflecting on this, do as you wish. (18.63)

PATH OF SURRENDER IS THE ULTIMATE PATH TO GOD

सर्वगुह्यतमं भूयः शृणु मे परमं वचः ।
इष्टोऽसि मे दृढम् इति ततो वक्ष्यामि ते हितम् ॥६४॥

sarvaguhyatamaṁ bhūyaḥ śṛṇu me paramaṁ vacaḥ
iṣṭo'si me dṛḍham iti tato vakṣyāmi te hitam

Hear once again My most secret, supreme word. You are very dear to Me; therefore, I shall tell this for your benefit. (18.64)

मन्मना भव मद्भक्तो मद्याजी मां नमस्कुरु ।
माम् एवैष्यसि सत्यं ते प्रतिजाने प्रियोऽसि मे ॥६५॥

manmanā bhava madbhakto madyājī māṁ namaskuru
māṁ evai'ṣyasi satyaṁ te pratijāne priyo'si me

Fix your mind on Me, be devoted to Me, offer service to Me, bow down to Me, and you shall certainly reach Me. I promise you because you are My very dear friend. (18.65)

सर्वधर्मान् परित्यज्य मामेकं शरणं व्रज ।
अहं त्वा सर्वपापेभ्यो मोक्षयिष्यामि मा शुचः ।।६६।।

sarvadharmān parityajya mām ekaṁ śaraṇaṁ vraja
ahaṁ tvā sarvapāpebhyo mokṣayiṣyāmi mā śucaḥ

Set aside all meritorious deeds and religious rituals, and just surrender completely to My will with firm faith and loving devotion. I shall liberate you from all sins, the bonds of Karma. Do not grieve. (18.66)

The meaning of abandoning all duties and taking refuge in the Lord is that a seeker should perform all duties without selfish attachment as an offering to the Lord and totally depend only on the Lord for help and guidance. The Lord takes full responsibility for a person who totally depends on Him. If you find a good solution and get attached to it, the solution will soon become your next problem. The scripture says: The wise should not be attached even to righteous deeds for their entire life, but should engage their mind and intellect in contemplation of the Supreme Being (MB 12.290.21). One should develop a spirit of genuine self-surrender to the Lord by offering everything to Him, including the fruits of spiritual discipline. We should connect all our work with the divine. The world is controlled by the laws or will of God. One has to learn to abide by His will. Be thankful in prosperity and resigned to His will in adversity.

In order to be free from pious or impious results that bind one to this material world, it is necessary to offer every action to God. When a devotee sincerely works for God, God protects that devotee from the touch of Maya, the external energy of the Lord. If one voluntarily depends on the supreme Lord under all circumstances, then the good and bad results (sins) of work automatically go to Him, and one is free from sin.

A true devotee perceives: O Lord, I remembered You because You remembered me first. One breaks away every yoke of bondage and becomes free in this very life as soon as one gains the knowledge and a firm conviction that everything is done by the will of God, that it is His world, His sport, and His battle, not ours, and regards oneself as a mere actor in the divine play and the Lord as the great director in the cosmic drama of the soul on the stage of creation. Surrendering of individual will to divine will is the culmination of all spiritual practices, resulting in joyful participation in the drama of joys and sorrows of life. This is called liberation, or Mahayana in Buddhism. One cannot see God as long as one does not completely get rid of the notion of doership and ownership. The grace of God is triggered when one becomes firmly convinced that one is not the doer and at once becomes free in this very life. Lord arranges for the science of Self-realization to be revealed to a surrendered soul.

Surrendering to God does not involve leaving the world, but realizing that everything happens in accordance with His laws and by His direction and power. To fully recognize that everything is controlled and governed by a divine plan is to surrender to Him. In surrender one lets the divine plan rule one's life without giving up one's best effort. It is the complete renunciation of individual existence or the ego. It is the feeling: O my beloved Lord, nothing is mine, everything — including my body, mind, and ego — is Yours. I am not God, but a servant of God; save me from the ocean of transmigration. I tried to get out of the ocean of the material world using all the methods given in the scriptures, and failed. Now I have discovered the ultimate process — the process of seeking divine grace through prayer and surrender. God can be discovered by seeking His help in discovering Him and not by spiritual practices alone. Thus, one should start the spiritual journey as a dualist, experience monism, and again come back to dualism. A successful journey begins and ends at the same place.

The process of surrender may be called the fifth or the ultimate path of yoga — the other four being the path of selfless service, metaphysical knowledge, devotion, and meditation. The Good Lord directs the mind and senses of the living entities according to their Karma-born desires. But in case of surrendered devotees, however, He controls the senses directly according to His desires and in the best interest of the devotee. Let Him be the driver of your spiritual journey and you just enjoy the ride. Muniji beautifully explains this process. He says: Every pain, every ache, every discomfort becomes His gift and grace when you lay it in His lap. If you put the reins of your life-chariot in His hands, you will be ever happy, ever peaceful. This is the lesson of ultimate surrender.

It is the divine grace or power that comes in the form of self-effort. The divine grace and self-effort, as well as dualism and monism, are nothing but two sides of the same coin of Reality. The grace of God is always available — one has to collect it. To win the grace is not easy. One has to earn it by sincere, spiritual discipline and effort. Grace is the cream of that effort — our own good Karma. It is said that self-effort is absolutely necessary, but the last rung of the ladder to the Supreme is not self-effort, but praying for His grace in the spirit of surrender. When everything is surrendered to Him and one truly understands that He is the goal, the path, the traveler, as well as the obstacles on the path, vice and virtue become powerless and harmless as a cobra with fangs removed.

According to Shankara, if any object other than the Supreme Being — the Cosmic Energy Field — appears to exist, it is unreal like a mirage or like the presence of a snake in the rope. When one firmly understands that there is nothing else except the Supreme Being and His sport, all Karma gets exhausted; one surrenders to His will, and attains salvation. Yukteshwar said: Human life is beset with sorrow until we know how to surrender or tune in with the divine will that baffles our intellect. The Koran says: Whoever follows My guidance, no fear shall come upon them; neither shall they grieve (Surah 2.38). The Upanishad says: The knower of the Supreme goes beyond grief.

इदं ते नातपस्काय नाभक्ताय कदाचन ।
न चाशुश्रूषवे वाच्यं न च मां योऽभ्यसूयति ।।६७।।

idaṁ te nā'tapaskāya nā'bhaktāya kadācana
na cā'śuśrūṣave vācyaṁ na ca māṁ yo'bhyasūyati

This knowledge should never be spoken by you to one who is devoid of austerity, who is without devotion, who does not desire to listen, or who speaks ill of Me. (18.67)

To speak of wisdom to a deluded person, to glorify sacrifice to a greedy person, to advise sense control to an irascible person, and to discourse on Lord Rama's exploits to a lecher, is as useless as sowing seed on barren ground (TR 5.57.01-02). It is not for any soul to believe, save by the permission of Allah. You should not compel one to believe (Surah 10.100-101). Anyone to whom God has not granted the light (of knowledge) will have no light (Surah 24.40). The study of Gita is meant only for sincere persons. According to Ramakrishna, one can understand Him as much as He makes one understand. Guru Nanak said: O Beloved; only they to whom You give the divine knowledge, obtain it.

According to the Bible: Do not give what is holy to dogs. Do not throw your pearls in front of pigs. They will only trample them under their feet (Matthew 7.06). No one can come to me unless the Father who sent me draws him or her to me (John 6.44). The recipient of knowledge must have spiritual inclination and sincerely seek it. Knowledge given without being asked for serves no purpose and should be avoided. There is a time for everything under the heaven. We cannot change the world; we can change only the lives of a few sincere souls whose time for a change has come by His grace.

THE HIGHEST SERVICE TO GOD, AND THE BEST CHARITY

य इमं परमं गुह्यं मद्भक्तेष्व् अभिधास्यति ।
भक्तिं मयि परां कृत्वा माम् एवैष्यत्य् असंशयः ॥६८॥

ya imaṁ paramaṁ guhyaṁ madbhakteṣv abhidhāsyati
bhaktiṁ mayi parāṁ kṛtvā mām evai'ṣyaty asaṁśayaḥ

न च तस्मान् मनुष्येषु कश्चिन् मे प्रियकृत्तमः ।
भविता न च मे तस्माद् अन्यः प्रियतरो भुवि ॥६९॥

na ca tasmān manuṣyeṣu kaścin me priya kṛttamaḥ
bhavitā na ca me tasmād anyaḥ priyataro bhuvi

One who shall propagate this supreme secret philosophy — the transcendental knowledge of the Gita — amongst My devotees, shall be performing the highest devotional service to Me and shall certainly come to Me. No other person shall do a more pleasing service to Me, and no one on the earth shall be more dear to Me. (18.68-69)

Ignorance is the mother of all sins. All negative qualities, such as lust, anger, and greed, are nothing but a manifestation of ignorance. The giving of the gift of knowledge is the best charity. It is equivalent to giving the whole world in charity (MB 12.209.113). The best welfare is to help others discover their real nature that is the source of everlasting happiness rather than to provide material goods and comforts for temporary happiness. The Bible says: Whoever obeys the law, and teaches others to do the same, will be great in the Kingdom of Heaven (Matthew 5.19). Happiness is not attained through wealth and sense gratification, but through fidelity to a worthy cause (Helen Keller).

GRACE OF THE GITA

अध्येष्यते च य इमं धर्म्यं संवादम् आवयोः ।
ज्ञानयज्ञेन तेनाहम् इष्टः स्याम् इति मे मतिः ॥७०॥

adhyeṣyate ca ya imaṁ dharmyaṁ saṁvādam āvayoḥ
jñānayajñena tenā'ham iṣṭaḥ syām iti me matiḥ

Those who study our sacred dialogue shall be performing a holy act of propagation and acquisition of self-knowledge. This is My promise. (18.70)

God and His words are one and the same. The study of the Gita is equivalent to worship of God. Life in modern society is all work and no spirituality. Swami Harihar says: "Daily study of only a few verses of the Gita will recharge mental batteries and add meaning to the dull routine life of modern society." For serious students, daily study of one chapter of the Gita or several verses from the forty selected verses given in the end of this book is highly recommended.

श्रद्धावान् अनसूयश्च शृणुयाद् अपि यो नरः ।
सोऽपि मुक्तः शुभाँल् लोकान् प्राप्नुयात् पुण्यकर्मणाम् ॥७१॥

śraddhāvān anasūyaś ca śṛṇuyād api yo naraḥ
so'pi muktaḥ śubhāṁl lokān prāpnuyāt puṇyakarmaṇām

Whoever hears this sacred dialogue with faith and without cavil becomes free from sin, and attains heaven — the higher worlds of those whose actions are pure and virtuous. (18.71)

A summary of the Glory of the Gita as elaborated in the scriptures is given below. Reading this Glory of the Gita generates faith and devotion in the heart that is essential for reaping the benefits of the study of the Gita.

The goal of human birth is to master the mind and senses and reach one's destiny. A regular study of the Gita is sure to help achieve this noble goal. One who is regular in the study of the Gita becomes happy, peaceful, prosperous, and free from the bondage of Karma, though engaged in the performance of worldly duties. Sins do not taint those who regularly study the Gita, just as water does not stain a lotus leaf. The Gita is the best abode of Lord Krishna. The spiritual potency of the Lord abides in every verse of the Gita. The Bhagavad-Gita is the storehouse of spiritual knowledge. The Lord Himself spoke this supreme science of the Absolute containing the essence of all the scriptures for the benefit of humanity. All the Upanishads are the cows; Arjuna is the calf; Krishna is the milker; the nectar of the Gita is the milk; and persons of purified intellects are the drinkers. One need not study any other scripture if one seriously studies the Gita, contemplates the meaning of the verses, and practices its teachings in one's daily life.

The affairs of the world are run by the first commandment of the Creator — the teachings of selfless service — so beautifully expounded in the Gita. The sacred knowledge of doing one's duty without looking for a reward is the original teaching that alone can lead to salvation. The Gita is like a ship by which one can easily cross the ocean of transmigration and attain liberation. It is said that wherever the Gita is chanted or read with love and devotion, Lord makes Himself present there to listen and enjoy the company of His devotees. Going to a place where Gita is regularly chanted or taught is like going to a holy place of pilgrimage. One who regularly reads, recites to others, hears, and follows the sacred knowledge contained in the Gita is sure to attain liberation from the bondage of Karma and attain Nirvana.

Though engaged in the performance of worldly duties, one who is regular in the study of the Gita becomes happy and free from Karmic bondage. All the sacred centers of pilgrimage, gods, sages, and great souls dwell in the place where the Gita is kept and read. Help during troubles comes quickly where the Gita is recited, and the Lord dwells where it is read, heard, taught, and contemplated. By repeated reading of the Gita, one attains bliss and liberation. One who contemplates the teachings of the Gita at the time of death becomes free from sin and attains salvation. Lord Krishna personally comes to take such a person to His Supreme Abode — the highest transcendental plane of existence.

The grace of the Gita cannot be described. Its teachings are simple as well as abstruse and profound. New and deeper meanings are revealed to a serious student of the Gita, and the teachings remain ever inspirational. The interest in a serious study of the Gita is not available to all but only to those with good Karma. One should be very earnest in the study of the Gita.

The Gita is the heart, the soul, the breath, and the voice of the Lord. No austerity, penance, sacrifice, charity, pilgrimage, vow, fasting, or continence equals the study of the Gita. It is difficult for any ordinary person, or even for the great sages and scholars, to understand the deep, secret meaning of the Gita. To understand the Gita completely is like a fish trying to fathom the extent of the ocean, or a bird trying to measure the sky. The Gita is the deep ocean of the knowledge of the Absolute; only the Lord has a complete understanding of it. Nobody, other than Lord Krishna, should claim authority on the Gita.

कच्चिद् एतच् छ्रुतं पार्थ त्वयैकाग्रेण चेतसा ।
कच्चिद् अज्ञानसंमोहः प्रनष्टस् ते धनंजय ॥७२॥

kaccid etac chrutaṁ pārtha tvayai'kāgreṇa cetasā
kaccid ajñānasaṁmohaḥ pranaṣṭas te dhanaṁjaya

O Arjuna, did you listen to this with single-minded attention? Has your delusion born of ignorance been completely destroyed? (18.72)

अर्जुन उवाच
नष्टो मोहः स्मृतिर् लब्धा त्वत्प्रसादान् मयाऽच्युत ।
स्थितोऽस्मि गतसंदेहः करिष्ये वचनं तव ॥७३॥

arjuna uvāca
naṣṭo mohaḥ smṛtir labdhā tvatprasādān mayā'cyuta
sthito'smi gatasaṁdehaḥ kariṣye vacanaṁ tava

Arjuna said: By Your grace my delusion is destroyed; I have gained Self-knowledge; my confusion with regard to body and Spirit is dispelled; and I shall obey Your command. (18.73)

When one realizes Him by His grace, the knots of ignorance are loosened, all doubts and confusions are dispelled, and all Karma is exhausted (MuU 2.02.08). The true knowledge of the Supreme Being comes only by His grace.

संजय उवाच
इत्य् अहं वासुदेवस्य पार्थस्य च महात्मनः ।
संवादम् इमम् अश्रौषम् अद्भुतं रोमहर्षणम् ॥७४॥

saṁjaya uvāca
ity ahaṁ vāsudevasya pārthasya ca mahātmanaḥ
saṁvādam imam aśrauṣam adbhutaṁ romaharṣaṇam

Sanjaya said: Thus, I heard this wonderful dialogue between Lord Krishna and Arjuna, causing my hair to stand on end. (18.74)

व्यासप्रसादाच् छ्रुतवान् एतद् गुह्यम् अहं परम् ।
योगं योगेश्वरात् कृष्णात् साक्षात् कथयतः स्वयम् ॥७५॥
vyāsaprasādāc chrutavān etad guhyam ahaṁ param
yogaṁ yogeśvarāt kṛṣṇāt sākṣāt kathayataḥ svayam

By the grace of sage Vyasa, I heard this most secret and supreme yoga directly from Krishna, the Lord of yoga, Himself speaking to Arjuna before my very eyes of clairvoyance granted by sage Vyasa. (18.75)

राजन् संस्मृत्य संस्मृत्य संवादम् इमम् अद्भुतम् ।
केशवार्जुनयोः पुण्यं हृष्यामि च मुहुर् मुहुः ॥७६॥
rājan saṁsmṛtya saṁsmṛtya saṁvādam imam adbhutam
keśavārjunayoḥ puṇyaṁ hṛṣyāmi ca muhur muhuḥ

O King, by repeated remembrance of this marvelous and sacred dialogue between Lord Krishna and Arjuna, I am thrilled at every moment. (18.76)

तच् च संस्मृत्य संस्मृत्य रूपम् अत्यद्भुतं हरेः ।
विस्मयो मे महान् राजन् हृष्यामि च पुनः पुनः ॥७७॥
tac ca saṁsmṛtya saṁsmṛtya rūpam atyadbhutaṁ hareḥ
vismayo me mahān rājan hṛṣyāmi ca punaḥ punaḥ

Recollecting again and again, O King, that marvelous form of Krishna, I am greatly amazed, and I rejoice over and over again. (18.77)

BOTH TRANSCENDENTAL KNOWLEDGE AND ACTION ARE NEEDED FOR A BALANCED LIVING

यत्र योगेश्वरः कृष्णो यत्र पार्थो धनुर्धरः ।
तत्र श्रीर् विजयो भूतिर् ध्रुवा नीतिर् मतिर् मम ॥७८॥

yatra yogeśvaraḥ kṛṣṇo yatra pārtho dhanurdharaḥ
tatra śrīr vijayo bhūtir dhruvā nītir matir mama

Wherever there will be both Krishna, the Lord of yoga (or Dharma in the form of the scriptures), and Arjuna with the weapons of duty and protection, there will be everlasting prosperity, victory, happiness, and morality. This is my conviction. (18.78)

Where there is Dharma (righteous duty), there is the grace of Lord Krishna; where there is the grace of Lord Krishna, there will be peace and victory (MB 6.43.60). Everlasting peace and prosperity in the family are possible only by performing one's duty with full metaphysical knowledge of the Absolute. Peace and prosperity of a nation depend on mastering both the knowledge of scriptures and the knowledge of the use of weapons of protection, as well as science and technology. It is said that science and technology without spirituality are blind, and spirituality without technology is lame.

ॐ तत्सदिति श्रीमद्भगवद्गीतासूपनिषत्सु ब्रह्मविद्यायां योगशास्त्रे
श्रीकृष्णार्जुनसंवादे मोक्षसंन्यासयोगो नाम अष्टादशोऽध्यायः ॥

हरिः ॐ तत्सत् हरिः ॐ तत्सत् हरिः ॐ तत्सत्
श्रीकृष्णार्पणं अस्तु शुभं भूयात्
ॐ शान्तिः शान्तिः शान्तिः

OM tatsaditi śrīmadbhagavadgītāsūpaniṣatsu brahmavidyāyāṁ
yogaśāstre śrīkṛṣṇārjuna saṁvāde mokṣasaṁnyāsayogo
nāma aṣṭādaśo'dhyāyaḥ

hariḥ aum tatsat hariḥ aum tatsat hariḥ aum tatsat
śrīkṛṣṇārpaṇaṁ astu śubhaṁ bhūyāt
OM śāntiḥ śāntiḥ śāntiḥ

Thus ends the eighteenth chapter named "Nirvana Through Renunciation" of the Upaniṣad of the Bhagavadgītā, the scripture of yoga, dealing with the science of the Absolute in the form of the dialogue between Śrīkṛṣṇa and Arjuna.

This book is offered to Lord Shri Krishna. May He bless us all with Goodness, Prosperity, and Peace.

EPILOGUE

The Farewell Message of Lord Krishna

Lord Krishna on the eve of His departure from the arena of this world, after finishing the difficult task of establishing righteousness (Dharma), gave His last parting discourse to His cousin brother Uddhava, who was also His dearest devotee and follower. At the end of a long sermon comprising more than one thousand verses Uddhava said: O Lord, I think the pursuit of yoga as You narrated to Arjuna, and now to me, is very difficult, indeed, for most people because it entails control of the unruly senses. Please tell me a short, simple, and easy way to God-realization. Lord Krishna, upon Uddhava's request, gave the essentials of Self-realization (BP 11.06-29) for the modern age as follows:

(1) Do your duty, to the best of your abilities, for Me without any selfish motive, and remember Me at all times — before starting a work, at the completion of a task, and while inactive. (2) Practice to look upon all creatures as Myself in thought, word, and deed; and mentally bow down to them. (3) Awaken your dormant Kundalini power and perceive — through the activities of mind, senses, breathing, and emotions — that the power of God is within you at all times, and is constantly doing all the work, using you as a mere instrument.

Yogi Mumtaz Ali says: One who fully knows oneself as a mere instrument and a playground of mother Nature, knows the Truth. Cessation of all desires by realizing the true essence of the world and the human mind is Self-realization. Hariharananda Giri says: God is in everything as well as above everything. So if you want to realize Him, you must seek and see Him in every atom, in every matter, in every bodily function, and in every human being, with an attitude of surrender.

Muniji says: You must be God's gardener, carefully tending the garden, but never becoming attached to what will blossom, what will flower, what will give fruit or what will wither and die. Expectation is the mother of frustration, and acceptance gives peace.

Lord Krishna also summarized the essence of God-realization (BP 2.09.32-35) as follows:

The Supreme Lord Krishna said: One who wants to know Me, the Supreme Personality of Godhead, should only understand that I existed before creation; I exist in the creation, as well as after complete dissolution. Any other existence is nothing but My illusory energy (Maya). I exist within the creation and at the same time outside the creation. I am the all-pervading Supreme Lord who exists everywhere, in everything, and at all times.

श्री गीता चालीसा
FORTY VERSES OF THE GITA
(For Daily Reading and Contemplation)

ॐ श्री परमात्मने नमः
वसुदेवसुतं देवं कंसचाणूरमर्दनम् ।
देवकीपरमानन्दं कृष्णं वन्दे जगद्गुरुम् ॥१॥
मूकं करोति वाचालं पङ्गुं लङ्घयते गिरिम् ।
यत्कृपा तमहं वन्दे परमानन्दमाधवम् ॥२॥

Om śrī paramātmane namaḥ
vasudeva sutaṁ devaṁ kaṁsa cāṇūra mardanam
devakī paramānandaṁ kṛṣṇaṁ vande jagadgurum
mūkaṁ karoti vācāDṁaṁ paṅguṁ Dṁaṅghayate girim
yatkṛpā tamahaṁ vande paramānanda mādhavam

Obeisance To The Supreme Lord
I offer my obeisance to Lord Kṛṣṇa, the world teacher, who is the son of Vasudeva, the remover of all obstacles, the supreme bliss of His mother Devakī, and whose grace makes the dumb eloquent and the crippled cross the mountains.

धृतराष्ट्र उवाच
धर्मक्षेत्रे कुरुक्षेत्रे समवेता युयुत्सवः ।
मामकाः पाण्डवाश्चैव किम् अकुर्वत संजय ॥१॥

dhṛtarāṣṭra uvāca
dharmakṣetre kurukṣetre samavetā yuyutsavaḥ
māmakāḥ pāṇḍavāś cai'va kim akurvata Saṁjaya

The King inquired: Sanjaya, please now tell me, in details, what did my people (the Kauravas) and the Pandavas do in the battlefield before the war started? (1.01)

संजय उवाच
तं तथा कृपयाविष्टम् अश्रुपूर्णाकुलेक्षणम् ।
विषीदन्तम् इदं वाक्यम् उवाच मधुसूदनः ॥१॥
saṁjaya uvāca
taṁ tathā kṛpayāviṣṭam aśrupūrṇākulekṣaṇam
viṣīdantam idaṁ vākyam uvāca madhusūdanaḥ

Sanjaya said: Lord Krishna spoke these words to Arjuna whose eyes were tearful and downcast, and who was overwhelmed with compassion and despair. (2.01)

श्रीभगवानुवाच
अशोच्यान् अन्वशोचस् त्वं प्रज्ञावादांश्च भाषसे ।
गतासून् अगतासूंश्च नानुशोचन्ति पण्डिताः ॥११॥
śrī bhagavān uvāca
aśocyān anvaśocas tvaṁ prajñāvādāṁśca bhāṣase
gatāsūn agatāsūṁśca nānuśocanti paṇḍitāḥ

Lord Krishna said: You grieve for those who are not worthy of grief and yet speak words of wisdom. The wise grieve neither for the living nor for the dead. (2.11)

देहिनोऽस्मिन् यथा देहे कौमारं यौवनं जरा ।
तथा देहान्तरप्राप्तिर् धीरस् तत्र न मुह्यति ॥१३॥
dehino'smin yathā dehe kaumāraṁ yauvanaṁ jarā
tathā dehāntaraprāptir dhīras tatra na muhyati

Just as the soul acquires a childhood body, a youth body, and an old-age body during this life, similarly, the soul acquires another body after death. This should not delude the wise. (See also 15.08) (2.13)

वासांसि जीर्णानि यथा विहाय
नवानि गृह्णाति नरोऽपराणि ।
तथा शरीराणि विहाय जीर्णान्य्
अन्यानि संयाति नवानि देही ।।२२।।

vāsāṁsi jīrṇāni yathā vihāya
navāni gṛhṇāti naro'parāṇi
tathā śarīrāṇi vihāya jīrṇāny
anyāni saṁyāti navāni dehī

Just as a person puts on new garments after discarding the old ones, similarly, the living entity or the individual soul acquires new bodies after casting away the old bodies. (2.22)

सुखदुःखे समे कृत्वा लाभालाभौ जयाजयौ ।
ततो युद्धाय युज्यस्व नैवं पापम् अवाप्स्यसि ।।३८।।

sukha duḥkhe same kṛtvā lābhālābhau jayājayau
tato yuddhāya yujyasva naivaṁ pāpam avāpsyasi

Treating pleasure and pain, gain and loss, and victory and defeat alike engage yourself in your duty. By doing your duty this way, you will not incur any sin. (2.38)

कर्मण्येवाधिकारस्ते मा फलेषु कदाचन ।
मा कर्मफलहेतुर् भूर् मा ते सङ्गोऽस्त्व् अकर्मणि ।।४७।।

karmaṇy evādhikāraste mā phaleṣu kadācana
mā karma phala hetur bhūr mā te saṅgo'stv akarmaṇi

You have control over doing your respective duty only, but no control or claim over the results. The fruits of work should not be your motive, and you should never be inactive. (2.47)

बुद्धियुक्तो जहातीह उभे सुकृतदुष्कृते ।
तस्माद् योगाय युज्यस्व योगः कर्मसु कौशलम् ।।५०।।
buddhiyukto jahātīha ubhe sukṛta duṣkṛte
tasmād yogāya yujyasva yogaḥ karmasu kauśalam

A KarmaYogi or the selfless person becomes free from both vice and virtue in this life itself. Therefore, strive for selfless service. Working to the best of one's abilities without becoming selfishly attached to the fruits of work is called KarmaYoga or Seva. (2.50)

इन्द्रियाणां हि चरतां यन् मनोऽनुविधीयते ।
तदस्य हरति प्रज्ञां वायुर् नावम् इवाम्भसि ।।६७।।
indriyāṇāṁ hi caratāṁ yan mano'nuvidhīyate
tad asya harati prajñāṁ vāyur nāvam ivāmbhasi

The mind, when controlled by the roving senses, steals away the intellect as a storm takes away a boat on the sea from its destination — the spiritual shore of peace and happiness. (2.67)

प्रकृतेः क्रियमाणानि गुणैः कर्माणि सर्वशः ।
अहंकारविमूढात्मा कर्ताहम् इति मन्यते ।।२७।।
prakṛteḥ kriyamāṇāni guṇaiḥ karmāṇi sarvaśaḥ
ahaṁkāra vimūḍhātmā kartāham iti manyate

The forces (Gunas) of Nature do all work, but due to delusion of ignorance people assume themselves to be the doer. (See also 5.09, 13.29, and 14.19) (3.27)

एवं बुद्धेः परं बुद्ध्वा संस्तभ्यात्मानम् आत्मना ।
जहि शत्रुं महाबाहो कामरूपं दुरासदम् ।।४३।।

evaṁ buddheḥ paraṁ buddhvā saṁstabhyā'tmānam ātmanā
jahi śatruṁ mahābāho kāmarupaṁ durāsadam

Thus, knowing the Self to be the highest, and controlling the mind by the intellect that is purified by spiritual practices, one must kill this mighty enemy, lust, O Arjuna, with the sword of true knowledge of the Self. (3.43)

यदा यदा हि धर्मस्य ग्लानिर् भवति भारत ।
अभ्युत्थानम् अधर्मस्य तदात्मानं सृजाम्यहम् ॥७॥

yadā yadā hi dharmasya glānir bhavati bhārata
abhyutthānam adharmasya tadā'tmānaṁ sṛjāmy aham

परित्राणाय साधूनां विनाशाय च दुष्कृताम् ।
धर्मसंस्थापनार्थाय संभवामि युगे युगे ॥८॥

paritrāṇāya sādhūnāṁ vināśāya ca duṣkṛtām
dharma saṁsthāpanārthāya saṁbhavāmi yuge yuge

Whenever there is a decline of Dharma (Righteousness) and a predominance of Adharma (Unrighteousness), O Arjuna, I manifest Myself. I appear from time to time for protecting the good, for transforming the wicked, and for establishing world order (Dharma). (4.07-08)

चातुर्वर्ण्यं मया सृष्टं गुणकर्मविभागशः ।
तस्य कर्तारम् अपि मां विद्ध्य् अकर्तारम् अव्ययम् ॥१३॥

cāturvarṇyaṁ mayā sṛṣṭaṁ guṇakarma vibhāgaśaḥ
tasya kartāram api māṁ viddhy akartāram avyayam

I created the four divisions of human society based on aptitude and vocation. Though I am the author of this system of division of labor, one should know that I do nothing directly, and I am eternal. (See also 18.41) (4.13)

कर्मण्य् अकर्म यः पश्येद् अकर्मणि च कर्म यः ।
स बुद्धिमान् मनुष्येषु स युक्तः कृत्स्नकर्मकृत् ॥१८॥

karmaṇy akarma yaḥ paśyed akarmaṇi ca karma yaḥ
sa buddhimān manuṣyeṣu sa yuktaḥ kṛtsnakarmakṛt

One who sees inaction in action and action in inaction, is a wise person. Such a person is a yogi and has accomplished everything. (See also 3.05, 3.27, 5.08 and 13.29) (4.18)

ब्रह्मार्पणं ब्रह्म हविर् ब्रह्माग्नौ ब्रह्मणा हुतम् ।
ब्रह्मैव तेन गन्तव्यं ब्रह्मकर्मसमाधिना ॥२४॥

brahmā'rpaṇaṁ brahma havir brahmāgnau brahmaṇā hutam
brahmaiva tena gantavyaṁ brahmakarma samādhinā

The divine Spirit has become everything. The Divinity (Brahma, Self, Spirit) shall be realized by one who considers everything as a manifestation (or an act) of Divine. (Also see 9.16) (4.24)

न हि ज्ञानेन सदृशं पवित्रम् इह विद्यते ।
तत् स्वयं योगसंसिद्धः कालेनात्मनि विन्दति ॥३८॥

na hi jñānena sadṛśaṁ pavitram iha vidyate
tat svayaṁ yogasaṁsiddhaḥ kālenā'tmani vindati

Truly, there is no purifier in this world like the true knowledge of the Supreme Being. One discovers this knowledge within, naturally, in course of time when one's mind is cleansed of selfishness by KarmaYoga. (See also 4.31, 5.06, and 18.78). (4.38)

संन्यासस् तु महाबाहो दुःखम् आप्तुम् अयोगतः ।
योगयुक्तो मुनिर् ब्रह्म नचिरेणाधिगच्छति ॥६॥

saṁnyāsas tu mahābāho duḥkham āptum ayogataḥ
yogayukto munir brahma nacireṇā'dhigacchati

But true renunciation (the renunciation of doership and ownership), O Arjuna, is difficult to attain without KarmaYoga. A sage equipped with KarmaYoga quickly attains Nirvana. (See also 4.31, 4.38, 5.08) (5.06)

ब्रह्मण्य् आधाय कर्माणि सङ्गं त्यक्त्वा करोति यः ।
लिप्यते न स पापेन पद्मपत्रम् इवाम्भसा ॥१०॥

brahmaṇy ādhāya karmāṇi saṅgaṁ tyaktvā karoti yaḥ
lipyate na sa pāpena padma patram ivāmbhasā

One who does all work as an offering to God — abandoning selfish attachment to results — remains untouched by Karmic reaction or sin, just as a lotus leaf never gets wet by water. (5.10)

यो मां पश्यति सर्वत्र सर्वं च मयि पश्यति ।
तस्याहं न प्रणश्यामि स च मे न प्रणश्यति ॥३०॥

yo māṁ paśyati sarvatra sarvaṁ ca mayi paśyati
tsyā'haṁ na praṇaśyāmi sa ca me na praṇaśyati

Those who perceive Me in everything, and behold everything in Me, are not separated from Me, and I am not separated from them. (6.30)

चतुर्विधा भजन्ते मां जनाः सुकृतिनोऽर्जुन ।
आर्तो जिज्ञासुर् अर्थार्थी ज्ञानी च भरतर्षभ ॥१६॥

caturvidhā bhajante māṁ janāḥ sukṛtino'rjuna
ārto jijñāsur arthārthī jñānī ca bharatarṣabha

Four types of virtuous ones worship or seek Me, O Arjuna. They are: the distressed, the seeker of Self-knowledge, the seeker of wealth, and the enlightened one who has experienced the Supreme Being. (7.16)

बहूनां जन्मनाम् अन्ते ज्ञानवान् मां प्रपद्यते ।
वासुदेवः सर्वम् इति स महात्मा सुदुर्लभः ॥१९॥
bahūnāṁ janmanām ante jñānavān māṁ prapadyate
vāsudevaḥ sarvam iti sa mahātmā sudurlabhaḥ

After many births, the enlightened one resorts to Me by realizing that everything is, indeed, My manifestation. Such a great soul is very rare. (7.19)

अव्यक्तं व्यक्तिम् आपन्नं मन्यन्ते माम् अबुद्धयः ।
परं भावम् अजानन्तो ममाव्ययम् अनुत्तमम् ॥२४॥
avyaktaṁ vyaktim āpannaṁ manyante mām abuddhayaḥ
paraṁ bhāvam ajānanto mamā'vyayam anuttamam

The ignorant ones — unable to understand My immutable, incomparable, incomprehensible, and transcendental form — assume that I, the Supreme Being, am formless and take forms or incarnate. (7.24)

यं यं वापि स्मरन् भावं त्यजत्य् अन्ते कलेवरम् ।
तं तं एवैति कौन्तेय सदा तद्भावभावितः ॥६॥
yaṁ yaṁ vā'pi smaran bhāvaṁ tyajaty ante kalevaram
taṁ taṁ evaiti kaunteya sadā tadbhāvabhāvitaḥ

Whatever object one remembers as one leaves the body at the end of life, that object is attained. Thought of whatever object prevails during one's lifetime, one remembers only that object at the end of life and achieves it. (8.06)

तस्मात् सर्वेषु कालेषु माम् अनुस्मर युध्य च ।
मय्य् अर्पितमनोबुद्धिर् माम् एवैष्यस्य् असंशयम् ॥७॥
tasmāt sarveṣu kāleṣu mām anusmara yudhya ca
mayy arpitamanobuddhir mām evai'ṣyasy asaṁśayam

Therefore, always remember Me and do your duty. You shall certainly attain Me if your mind and intellect are ever focused on Me. (8.07)

अनन्यचेताः सततं यो मां स्मरति नित्यशः ।
तस्याहं सुलभः पार्थ नित्ययुक्तस्य योगिनः ॥१४॥

ananyacetāḥ satataṁ yo māṁ smarati nityaśaḥ
tasyā'haṁ sulabhaḥ pārtha nityayuktasya yoginaḥ

I am easily attainable, O Arjuna, by that ever steadfast devotee who always thinks of Me and whose mind does not go elsewhere. (8.14)

अनन्याश् चिन्तयन्तो मां ये जनाः पर्युपासते ।
तेषां नित्याभियुक्तानां योगक्षेमं वहाम्य् अहम् ॥२२॥

ananyāś cintayanto māṁ ye janāḥ paryupāsate
teṣāṁ nityābhiyuktānāṁ yogakṣemaṁ vahāmy aham

I personally take care of both the spiritual and material welfare of those ever-steadfast devotees who always remember and adore Me with single-minded contemplation. (9.22)

पत्रं पुष्पं फलं तोयं यो मे भक्त्या प्रयच्छति ।
तद् अहं भक्त्युपहृतम् अश्नामि प्रयतात्मनः ॥२६॥

patraṁ puṣpaṁ phalaṁ toyaṁ yo me bhaktyā prayacchati
tad ahaṁ bhakty upahṛtam aśnāmi prayatātmanaḥ

Whosoever offers Me a leaf, a flower, a fruit, or water with devotion, I accept and eat the offering of devotion by the pure-hearted. (9.26)

मन्मना भव मद्भक्तो मद्याजी मां नमस्कुरु ।
माम् एवैष्यसि युक्त्वैवम् आत्मानं मत्परायणः ॥३४॥

manmanā bhava madbhakto madyājī māṁ namaskuru
mām evai'ṣyasi yuktvai'vam ātmānaṁ matparāyaṇaḥ

Always think of Me, be devoted to Me, worship Me, and bow down to Me. Thus, uniting yourself with Me by setting Me as the supreme goal and the sole refuge, you shall certainly come to Me. (9.34)

अहं सर्वस्य प्रभवो मत्तः सर्वं प्रवर्तते ।
इति मत्वा भजन्ते मां बुधा भावसमन्विताः ॥८॥
ahaṁ sarvasya prabhavo mattaḥ sarvaṁ pravartate
iti matvā bhajante māṁ budhā bhāvasamanvitāḥ

I am the origin of all. Everything emanates from Me. The wise who understand this adore Me with love and devotion. (10.08)

मत्कर्मकृन् मत्परमो मद्भक्तः सङ्गवर्जितः ।
निर्वैरः सर्वभूतेषु यः स माम् एति पाण्डव ॥५५॥
matkarmakṛn matparamo madbhaktaḥ saṅgavarjitaḥ
nirvairaḥ sarvabhūteṣu yaḥ sa mām eti pāṇḍava

One who dedicates all works to Me and to whom I am the supreme goal, who is my devotee, who has no attachment or selfish desires and who is free from malice towards any creature; attains Me, O Arjuna. (See also 8.22) (11.55)

मय्येव मन आधत्स्व मयि बुद्धिं निवेशय ।
निवसिष्यसि मय्येव अत ऊर्ध्वं न संशयः ॥८॥
mayyeva mana ādhatsva mayi buddhiṁ niveśaya
nivasiṣyasi mayyeva ata ūrdhvaṁ na saṁśayaḥ

Therefore, focus your mind on Me and let your intellect dwell upon Me alone through meditation and contemplation. Thereafter, you shall certainly attain Me. (12.08)

समं सर्वेषु भूतेषु तिष्ठन्तं परमेश्वरम् ।
विनश्यत्स्व् अविनश्यन्तं यः पश्यति स पश्यति ।।२७।।

samaṁ sarveṣu bhūteṣu tiṣṭhantaṁ parameśvaram
vinaśyatsv avinaśyantaṁ yaḥ paśyati sa paśyati

One who sees the same eternal Supreme Lord dwelling as Spirit equally within all mortal beings, truly sees. (13.27)

मां च योऽव्यभिचारेण भक्तियोगेन सेवते ।
स गुणान् समतीत्यैतान् ब्रह्मभूयाय कल्पते ।।२६।।

māṁ ca yo'vyabhicāreṇa bhaktiyogena sevate
sa guṇān samatītyai'tān brahmabhūyāya kalpate

One who serves Me with love and unswerving devotion, transcends the three modes of material Nature and becomes fit for Brahm-Nirvana. (See also 7.14 and 15.19) (14.26)

सर्वस्य चाहं हृदि संनिविष्टो
मत्तः स्मृतिर् ज्ञानम् अपोहनं च ।
वेदैश्च सर्वैर् अहम् एव वेद्यो
वेदान्तकृद् वेदविद् एव चाहम् ।।१५।।

sarvasya cā'haṁ hṛdi saṁniviṣṭo
mattaḥ smṛtir jñānam apohanaṁ ca
vedaiśca sarvair aham eva vedyo
vedāntakṛd vedavid eva cā'ham

And I am seated in the inner psyche of all beings. Memory, Self-knowledge, and removal of doubts and wrong notions about God come from Me. I am, in truth, that which is to be

known by the study of all the Vedas. I am, indeed, the author as well as the student of the Vedas. (See also 6.39) (15.15)

त्रिविधं नरकस्येदं द्वारं नाशनम् आत्मनः ।
कामः क्रोधस् तथा लोभस् तस्माद् एतत् त्रयं त्यजेत् ॥२१॥
trividhaṁ narakasye'daṁ dvāraṁ nāśanam ātmanaḥ
kāmaḥ krodhas tathā lobhas tasmād etat trayaṁ tyajet

Lust, anger, and greed are the three gates of hell leading to the downfall (or bondage) of the individual. Therefore, one must learn to give up these three. (16.21)

अनुद्वेगकरं वाक्यं सत्यं प्रियहितं च यत् ।
स्वाध्यायाभ्यसनं चैव वाङ्मयं तप उच्यते ॥१५॥
anudvegakaraṁ vākyaṁ satyaṁ priyahitaṁ ca yat
svādhyāyā'bhyasanaṁ cai'va vāṅmayaṁ tapa ucyate

Speech that is non-offensive, truthful, pleasant, beneficial, and is used for the regular reading aloud of scriptures is called the austerity of word. (17.15)

भक्त्या माम् अभिजानाति यावान् यश् चास्मि तत्त्वतः ।
ततो माम् तत्त्वतो ज्ञात्वा विशते तदनन्तरम् ॥५५॥
bhaktyā mām abhijānāti yāvān yaś cā'smi tattvataḥ
tato mām tattvato jñātvā viśate tadanantaram

By devotion one truly understands what and who I am in essence. Having known Me in essence, one immediately merges with Me. (See also 5.19) (18.55)

ईश्वरः सर्वभूतानां हृद्देशेऽर्जुन तिष्ठति ।
भ्रामयन् सर्वभूतानि यन्त्रारूढानि मायया ॥६१॥
īśvaraḥ sarvabhūtānāṁ hṛddeśe'rjuna tiṣṭhati
bhrāmayan sarvabhūtāni yantrārūḍhāni māyayā

The Supreme Lord — as the controller abiding in the inner psyche of all beings — causes them to work out their Karma like a puppet (of Karma created by the free will) mounted on a machine. (18.61)

सर्वधर्मान् परित्यज्य मामेकं शरणं व्रज ।
अहं त्वा सर्वपापेभ्यो मोक्षयिष्यामि मा शुचः ।।६६।।
sarvadharmān parityajya mām ekaṁ śaraṇaṁ vraja
ahaṁ tvā sarvapāpebhyo mokṣayiṣyāmi mā śucaḥ

Set aside all meritorious deeds and religious rituals, and just surrender completely to My will with firm faith and loving devotion. I shall liberate you from all sins, the bonds of Karma. Do not grieve. (18.66)

य इमं परमं गुह्यं मद्भक्तेष्व् अभिधास्यति ।
भक्तिं मयि परां कृत्वा माम् एवैष्यत्य् असंशयः ।।६८।।
ya imaṁ paramaṁ guhyaṁ madbhakteṣv abhidhāsyati
bhaktiṁ mayi parāṁ kṛtvā mām evai'ṣyaty asaṁśayaḥ

One who shall propagate this supreme secret philosophy — the transcendental knowledge of the Gita — amongst My devotees, shall be performing the highest devotional service to Me and shall certainly come to Me. (18.68)

संजय उवाच
यत्र योगेश्वरः कृष्णो यत्र पार्थो धनुर्धरः ।
तत्र श्रीर् विजयो भूतिर् ध्रुवा नीतिर् मतिर् मम ।।७८।।
yatra yogeśvaraḥ kṛṣṇo yatra pārtho dhanurdharaḥ
tatra śrīr vijayo bhūtir dhruvā nītir matir mama

Wherever there will be both Krishna, the Lord of yoga (or Dharma in the form of the scriptures), and Arjuna with the weapons of duty and protection, there will be everlasting prosperity, victory, happiness, and morality. This is my conviction. (18.78)

हरिः ॐ तत्सत् हरिः ॐ तत्सत् हरिः ॐ तत्सत्
श्रीकृष्णार्पणं अस्तु शुभं भूयात्
ॐ शान्तिः शान्तिः शान्तिः

Hariḥ AUM tatsat Hariḥ AUM tatsat Hariḥ AUM tatsat
Śrī Kṛṣṇārpaṇaṁ astu śubhaṁ bhūyāt
AUM Śāntiḥ Śāntiḥ Śāntiḥ

This is offered to Lord Śrī Kṛṣṇa. May He bless us all with goodness, prosperity, and peace.

Index

ABOUT THE AUTHOR

Dr. Prasad is a charter member of several non-profit organizations in the San Francisco Bay Area. He founded the American/International Gita Society whose aim is to serve the humanity through the teachings of the holy Bhagavad-Gita and other Hindu scriptures, and to establish unity amongst all cultures, races, religions, and faiths of the world through the immortal teachings of all great masters, and major world scriptures.

He is a graduate of the Indian Institute of Technology, Kharagpur, India. He obtained his M.S. degree from the University of Toronto, and a Ph.D. in Civil Engineering from the University of Illinois. Dr. Prasad has worked in research, teaching, engineering consulting, as well as State and Federal Governments, including U.S. Navy and Army Corps of Engineers.

At present he is a professor of Civil Engineering at the San Jose State University, CA and an adjunct professor of Religion and Psychology at the Graduate College of the Union Institute of Cincinnati, Ohio.